P9-DVU-380

Cascading Style Sheets (CSS)

BY EXAMPLE

201 West 103rd Street
Indianapolis, Indiana 46290

Steve Callihan

Cascading Style Sheets (CSS) By Example

International Standard Book Number: 0-7897-2617-3

Library of Congress Catalog Card Number: 2001094314

Printed in the United States of America

First Printing: November 2001
Second printing with corrections December 2002

04   03   02   01   4   3   2

Trademarks

Warning and Disclaimer

Associate Publisher
Dean Miller

Senior Acquisitions Editor
Jenny L. Watson

Development Editor
Mark Cierzniak

Managing Editor
Thomas F. Hayes

Project Editor
Karen S. Shields

Indexer
D&G Limited, LLC

Proofreader
D&G Limited, LLC

Team Coordinator
Cindy Teeters

Interior Designer
Karen Ruggles

Cover Designer
Rader Design

Page Layout
D&G Limited, LLC

Contents at a Glance

Table of Contents

About the Author

Steve Callihan is a freelance technical writer and has written several books on Web design. He has had articles published in major computer and Internet magazines and has extensive experience designing, writing, and producing hardware and software user guides.

Dedication

In memory of my brother, Don.

Acknowledgments

Creating a book is much more than just a one-person job. As the author, I owe a large debt to the many helpers who have contributed to the planning and production of a book that is both a quality product and one that will find favor among readers. Special thanks are due to Debbie Abshier, for without her strong efforts for and belief in this project, it might never have come to fruition. The whole crew from Que also deserves effusive thanks, especially Jenny Watson (Acquisition Editor), Mark Cierzniak (Development Editor), Kynn Bartlett (Technical Editor), and Molly Schaller (Copy Editor), for the strong contributions they've made to this project. Thanks are also due to the many posters to the newsgroup, comp.infosystems.www.authoring.stylesheets, who proved to be of invaluable assistance in sorting out the many nuances and implementation issues that CSS presents.

Tell Us What You Think!

As the reader of this book, *you* are our most important critic and commentator. We value your opinion and want to know what we're doing right, what we could do better, what areas you'd like to see us publish in, and any other words of wisdom you're willing to pass our way.

As an associate publisher for Que, I welcome your comments. You can fax, e-mail, or write me directly to let me know what you did or didn't like about this book—as well as what we can do to make our books stronger.

Please note that I cannot help you with technical problems related to the topic of this book and that due to the high volume of mail I receive, I might not be able to reply to every message.

When you write, please be sure to include this book's title and author as well as your name and phone or fax number. I will carefully review your comments and share them with the author and editors who worked on the book.

Fax: 317-581-4666

E-mail: feedback@quepublishing.com

Mail: Associate Publisher
            Que
            201 West 103rd Street
            Indianapolis, IN 46290 USA

Introduction

HTML has opened up the world of publishing on the World Wide Web to anyone who cares to learn its tags and attributes, but it provides limited facility for the kind of layout control that some users (desktop publishers, for instance) are used to having. That's because the initial design philosophy behind HTML largely focuses on designating the structural elements of a document, while leaving the individual layout decisions up to the Web browser to figure out. As HTML and Web browser technology have progressed over time, however, a certain amount of control over the appearance of a Web page has been added into HTML, primarily in an *ad hoc* fashion in the form of extensions to HTML developed by Netscape and Microsoft. These extensions to HTML, however, run contrary to the original philosophy behind HTML (which is to specify the structure, and not the appearance, of a document), while still falling far short of the kind of precise control desktop publishers are used to having.

Part of the reason for this focus on structure versus appearance goes back to the bandwidth-starved early days of Web publishing, when most people were still connecting at 14 kbps or less and the Internet backbone had considerably less capacity than it has today. The thinking was that allowing Web publishers to individually design their own Web pages, rather than rely on browsers to largely do it for them, would lead to over-consumption of a scarce resource, bandwidth, that we all have to share. This is not a concern that desktop publishers have, in that their DTP documents only need to consume resources available on their local machines.

Although bandwidth is much more plentiful than it was in the early days, bandwidth-availability is still a concern on the Web and the Internet. Even broadband connections using DSL and cable modems are often slowed to a crawl due to traffic jams on the information superhighway.

The solution to the problem of providing more formatting control while continuing to conserve bandwidth is one that desktop publishers are already very familiar with: style sheets. The initial standard for using style sheets on the Web, Cascading Style Sheets, level 1 (CSS1), was recommended as early as December of 1996, although it is only now being fully supported by current Web browsers. A second level, Cascading Style Sheets, level 2 (CSS2), was recommended in May of 1998, but it is only partially supported by current Web browsers.

Another reason behind separating appearance from content is accessibility. If HTML is handling both the structure and the appearance of a document, a non-graphical or non-visual browser, such as a text browser, speech browser, or Braille browser, might have difficulty separating structure from appearance, making access to the document for visually impaired individuals more difficult. However, if HTML is used only to control the structural elements of a page, while style sheets are used to control its appearance, then a non-visual browser, for instance, can easily ignore the document's appearance and focus in on its structural content. Style sheets can also be used to add in presentation features that are specifically aimed at non-visual browsers, for instance, such as specifying pauses prior to, or pitch or tonal changes for, major headings within a document.

Cascading Style Sheets (CSS) also helps to enable the creation of fluid Web page designs that can be scaled in relation to a user's default settings. For instance, a user may reset his browser's default settings to display a larger default font size, due to a visual impairment that makes reading the usual default font size difficult or impossible. Using CSS, Web authors and designers can create Web page designs and layouts that use relative font sizes and other measurements that will be based on a user's default preferences. CSS also allows users to specify their own style sheet, thus participating in the determination of how Web pages will be displayed on their local computer.

What's the *by Example* Advantage

There are two distinct advantages in learning CSS when it's done *by Example*. First, by completing the examples as you read through the chapters, the concepts are reinforced for you immediately; much more so than just reading about a technique.

Second, with the CSS and HTML examples available for download from this book's Web site, *Cascading Style Sheets (CSS) by Example*, you can focus right in on learning how to use CSS, without having to spend a lot of extra time typing in HTML code examples. Because all of the HTML code you use in this book's examples is provided for you, you don't even have to know HTML to do this book's examples (although in order to practically apply CSS, you will need some familiarity with HTML). The CSS and HTML examples provided in this book can also be used to give you a leg up on developing your own individualized CSS-styled Web pages or sites in the future.

Who Should Use This Book?

Although some experience using HTML is helpful in using this book, it isn't required. Anybody can learn how to use CSS. You don't need to be a programmer, developer, or "techie" to learn how to design Web pages using CSS.

This book provides abundant examples, starting with the basics and progressing to more advanced topics, illustrated with screen grabs that show real-world results as they appear in the latest CSS-supporting browsers.

The examples in this book primarily utilize screen grabs made on a Windows system, but users of other platforms, such as the Macintosh or Linux, can also use this book. All of the example files used in this book are available for download from this book's Web site at http://www.callihan.com/cssbook/.

Why Learn to Use CSS?

CSS is the key to being able to create visually richer and more efficient Web pages, as well as more easily accessible Web pages that don't penalize individuals with handicaps that make viewing the usual graphical presentation of a Web page either more difficult or impossible. CSS opens the way to producing more advanced and interactive Web page designs, including DTP-like control over font sizes, margins, and positioning, for instance, that is just impossible to achieve in straight HTML, while at the same time helping to ensure that no one need be excluded from viewing and understanding your Web page's content due to a visual impairment.

You can create Web pages without using CSS, but CSS opens up new possibilities that are simply impossible to achieve using straight HTML. For instance, you can specify any size font you like, instead of being stuck with the seven stock font sizes provided by HTML. You can also specify custom margins and indents, the exact space you want above and below elements, easy drop-caps, absolute or relative positioning of elements, and much more. You can also save your style sheet as a separate file and then link to it to apply it to any Web page in your site, thus making maintaining the layout of a complex Web site a much easier and less onerous task.

In the past, Web designers have resorted to all sorts of HTML tricks to present more versatile and complex Web page designs, including using such HTML elements as block quotes and tables, for instance, to create layout effects, rather than for their purported purposes (formatting block quotes and presenting data in a tabular format using rows and columns). Web designers have also utilized extensions to HTML to control font sizes, colors, and typefaces. The result is that many current Web pages are a mass of multiple nested tables, block quote elements, and font tags, or what is often termed as *spaghetti code*. While many of these pages may be visually appealing (or at least as visually appealing as straight HTML will allow), they can be a nightmare for visually handicapped surfers to peruse, as well as wasteful consumers of bandwidth. Using CSS, Web designers can create visually rich Web page designs that are also accessible and efficient.

While many Web designers still continue to utilize the old "tricks of the trade," with all current major Web browsers now supporting CSS, increasingly, now and into the future, all serious Web designers will want to know how to use CSS. All professional Web designers will *need* to know CSS. CSS, however, is not just for professional Web designers or developers; like HTML, CSS can be used by anyone who wants to have greater control over the appearance and display of his or her Web page or site.

CSS also works well with the latest XHTML/XML standards, so you don't need to worry that CSS will become obsolete in the future. The latest XHTML standard even mandates the use of style sheets.

What Tools Do You Need?

No special software tools are required to create your own CSS style sheets. Whether embedded in an HTML file or saved separately, style sheets are saved as straight text files. All operating systems include text editors—such as Notepad in Windows, SimpleText on the Macintosh, or vi for Linux—that can be used to create and save your own style sheets.

To preview and dynamically debug your work, you also need to have one of the latest Web browsers installed. If you're a Windows user, I recommend that you have Microsoft Internet Explorer 5.5 or 6 installed, but you can also use Netscape 6 or Opera 5. If you're a Macintosh user, I recommend you have Internet Explorer 5 installed, but you can also use Netscape 6. If you're a Linux user, you can use Netscape 6. In Chapter 1, "Getting Oriented," I tell you where you can download the latest Web browsers.

While not absolutely necessary, a connection to the Internet will make learning CSS much easier. Although you don't need to log on to the Internet to create and preview your local HTML files and style sheets, you may need a connection to download one of the latest CSS-supporting Web browsers, if you don't already have one installed on your computer. (In Chapter 1, however, I show you how you can order a copy of Netscape 6 on CD-ROM.) You also need a connection to the Internet to download the example files that are used in this book. You will also need an Internet connection to access any of the Web sites referenced in this book, many of which provide additional information and in-depth details about particular CSS features and capabilities.

Downloading the Example Files

This book doesn't come with a CD-ROM, but I've created a Web site from which you can download all of the example files used in this book. You can find the Web site for this book located at http://www.callihan.com/cssbook/.

At the site are step-by-step instructions on how to download and extract the example files. Separate example files are available for download for Windows, Macintosh, and Linux/Unix users. You'll also find additional downloads available, including Web art images (balls, buttons, bars, backgrounds, and so on), Web page templates, and additional style sheet templates.

You can also find many other resources at this book's site, including an FAQ, Web site promotion tips and tricks, links to HTML tutorials (if you need to learn HTML) and Web publishing software tools, and a page detailing how to find a home for your Web site and upload your site's files using FTP.

What This Book Covers

This book is organized to provide a graduated, but fast-track, introduction to using Cascading Style Sheets to create visually rich, accessible, and efficient

Web pages. The topics and examples start with the basics and then progress to more advanced subject matter. The book covers most of what comprises the initial level of CSS, or CSS1 (Cascading Style Sheets, level 1), along with several key features of CSS2 (Cascading Style Sheets, level 2) supported by current browsers. Additional information is also included on using CSS with XHTML/ XML, JavaScript, and Dynamic HTML. Here is a specific breakdown of what is covered:

Part I: Creating Your First Style Sheet

Chapter 1, "Getting Oriented," provides background on style sheets and CSS, instructions for downloading and using the examples files, and an introduction to using CSS with HTML.

Chapter 2, "Setting Your Page's Base Styles," provides an explanation of the basic building block of all style sheets, the "style rule," before walking you through setting style rules to control the overall appearance of your page. Various examples are provided for setting style characteristics for your page's body and paragraphs, including setting margins, indents, fonts, colors, backgrounds, and more.

Chapter 3, "Setting Your Page's Other Styles," covers setting styles for the other elements in your example page, including heading, list, address, and link styles.

Part II: Understanding Basic Concepts

Chapter 4, "Using CSS with HTML," covers using CSS with HTML in more depth, including containment of CSS in HTML documents, the "true" HTML 4 (which requires use of CSS), the philosophy of separating appearance and structure, deprecated HTML elements and attributes that have been superceded by CSS, and the significance of the accessibility and device-independence features included in CSS.

Chapter 5, "Cascading, Grouping, and Inheritance" provides discussion and examples of key concepts that are integral to understanding the "why and what for" of CSS. *Cascading* provides for the application of modular style sheets, *grouping* for the assignment of the same characteristics to groups of elements, and *inheritance* allows for the inheritance of characteristics by "child" elements from "parent" elements.

Part III: Working with Colors, Fonts, and Text

Chapter 6, "Working with Colors and Backgrounds," covers setting foreground and background colors for any element using the 16 standard color keywords, as well as numerical and percentage RGB color values that let you specify any of 16.7 million unique colors. You also learn how to use CSS to set a background image for any element within your page, as well as how to control the repetition (or tiling), position, and scrolling of a background image in your page's background.

Chapter 7, "Working with Fonts," covers setting font characteristics, including font colors, families, sizes, weights, styles, and variants. Discussion of "font realities," font matching, and the use of the shorthand FONT property are also included.

Chapter 8, "Working with Text and Links," covers setting the characteristics of strings and blocks of text, including setting alignment and indents, line height, text decoration and transformation, and word and letter spacing. It also covers setting the characteristics of hypertext links, including setting colors and fonts for links; turning underlining off; controlling the appearance of unvisited, visited, active, and hover links; and creating roll-over links. Use of the SPAN element to create your own custom inline HTML elements is also covered.

Part IV: Working with Block Elements and Objects

Chapter 9, "Formatting Block Elements," covers setting display characteristics for block elements (headings, paragraphs, lists, and so on). Topics covered include understanding the CSS block formatting model, setting vertical and horizontal margins and padding, turning on different border styles, widths, and colors, and using the DIV element to create your own custom block elements.

Chapter 10, "Aligning, Floating, and Positioning," covers working with block elements and objects, including horizontally aligning them on the page, floating them on the page (while flowing text and other elements around them), and positioning them, absolutely or relatively, on the page. You also learn how to control the stacking order of overlapping elements.

Part V: Working with Lists and Tables

Chapter 11, "Working with Lists," covers setting the characteristics for bulleted, numbered, and glossary lists, including setting bullet and number types, specifying list positioning, controlling the display of nested lists, and creating a multilevel outline.

Chapter 12, "Working with Tables," provides extensive coverage of using CSS with tables. Topics covered include controlling the width and horizontal alignment of tables, setting cell padding, cell spacing, and cell borders, aligning cell contents, and setting formatting characteristics for cells, rows, columns, row groups, and column groups. You also learn how to use borders and backgrounds to make your tables more visually appealing.

Part VI: Getting Deeper into Using Styles

Chapter 13, "Creating Menus and Interfaces," covers creating interactive menus and user interfaces, including simple, boxed, and floating interactive menus, and designing sidebar and ribbon menu interfaces. You learn to use CSS to create menus using interactive roll-over effects, without having to use any JavaScript.

Chapter 14, "Creating Page Layouts and Site Designs," covers combining lessons already learned to create layouts using fixed sidebar backgrounds, newspaper columns, as well as more sophisticated three-column layouts. You also gain hands-on experience using an external style sheet to control the formatting of multiple pages within your site.

Part VII: Validation and Compatibility

Chapter 15, "Validating Your Style Sheet," covers why validation is important and provides hands-on guidance for using the CSS validators provided by the W3C and the Web Design Group (WDG). Guidance is also provided for the HTML validators offered by these organizations to test the validity of your page's HTML.

Chapter 16, "Providing for Backward Compatibility," discusses issues presented by older browsers that either don't support CSS at all or do so badly. Covered are redirecting, forewarning, or shielding users using non-conforming browsers, including using gateway pages, browser sniffers, participation in the Web Standards Project's Browser Upgrade Initiative, and shielding non-conforming browsers from parsing styles they have trouble with. You gain hands-on experience using an external style sheet to shield Netscape Navigator 4 from parsing styles that have a deleterious effect in that browser. The subject of DocType switching in the latest browsers is also discussed.

Part VIII: Appendixes

Appendix A, "CSS Quick Reference," includes a rundown on all CSS1 features and properties, as well as on CSS2 positioning properties. A look ahead to CSS3 is also included.

Appendix B, "Using CSS with Other Technologies," covers using JavaScript with CSS, creating Dynamic Styles with Dynamic HTML, and using CSS with XML (Extensible Markup Language). Hands-on examples are provided of creating Dynamic Styles that dynamically change in response to mouse actions (mouse over, mouse off, and so on).

Appendix C, "Overview of CSS Software Tools," includes a quick rundown on currently available CSS software tools that you can download and try, including CSS style sheet editors, CSS-supporting HTML editors and Web suites, text editors, and other utilities. Web addresses are provided for Windows, Macintosh, and Linux/Unix software tools.

Conventions Used in This Book

To make it easier for you to use the examples included in this book, a number of typographical conventions are used.

Convention	When Used
San serif font	Example text and code
Bold font	Text you type in
Italic font	Text to be substituted (*Type Your Name*, for instance, indicates you should type your name)
Monospace font	Code fragments presented within regular text
ALL CAPS	HTML element and attribute names when presented within regular text (not included in HTML code examples, where they are lowercase)

Notes, Tips, and Cautions are inserted at various points within the text. Here's how they look.

NOTE
Notes provide additional information related to a particular topic.

TIP
Tips provide additional useful suggestions and tricks not directly covered in the regular text or examples.

CAUTION
Cautions alert you to things to watch out for, whether possible negative consequences of certain procedures or actions to be avoided.

Visit This Book's Web Site

I've created a Web site dedicated to supporting the readers of this book. You can find it at http://www.callihan.com/cssbook/. It provides all of the example files used for this book, available for download, as well as Web art, fonts, and style sheet and HTML templates. If you run into any problems, first check out the FAQ (Frequently Asked Questions) page to see if your question has already been answered—if your question's not there, feel free to query me, the author, for an answer or solution to your question or problem.

Part I

Creating Your First Style Sheet

Getting Oriented

Setting Your Page's Base Styles

Setting Your Page's Other Styles

Getting Oriented

Before you jump into creating your first style sheet, it doesn't hurt to get oriented. Just jumping directly into creating styles can be pretty confusing, if you don't first develop some basic understandings of what styles sheets are and how they work. I'll also be including directions for how to download and extract the example files you'll be using to create this book's examples, as well as information on choosing a text editor to work with the examples. In this chapter you'll learn about the following:

- What a style sheet is

  The use of style sheets in word processing programs, desktop publishing programs, and on the World Wide Web is discussed.

- How CSS is implemented in browsers

  You'll learn about first-generation and second-generation CSS-supporting browsers and how their implementations of CSS impact the utilization of CSS in Web pages.

- The relation between CSS and HTML

  You'll learn how style sheets have been implicit in HTML from the very beginning.

- Downloading and extracting the example files

  The example files used in this book are available for download from this book's Web site. Guidance is provided for downloading and extracting the example files, as well as creating and locating your working folder.

- Using a text editor to work with the examples

  You don't need anything fancy to work with HTML and CSS files—a simple text editor works just fine. Text editors available on different platforms (Windows, Macintosh, and Unix) are discussed, as well as where to find and download other, more sophisticated, text editors.

What Is a Style Sheet?

Style sheets are nothing new. They've actually been around for quite some time. If you've had any experience working with word processing or desktop publishing programs (such as Microsoft Word or Adobe PageMaker), you've already used style sheets—you just might not have been aware that you were using them.

Style sheets have their origin in the world of desktop publishing. Programs such as PageMaker, Quark Xpress, and Ventura Publisher allow you to assign formatting characteristics to what are variously called *styles* or *tags*. The formatting characteristics that are assigned can then be applied to a document by applying the style, rather than having to re-apply the same formatting characteristics each and every time.

Styles enable you to define the formatting characteristics of the different elements that comprise a document. They enable you to control, for instance, the size of the margins around a page, specify the typeface and font color of heading and paragraph elements, set indents, or increase or decrease the amount of space (the *leading*) above or below an element. Other common features that might be controlled using a style are the line height, word spacing, and letter spacing (which is also called *kerning*). You can also specify that you want a particular element (a main-topic heading, for instance) to be centered on the page, or you might want to have it right-aligned.

A collection of styles is commonly referred to as a *style sheet,* although different desktop publishing or word processing programs might have their own individual terminology to designate this. In Microsoft Word for Windows, for instance, a style sheet is referred to as a document template.

A style sheet might also be saved as a separate file or document template, allowing multiple documents to share the same styles. For example, let's say that in Word you're writing a book or other long document consisting of chapters. Because it is cumbersome to type all your chapters into a single document, you're saving the chapters as separate documents. By creating a separate document template in which you define a style for controlling the display characteristics of a top-level heading (or chapter title), for instance, and attaching it to the separate chapter files, you can then have those characteristics globally applied within your chapter files wherever that style is specified.

Style Sheets in Word Processing Programs

If you've worked with recent versions of Microsoft Word, you've probably been using style sheets or document templates all along. Every document utilizes a template—for a blank document, Word automatically attaches the Normal template (Normal.dot) to the document. In Word 2000, for instance, you can see where the Normal template is actually attached if you select Tools, Templates and Add-Ins (see Figure 1.1). A template defines the formatting characteristics to be applied to certain predefined elements (or styles).

Figure 1.1: *Microsoft Word automatically attaches the Normal template to a blank document.*

The default template that is applied to blank documents in Word is actually very simple; it defines the formatting characteristics for five different styles: two text (Default Paragraph Font and Normal) and the top three heading levels (Heading 1, Heading 2, and Heading 3).

In Word you can also attach a document template or add your own styles to your document's default template, so many styles may be available for a particular document in addition to the default styles. Figure 1.2 shows the default styles, and additional styles that have been attached to the document.

Figure 1.2: *In Word, a document template is a collection of styles that can be used in formatting a document.*

Word's default template actually includes many additional styles that you can use and apply to your documents—they just aren't displayed on the drop-down menu unless they've been inserted into the document. For instance, in Word 2000 for Windows, when you select Format, Style, and then from the List menu choose All Styles, you see the full-range of styles that are available displayed in the Styles list (see Figure 1.3). Just click the style you want to apply (the Heading 4 style, for instance) and then click the Apply button. After you've applied a style to a document it is automatically listed in the Style box on the Formatting toolbar and is available there for reuse.

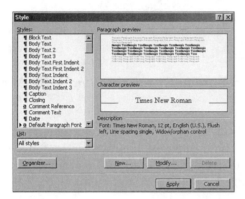

Figure 1.3: *In Word 2000, all the styles available within a template can be viewed and applied from the Styles dialog box.*

You can also easily modify existing styles or create new ones. Additionally, you can save your file as a new document template (as MyTemplate.dot, for instance) and then attach it to any other Word document in which you want to use those styles.

This should work similarly for other versions of Word. Most other modern word processing programs, such as Corel WordPerfect or Lotus Word Pro, also include the ability to select, modify, save, and attach styles.

Style Sheets in Desktop Publishing Programs

Style sheets originated in the desktop publishing world. The basic mechanism is exactly the same as with word processing programs: A collection of styles (a style sheet) is created that can then be used for applying to documents the predefined formatting characteristics assigned to those styles. Examples of desktop publishing programs that utilize style sheets and styles are Adobe PageMaker, Quark Xpress, and Ventura Publisher. The only differences between how this works in DTP programs and in word processing programs, is that DTP programs usually provide you with more formatting characteristics that can be controlled and finer control over those formatting characteristics.

Style Sheets on the Web

For use in the world of Web publishing, style sheets have also been around for a while. The first draft proposal for the use of style sheets with HTML was actually proposed in 1994, before Netscape had even released its first browser. The initial official recommendation for Cascading Style Sheets, level one (or CSS1) was released by the World Wide Web Consortium (W3C) in 1996. Since then, a second level, CSS2, has been recommended, and the W3C is currently at work on formulating the next level, CSS3.

You may be wondering what *cascading* means in Cascading Style Sheets. That is an important concept that relates to how CSS style sheets work and function. In the simplest terms, cascading allows styles to cascade (or fall) from one style sheet to another, sort of like a cascading waterfall, enabling the use of multiple style sheets (and interoperation between them) in a document. There is a good deal more to this concept, but at this point you don't really need to know what cascading is in any depth—after you've gained some hands-on familiarity with what styles are and how they work, you'll be better situated to understand exactly what cascading is.

✔ For more detailed coverage of what cascading is, see "How Cascading Works," p. 90 (chapter 5).

NOTE

The World Wide Web Consortium (or W3C) is in charge of recommending specifications for the World Wide Web. You can find out more about the W3C, CSS, and HTML at `http://www.w3.org/`. The W3C site on CSS can be found at `http://www.w3.org/Style/CSS/`. This should be your first Web stop when seeking information and guidance on using CSS.

CSS1 is sometimes referred to as *core CSS*, because it forms the root or core of any future CSS recommendation. CSS1 is almost completely preserved, except for some minor changes, within CSS2, for instance. Both CSS1 and CSS2 should also be almost entirely preserved inside of CSS3, when that specification is eventually released. CSS2 and CSS3 are not replacements for CSS1; instead, they are supplements to it.

CSS on the Web works in conjunction with HTML documents, which can be either HTML 4 or XHTML documents. HTML 4 is the latest version of the traditional form of HTML that has grown up from its roots over the last several years. Using CSS in HTML documents (HTML 4 or XHTML), lets you apply and display characteristics to your pages that can't be achieved by HTML alone. The W3C's site on styles, which can be seen at `http://`

www.w3.org/Style, is a good example of some of the visual effects that can be achieved using styles (see Figure 1.4).

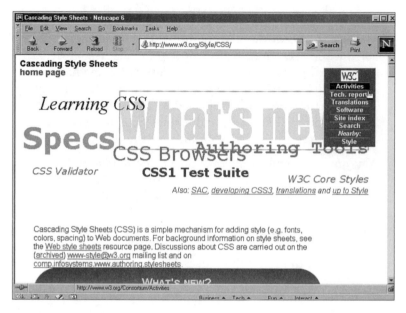

Figure 1.4: *Using CSS, you can create visual effects that can't be created in HTML alone, as shown here in Netscape 6.*

There are actually two style sheet languages that are currently recommended by the W3C. The other style sheet language is Extensible Stylesheet Language (or XSL) and can be used in XML and XHTML documents, but not in HTML 4 documents. CSS, on the other hand, can be used in HTML 4, XHTML, and XML documents. In a nutshell, XML (Extensible Markup Language) is a W3C technology for enabling more complex and interactive serving, reception, and processing of structured data over the Web than is currently possible using HTML alone. XHTML (Extensible HyperText Markup Language) is a next-generation version of HTML, reformulated as a suite of XML tag sets and allowing for easy migration from HTML 4.

NOTE

Don't worry if you find all those acronyms a bit confusing. You don't need to know anything about XSL, XML, or XHTML to use CSS with HTML 4 documents, but knowing that those other related technologies exist helps to put things into context. Currently, HTML 4 is still the most widely used technology, by far, for publishing information over the Web, but in the future you'll see these other next-generation technologies play a larger and larger role.

You can find out more about XSL, XML, and XHTML at the W3C's site at http://www. w3.org/.

In this book, I'll be sticking primarily to examples and explanations of using CSS in HTML 4 documents. There are a couple of reasons for this. First, the vast majority of Web publishers still use HTML 4 and will likely continue to do so for quite some time. Second, CSS works the same way in both HTML 4 and XHTML documents, so pretty much all of what you'll be learning in using CSS in HTML 4 documents should apply equally to XHTL documents—the main differences are between the two versions of HTML and not between how CSS works with them. If you want to use CSS with XHTML documents, I include notes where specific XHTML-related information is required, although that will be relatively seldom.

Implementation of CSS in Browsers

Until quite recently, the main barrier to the acceptance of CSS on the World Wide Web by Web designers has been faulty and less than complete implementations of CSS in browsers. For instance, while Internet Explorer 5 for Windows supported about 70 percent of CSS1, Netscape Navigator 4, the next most popular browser, supported less than 30 percent of CSS1. The implementation of CSS in Netscape Navigator 4 is a particularly faulty one, as well. More recently, however, new versions of the most widely used browsers have been released that support most (at least 90 percent) of the CSS1 standard and parts of the CSS2 standard: Internet Explorer 5.5 for Windows, Internet Explorer 5 for the Macintosh, Netscape 6 (for Windows, Macintosh, and Linux), and Opera 5 (for Windows).

It may be helpful to think of these two groupings of browsers as comprising the *first-generation* and *second-generation* of CSS browsers, with a *third-generation* of CSS browsers still to come. First-generation CSS browsers only partially and imperfectly implement CSS1. Second-generation CSS browsers almost completely support CSS1 (at least 90 percent) and support parts of CSS2. Third-generation CSS browsers, such as Internet Explorer 6 and Netscape 7, for instance, will support all of CSS1 and most of CSS2, and so on.

CSS-Browser Generations	Browsers
First-Generation	Internet Explorer 3 and 4
	Internet Explorer 5/Win
	Netscape Navigator 4
	Opera 3 and 4
Second-Generation	Internet Explorer 5/Mac
	Internet Explorer 5.5 and 6/Win
	Netscape 6 (and Mozilla)
	Opera 5 and Opera 6

continues

continued

CSS-Browser Generations	Browsers
Third-Generation	Internet Explorer 6/Mac and Win
	Netscape 7
	Opera 6

This is just a partial list of CSS-supporting browsers, but includes the major ones that are in common use. For a listing of all CSS-supporting browsers, see the W3C's CSS site at `http://www.w3.org/Style/CSS/`.

Currently, users have access to second-generation CSS browsers on all the major platforms. Internet Explorer 5.5, Netscape 6, and Opera 5 are all available to Windows users; Internet Explorer 5 and Netscape 6 are available to Macintosh users; and Netscape 6 and Opera 5 are available to Linux users.

Because of multiple bugs, quirks, and un-implemented features, trying to write CSS style sheets of any sophistication for first-generation CSS browsers is challenging and difficult. In my opinion, while I don't think that users of these browsers should be ignored, I do think it is a waste of time to expend a lot of effort in trying to jerry-rig CSS style sheets to work reliably for them. There are several approaches that can be used to not leave these users in the lurch; however, I'll be covering them later in this book, in Chapter 16, "Providing for Backward Compatibility."

In this book, I'll be primarily focusing on the second-generation of CSS-supporting browsers. While these browsers do have some bugs and quirks in their implementations of CSS1, they do define the starting point at which browsers can be expected to substantially and reliably support the CSS1 specification, as well as parts of the CSS2 specification. They form a bottom line, in other words, relative to which you should expect your CSS-enabled Web pages to display properly and reliably, with only a minimal use of workarounds to avoid or counteract bugs and quirks. Thus, even once a third-generation of CSS-browsers is on the scene, you'll still need to know how to code your pages so they display properly and reliably in both the second- and third-generations of CSS-browsers.

CSS and HTML

Although the initial implementations of HTML did not allow for the specification of style sheets, the original philosophy behind the design of HTML, as formulated by Tim Berners-Lee, the inventor of the World Wide Web, is actually implicative of the use of style sheets.

The original philosophy behind HTML utilized tags to mark elements (headings, paragraphs, lists, images, links, and so on) that to indicate the structure of a page, while leaving the actual appearance of those elements up to the individual browser being use to display them. Each browser, thus, contains its own set of directives, a kind of internal style sheet, on how to display the different HTML elements. That browsers mostly tend to display the different HTML elements in similar, and frequently identical, fashion is more a tribute to market forces, rather than any particular directive compelling uniformity in how browsers display HTML elements.

The real point here, in other words, is that style sheets have really been implicit in HTML from the very beginning and are not just some add-on that got tacked on later.

More recent browsers allow users to set some of the default display characteristics of Web pages, such as specifying default typefaces, font sizes, and text, link, and background colors. Users can even override formatting choices specified by the Web designer. This is a theme I return to later at various points within this book, as the tension between display characteristics specified by users and those specified by Web designers is a very important issue when implementing CSS in Web pages.

Downloading and Extracting the Example Files

At the Web site I've created for this book, you'll find all the example HTML and other files used in this book available for download. Just go to `http://www.callihan.com/cssbook/` to download the example files. Separate downloads are available for Windows, Macintosh, and Linux (or Unix) users.

How to Download the Example Files

The example files can be downloaded in one of two basic ways (if the first doesn't work for you, try the second):

- Click the download link and then select to either open the example file in your default file compression software or, if provided with the option, save the example file to your hard drive.

- If that doesn't work, you can choose to save the file directly to your hard drive. In Windows and Linux, in any browser, just right-click on the download link and select to save the link (or target) to a location of your choosing; In Netscape Navigator, you can also hold down the Shift key when clicking on a download link to go directly to the Save dialog box. On the Macintosh, just hold down the mouse button (or the Control key) while clicking on the link and select to save the link (or target) to a location of your choosing.

If you've chosen to save the example Zip file to a location on your computer (rather than have it opened automatically by your default file compression software), you need to have file compression software installed that is capable of handling Zip files in order to be able to extract (or expand) the contents of the Zip file. If you need to install file compression software, there are several shareware or trialware programs available for Windows, the Macintosh, or Linux, that can expand the contents of Zip files. These include WinZip or PKZip for Windows, Stuffit Deluxe or Expander for the Macintosh, and the Cool Zippi Tool or GnomeZip for Linux (or Unix).

For lots of links to file compression programs that you can download and use for Windows, the Macintosh, and Linux, go to the TuCows directory of shareware and trialware software programs at `http://www.tucows.com/`.

Whether you've opened the example Zip file directly in your file compression software or have chosen to download it to a location on your computer, you'll need to use your file compression software to extract (or expand) the contents of the example Zip file to a location on your computer. If you're using Windows, you may find it easier to first run your file compression software, open the example Zip file from where you saved it, and then choose to extract or expand its contents. If you're using the Macintosh, you may find it easier to just drop the example Zip file on the file compression program's icon to expand its contents, which should create a separate folder (named after the Zip file's name) containing the unzipped files located in the same folder or location as the Zip file that is being expanded.

You can also use an FTP program to download the example file: The example files are available for the different platforms (Windows, Macintosh, and Linux/Unix) via FTP at `ftp://ftp.callihan.com/pub/cssbook/`. Some FTP programs that can be used include CoffeeCup Free FTP and WS_FTP for Windows, Transmit or Fetch for the Macintosh, and Gwget or qFTP for Linux (or Unix). To find FTP programs that you can download, just go to TuCows at `http://www.tucows.com/`.

Extracting the Example Files to Your Working Folder

You can either extract the example files directly to a folder that you'll use as your working folder or you can copy the example files after extracting them to another folder you want to use as your working folder. If you're working on the Macintosh, you can just rename the extraction folder created by your file compression software and use it as your working folder.

In this book, I'll be referring to your working folder as the CSS Examples folder, although you can name it whatever you want. If you're using Windows, it may be most convenient to locate your working folder in your

My Documents folder. If you're using the Macintosh, it may be most convenient to locate your working folder on your Desktop. If you're using Linux, it might be most convenient to locate your working folder in your home directory.

NOTE

The example files include example graphics that are used in some of the CSS and Web page examples included in this book. For those graphics to show up when you preview your example document in your browser, they must be located in the same folder as the document that is displaying them. If you get broken image icons when previewing examples that include graphics, it is because the example graphics are not located in the folder where you're saving your example document. To fix the situation, either resave your example document in a folder that contains the example files or copy the example files into the folder where you're saving your example document.

Using a Text Editor to Work with the Examples

HTML and CSS files are just straight text files, so you don't need anything more than a simple text editor to create or edit the examples used in this book.

If you use Windows, you can use Windows Notepad to create and edit HTML files and style sheets. For a shortcut for running Notepad, just click the Start button, select Run, and enter notepad.

NOTE

In Notepad, Word Wrap is not automatically turned on. In Windows 98 and later versions of Windows, you only have to turn Word Wrap on once—it stays on until you turn it off. In Windows 95, you have to turn Word Wrap on every time you run Notepad. In Notepad you can toggle Word Wrap on and off by selecting Edit and Word Wrap (if already toggled on, the Word Wrap option displays a check).

If you're using a Macintosh, you can use the SimpleText text editor. You should be able to find SimpleText located in the Macintosh HD > Applications folder. (Users of earlier Macintosh systems can use the TeachText text editor.)

If you're using Linux, or any other version of Unix, the vi text editor is available for you to use, if you want. The vi text editor is a little arcane to use (you have to toggle between insert and command mode, for instance). See the note that follows for where you can find and download additional, more user-friendly, text editors for Linux or Unix.

NOTE

Many other text editors are available for Windows, the Macintosh, and Linux; and many have additional features such as spell-checking, global search and replace, and so on. For completing this book's examples, you might want to just stick with using the text editor that is available with your system. Later, however, you might want to check out some of the other text editors that are available. For a selection of available freeware, shareware, and trialware text editors for Windows, the Macintosh, and Linux, see the TuCows software archive at http://www.tucows.com/.

✔ At the start of the next chapter, "Setting Your Page's Base Styles," see "Using This Chapter's Example File," p. 27 (chapter 2) for a specific rundown on how to open, edit, and preview the example files that are used in this book.

TIP

If you're using Windows, display of the file extensions for known file types is turned off by default. The file extension identifies the file type (.doc, .txt, .css, .html, .htm, .jpg, .gif, and so on). I personally find it much easier to work with files in Windows if display of all file extensions is turned on, rather than relying on the (often quite cryptic) file icon to identify the file type. The file extensions are actually still there, but they're hidden. In this book, I always refer to the full filename, including the file extension (example.html, for instance).

For example, to turn on display of file extensions in Windows 98, double-click the My Computer icon on your desktop, select View, select Folder Options, and then click the View tab. For Windows 98, make sure that the check box, Hide File Extensions for Known File Types, is unchecked. If you're using a version of Windows other than 98, the procedure for doing this should be quite similar (consult Windows Help if you need more information).

Turning on display of file extensions can also help you to identify possibly malicious virus programs that are attached to e-mail messages. A certain type of virus attachment tries to masquerade as a legitimate file type by using a filename such as imagename.jpg.exe, for instance. If you have display of file extensions turned off, this is displayed simply as imagename.jpg, making you think that it is simply a link to an innocent image. If you don't recognize that the file icon doesn't belong to the JPEG file type, you could click the link without thinking and face some disastrous results.

What's Next?

You should now have a good grip on what style sheets are, and specifically what Cascading Style Sheets are, as well as at least a starting understanding about how CSS relates to and is used with HTML. You should also know now how to download the example files from this book's Web site and extract (or expand) them to a folder you'll be using as your working folder while doing this book's examples.

In the next chapter, Chapter 2, "Creating Your Page's Base Styles," you start creating your first style sheet. You'll start out with a rundown on how to open and edit the HTML example files, as well as an explanation of some of their contents. That done, you then go on to learn how style rules are inserted in HTML documents and how to use them to apply various display characteristics, including colors, backgrounds, margins, and more, to your page's body and paragraphs.

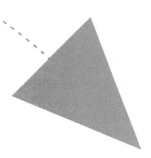

2

Setting Your Page's Base Styles

In this and the following chapter, you'll be creating a sample style sheet for a type of Web page that is fairly commonly found on the Web, a family home page. The purpose of this is not to show or tell you everything that there is to know about creating style sheets, but just to let you get your feet wet and get a sense of what a style sheet is and what it can do. While you'll be utilizing a fair number of CSS features in this and the next chapter, I'm not going to be spending any more time than necessary to explain what any particular feature is or what all the possible options are—I will provide cross-references, however, to where in the following chapters more complete and detailed explanations can be found for the CSS features presented in this chapter.

In this chapter, you will be doing the following:

- Checking to see if you need to download a more recent browser.

- Learning how to use this chapter's example file and preview your work in your browser.

- Getting a brief rundown on the basic constituents of CSS style sheets and HTML files.

- Setting styles to control the presentation of the body of your page, including setting page margins, fonts, colors, and background.

- Setting styles to control the presentation of your page's paragraphs, including setting horizontal and vertical margins, creating text indents, and setting the line heights.

Checking Which Browser You're Using

In the previous chapter, you read about the implementation of CSS in Web browsers. To guarantee the best results when doing the examples in this book, you should use a browser version (or later version) characterized in Chapter 1 as a *second-generation (page xxx)* CSS-browser. You can use a later version of these browsers, but if you're using an earlier browser version, you should update the browser you're using before trying to do the examples in this book. For doing the examples in this book, you should be using one of these (or later) browser versions (download addresses are included if you need to update your browser):

- Microsoft Internet Explorer 5.5 or 6 for Windows—you can download the most recent version of Internet Explorer for Windows at `http://www.microsoft.com/windows/IE/`.

- Microsoft Internet Explorer 5 for the Macintosh—you can download the most recent version of Internet Explorer for the Macintosh at `http://www.microsoft.com/mac/`.

- Netscape 6 for Windows, Macintosh, or Linux—you can download the most recent version of Netscape 6 at `http://www.netscape.com/` (just click the Downloads button).

- Opera 5 for Windows or Linux—you can download the most recent version of Opera 5 at `http://www.opera.com/`. A beta version of Opera 5 is also available for the Macintosh.

Most of the screen captures for this book's figures were created using Internet Explorer 5.5 for Windows. Part of the reason for this is that, of all the second-generation CSS browsers, it provides the lowest level of CSS support (supporting about 90 percent of CSS1), thus forming a kind of bottom line for functional, if not complete, support of CSS. All the examples provided in this book work at least reasonably well in all of the browsers listed previously, so if you're currently using Internet Explorer 5.5 for Windows as your browser, for instance, you shouldn't need to upgrade your browser to do this book's examples.

Of the browsers listed previously, only Internet Explorer for Windows doesn't clearly identify its version number. If you're not sure which version of Internet Explorer you're using, just select Help from the menu bar, and then select About Internet Explorer.

Using This Chapter's Example File

I've created example HTML files for you that you can use to do the examples in this book. For this and the next chapter, you'll be working with an example file, **kochanski.html**, for a fictional family page ("The Kochanski Family Page"). Feel free to substitute your own family name, of course.

✔ If you haven't downloaded the example files yet from this book's site and extracted them to your working folder, see "Downloading and Extracting the Example Files," p. 19 (chapter 1).

Opening the Example File in Your Text Editor

To work with the example file, you need to open it in your text editor. Any text editor will do.

✔ If you're not sure of which text editor to use to work with the example files, see "Using a Text Editor to Work with the Examples," Page 21 (chapter 1).

Just run your text editor and open **kochanski.html** from the folder that you're using as your working folder and to which you have extracted the example files.

TIP

If you're using Windows, Windows Notepad defaults to only listing text files with a .txt file extension. For Notepad to also list files with an .html file extension when you select File and Open, you need to select All Files [*.*] from the Files of Type list.

You can also type this file into your text editor from scratch, if you wish, as shown in Listing 2.1:

Listing 2.1: KOCHANSKI.HTML—The Kochanski Family Page

```
<!DOCTYPE HTML PUBLIC "-//W3C//DTD HTML 4.01 Transitional//EN"
"http://www.w3.org/TR/html4/loose.dtd">

<html>
<head>
<title>Kochanski Family Page</title>
<style type="text/css">
</style>
</head>
<body>
```

Listing 2.1   continued

```
<h1>The Kochanski Family Page</h1>

<p>Welcome to the Kochanski Family page! Look here for information on birthdays,
anniversaries, milestones, graduations, family gatherings, and other stuff
related to our immediate and extended family.</p>

<p>George and I will also be presenting the latest information and details about
our own lives and careers, as well as the latest info on our two wonderful kids,
Joe and Sue (or at least what we've been able to wring out of them!).</p>


<h2>The Kochanski Family Gathering</h2>

<p>You'll all be pleased to know that the annual Kochanski family gathering has
been scheduled for next July 1st. It will be held at Ford Park at Stove #24
starting at 12 noon. Back by popular demand, George will be handling the barbecue
(ribs and hot dogs), but others are encouraged to contribute other dishes and
items to eat or drink.</p>

<p>Please, however, follow safe food preparation practices — we don't want any
more outbreaks like we had last year! Remember, if bringing food to the
gathering, it is important to keep cold food cold and hot food hot. If in doubt,
see the Department of Agriculture's <a
href="http://www.fsis.usda.gov/OA/pubs/facts_barbecue.htm">Barbecue Food
Safety</a> tips.</p>


<h3>Coming Attractions</h3>

<p>We're still in the process of building this new home on the Web, so we haven't
entirely finished moving in yet! Coming up, however, look for these additions to
our new home on the Web:</p>
<ul>
<li>George and Kristine's Family Room
<li>Sue's Teddy Bear Haven
<li>Joe's Hideaway (we hardly ever see him!)
<li>Other Family News and Events
</ul>


<hr>
<address>
Kristine Kochanski<br>
E-Mail: <a href="mailto:kristine@kochanski-family.com">kristine@kochanski-
family.com</a><br>
Web Address: <a href="http://www.kochanski-
family.com/">http://www.kochanski.com/</a>
</address>


</body>
</html>
```

Opening the Example File In Your Browser

To view the example file, you need to open it in your browser. The steps for
doing this vary somewhat from browser to browser, but the basic procedures are very similar. For instance, to open **kochanski.html** in Internet
Explorer 5.5 for Windows:

1. Select File, Open, and click the Browse button.

2. In the My Documents folder, double-click your working folder (CSS Examples, if you heeded my suggestion) and then double-click on **kochanski.html**. Click OK.

Figure 2.1 shows **kochanski.html** opened in Internet Explorer 5.5 for Windows.

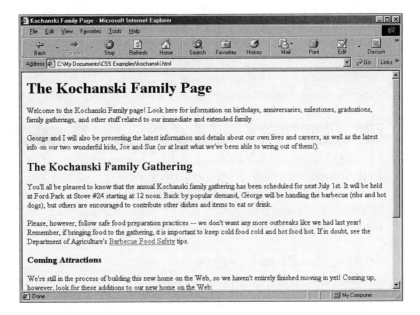

Figure 2.1: *The Kochanski Family Page is opened in Internet Explorer 5.5 for Windows.*

The steps for opening local HTML files in other browsers are quite similar to those used with Internet Explorer 5.5 for Windows. In Opera 5 for Windows, for instance, just select File, Open, and then click the Open button. In Internet Explorer 5 for the Macintosh and Netscape 6 (for Windows or the Macintosh), just select File, Open File, and then click the Open button.

You can also drag the example HTML file from a local folder on your computer and drop it on a browser's open window to open it in your browser. It is debatable, however, whether this is actually easier than simply directly opening the HTML file using the menu options.

A Quick Word About Using the Example File

The starting example HTML file, **kochanski.html**, includes all the HTML codes for the page, including the STYLE element in which you'll be adding some CSS styles soon. If you're not real familiar with HTML, don't worry if you don't understand everything that's included within the file. The point of this current example is just to give you some "do and see" experience in creating and previewing an example CSS style sheet.

✔ For an explanation of the codes at the top of the example HTML file ("`<!DOCTYPE HTML PUBLIC...`") see "The Three flavors of HTML," page 84 (chapter 4). For an explanation of the content of the STYLE start tag (`type="text/css"`), see "Embedding Style Sheets Using the STYLE Element," page 68 (chapter 4). For the purposes of this chapter, however, it isn't necessary for you to understand what these codes mean or do.

Controlling the Body of Your Page

In HTML documents, all displayable elements are nested inside of the BODY element (between the `<body>` start tag and the `</body>` end tag). By setting a style rule for the BODY element, you can control the global characteristics of your page, such as the page margins, the default font, and the foreground and background colors, for instance.

Setting the Page Margins

Using styles, you can control all four margins on your page. To set the width of all four margins, just type the following bold text:

```
<style type="text/css">
body { margin-top: 25px; margin-bottom: 25px; margin-left: 25px; margin-right:
25px; }
</style>
```

To check this out in your browser, first resave **kochanski.html**—in most cases, you can just select File and Save in your text editor (if you're using Windows Notepad, pressing Ctrl+S just emits a loud beep, without saving your file). With **kochanski.html** already open in your browser, just click the Refresh button (in Internet Explorer) or the Reload button (in Netscape 6 or Opera 5) to refresh the display of your page. This should display the changes you've just saved in your text editor, as shown in Figure 2.2. As you go through the rest of the examples in this chapter, you should frequently save your example file and hop over to refresh the display of the page in your browser. Only by actually seeing your results in your browser can you be sure that you're doing it right. Feel free to use the figures as prompts to save your file and hop over to your browser to see what's going on for yourself.

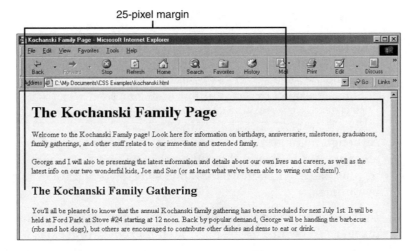

Figure 2.2: *Using a style, you can reset the margins for your page.*

A CSS style is composed of two basic parts: at least one *selector* (or a list of selectors) and at least one *property* (or a list of properties).

A selector generally identifies the HTML *element* to which a style property or properties are to be applied. In the example text you just typed in, the page's BODY element is selected, in other words, to have the different margin property values applied to it.

A property in CSS controls is a particular presentation characteristic (or property)—in this case, any of the four margins that surround the page.

A CSS property has two parts, first the property label (margin-top, as shown in the previous code example) and then the *value* (25px) that is being assigned to that property. A colon separates a property's label and value: margin-top: 25px. A semicolon separates the individual properties in a list of properties: margin-top: 25px; margin-bottom: 25px; margin-left: 25px; margin-right: 25px;.

Squiggly brackets, { and }, surround any properties that are assigned to a style, setting them off from the selector (or selectors) for which those property values are being declared: { margin-top: 25px; margin-bottom: 25px; margin-left: 25px; margin-right: 25px; }, for instance two basic parts: at least.

TIP

If you don't see the result you expect, or if what you see in your browser doesn't come close to matching what's shown in the figures, double-check to make sure you haven't mistyped the CSS code example. Very common errors (I even commit them fairly frequently) include typing regular parentheses, (and), instead of squiggly brackets, { and }, to set off a style's properties, as well as typing a colon when you need to type a semicolon (and vice versa).

Although not shown in this example, you can also specify a list of selectors, allowing you to assign the same property values to more than one element in your page. When more than one selector is specified, they are separated by commas.

In the example you just created, margin-top: 25px assigns a value of 25 pixels as the width of the page's top margin, while margin-left: 25px assigns a value of 25 pixels as the width of the page's left margin.

A *pixel* is the fundamental element of a computer display, a single dot that conveys both color and intensity (or brightness). The higher the *resolution* of the computer screen, the higher the density of the field of pixels (or dots) that compose it. For instance, currently the most commonly used screen resolution is 800×600 pixels (800 pixels across and 600 pixels from top to bottom of the screen). Depending upon the capabilities of your system, you may be using a higher or lower screen resolution, such as 640×480 or 1024×768 pixels. The screen captures for this book's figures were mostly captured in an 800×600 screen resolution. A 25-pixel top margin, for instance, means that the margin (below which the page's content is displayed) is located 25 pixels down from the top of the browser window.

✔ Other measuring units can be used to set CSS length dimensions, including ems, ens, x-heights, percentages, and other measurements. For a more in-depth explanation of CSS measuring units and how they work, see "Setting Font Sizes," page 130 (chapter 7).

Setting Your Page's Text Font

To give your page a bit of a different look, you can set a different font to be displayed as your page's default text font. In CSS, the font-family property can be used to specify the font in which an element may be displayed. You set fonts in CSS by specifying generic or specific font families. You can also specify a list of fonts that a browser can choose from, as well as combine generic and specific font families.

SETTING A GENERIC FONT FAMILY

In CSS, there are several keyword values that can be used with the `font-family` property to denote generic font families to be displayed as your preferred text font: `serif`, `sans-serif`, `monospace`, `cursive`, and `fantasy`. Of these, the last two, `cursive` and `fantasy`, produce unpredictable results in current browsers and should be avoided.

If you specify a serif font, browsers generally display Times New Roman or Times, while if you specify a sans serif font, browsers generally display Arial or Helvetica. A *serif font* has strokes that extend out from the top or bottom of the letterforms, while a *sans serif font* lacks any such strokes. (To see what a serif font looks like, just look at the text font (Times New Roman) that is shown in Figures 2.1 or 2.2; see Figure 2.3 for an example of what a sans serif font looks like.)

If you specify a monospace font, browsers generally display Courier New or Courier. A *monospace font* is a font in which all the characters are of the same width. Fonts such as Times or Helvetica, for instance, are proportional fonts, in that the widths of the different characters vary, with an "M" being wider than an "i," for instance.

For instance, here's an example of using the `font-family` property to specify the `sans-serif` generic font family (see Figure 2.3):

```
<style type="text/css">
body { font-family: sans-serif; margin-top: 25px; margin-bottom: 25px; margin-
left: 25px; margin-right: 25px; }
```

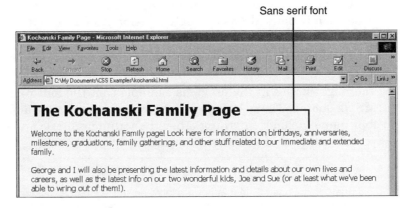

Figure 2.3: *You can change the default base font for a page to a sans serif font to get a different look.*

In publishing, a serif font is often used for *body text* (the paragraph text in a book or magazine article, for instance) because it is thought to be easier to read. That's because the serifs in the font faces provide cues for the eye as the text is scanned.

You may notice in many magazines, for instance, that while the body text for articles is set in a serif font, text in many of the advertisements is set in a sans serif font.

Designers, for instance, often prefer using a sans serif font when text is functioning as a design element, and not just as a conveyor of information, since that is thought to give the text a more stylish and graphically purer look.

Generally, if you're presenting a lot of text, where your text font is primarily being used to convey information, rather than perform as an element within a design, you're best off sticking to using serif fonts for your page's body text. Otherwise, use whatever type of font, sans serif or serif, that you feel looks best for your page. You might want to set your headings in a sans serif font, while leaving your paragraphs set in a serif font, for instance.

SETTING A SPECIFIC FONT FAMILY

When you specify a generic font family, a browser displays whatever font it defaults to for displaying that type of font. On a Windows system, for instance, a browser may display an Arial font if the `sans-serif` generic family name is specified, while a Macintosh system might display a Helvetica font.

You can also specify a font family, such as Arial, Verdana, Comic Sans MS, Helvetica, and so on. Here's an example of using the `font-family` property to set Comic Sans MS as the BODY element's font (see Figure 2.4):

```
<style type="text/css">
body { font-family: "comic sans ms"; margin-top: 25px; margin-bottom: 25px;
margin-left: 25px; margin-right: 25px; }
```

You might notice in the previous example that the font name, Comic Sans MS, is quoted. That's because there are spaces within the font name. If a font name includes anything other than alphanumeric and dash characters, you should always put quotes around it.

NOTE

If the Comic Sans MS font is not available on your system (you'll see the default serif font displayed instead), in the previous example, feel free to substitute the name of any other font that you have available on your system instead.

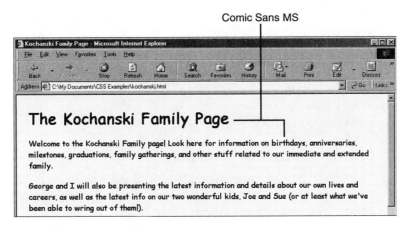

Comic Sans MS

Figure 2.4: *You can specify a font, such as Comic Sans MS, for an element.*

The problem with specifying a specific font name, such as Comic Sans MS, is that you can't depend on every system having it among its installed fonts. If the font isn't available locally, it isn't displayed, and the browser defaults to whatever its default font is.

COMBINING SPECIFIC AND GENERIC FONT FAMILIES

One way around this limitation of unavailable fonts is to combine the name of a specific font family with a generic font family. For instance, here's an example of combining an Arial font family with a sans-serif font family:

```
<style type="text/css">
body { font-family: arial, sans-serif; margin-top: 25px; margin-bottom: 25px;
margin-left: 25px; margin-right: 25px; }
```

In this case, if the Arial font isn't available on a system, rather than displaying the default font, the browser displays its default sans-serif font instead. On a Macintosh without the Arial font available, the Helvetica font would most likely be displayed.

SPECIFYING A FONT LIST

You can gain even more control over the fonts that are displayed on your page by specifying a list of preferred font families. Here's an example of specifying a list of fonts:

```
<style type="text/css">
body { font-family: verdana, arial, helvetica, sans-serif; margin-top: 25px;
margin-bottom: 25px; margin-left: 25px; margin-right: 25px; }
```

In this case, the Verdana font is displayed if it's available. If Verdana is not available, Arial is displayed if it's available. If Arial is not available,

Helvetica is displayed if it's available. If none of the three specific fonts are available, then the default sans-serif font is displayed.

If you want to specify a font family, you're best off doing it this way, rather than leaning on just one font being available.

✔ For a more detailed explanation of setting font families using CSS, see "Setting Font Families," p. 142 (chapter 7).

Setting the Default Text Color

Another way to change the over look of your page is to change the default color of your text. Here's an example of using the color property to set the default text color to a teal color (see Figure 2.5):

```
body { color: teal; font-family: Verdana, Arial, Helvetica, sans-serif; margin-
top: 1.5em; margin-bottom: 1.5em; margin-left: 5%; margin-right: 5%; }
```

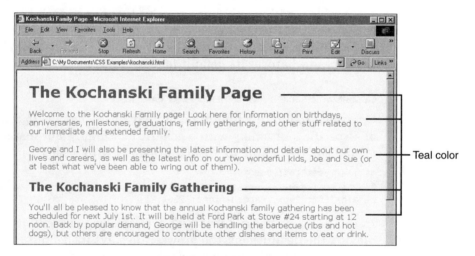

Figure 2.5: *You can change your page's default text color.*

The previous example specifies the color using one of the 16 color keywords named in the CSS specification. These color keywords are aqua, black, blue, fuchsia, gray, green, lime, maroon, navy, olive, purple, red, silver, teal, white, and yellow. Other color keywords work in some browsers, such as "orange," for instance, but some browsers are not required by the CSS or HTML standards to support any other than the 16 standard color keywords.

You can also specify colors using numerical RGB color values. This can provide you with a much wider range of colors at your disposal, although finding the right color can still be a challenge. You can set numerical RGB color values using hexadecimal, decimal, and percentage values. Hexadecimal values are the most efficient, in that only two numerals are required to count from 0 to 255. In the next example I show you how to set a background color for your page using hexadecimal values.

Setting the Background Color

You can set a background color for any element, including the document's BODY element. As with setting the foreground text color, you can set a background color by using any of the 16 standard color keywords, numerical values (hexadecimal or decimal), or percentage values. Here's an example of using the background-color property to set a light-yellow background color for your page using hexadecimal numerical values (see Figure 2.6):

```
body { background-color: #ffffcc; color: teal; font-family: verdana, arial,
helvetica, sans-serif; margin-top: 25px; margin-bottom: 25px; margin-left: 25px;
margin-right: 25px; }
```

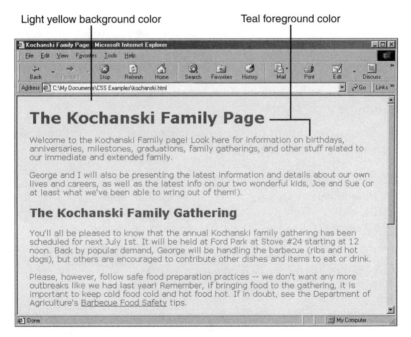

Figure 2.6: *You can change your page's default background color.*

This same property could be set using background-color: #ffc;—the first two characters are shortcuts for ff, and the third character is a shortcut for cc.

The hexadecimal numbering system uses a base of 16 numbers, using the numerals 0 through 9 and the letters A through F. Using this system, you can count from 0 to 255 using only two digits, which is why it is popularly used by programmers, instead of the decimal system, which requires three digits to count from 0 to 255. Here are some examples of hexadecimal numbers and their decimal equivalents:

Hexadecimal	Decimal
00	000
33	051
66	102
99	153
CC	204
FF	255

If you don't already know how to count in hexadecimal, there's really no need to do so just to enter color values. On the Web there are lots of color charts available that provide the hexadecimal color values for a wide range of colors. There are also online utilities available that convert decimal values to hexadecimal values for you. See this book's Web site for links to where you can find color charts and other color resources on the Web.

Alternatively, you can also use decimal or percentage values to set RGB colors for your page.

The basic layouts for setting color values using numerical and percentage values are shown here:

Number Type	Format
Hexadecimal	#rrggbb or #rgb
Decimal	rgb(rrr,ggg,bbb)
Percentage	rgb(rrr%,ggg%,bbb%)

For instance, to set the same background color specified in the previous example using an RGB decimal value (from 0 to 255), just use the following: `background-color: rgb(255,255,204);`.

To set it using percentage values (from 0% to 100%), just use the following: `background-color: rgb(100%,100%,80%);`.

TIP

If you choose to specify a foreground text color for your page's BODY element, it is a good idea to also set a background color, even if only white. The reason for this is that just because your browser defaults to a white background color doesn't mean that someone else's browser will do the same. Some browsers, for instance, default to a gray background color. Users may also specify their own preference, even choosing a light pink background color, for instance, if that's their druthers. CSS also lets users set their own *user style sheets*, giving users much more control over how their browser displays Web pages that they view. At this point, only Internet Explorer 5.5 provides this feature to users, but you can expect all other browsers to follow suit in the future.

There are some cases where you won't want to set a background color for an element. You might want to set the foreground color for a heading element that is displayed against a background image set in the page's body element, for instance. Setting a background color would overlay the background image, which you might not want to happen. In that case, just set the background color as transparent (`background-color: transparent;}`.

You'll find a chapter later in this book, Chapter 6, "Working with Colors and Backgrounds," that will focus in much more detail on using colors, background colors, and background images in your CSS style sheets.

Setting the P Rule for Paragraphs

In HTML files, the P element is used to specify text to be formatted as text paragraphs (that is, as paragraph elements). As you'll notice in the example HTML file, each P element starts with a `<p>` start tag and ends with a `</p>` end tag, with text to be formatted as a text paragraph enclosed within the start and end tags.

You can add a style to your style sheet that specifies the formatting for all the paragraph elements within your page. In this section I show you examples you can try for setting left and right margins, top and bottom margins, first-line indents, and the line height for your page's paragraphs elements.

Setting Left and Right Paragraph Margins

Using styles, you have complete control over the left and right margins for your paragraph elements. The P element inherits the left and right margins that you previously set for the BODY element. Any margin spacing you set for the P element is in addition to the margins already set in for the BODY element. Here's an example of setting left and right margins of 20 pixels for your page's paragraph elements (see Figure 2.7):

```
<style type="text/css">
body { background-color: #ffffcc; color: teal; font-family: verdana, arial,
helvetica, sans-serif; margin-top: 25px; margin-bottom: 25px; margin-left: 25px;
margin-right: 25px; }
p { margin-left: 20px; margin-right: 20px; }
</style>
```

Because left and right margin spacing of 25 pixels is already set for the BODY element, setting left and right margins of 20 pixels for the P element actually results in the horizontal spacing of 45 pixels (25 pixels + 20 pixels) separating the paragraph elements from the edge of the browser window.

20-pixel left margin   20-pixel right margin

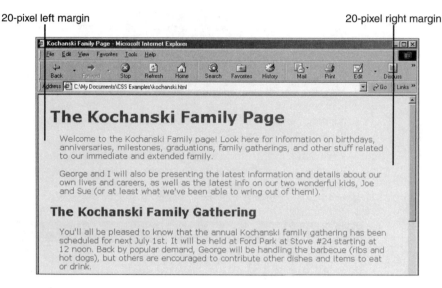

Figure 2.7: *You can control the left and right margins for any element.*

NOTE

In HTML, elements may be nested inside of each other. In the example HTML file, notice that the P elements are nested inside of the BODY element, making each P element a *child element* of the BODY element and the BODY element the *parent element* of each P element.

Generally in CSS, a child element may *inherit* characteristics that have been assigned to its parent element (whether by a browser or within a style sheet). There are a some exceptions to this—element backgrounds are not inherited, for instance (although element backgrounds do default to transparent). In many more cases than not, however, a child element will inherit the characteristics assigned to its parent element. You've already seen some examples of this. When you set the color and font-family characteristics for the BODY element, for instance, those characteristics were inherited by all the elements nested inside of the BODY element.

✔ For a more detailed explanation of the subject of inheritance, see "How Inheritance Works," p. 99 (chapter 5).

Setting Top and Bottom Margins

Using styles you can also gain full control over the top and bottom margins of elements. Here's an example you can try to set the top and bottom margins of the P element (see Figure 2.8):

```
p { margin-top: 25px; margin-bottom: 25px; margin-left: 20px; margin-right: 20px;
}
```

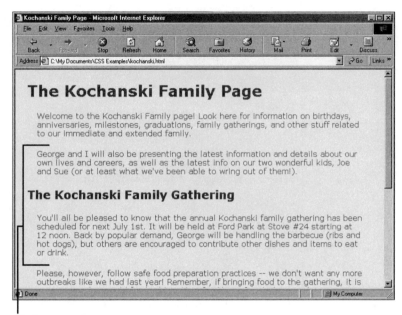

25-pixel top and bottom margins

Figure 2.8: *You can increase the margin space above and below an element, in this case for the P element.*

Unlike with the left and right margins of nested elements, which concatenate, the top and bottom margins of abutting elements collapse to the largest margin value of the two. Thus, while there are paragraphs in the example file, as shown in Figure 2.7, that follow one after the other, even though the first paragraph has a bottom margin of 25 pixels and the second paragraph has a top margin of 25 pixels, the total margin space between the two paragraph elements is still only 25 pixels, since the two values collapse to the maximum value of the two (25 pixels in either case, in this instance).

DECREASING THE TOP AND BOTTOM MARGINS

Not only can you increase the margin spacing above and below elements, but you can also decrease it. Here's an example that eliminates the vertical margins between text paragraphs (P elements), while leaving the vertical margins set as they are for other elements (see Figure 2.9):

```
p { margin-top: 0; margin-bottom: 0; margin-left: 20px; margin-right: 20px; }
```

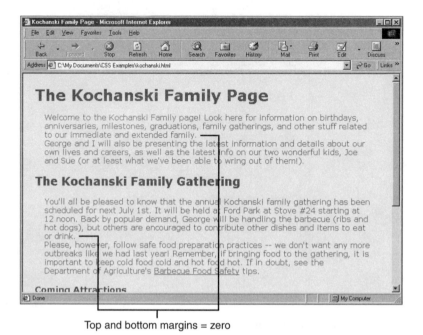

Top and bottom margins = zero

Figure 2.9: *You can eliminate the adjoining vertical spacing between paragraph elements.*

In this case, the top and bottom margins for all P elements within the document are reduced to zero. That's because a browser starts out by setting its own default top and bottom margins for P elements. By saying you want those values to be set to zero, you're telling the browser to eliminate the default margins that it would normally set. You could also set the top and bottom margins for paragraph elements at eight pixels, which would reduce the amount of horizontal margin spacing between the elements, but would not eliminate it.

Notice, however, that the top and bottom margins that abut other elements (the heading-level elements, H1 and H2, for instance) are not reduced in this case. That's because, as discussed earlier, the vertical margin value between the elements is collapsed to the maximum value between the two, meaning that the default margins displayed for the H1 and H2 elements would continue to be respected, regardless of whatever vertical margins are set for surrounding P elements.

✔ For a more detailed explanation of setting margins, including setting negative margins, see "Setting Margins," p. 184 (chapter 9).

Setting Text Indents

In HTML, paragraphs and other block elements are separated by a default amount of vertical spacing that is set by the browser. You've undoubtedly noticed, however, that paragraphs in books and newspapers often use a tabbed indent on the first line to signal the start of a new paragraph. That method is used so that more content can be crammed into a set amount of vertical space (where only so much vertical space is available).

CSS provides the text-indent property, which indents the first line of a block of text by a specified amount. Here's an example of indenting the first line of the page's paragraphs by 25 pixels (see Figure 2.10):

```
p { text-indent: 25px; margin-top: 0; margin-bottom: 0; margin-left: 20px;
margin-right: 20px; }
```

25-pixel text indent

Figure 2.10: *By applying the text-indent property to an element, you can indent the first line of a block of text by a specified amount.*

Controlling the Line Height

You've already learned how to set the vertical margins for an element. You can also control the spacing between text lines within an element by setting the line height. In the following example, go ahead and eliminate the text-indent property from the previous example, reset the margin-top and margin-bottom properties to positive values, and then use the line-height property to set the line height (see Figure 2.11):

```
p { line-height: 25px; margin-top: 20px; margin-bottom: 20px; margin-left: 20px;
margin-right: 20px; }
```

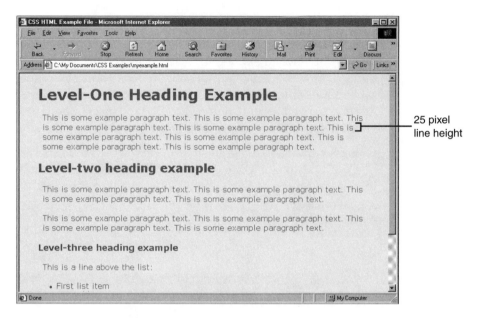

25 pixel line height

Figure 2.11: *Using styles, you can control the line height of any element.*

What's Next?

In this chapter you learned what style rules are and how to apply them to control the overall look and appearance of your page. You should now at least be familiar with setting page and paragraph margins, as well as controlling foreground and background colors, text indents, and an element's line height.

In the next chapter, "Setting Your Page's Other Styles," you learn how to set style properties for the other HTML elements that are included in the Kochanski Family Page example file, including headings, lists, address blocks, and hypertext links.

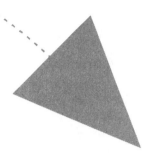

3

Setting Your Page's Other Styles

In the previous chapter, you gained some experience setting the base characteristics for your page using styles, including specifying the appearance of your page's body and paragraphs. In this chapter, you create styles for controlling the appearance of some of the more commonly used HTML elements, including:

- Setting the font size, color, and horizontal alignment of your page's H1 (level-one heading) element.

- Using a group selector to set font and margin properties for your page's H2 and H3 elements.

- Controlling the vertical spacing and bullet type of your page's bulleted lists.

- Setting the color of your page's address block and hypertext links.

Using the Example File

For doing the examples in this chapter, you'll be using the same example that you used in the previous chapter, the Kochanski Family Page example. Just reopen in your text editor the final version of **kochanski.html** that you saved and continue using that example file to create this chapter's examples. If you haven't yet created the examples from the last chapter, you should first return to and complete Chapter 2, "Creating Your Page's Base Styles," before continuing with this chapter.

Setting the H1 Rule

In HTML, the H1 element specifies the top-level (or level-one) heading for a page. Generally, there should only be one H1 element included in a page and it should be at or near the top of the page.

Setting the Font Size

By default, browsers display the H1 element in a font size that is larger than any of the other elements, because it is the top-level heading within an HTML document (see Figure 3.1).

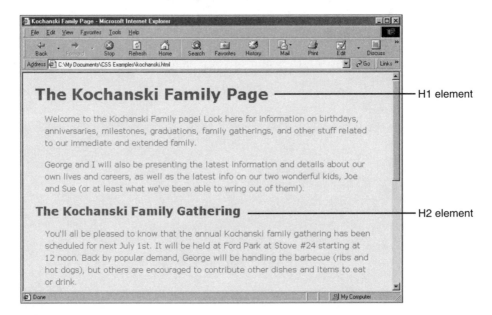

Figure 3.1: Prior to any style being applied, the browser determines the size of an H1 element.

HTML also allows you to change the font size of the H1 and other elements, using the FONT element. The FONT element allows the setting of seven font sizes, from very small to fairly large, numbered from 1 to 7. A font size of 7 is larger than the font size generally used by browsers to display the H1 element. For instance, here's how you would specify a font size of 7 using the FONT attribute for the H1 element:

```
<h1><font size="7">The Kochanski Family Page</font></h1>
```

One of the limitations, however, of setting font sizes in this fashion is that you can only specify seven different stock font sizes, of which only four will increase the font size. You should also be aware that the FONT element has been deprecated in HTML 4, meaning that it is recommended that you avoid it. Although you can use the FONT element, you are strongly encouraged to avoid using it, since you can use styles to achieve the same or better results. Liberal use of the FONT element can also make it difficult for visitors using speech, Braille, or other nonvisual browsers to access the content of your page.

✔ For further discussion of the deprecation of HTML 4 elements and attributes, see "CSS and Deprecated Elements and Attributes," p. 82 (chapter 4).

When you use styles to set font sizes, however, you're not limited to setting just seven font sizes, but you can specify an unlimited range of font sizes. For instance, here's an example of setting the size of your page's H1 element to 36 pixels (see Figure 3.2):

```
<style type="text/css">
body { background-color: #ffffcc; color: teal; font-family: verdana, arial,
helvetica, sans-serif; margin-top: 25px; margin-bottom: 25px; margin-left: 25px;
margin-right: 25px; }
p { line-height: 25px; margin-top: 20px; margin-bottom: 20px;  margin-left: 20px;
margin-right: 20px; }
h1 { font-size: 36px; }
```

Figure 3.2: The size of the H1 element's font is set to 36 pixels.

NOTE

I'm having you use *pixels (page 32)* here to set the font size of the H1 element, primarily because they are easier to understand and visualize for users just starting to learn to use CSS. You should be aware, however, that using pixels to set font sizes can be somewhat problematical. That's because doing so counteracts any font size setting a user may have set for that element in their browser preferences or user style sheet. For that reason, using a relative size measurement, such as ems, is usually preferable when setting font sizes.

You should also be aware that reducing the font-size of a page's BODY element or P element, whether using pixels or ems, can cause their content to be rendered unreadable in some circumstances.

✔ For a full discussion of using ems, percentages, and other relative measuring units to set font sizes, see "Setting Font Sizes," p. 130 (chapter 7).

Setting the Text Color

You had some practice setting the text color in the previous chapter. You applied the color property to the BODY element; you set the text color (or foreground color) of the H1 element in exactly the same way (see Figure 3.3):

```
h1 { color: red; font-size: 36px; }
```

Figure 3.3: *The color of the top-level heading is changed to red.*

You can't actually see the red color you've just seen represented in Figure 3.3, other than in the form of the callout I've included. To see any colors that you set, be sure to save your file and hop over to your browser to check the results out for yourself.

✔ For a full discussion of using RGB and percentage color values, see "Setting Foreground and Background Colors," p. 111 (chapter 6) .

TIP

When setting a foreground color for an element, you should always also set a background color. That's because you have no way of knowing whether the element's background color has been set in a browser's preferences or a user style sheet. You could end up with navy blue text, set by you, displayed against a navy blue background, set in a browser or by a user. In the current example, you can either set the same background color that you set for the BODY element (the parent element of the H1 element) or you can set a transparent background color, to avoid this problem. Here's an example of setting the H1 element's background color to be transparent:

```
h1 { color: red; background-color: transparent; font-size: 36px; }
```

Setting the Horizontal Alignment

You can easily set the horizontal alignment of an element. You do this by using the text-align property. Here's an example of centering the H1 element in your example page (see Figure 3.4):

```
h1 { text-align: center; color: red; background-color: transparent; font-size: 36px; }
```

Figure 3.4: *The top-level heading is centered.*

Other allowable property values here are text-align: left, text-align: right, and text-align: justify. Left-alignment is the default (or initial) setting and aligns the heading flush with the left margin. Generally, you won't need to set left-alignment for an HTML element, unless a different horizontal alignment is inherited from a parent element. Right-alignment aligns an element with the right margin; when applied to headings, for instance, it provides a way to give your page a different look. Justification aligns all the wrapping text lines in an element with both the left and right margins, although this is generally only used with paragraph text.

Using a Group Selector to Set the Other Heading Characteristics

The example file includes three different heading elements: H1, H2, and H3. Instead of separately setting the display properties for the H2 and H3 elements, you can set properties for both of these elements at the same time, using a group selector. In CSS, a *group selector* lets you select the properties you want applied to a group of elements (in this case, the H2 and H3 elements).

✔ For a fuller discussion of what grouping is and how it works, see "How Grouping Works," p. 96 (chapter 5).

To group selectors within a single style rule, you just insert them as comma-separated lists. Here's an example of using an RGB hexadecimal color code to set a slate blue text color for both the H2 and H3 elements (see Figure 3.5):

```
h1 { text-align: center; color: red; background-color: transparent; font-size:
36px; }
h2, h3 { color: #0066cc; background-color: transparent; }
```

Slate blue color (#0066cc)

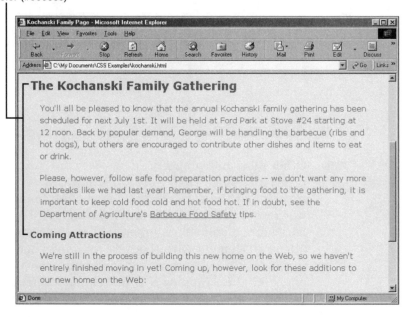

Figure 3.5: *A slate blue color is set for both the H2 and H3 headings.*

As with the H1 element previously, a transparent background color is also set for the H2 and H3 elements here. Whenever you set a foreground color, you should also set a background color, if only a transparent background color.

✔ The previous example uses a hexadecimal numerical color value to set a slate blue color. For a full discussion of using numerical RGB color values, see "Using Numerical RGB Values to Set Colors," p. 114 (chapter 6).

Setting a Monospace Font

You can give headings a bit of a different look by specifying that they be displayed using a monospace font. A *monospace* font is a font in which all the characters (including spaces) are the same width. Most browsers display monospace text in a Courier font or some variation of it. Here's an example of setting both the H2 and H3 elements in your page to be displayed using a monospace font (see Figure 3.6):

```
h2, h3 { font-family: monospace; color: #0066cc; background-color: transparent; }
```

Monospace font

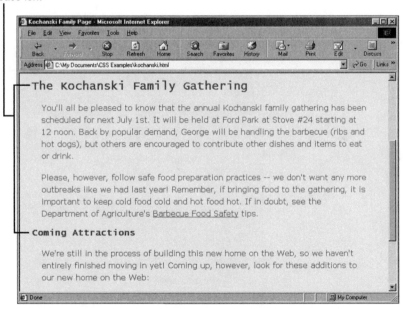

Figure 3.6: *The H2 and H3 headings are set in a monospace font.*

Setting a Negative Margin

In the previous chapter, you set the BODY element's left margin to a value of 25 pixels (left-margin: 25px;). While the other elements that are nested inside of the BODY element do not directly inherit this value, their margins are nested inside of whatever margin has been set for the BODY element. Thus, while your H2 and H3 elements do not have a left margin set, they are still spaced in 25 pixels from the left margin, since that is the width of the margin set for the page's body. Any left margin that you set for those elements would be in addition to the margin already set for your page's body.

But what if you want the horizontal spacing separating your H2 and H3 elements from the left side of the browser window to be less than 25 pixels (the value set for the BODY element's margin)? The solution is to set a negative margin value. Here's an example of setting a negative margin value for the H2 and H3 elements that causes them to be displayed flush to the left margin (see Figure 3.7):

```
h2, h3 { margin-left: -25px; font-family: monospace; color: #0066cc; background-
color: transparent; }
```

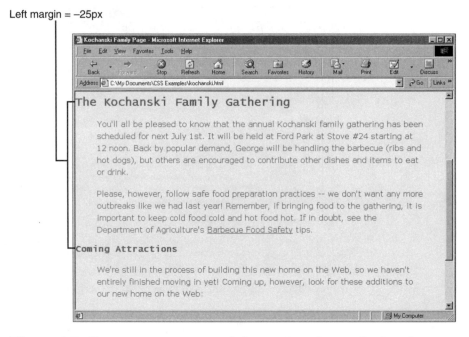

Figure 3.7: *You can use a negative left margin value to display the start of your H2 and H3 elements inside of their parent element's left margin.*

If you don't want the left margins for the H2 and H3 elements to be flush with the left side of the page, just set a value that is less than the current body margin. Here's an example of setting a negative left margin of 10 pixels (see Figure 3.8):

```
h2, h3 { margin-left: -10px; font-family: monospace; color: #0066cc; background-
color: transparent; }
```

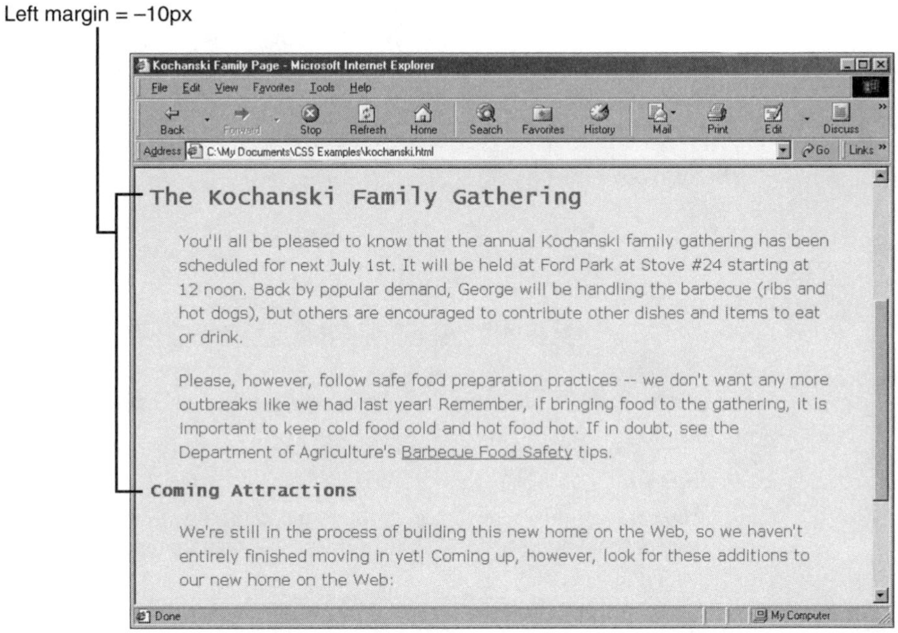

Left margin = –10px

Figure 3.8: *The left margin of the H2 and H3 elements subtracts 10 pixels from the BODY element's left margin (set at 25 pixels).*

Setting the List Characteristics

After headings and paragraphs, probably the most common element used in Web pages is the bulleted list. In HTML, a bulleted list is created using the UL (Unordered List) element in combination with LI (List Item) elements. In the example file are the codes for the bulleted list as shown here (see Figure 3.9):

```
<p>This is a line above the list:</p>
<ul>
<li>George and Kristine's Family Room
<li>Sue's Teddy Bear Haven
<li>Joe's Hideaway (we hardly ever see him)
</ul>
```

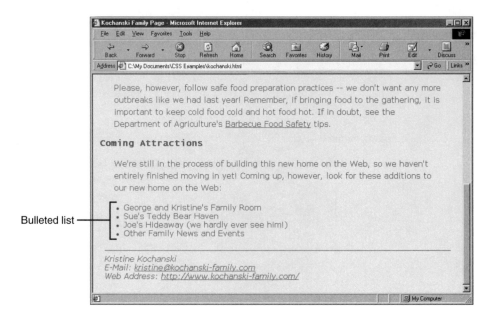

Bulleted list

Figure 3.9: *A bulleted list before any style is applied to it.*

NOTE

You create a numbered list in HTML in the same way that you create a bulleted list, except that you use the OL (Ordered List) element instead of the UL (Unordered List) element.

Setting the Horizontal Margins for Your List

You may notice in Figure 3.9 that the bullets for your bulleted list are practically flush with the left margin of the preceding paragraph element. Normally, a bulleted list (or a numbered list) would be indented from the left margin of a page's paragraph elements. However, when you increase the left margin of your paragraph elements, the left margin of any lists you've included remain at their default settings.

The problem, however, is that different browsers space in lists from the margin in different ways. Internet Explorer 5.5 for Windows and Opera 5, for instance, use margin spacing to space in a list from the margin, while Netscape 6 uses padding. In CSS, *padding* adds spacing inside of an element, while margins add spacing outside of an element. Neither way is really wrong; they're just different interpretations of the specification. However, if you want this to look the same way in all browsers, you need to set both margin and padding values. For instance, the following example sets `margin-left` and `padding-left` property values of 25 pixels, to space in the list from the margin of the page's body by a total of 50 pixels (see Figure 3.14):

```
h2, h3 { margin-left: -10px; font-family: monospace; color: #0066cc; background-
color: transparent; }
ul { margin-left: 25px; padding-left: 25px; }
```

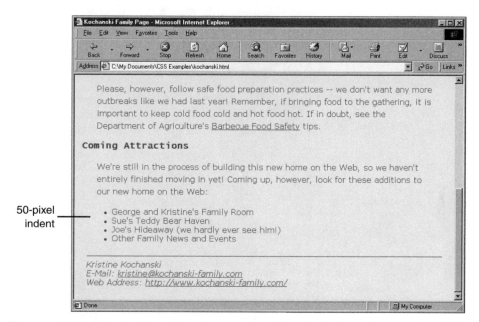

50-pixel indent

Figure 3.10: *The bulleted list is spaced in 50 pixels from the margin of the page's body.*

✔ For a detailed explanation of the relationship between padding and margins, see "Understanding the CSS Formatting Model," p. 182 (chapter 9).

Setting Vertical Margins for Your List

You've already had some experience setting vertical margins for the P element. Vertical margins work the same way for a list, adding vertical space above or below the list.

As discussed in the previous chapter, the vertical margins of elements do not concatenate, as is the case with horizontal margins, but collapse to the larger margin value. Thus, if the bottom margin of the paragraph element is set at 20 pixels, while the top margin of a following list is set at 15 pixels, the total vertical margin spacing between the two elements will be 20 pixels, since that is the larger of the two margin values.

INCREASING THE VERTICAL SPACING

To increase the amount of vertical spacing that is inserted above a list, just set a top margin value for your list that is greater than the P element's bottom margin setting. For instance, if you set a top margin of 30 pixels for the UL element, that amount of space is inserted between the two elements, because it is larger than the 20 pixels of bottom margin spacing that is assigned to the preceding P element. Here's an example (see Figure 3.11):

```
ul { margin-top: 30px; margin-left: 25px; padding-left: 25px; }
```

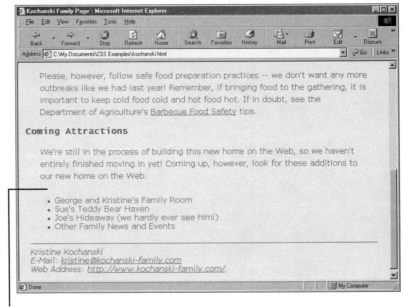

Top margin = 30 pixels

Figure 3.11: *The margin space above the bulleted list is increased to 30 pixels.*

DECREASING THE VERTICAL SPACING

So, how do you decrease the vertical spacing beyond what is set for the preceding element's bottom margin setting? Let's say you want to keep 20 pixels as the setting for the P element's bottom margin, but would like to have less vertical spacing set between the P element and a following UL element. To do that, you just need to set a negative top margin value for the UL element. For instance, here's an example of decreasing the vertical spacing above the UL element by 12 pixels (see Figure 3.12):

```
ul { margin-top: -12px; margin-left: 25px; padding-left: 25px; }
```

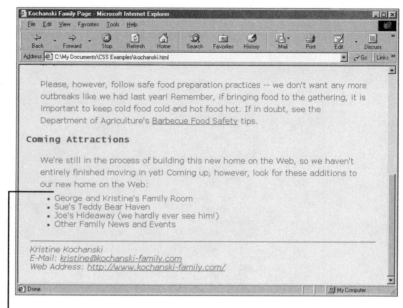

Top margin = −12px

Figure 3.12: *The vertical spacing above the list has been decreased by 12 pixels.*

Since you earlier set the bottom margin for paragraphs to 20 pixels, setting a negative top margin of 12 pixels for the following list element has the effect of causing eight pixels of vertical margin spacing to be displayed between the two elements (20 pixels minus 12 pixels).

Setting the Vertical Margins for the List Items

The individual list items are specified by LI (List Item) elements. List items are single-spaced (without additional margin space added above or below), unless you reset them in your style sheet. This is because, despite the UL element being the parent element of the LI element, the second does not inherit vertical margin values from the former.

You might want to have your list items vertically spaced out more on the page, however. Enter the following in your style sheet to set the bottom margin of six pixels for each list item (see Figure 3.13):

```
ul { margin-top: -12px; margin-left: 25px; padding-left: 25px; }
li { margin-bottom: 6px; }
```

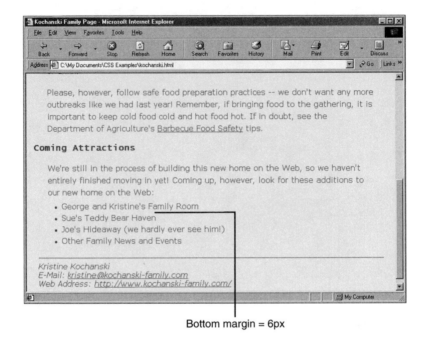

Bottom margin = 6px

Figure 3.13: *A bottom margin of six pixels is set for each list item.*

Specifying the Bullet Type

When displaying a bulleted list, browsers should display a bullet in the form of a filled disc. There might be a browser out there that displays a different default bullet, but I'm not aware of it. You can change the type of bullet that is displayed, however, if you wish. This can be done in HTML and by using styles. Because the HTML feature is deprecated in favor of using styles, I'll show you how to do this by using styles.

Use the `list-style-type` property to specify a different bullet type. You can choose between `disc` (the default), `circle`, `square`, and `none` as the property values. The first is displayed as a filled disc, the second as a hollow circle, the third as a filled square, and the fourth is displayed as a blank space. For instance, to change the list element's bullet type to a hollow circle, enter the following (see Figure 3.14):

```
ul { list-style-type: circle; margin-top: -12px; margin-left: 25px; padding-left:
25px; }
li { margin-bottom: 6px; }
```

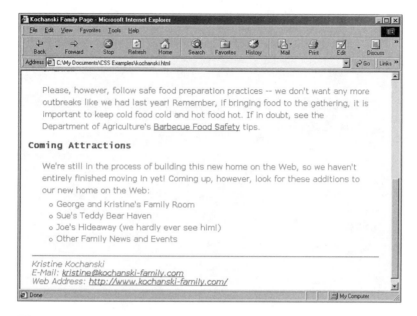

Figure 3.14: *The list's bullet is changed to a hollow circle.*

NOTE

You can also use the `list-style-type` property to specify different number types for numbered lists (using OL rather than the UL elements). The possible values are `decimal` (1, 2, 3, and so on; the default), `upper-roman` (I, II, III, and so on), `lower-roman` (i, ii, iii, and so on), `upper-alpha` (A, B, C, and so on), and `lower-alpha` (a, b, c, and so on).

✔ For examples of changing the number type for numbered lists, see "Creating Numbered Lists," p. 260 (chapter 11).

Later, in Chapter 11, "Working with Lists," you'll be working much more extensively with both bulleted and ordered lists.

Setting the Address Characteristics

In HTML the ADDRESS element is used to designate your address block, within which you may include information identifying the author or owner of a site, as well as provide contact information and links. An address block is often separated from the rest of the page by an HR (Horizontal Rule) element. Here's the address block section of the example file (see Figure 3.15):

```
<hr>
<address>
Kristine Kochanski<br>
```

```
E-Mail: <a href="mailto:kristine@kochanski-family.com">kristine@kochanski-
family.com</a><br>
Web Address: <a href="http://www.kochanski-family.com/">http://www.kochanski-
family.com/</a>
</address>
```

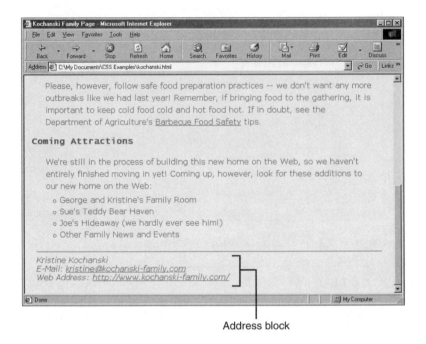

Address block

Figure 3.15: *An address block identifies and provides a means to contact the author or owner of a site.*

Centering Your Address Block

The ADDRESS element is left-aligned by default. Centering your address block is one way to give your page a bit of a different look. Go ahead and center the ADDRESS element (see Figure 3.16):

```
li { margin-bottom: 6px; }
address { text-align: center; }
```

Changing Your Address Block's Text and Link Colors

Changing the color of your address block's font helps to set it off from the rest of your page. Go ahead and change the text color for your address block to a brick red color:

```
address { color: #cc0000; background-color: transparent; text-align: center; }
```

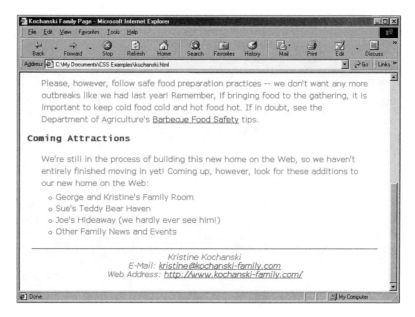

Figure 3.16: *You can center your address block.*

Changing the foreground color of your address block only changes the color of the text, but not the hypertext links. To also change the color of your links, to a green color, for example, just add the following style rule for the A (Anchor) element:

```
address { color: #cc0000; background-color: transparent; text-align: center; }
a { color: green; background-color: transparent; }
```

✔ For more guidance on setting colors for hypertext links, including examples of setting different colors for the different link states (unvisited, visited, active, and hover), see "Controlling the Appearance of Links," p. 171 (chapter 8).

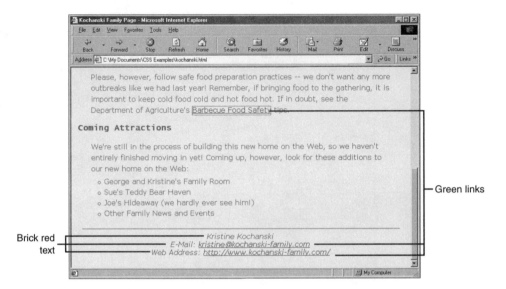

Figure 3.17: *You can set the foreground colors of your address block and hypertext links to whatever colors you prefer.*

What's Next?

This is the end of Part I, "Creating Your First Style Sheet." In this chapter you finished creating your first style sheet and should now have some understanding and feeling for what a style sheet is and how it works. The intention of the first part of this book is to provide you with an introduction to creating and using style sheets without going too deeply into any one feature.

In Part II, "Understanding Basic Concepts," you go deeper into some of the key concepts behind CSS. In Chapter 4, "Using CSS with HTML," you learn more about using CSS in HTML, including: containment in HTML, what elements and attributes have been deprecated in HTML and what features in CSS replace them, accessibility and device-independence features of CSS, using CSS with XHTML, and more.

Part II

Understanding Basic Concepts

Using CSS with HTML

Cascading, Grouping, and Inheritance

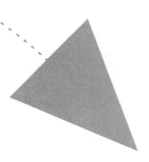

Using CSS with HTML

In the first part of this book, you created your first style sheet. This gave you some hands-on experience working with CSS, as well as a global feel for the language, without getting into extra details.

The remaining parts of this book are designed to give you a more in-depth and detailed review and examples of using CSS. In this chapter, you learn about:

- Using the STYLE element to embed CSS style sheets in HTML documents

- Linking and importing external style sheets within HTML documents

- Inserting inline styles directly into HTML elements

- Using class, ID, and contextual selectors to create your own specialized styles

- Using HTML comments and CSS comments in your pages

- The importance of separating appearance from structure

- The meaning and importance of deprecation and which elements and attributes are deprecated in HTML 4

- What the three flavors of HTML are and how to use the correct DOCTYPE declaration in your page

Containment in HTML

CSS doesn't really do anything by itself. To take effect, it needs to be mated with a markup language such as HTML, XHTML, or XML. A *markup language* is a system of instructions that are incorporated into a document that direct how the content is to be presented. HTML, XHTML, and XML are all based on SGML (Standard Generalized Markup Language), which is generally used in the desktop publishing world to markup computer documents for printing.

NOTE

Because the vast majority of Web publishers use HTML to code Web pages, and are likely to do so far into the future, this book primarily deals with using CSS with HTML documents. CSS can also be used with XHTML documents.

In most cases, the examples and material provided in this book apply equally to both HTML and XHTML.

CSS can be included in an HTML document in the following four ways:

- Using the STYLE element in HTML to directly embed style rules in an individual HTML document.

- Using the LINK element to link an HTML document to an external style sheet file.

- Using CSS' @import notation to import a style sheet into an HTML document.

- Using the STYLE attribute to apply "inline styles" to specific elements within the body of any HTML document.

Embedding Style Sheets Using the STYLE Element

You used this method when creating your first style sheet in the previous chapters in this book. Beginning users need to understand how styles work before learning how the intricacies of styles can be applied to HTML documents. In other words, learn to ride the bicycle before trying to do handstands on the handlebars!

You *embed* a style sheet in an HTML file using the STYLE element, nesting the styles that make up your style sheet within that element. The STYLE element was incorporated into the HTML 3.2 specification to allow the inclusion of style sheets within an HTML document. The STYLE element is a container element within which individual style rules are nested. In HTML, many elements can take attributes to further qualify the function of the element. An *attribute* is a code inserted into the start tag of an HTML element that further qualifies the function of the element, in most cases in the form of the name of the attribute and a value assigned to it.

Each HTML element has a specific set of attributes that can be used with it, some of which may be required, while others are optional. The two most important attributes that are used with the STYLE element are the TYPE attribute and the MEDIA attribute, the first of which is required, while the second is optional.

THE TYPE ATTRIBUTE

You'll notice in the example HTML file you worked with in the previous two chapters that the start tag for the STYLE element contains an attribute, `type="text/css"`, as shown here:

```
<style type="text/css">
```

The TYPE attribute is a required element that must be included in the STYLE element's start tag. If you don't include it, some browsers may not recognize your style sheet. The specific content of the TYPE attribute in this case specifies that the content of the STYLE element is a CSS style sheet. This must be included, exactly as shown above, whenever you want to embed a CSS style sheet in an HTML document.

NOTE

Only CSS style sheets can be used with HTML documents, so the content of the STYLE element's TYPE attribute in HTML documents will always be the same (`type="text/css"`). XHTML documents, however, can utilize two different style sheet languages, CSS or XSL (Extensible Stylesheet Language), with the TYPE attribute taking different values depending on the type of style sheet being used. XSL style sheets can be used with XHTML or XML documents, but not with HTML documents, while CSS style sheets can be used with HTML, XHTML, or XML documents.

You embed a CSS style sheet in an XHTML document in exactly the same way as in an HTML document (including the `type="text/css"` attribute in the STYLE element). Any detailed discussion of XSL or XML is beyond the scope of this book and is not directly relevant to using CSS style sheets with HTML documents. You can find out more about XSL and XML at the W3C's site (`http://www.w3.org/`).

THE MEDIA ATTRIBUTE

The MEDIA attribute can be included in the STYLE tag to specify the target medium or media in which the document is to be presented or displayed. CSS can be used not only to specify how an HTML document is presented on a computer screen (through a browser window), for instance, but also how it might be presented in a variety of other media or devices. One set of styles might be included directing how the document should be displayed on a computer screen, while another might be included directing how the same document should be printed on a printer, for instance.

The HTML 4.01 specification refers to these different MEDIA attribute values as *media-descriptors*, indicating they are values that describe the different media for which style sheets may be used to specify media-specific presentation. Table 4.1 shows the allowable media-descriptors that can be used with the MEDIA attribute, along with descriptions of their functions:

Table 4.1   MEDIA Attribute Values

Media-Descriptor	Target Media Description
screen	Non-paged computer screens
print	Paged printed documents
projection	Paged projected documents (presentations)
handheld	Handheld devices, such as PDAs or cell phones
tv	Television-type devices (WebTV, for instance)
tty	Teletypes, terminals, and other fixed-pitch displays
aural	Speech browsers and synthesizers
braille	Braille tactile feedback devices
embossed	Paged Braille printers
all	All devices

By default, a media-descriptor of screen (referring to a nonpaged computer display), is assumed. Multiple media-descriptors can be included in the form of a comma-delimited list to indicate that a style sheet is targeted for multiple media types.

Including a separate style sheet for printing, for instance, can be quite useful. Web designers often have to create two separate versions of a page, one for displaying in a browser and the other for printing on a printer, because the version for the Web doesn't print well or includes lots of extraneous information that doesn't need to be printed. If you have a printer connected to your computer, you can try this out. First, open the example file you created in the previous chapter, **kochanski.html**, and edit it as follows:

```
<head>
<title>Kochanski Family Page</title>

<style type="text/css" media="print">
body { font-family: verdana, helvetica, sans-serif; margin: 0.5in; }
h1 { font-family: impact, avantgarde, arial, sans-serif; text-align: center;
font-size: 26pt; }
h2, h3 { font-family: avantgarde, arial, sans-serif; font-style: italic; }
p { text-align: justify; }
address { text-align: center; }
</style>
```

```
<style type="text/css" media="screen">
body { background-color: #ffffcc; color: teal; font-family: verdana, arial,
helvetica, sans-serif; margin-top: 25px; margin-bottom: 25px; margin-left: 25px;
margin-right: 25px; }
```

You'll notice in this example that a mixture of different fonts are specified. Verdana, Impact, and Arial are TrueType fonts, for instance, while Helvetica and AvantGarde are PostScript fonts. Substitute different fonts, if you want, specifying fonts that you know are available on your system or from your printer.

Next, save your document, open it in your browser, and then click the Print button to print it. Figures 4.1 and 4.2 show the results of these style sheets when the page is displayed in a browser window and when it is printed from the same browser. Depending on which fonts you have available, the actual fonts that are printed may be different than those shown in Figure 4.2 (if you don't have Impact or AvantGarde available, for instance, the heading elements will be printed using whatever font is specified as the default sans serif font on your system).

Figure 4.1: *A Web browser is just one medium in which a CSS/HTML document can be displayed.*

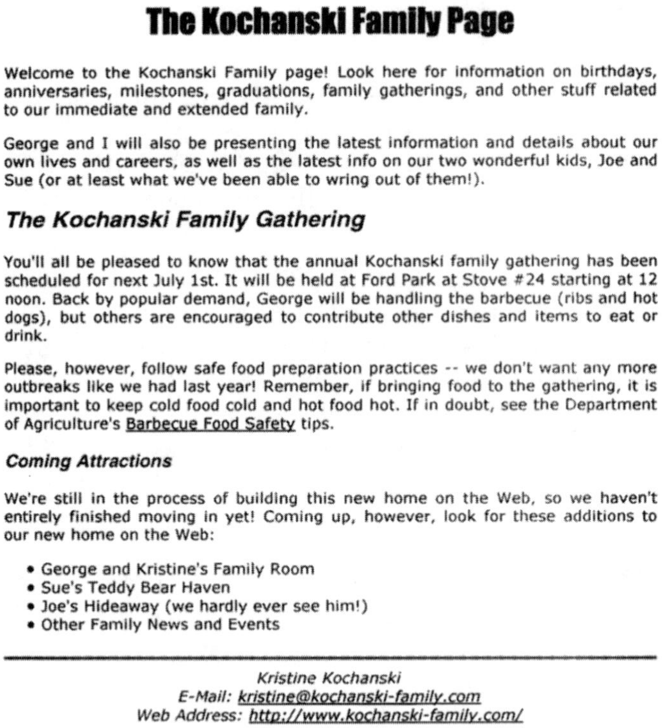

The Kochanski Family Page

Welcome to the Kochanski Family page! Look here for information on birthdays, anniversaries, milestones, graduations, family gatherings, and other stuff related to our immediate and extended family.

George and I will also be presenting the latest information and details about our own lives and careers, as well as the latest info on our two wonderful kids, Joe and Sue (or at least what we've been able to wring out of them!).

The Kochanski Family Gathering

You'll all be pleased to know that the annual Kochanski family gathering has been scheduled for next July 1st. It will be held at Ford Park at Stove #24 starting at 12 noon. Back by popular demand, George will be handling the barbecue (ribs and hot dogs), but others are encouraged to contribute other dishes and items to eat or drink.

Please, however, follow safe food preparation practices -- we don't want any more outbreaks like we had last year! Remember, if bringing food to the gathering, it is important to keep cold food cold and hot food hot. If in doubt, see the Department of Agriculture's Barbecue Food Safety tips.

Coming Attractions

We're still in the process of building this new home on the Web, so we haven't entirely finished moving in yet! Coming up, however, look for these additions to our new home on the Web:

- George and Kristine's Family Room
- Sue's Teddy Bear Haven
- Joe's Hideaway (we hardly ever see him!)
- Other Family News and Events

Kristine Kochanski
E-Mail: kristine@kochanski-family.com
Web Address: http://www.kochanski-family.com/

Figure 4.2: *By including a print style sheet, you can specify how you want a CSS/HTML document to be printed.*

You can find out more about using the MEDIA attribute on the W3C's page on Media Types at `http://www.w3.org/TR/REC-CSS2/media.html`.

Other STYLE Attributes

Three other HTML attributes—the TITLE, LANG, and DIR attributes—might also be included in the STYLE element, but are neither required nor commonly used. For more information on these attributes, see the W3C's HTML 4.01 specification at `http://www.w3.org/TR/html4/`.

Linking and Importing Style Sheets

You're not limited to just embedding styles sheets in HTML files using the STYLE element. You can also link to or import external style sheets using the LINK element or the `@import` rule. By *linking* or *importing* an external style sheet, for instance, you can control the presentation of a whole Web site from a single external style sheet. An *external style sheet* is a text document, saved with .css as the file extension, containing a list of styles that can then be linked to or imported into an HTML document. Here is a simple hypothetical example that utilizes both of these methods:

```
<link rel="stylesheet" type="text/css"
href="http://www.domain.com/mystyles/default.css">
<style type="text/css">
@import { url("mystyle.css"); }
H1 { color: blue }
</style>
```

When using linked, imported, and embedded style sheets within the same document, it is important to be aware of the rules of precedence between them. These can be fairly simply stated in the following fashion:

- Embedded styles have precedence over imported or linked styles.

- Imported styles have precedence over linked styles.

Thus, if an embedded style declares that the color of the H1 element is blue, that's what it will be, even if other colors are declared for the H1 element via an imported or linked style sheet. In the absence of an embedded style, however, an imported style rule declaring the color of the H1 element to be purple, for instance, wins out over a linked style rule declaring the color of the H1 element to be green.

While you're still learning CSS, however, you're best off sticking to experimenting with embedded style sheets. Later, after you've gained more experience working with embedded style sheets, see Chapter 14, "Creating Page Layouts and Site Designs" to create and link an external style sheet to the pages of a Web site. In Chapter 16, "Providing for Backward Compatibility," you'll learn how to use the @import rule to shield Netscape Navigator 4 (which doesn't support the @import rule) from styles that are not compatible with that browser, while allowing other browsers (which do support the @import rule) to have access to the styles.

NOTE

To create an external style sheet, just type the style rules directly in a text file, saving it with a .css extension. Don't include a STYLE element in an external style sheet—just include the style rules.

Inserting Inline Styles Using the STYLE Attribute

You can also insert styles directly into HTML elements by using the STYLE attribute. This is handy when you only need to apply a particular format in one place within your document.

Here's an example of using an inline style to specify a bold-weight font for the first paragraph in the Kochanski Family Page (see Figure 4.3):

```
<h1>The Kochanski Family Page</h1>
```

```
<p style="font-weight: bold">Welcome to the Kochanski Family page! Look here for
information on birthdays, anniversaries, milestones, graduations, family
gatherings, and other stuff related to our immediate and extended family.</p>
```

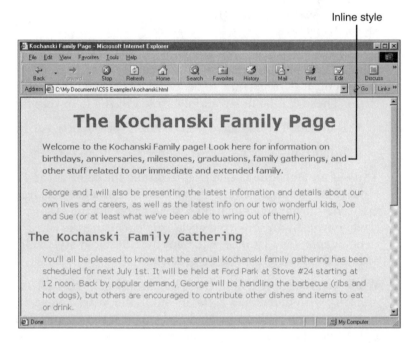

Figure 4.3: Inline styles are handy if you only need a particular format once.

The syntax for expressing inline styles is the same as for style rules created using the STYLE element. The style properties and their values are quoted rather than enclosed within squiggly brackets. As long as you remember that, you shouldn't have any problem using inline styles. The STYLE attribute can be applied to all elements, except for the HTML, HEAD, TITLE, META, SCRIPT, PARAM, and STYLE elements.

TIP

When using inline styles, you might run into a situation in which you need to quote a text string within a style declaration. For instance, you might want to include a style declaration such as `font-family: "Bookman Old Style"`, where the font-family name needs to be quoted because of spaces within the text string. The problem here is that you need to use quotes when specifying the inline style and can't nest the same quotation marks within each other. To address this, replace the nested double-quotes with single quotes, like this:

```
<p style="font-family: 'Bookman Old Style'">Welcome to the
Kochanski Family page!</p>
```

Because inline styles involve specifying formatting for individual elements, they also go somewhat against the philosophy of CSS, which is to promote both richness and efficiency in the coding of Web pages. Generally, you should use inline styles in single instances where you need to override an element's style or default display. If you find yourself repeating the same inline style within a document more than a couple of times, then you should consider creating a non-inline style rule to handle the styling. The two most common ways of doing this are by using a class selector or an ID selector. The next section, "Using Class and ID Selectors," covers doing that.

Using Class and ID Selectors

In HTML, you can apply CLASS or ID attributes to HTML elements. A *CLASS attribute* assigns a class name to an element, while an *ID attribute* assigns a unique name to an element. You can include a particular CLASS attribute as many times as you wish, even to dissimilar elements. ID attribute values, however, must be unique and should not be repeated in the same document. Using the Kochanski Family Page example you've been working with, here are some examples of adding CLASS and ID attributes to HTML elements:

```
<h1>The Kochanski Family Page</h1>
<p class="first">Welcome to the Kochanski Family page! Look here for information
on birthdays, anniversaries, milestones, graduations, family gatherings, and
other stuff related to our immediate and extended family.</p>
<p>George and I will also be presenting the latest information and details about
our own lives and careers, as well as the latest info on our two wonderful kids,
Joe and Sue (or at least what we've been able to wring out of them!).</p>

<h2 id="special">The Kochanski Family Gathering</h2>
<p class="first">You'll all be pleased to know that the annual Kochanski family
gathering has been scheduled for next July 1st. It will be held at Ford Park at
Stove #24 starting at 12 noon. Back by popular demand, George will be handling
the barbecue (ribs and hot dogs), but others are encouraged to contribute other
dishes and items to eat or drink.</p>
```

In CSS, two special types of selectors let you apply styles to elements marked with CLASS or ID attributes: class selectors and ID selectors. A *class selector* lets you assign styles to elements that are included within a particular class, while an *ID selector* lets you assign styles to an element with a unique ID.

For instance, here's an example of creating a class selector to apply style properties to P elements that contain a class="first" attribute (eliminate the line-height property from the P element rule):

```
p { margin-top: 20px; margin-bottom: 20px;  margin-left: 20px; margin-right:
20px; }
```
p.first { font-style: italic; font-weight: bold; }

You'll notice that a class selector is specified using a period followed by the name of the class. In this case, all P elements that contain a class="first" attribute are displayed bolded and in italic.

Here's an example of creating an ID selector to apply style properties to an H2 element marked with an id="special" attribute:

```
h2, h3 { margin-left: -10px; font-family: monospace; color: #0066cc; }
```
h2#special { font-family: sans-serif; text-decoration: underline; }

You'll notice that an ID selector is specified using a hash mark (#) followed by the ID name. In this case, the H2 element containing the id="special" attribute is displayed in a sans serif font and underlined.

Figure 4.4 shows what the class and ID selectors you just created look like when displayed in a browser.

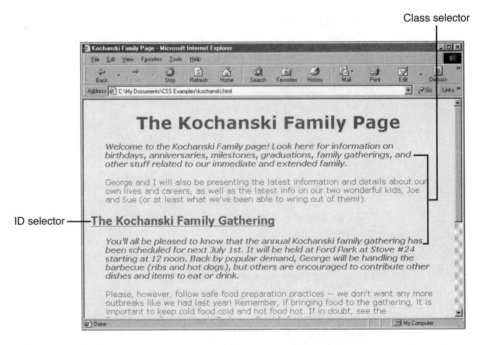

Figure 4.4: *You can create special formatting for a document using class selectors or ID selectors.*

✔ The previous example utilizes a new style property, the text-decoration property, that you haven't used before. For information on using the text-decoration property, see "Setting Underlining, Overlining, and Other Highlighting," p. 166 (chapter 8).

You can optionally leave out the element name when creating class and ID selectors. For instance, instead of p.first, you can just use .first. Instead of h2#special, you can just use #special. Here's what this looks like in your example style sheet:

```
p { margin-top: 20px; margin-bottom: 20px;  margin-left: 20px; margin-right:
20px; }
.first { font-style: italic; font-weight: bold; }
h1 { text-align: center; color: red; font-size: 36px; }
h2, h3 { margin-left: -10px; font-family: monospace; color: #0066cc; }
#special { font-family: sans-serif; text-decoration: underline; }
```

For ID selectors, since you can only use one ID attribute of the same name in a document, this just provides a shortened version you can use. For class selectors, this allows you to apply the same style properties to a class that may include more than one element type.

For an example of using a class selector to format two different elements, first change the ID selector you added to your style sheet earlier to a class selector (since your ID attributes need to be unique), like this:

```
h2, h3 { margin-left: -10px; font-family: monospace; color: #0066cc; }
.special { font-family: sans-serif; text-decoration: underline; }
```

Next, change the ID attribute you added to your page's H2 element to a class attribute, like this:

```
<h2 class="special">The Kochanski Family Gathering</h2>
```

Finally, add a class="special" attribute to your page's H3 element as well, like this:

```
<h3 class="special">Coming Attractions</h3>
```

Now, if you save your file and refresh the display of your page in your browser, you should see, as shown in Figure 4.5, that both the H2 and H3 elements now share the style properties assigned by the .special class selector.

Using Contextual Selectors

Another form of selector that allows you to style some instances of an element, but not others, is the contextual selector. A *contextual selector* applies style properties only to elements within a certain context. For instance, here's an example of only setting the display characteristics of hypertext links (the A element) that are nested inside of the ADDRESS element, while leaving hypertext links located elsewhere as they are (see Figure 4.6):

```
a { color: green; background-color: transparent; }
address a { font-weight: bold; color: yellow; background-color: navy; padding-
left: 5px; padding-right: 5px; }
```

Special class
selector

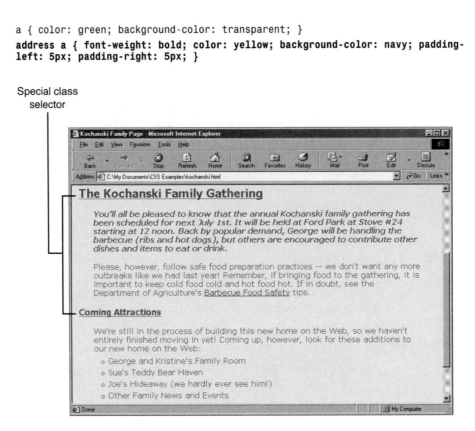

Figure 4.5: *You can style different elements using the same class selector.*

You'll notice that a contextual style is similar to a style group, except that the elements being selected are separated by a space, instead of a comma. You can create contextual styles that reach several levels deep, setting properties for a particular element that is nested within a particular element that is nested within even another element. Here's a hypothetical example:

```
blockquote p em { font-weight: bold; }
```

This would set the font weight to bold only for EM elements that are nested in a P element that is nested in a BLOCKQUOTE element. All other EM elements would remain unbolded.

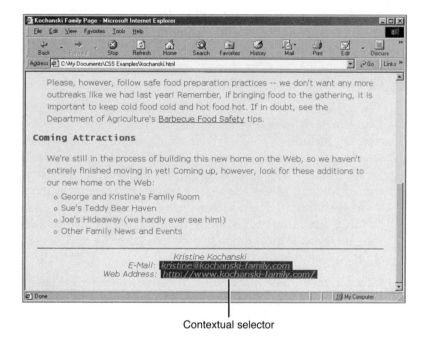

Contextual selector

Figure 4.6: *You can style different elements using the same class selector.*

Using Comments

Earlier browsers that don't recognize CSS might display text included in a STYLE element at the top of your page as untagged text. Some search engines might also try to index the content of a STYLE element or display its contents, rather then the initial text of the page, in a search engine query response list. To handle this situation, the W3C has instituted a special use for HTML comment codes when used with styles. In the following example, the HTML comment codes (<!-- and -->) function to shield non-supporting browsers from displaying the text nested within the STYLE element:

```
<style type="text/css">
<!--
body { font-family: "Bookman Old Style", serif; }
h1 { font-family: "Lucida Console", sans-serif; text-align: center; font-size:
24pt; }
-->
</style>
```

In this case, a nonsupporting browser simply treats everything within the HTML comment codes as a comment, ignoring it completely. Search engines should not display anything inserted between the comment codes in any search engine query response lists. A CSS-supporting browser, however, ignores the comment codes.

You might, however, want to include comments within your style sheets. CSS provides special codes you can use to bracket off comment text you want to include in your style sheet. By adding comments to your style sheets, you can leave notes to yourself, reminding yourself of what the different parts of the style sheet are doing, which can be helpful if you need to come back and revise the style sheet later. Others might also have to revise your work later—if you include comments, they'll have to spend less time figuring out what you're doing. Comments can also be handy for commenting out styles that you don't want to use in the current style sheet, but may want to use later.

CSS comments are inserted in the form of a forward slash and an asterisk (/*), which starts a comment, and an asterisk and a forward slash (*/), which ends a comment. Browsers will ignore anything placed between these codes. You can comment out text strings within a line, or one or several lines of text. Here are some examples of using both HTML and CSS comments in the Kochanski Family Page style sheets:

```
<head>
<title>Kochanski Family Page</title>

<style type="text/css" media="print">
<!--
/* This style sheet specifies formatting for printing. */
body { font-family: verdana, helvetica, sans-serif; margin: 0.5in; } /* Print
styling for body. */
h1 { font-family: impact, avantgarde, arial, sans-serif; text-align: center;
font-size: 26pt; } /* Print styling for level-one heading. */
h2, h3 { font-family: avantgarde, arial, sans-serif; font-style: italic; } /*
Print styling for level-two and level-three headings. */
p { text-align: justify; } */ Print styling for text paragraphs. */
address { text-align: center; } */ Print styling for address block. */
-->
</style>

<style type="text/css" media="screen">
<!--
/* This style sheet specifies formatting for display in a browser. */
body { background-color: #ffffcc; color: teal; font-family: verdana, arial,
helvetica, sans-serif; margin-top: 25px; margin-bottom: 25px; margin-left: 25px;
margin-right: 25px; }
```

```
p { margin-top: 20px; margin-bottom: 20px;  margin-left: 20px; margin-right:
20px; }

/* This style is commented out.
.first { font-style: italic; font-weight: bold; }
*/

h1 { text-align: center; color: red; font-size: 36px; }
h2, h3 { margin-left: -10px; font-family: monospace; color: #0066cc; }

/* This style is commented out.
.special { font-family: sans-serif; text-decoration: underline; }
*/

ul { list-style-type: circle; margin-top: -12px; margin-left: 25px; padding-left:
25px; }
li { margin-bottom: 6px; }
address { color: #cc0000; background-color: transparent; text-align: center; }
a { color: green; background-color: transparent; }
address a { font-weight: bold; color: yellow; background-color: navy; padding-
left: 5px; padding-right: 5px; }
-->
</style>
</head>
```

Separating Appearance from Structure

Separating appearance from structure is a key concept in CSS. The basic idea is that HTML should be responsible for specifying the structural elements of a document (headings, paragraphs, lists, hypertext links, and so on), while CSS should be responsible for specifying the appearance of those elements. Both HTML 4 and XHTML are formulated to facilitate this division of labor. There are some important reasons for separating appearance from structure in HTML documents:

- It facilitates visually richer presentations while conserving bandwidth, in that a style need only be stated once for an element and the same style sheet can be used for all the pages within a site. Web designers need no longer rely on using multiple FONT and TABLE elements to design their pages, which can be very wasteful of bandwidth.

- It makes Web pages and sites more accessible, in that nonvisual user agents (such as a speech or Braille browser, for instance) can simply ignore the visual styling of a page, while focusing on conveying the structure and content of the document. Style sheets can also be used to provide nonvisual styling, such as providing pause lengths before and after heading elements, changes in voice tone, pitch or volume, and so on, to provide cues for how a page's content might be rendered in a speech browser, for instance, to make it more understandable.

- It allows Web pages to be styled for multiple media. Using CSS style sheets can be used both for presenting information over the Web and for printing it on a laser printer, for instance, with separate formatting specified in each case. Without CSS, you need to maintain separate documents for this. You can also specify separate styling for presentations, TV displays, handheld devices (PDAs and cell phones), and other devices, all within the same document.

- Because a single style sheet, or set of style sheets, can be applied to multiple pages, or even to a whole site, using style sheets to control the appearance of your pages can also be much more efficient and less time-consuming for Web designers than having to change or update multiple instances of FONT elements, for instance, in multiple pages. Using styles makes enforcing a uniform look and appearance for a whole site a much more manageable task.

You've actually been working with using styles to separate appearance from content all along in this book. When you first started working with the example file for the Kochanski Family Page, for instance, it contained only the text for the page and HTML elements (headings, paragraphs, and so on) indicating the structural elements of the page (refer to Figure 2.1). No colors, alignment, font size changes, indents, or other visual formatting was included in the HTML coding for the page. When creating your first style sheet in the previous two chapters, you then had some hands-on experience of using styles to control the visual presentation of your page, without relying on using any HTML coding (such as FONT or TABLE elements) to control its appearance.

CSS and Deprecated Elements and Attributes

To help purge HTML of ad-hoc elements and attributes that were introduced over time, primarily by browser manufacturers, to govern the appearance and display of Web pages, the W3C has declared a number of elements and attributes as deprecated in HTML 4. A *deprecated* element or attribute is one which users are encouraged to avoid using, since the same or better results now can be produced using style sheets alone. Users are also warned that deprecated elements may be declared obsolete in future versions of HTML (although this is only really relevant to XHTML users, since HTML 4.01 is supposed to be the final version of HTML). An *obsolete* element or attribute should not be used, since current or future browsers are not required to support it.

Just because an element or attribute is deprecated doesn't mean that it can't be used in a Web page, however. They are still legal elements and attributes which current Web browsers are required to support. It is also unlikely elements or attributes deprecated in HTML 4.01 will be declared obsolete in the future, since HTML 4.01 is supposedly the final version of HTML. XHTML 1 is a different case, however—deprecated elements and attributes in XHTML 1 are highly likely to be declared obsolete in future versions of XHTML.

One of the goals of CSS is to enable Web designers to effectively design Web pages without the use of any deprecated elements or attributes. The examples in this book, for instance, do not include any deprecated elements or attributes. For your reference, Table 4.2 lists all the elements that have been deprecated in HTML 4, while Table 4.3 lists all the attributes that have been deprecated in HTML 4.

Table 4.2   Deprecated Elements in HTML 4.01

Element	Description
APPLET	Inserts Java applets in pages
BASEFONT	Specifies the base font size
CENTER	Centers nested elements and text
DIR	Creates a directory list
FONT	Specifies font sizes, colors, and faces
ISINDEX	Single-line prompt
MENU	Creates a menu list
S	Strikethrough text
STRIKE	Strikethrough text
U	Underlined text

Table 4.3   Deprecated Attributes in HTML 4.01

Attribute	Elements Where Deprecated
ALIGN	APPLET, CAPTION, DIV, Hn, HR, IFRAME, IMG, INPUT, LEGEND, OBJECT, P, TABLE (not deprecated in COL, COLGROUP, TBODY, TD, TFOOT, TH, THEAD, TR)
ALINK	BODY
BACKGROUND	BODY
BGCOLOR	BODY, TABLE, TD, TH, TR
BORDER	IMG, OBJECT (not deprecated in TABLE)
CLEAR	BR
COMPACT	DL, OL, UL
HEIGHT	TD, TH (not deprecated in IFRAME, IMG, OBJECT)
HSPACE	IMG, OBJECT

Table 4.3 continued

Attribute	Elements Where Deprecated
LANGUAGE	SCRIPT
LINK	BODY
NOSHADE	HR
NOWRAP	TD, TH
SIZE	HR (not deprecated in INPUT, SELECT)
START	OL
TEXT	BODY
TYPE	LI, OL, UL (not deprecated in A, BUTTON, INPUT, LINK, OBJECT, PARAM, SCRIPT, STYLE)
VALUE	LI
VERSION	HTML
VLINK	BODY
VSPACE	IMG, OBJECT
WIDTH	HR, TD, TH, PRE (not deprecated in COL, COLGROUP, IFRAME, IMG, OBJECT, TABLE

A Word About Frames

While frameset elements have not been deprecated in HTML 4, one of the goals of CSS is to enable the layout of framed pages without the use of any frameset elements or attributes. In HTML, the term *frameset element* refers to any element used to implement frames within a Web page (including the FRAMESET, FRAME, and other elements). The "strict" definitions for HTML 4 and XHTML 1, however, disallow the use of both deprecated and frameset elements and attributes. See the following section, "The Three Flavors of HTML," for information on the strict, transitional, and frameset definitions for HTML.

The Three Flavors of HTML

To help in the transition from the era of using HTML tags that have evolved in an ad-hoc fashion to control the appearance of Web pages to a new era in which the appearance of Web pages will be controlled entirely by the use of styles sheets, the W3C has formulated three different flavors of HTML 4: strict, transitional, and frameset. These are defined in the form of three separate DTDs (Document Type Definitions). A *DTD* is the formal definition of a specification by the W3C. Thankfully, the W3C also provides less formal and more easily comprehended explanations in the form of the official specifications, meaning that you don't have to know how to read the DTD (no easy task in itself) in order to understand the specification. If you want to learn how to read the HTML 4 DTDs, for instance, the W3C provides instructions on its "On SGML and HTML" page at `http://www.w3.org/TR/html4/intro/sgmltut.html`.

However, you only need to know that these three versions of HTML, strict, transitional, and frameset, conform to three separate formal DTDs of the same name. You do need to know what they signify, however, if you're going to be using styles. If you want to validate your CSS style sheets, you'll also need to include a DOCTYPE declaration at the top of your document. A *DOCTYPE declaration* declares the type of document that is being coded.

The *strict definition* of HTML 4 does not allow the use of any deprecated or frameset elements and attributes. To declare your document as adhering to the strict definition of HTML 4, you insert the following DOCTYPE declaration at the top of your document:

```
<!DOCTYPE HTML PUBLIC "-//W3C//DTD HTML 4.01//EN"
"http://www.w3.org/TR/html4/strict.dtd">
<html>
```

The *transitional definition* of HTML 4 allows the use of deprecated elements and attributes, but does not allow the use of frameset elements and attributes. To declare your document as adhering to the Transitional DTD, insert the following DOCTYPE declaration:

```
<!DOCTYPE HTML PUBLIC "-//W3C//DTD HTML 4.01 Transitional//EN"
"http://www.w3.org/TR/html4/loose.dtd">
```

The *frameset definition* of HTML 4 allows the use of both deprecated and frameset elements and attributes. To declare your document as adhering to the Frameset DTD, insert the following DOCTYPE declaration:

```
<!DOCTYPE HTML PUBLIC "-//W3C//DTD HTML 4.01 Frameset//EN"
"http://www.w3.org/TR/html4/frameset.dtd">
```

Browsers don't generally care whether you include a DOCTYPE declaration at the top of your page, but you'll need to include one if you want to validate your page's code using one of the HTML or CSS validators that are available.

If you declare that your page conforms to the strict definition of HTML 4, for instance, when validating your page you'll get error messages if any deprecated elements or attributes are included in the page.

If you declare that your page conforms to the transitional definition of HTML 4, when validating your page you won't get any error messages if deprecated elements or attributes are included in the page, but you will get error messages if any frameset elements or attributes are included in the page.

If you declare that your page conforms to the frameset definition of HTML 4, when validating your page you won't get any error messages if deprecated or frameset elements or attributes are included in the page.

✔ You'll be learning more about using DOCTYPE declarations and validating your HTML pages and style sheets in Chapter 15, "Validating Your Style Sheet."

You'll note in the Kochanski Family Page example you've been working with, that I've included the DOCTYPE declaration at the top of that page, declaring that the document conforms to the transitional definition of HTML 4. I could have just as easily declared it to be in conformance with the strict definition of HTML 4, since no deprecated elements or attributes are used in the examples I provide. However, since you may use this example page as a model for creating an actual page, and may decide to utilize deprecated elements or attributes in that page, I decided to allow for that possibility. There is no penalty for declaring your document as conforming to a less strict definition of HTML than it actually does. But if you want to validate your page later for conformance to the strict definition of HTML, however, you'll need to insert the appropriate DOCTYPE declaration for that.

XHTML DOCTYPE Declarations

XHTML 1 specifies the same three levels of conformity (strict, transitional, and frameset). The DOCTYPE declarations that you need to use with XHTML 1 documents are somewhat different from those used with HTML 4 documents. Following are the strict, transitional, and frameset DOCTYPE declarations that should be used in XHTML 1 documents.

The strict XHTML 1 DOCTYPE declaration:

```
<!DOCTYPE html PUBLIC "-//W3C//DTD XHTML 1.0 Strict//EN"
"http://www.w3.org/TR/xhtml1/DTD/xhtml1-strict.dtd">
```

The transitional XHTML 1 DOCTYPE declaration:

```
<!DOCTYPE html PUBLIC "-//W3C//DTD XHTML 1.0 Transitional//EN"
"http://www.w3.org/TR/xhtml1/DTD/xhtml1-transitional.dtd">
```

The frameset XHTML 1 DOCTYPE declaration:

```
<!DOCTYPE html PUBLIC "-//W3C//DTD XHTML 1.0 Frameset//EN"
"http://www.w3.org/TR/xhtml1/DTD/xhtml1-frameset.dtd">
```

For more information on using DOCTYPE declarations in XHTML 1, see the W3C's specification for XHTML 1 at http://www.w3.org/TR/xhtml1/.

What's Next?

In this chapter you learned about including CSS style sheets in HTML documents. You should now be familiar with how to embed, link to, and import style sheets in your pages, as well as with how to insert inline styles directly into HTML elements. You should also have a starting understanding of using class and ID selectors, as well as using contextual selectors, in your style sheets—I'll be providing lots more examples of using these as you go through the rest of the examples in this book.

You should also now be familiar with what elements and attributes are deprecated in HTML 4 and what that means, as well as what the three DOCTYPE declarations are and when and how to include them in your HTML documents.

In the next chapter, "Cascading, Grouping, and Inheritance," you learn more about the importance of the concept of cascading (as in Cascading Style Sheets), what grouping is and what it can do for you, and how style rules inherit qualities and characteristics.

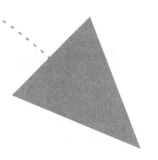

Cascading, Grouping, and Inheritance

In this chapter, you review three very important concepts in CSS: cascading, grouping, and inheritance. These concepts, by and large, have to do not with specific features or functions in CSS, but with how CSS functions as a whole. Here are the highlights of the ground you'll be covering in learning about these key concepts:

- What cascading is and how it works
- Modularity and author/user balance
- What grouping is and how it works
- Combining group and individual selectors
- What inheritance is and how it works
- Specified and computed values

How Cascading Works

As pointed out previously, the word cascading (p. 15) signifies that a CSS-styled document can derive style information from varying sources, rather than simply from a single style sheet. What is termed as the *cascade* is the mechanism by which styles from multiple sources can interact within the same document, with styles of higher weights falling (or cascading) through to be expressed in the document, while styles of lesser weights are caught up in the cascade and suppressed. If you think of the cascade as water flowing over a waterfall, cascading off of ledges and outcroppings, with gravity (or weight) entirely governing its course, that should give you a good visual hint of what the cascade is and how it works.

Modularity

In CSS, a closely related concept to cascading is *modularity*, which refers to the ability of a single document to incorporate style information originating from multiple sources and serving multiple purposes.

✔ You've already worked with one example of modularity, when you created separate style sheets, one targeted for printing on a printer and the other for display on a computer screen—see "Embedding Style Sheets Using the STYLE Element," p. 68 (Chapter 4).

Authors may also choose to modularize their own style sheets in other fashions, allowing them to apply separate style modules either individually or jointly to different documents. Thus, an author may have a separate style sheet that controls the presentation of the header and footer sections of pages, while incorporating different style sheets to control the presentation of the body sections of pages, depending upon their content and function.

The other end of this equation refers not only to the ability of an author to modularize his own style sheets, but also to the ability of sources other than the author to contribute to determining the presentation and styling of a CSS-styled document.

There are three general sources for style information:

- **Author**—The author of a Web page provides style information for a document through embedded, linked, or imported style sheets. The author can also insert inline styles directly into HTML elements.

- **User**—Users of a Web page may be able to provide their own style information by either creating their own user style sheet or through a wizard provided by a browser.

- **Browser**—The browser (or any user agent used to gather, or "browse," information or data from the Web) provides a default style sheet (or internal set of style rules) that is used to format HTML elements and attributes.

NOTE

A term you'll run into often when learning about CSS is *user agent*. A user agent is a broader and more generic term for a browser, but is inclusive of devices and media that you might not automatically associate with a "Web browser," but which might be used to gather (or browse) information and data from the Web. These might include devices for providing Braille tactile feedback, speech browsers (or synthesizers), a cell phone message window, and so on.

In general, element properties declared by the author have greater weight than those declared by a user through a user style sheet or by a browser through its own internal style sheet. Element properties declared by an author have greater weight than the default element properties determined by a browser. This forms a kind of decision tree, or cascade, that falls from author, to user, to browser. Any decisions not made by the author, in other words, cascade to the user; after which, any decisions not made by the user cascade to the browser.

THE AUTHOR

Thus, if the author declares that level-one headings are to be displayed as red, in most cases that trumps the user declaring that they are to be displayed as is. If the author omits to specify a color for level-one headings, however, and the user declares that they are to be displayed as green, then the heading is displayed as green on that user's system. Another user, however, might declare that they are to be displayed as blue, for instance. In other words, any element properties left undeclared are fair game for other players in the cascade to determine.

THE USER

The CSS specifications enable users to create their own style sheets. Internet Explorer 5.5 for Windows, Internet Explorer 5 for the Macintosh, and Opera 5 for Windows all enable users to specify a user style sheet.

For example, in Internet Explorer 5.5 for Windows you can specify your own personal style sheet by selecting Tools and Internet Options, clicking the Accessibility button, and then checking the bottom check box (Format documents using my style sheet). Next, click the Browse button and select the style sheet file (mystyles.css, for example) that you want to use (see Figure 5.1). If you are using Internet Explorer 5 for the Macintosh, you can achieve the same end by selecting Edit and Preferences, checking the check box, Use my style sheet, and then clicking the Select Style Sheet button to select the style sheet file. Users of Opera 5 for Windows can specify their own style sheet by selecting File and Preferences, clicking Documents in the sidebar, and then specifying a CSS file under the User CSS heading.

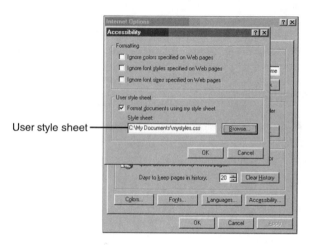

Figure 5.1: *Internet Explorer 5.5 is directed to use a user style sheet, mystyles.css, to format Web pages.*

Although Netscape 6 does not let you specify a user style sheet from within the program, it is the only browser—the only one at this point anyway—that makes available its own style sheet, ua.css. Users who know what they're doing can edit ua.css to change Netscape 6's default settings (be sure to back it up first, however, if you decide to fiddle with this).

Although most users are unlikely to create their own user style sheet, it is important that authors take into account that some users may do so. Remember, any undeclared property is fair game for a user to declare, so you need to be aware that just because a property is displayed in a certain way in your browser, or even by default in all browsers, that doesn't mean that a user can't change it. If you want to make sure that everyone has an equal chance to read your pages, you need to be aware of this. Otherwise you could end up with the text you designate as navy blue being displayed against a background that a user has designated also as navy blue, for instance.

✔ You'll be learning more about using foreground and background colors, as well as how to provide for users also potentially setting foreground and/or background colors for any element, in "Setting Foreground and Background Colors," p. 111 (Chapter 6).

THE BROWSER

Browsers must have a set of rules they follow in presenting elements and applying properties to them. HTML, by and large, leaves the initial display of different elements up to browsers. That most browsers tend to display almost all elements in a similar fashion isn't usually due to any established standard or requirement, but is simply a case of competition encouraging browsers to fall into line with each other, following and copying whichever is the lead browser (in terms of market share) at the time. Even so, there are still differences between browsers—Netscape Navigator 4 on the Macintosh defaults to a gray, rather than white, background, for instance, to mention just one fairly major difference.

Not only is there some variability between browsers in how they display different elements, browsers may also be impacted by system settings and configurations. Factors such as the monitor dimensions, screen resolution, default font size, and dot pitch (the dots per inch, or *dpi*, at which fonts are displayed) all contribute to how a browser displays particular elements. A user browsing at a screen resolution of 640×480 pixels, for instance, will see a different Web page from someone browsing at a 1024×768 screen resolution. Users with larger monitors who are running at larger screen resolutions are also much more likely to run their browser windows un-maximized, meaning that you have no control over the size or dimensions of a browser window used to view your pages.

Windows and Macintosh systems by default display fonts at a different dot pitch, with Windows systems defaulting to 96 dpi and Macintosh systems defaulting to 72 dpi. This has the impact of causing the same font sizes to appear smaller on a Macintosh system than on a Windows system, even though both might be using a similar sized monitor and running in the same screen resolution. Internet Explorer 4 for the Macintosh actually includes buttons on its navigation bar that allow users to bump the default font size up or down. Both Internet Explorer 5 and Netscape 6 for the Macintosh, however, specify a 16-point default font size, which approximates the default 12-point font on a Windows system (given similar monitor dimensions and the same screen resolution). Users of earlier versions of these browsers, as well as of many other Macintosh browsers that may be in use, will still see the smaller 12-point font when they view your pages.

Windows users can also choose to use small or large fonts, or select a custom font-size. In Windows, small fonts display at a dot pitch of 96 dpi, and large fonts display at 120 dpi. It is not uncommon for Windows users, for instance, to opt for running in a 1024×768 screen resolution, while bumping up the size of the default screen font to the large fonts setting (120 dpi) to make it more readable (especially when using a 17-inch or larger monitor).

Browsers also let users specify their own preferences for customizing which fonts, colors, backgrounds, and other characteristics they want their browsers to display. A user, for instance, might want to increase the base font size in which text is displayed because of a visual impairment or because they're running in a higher screen resolution that causes the default font size to be too small for comfortable reading. A user might want to specify different background, text, and link colors; or they might want to view their pages using a specific font on their system, either for improved readability or because of personal preference. Any of these choices can impact how a particular page will display in a browser, thus participating in the cascade that determines the appearance of a CSS-styled document.

Browsers also enable users to override the choices of the author, insisting that their own backgrounds, colors, and fonts are used instead of whatever is specified by an author (either through straight HTML or CSS style sheets). Thus, if a user insists on displaying white text against a black background, that's what he can get; the browser simply ignores any color suggestions made by the author (whether through HTML or a CSS style sheet). Once again, users might do this for reasons of readability or personal preference.

Figure 5.2 shows the dialog box for setting font preferences in Netscape 6 for Windows.

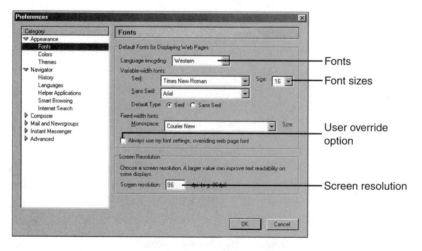

Figure 5.2: *In Netscape 6 for Windows, users can specify the fonts, font-sizes, and screen resolution they want to use when viewing Web pages.*

In Internet Explorer 5.5 for Windows, users can direct the browser to ignore author-specified colors, font styles, and font sizes, and use their own instead (see Figure 5.3).

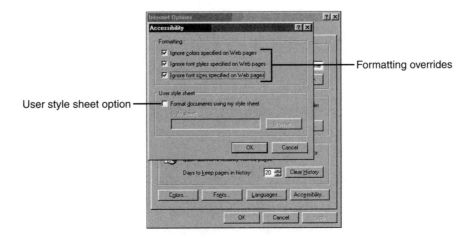

User style sheet option

Formatting overrides

Figure 5.3: In Internet Explorer 5.5, users can override colors, font styles, and font sizes specified by authors, as well as specify their own style sheet.

Author/User Balance

Both the browser and user are variables that need to be carefully considered when creating style sheets for your Web pages. You can't assume, in other words, that the preferences and characteristics displayed by your own system and browser are the same for everybody, or even anybody, else. In this book, one of my goals is to try to teach you how to create style sheets that interact gracefully with and respect the choices and preferences of users.

Cascading comes into play whenever there is a conflict between style sheets on how to present a particular element. The scheme sketched out above in the section, "Modularity," holds generally true whenever you have matching element properties, such as the same property for the H1 element in two different style sources. For instance, if the author declares that an H1 heading is red and a user declares that an H1 heading is blue, the author generally wins, and an H1 heading is displayed as red. The next section, however, deals with an exception to that general rule.

Specifying Importance

There is one key exception to this basic cascading scheme. CSS gives more weight to the designation of a property declaration by following it with an exclamation mark and the word "important." For example:

```
h1 { color: blue ! important; }
```

✔ As discussed previously in "Style Sheets on the Web," p. 15 (chapter 1), there are two current levels of CSS that have been recommended—CSS1 and CSS2. In CSS1, an author's important declaration trumps the user's, but in CSS2, a user's important declaration trumps the author's. Thus, as CSS2 becomes more generally supported in browsers, you should expect users to gain even more say over how they wish their Web pages to appear.

Other factors also determine how properties cascade. Although the previously discussed scheme holds generally true for matching style rule properties, CSS provides various means for applying style properties, with the possible result that an element could have conflicting values for the same property assigned through different mechanisms. CSS defines an actual weighting scheme that browsers are supposed to follow to adjudicate these differences. The actual details of this weighting scheme are quite complex and neither easy nor necessary for a beginning CSS-author to learn or comprehend. At this point, it is sufficient to understand that by declaring a property as important, you increase its weight (and thus the probability that it will win out against a conflicting property). I don't recommend that you take the time now, but after you've become more comfortable and familiar with creating CSS style sheets, you can find all about it at http://www. w3.org/TR/REC-CSS2/cascade.html#specificity, under the section, "Calculating a selector's specificity," in the W3C's CSS2 specification.

Some authors even go so far as to designate as important any element property declarations that they consider critical to the proper display of their page or site. However, since in CSS2 an author's choice here no longer trumps that of the user, with the user's choice trumping the author's instead, there really isn't much to be gained by doing this, at least in CSS2-conforming browsers. If a user declares a property to be important, they win hands down, regardless of whether the author also declares the same property to be important. Authors, in other words, just have to learn to live with the reality that users can have the final say, if they want to.

How Grouping Works

Another key concept in CSS is *grouping*. Grouping allows the creation of more efficient style sheets, in that selectors can be grouped in order to have the same style properties applied to all the selectors within the group. Similarly, properties can be listed in groups and applied to individual or grouped selectors.

✔ You also already worked with one example of creating a group selector in Chapter 3, "Setting Your Page's Base Styles," when you applied style properties to both the H1 and H2 elements—see "Using a Group Selector to Set the Other Heading Characteristics," p. 52 (chapter 3).

In CSS, selectors can be grouped by including them as a comma-separated list. Here's an example of grouping the H1, H2, H3, and H4 element selectors:

```
h1, h2, h3, h4 { font-family: sans-serif; color: blue; }
```

In this case, the H1, H2, H3, and H4 elements within a document will all be displayed as blue and in a sans serif font. This lets you group duplicate properties that you're applying to multiple elements. If you couldn't do this, you'd have to repeat all of the properties being assigned to each of the elements (or selectors) in your style sheet, which would make for much more cumbersome and less efficient style sheets.

Combining Group and Individual Selectors

You're not limited to listing the same selector just one time. By combining group and individual selectors, where the same selector may be both included within a group selector and expressed as an individual selector, you can gain even more flexibility and efficiency when designing your style sheets.

I've included an example document, Northwest Travel Ideas, as a real-world example you can try out of combining group and individual selectors in a style sheet. Just open **nwtravel.html** in your text editor from your working folder (the CSS Examples folder, if you followed my suggestion). You can also type in the text and codes for this document, if you like:

Listing 5.1 NWTRAVEL.HTML—Northwest Travel Ideas

```
<!DOCTYPE HTML PUBLIC "-//W3C//DTD HTML 4.01 Transitional//EN"
"http://www.w3.org/TR/html4/loose.dtd">

<html>
<head>
<title>Northwest Travel Ideas</title>
<style type="text/css" media="screen">

</style>
</head>
<body>

<h1>Northwest Travel Ideas</h1>
<p>You'll find here all sorts of possibilities for your next vacation trip to the
Pacific Northwest.</p>
<h2>Western Washington</h2>
<p>The west side of the state is quite different from the east side and
encompasses three main areas: the Puget Sound basin, Cascade Mountains (western
flanks), Olympic Peninsula, and Southwest Washington.
<h3>The Puget Sound Basin</h3>
```

Listing 5.1   continued

```
<p>The Puget Sound basin encompasses a wide range of different topological and
geographical regions and locales, including the lowlands and foothills running
along the western shore of Puget Sound, the Kitsap Peninsula on the eastern side
of Puget Sound, and the San Juan Islands. The major metropolitan area within the
Puget Sound basin is centered around the city of Seattle. Other important
metropolitan areas include Everett, Tacoma, Bellingham, Olympia, and Bremerton.
<h4>The Seattle Area</h4>
<p>The Seattle area encompasses the city of Seattle, two major satellite cities,
Bellevue and Renton, as well as a variety of different suburbs, including
Shoreline, Lynnwood, Bothell, Woodinville, Redmond, Kirkland, Kent, and Federal
Way, for instance. Here are some suggestions for things to do or places to go
when vacationing in the Seattle area:

<ul>
<li>Pike Place Market
<li>Seattle Center (and the Space Needle)
<li>The Monorail
<li>Seattle Art Museum
<li>The Waterfront
<li>Pioneer Square
<li>The International District
<li>Tillicum Village
<li>Woodland Park Zoo
<li>The University District
<li>Gas Works Park
</ul>

</body>
</html>
```

Next, add the following group and individual selectors to the page's style
sheet, as shown here:

```
<style type="text/css">
h1, h2, h3, h4 { font-family: sans-serif; color: blue; }
h1 { font-size: 32px; color: green; text-align: center; }
h2 { font-size: 24px; color: red; }
h3 { font-size: 20px; }
h4 { font-size: 18px; }
</style>
```

As shown in Figure 5.4, the group selector applies the sans-serif and blue
color to all four elements, and the individual selectors apply different font
sizes to each of the four heading elements, different colors (green and red)
to the H1 an H2 elements, as well as center-alignment to the H1 element.

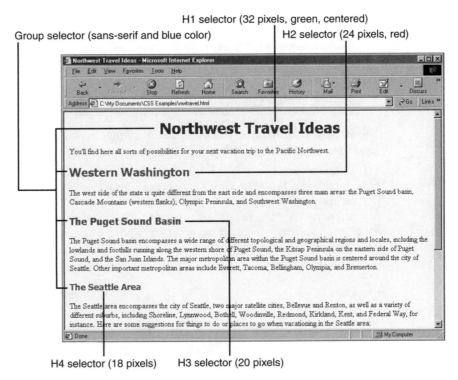

Group selector (sans-serif and blue color)

H1 selector (32 pixels, green, centered)

H2 selector (24 pixels, red)

H4 selector (18 pixels)   H3 selector (20 pixels)

Figure 5.4: *You can use both group and individual selectors to set properties for the same elements.*

In the preceding example, the group selector specifies a blue foreground color for each of the elements within the group, while the later H1 and H2 element selectors also specify foreground colors, green and red, respectively. A property declared later within a style sheet takes precedence over the same property declared earlier for the same element. As such, the later colors (green and red) declared in the individual selectors for the H1 and H2 elements take precedence over the earlier color (blue) declared in the group selector (for the H1, H2, H3, and H4 elements).

How Inheritance Works

Another key concept is inheritance. *Inheritance* is the method by which a child element inherits the property values of its parent element, if those property values aren't declared in the child element.

NOTE

A *child element* is an HTML element that is nested within another element, while a *parent element* is an element within which another element is nested. In CSS, the term *ancestor element* is also sometimes used and refers to any element from which an element inherits properties (which could be the parent, grandparent, great grandparent, and so on, of that element).

To see how inheritance works in action, add the following styles to the style sheet for the Northwest Travel Ideas page (see Figure 5.5):

```
<style type="text/css">
body { font-family: sans-serif; color: navy; background-color: white; }
p { margin-left: 3%; }
h1, h2, h3, h4 { font-family: sans-serif; color: blue; }
h1 { font-size: 32px; color: green; text-align: center; }
h2 { font-size: 24px; color: red; }
h3 { font-size: 20px; }
h4 { font-size: 18px; }
</style>
```

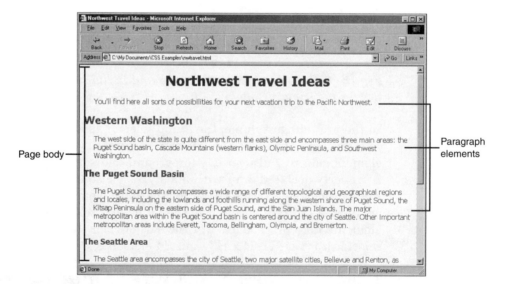

Figure 5.5: The paragraph elements inherit their sans serif font and navy blue color from their parent element (the BODY element).

However, if a paragraph element is nested inside of an element that is nested inside of the BODY element, it might inherit properties from that element instead of from the BODY element. For an example of this, first add the following style rule to your style sheet:

```
<style type="text/css">
body { font-family: sans-serif; color: navy; background-color: white; }
p { margin-left: 3%; }
h1, h2, h3, h4 { font-family: sans-serif; color: blue; }
h1 { font-size: 32px; color: green; text-align: center; }
h2 { font-size: 24px; color: red;}
h3 { font-size: 20px; }
h4 { font-size: 18px; }
div { color: green; background-color: aqua; }
</style>
```

Now, edit the body of your example file, bracketing the both the H4 element and the following paragraph element inside of a DIV (Division) element (see Figure 5.6):

```
<div>
<h4>The Seattle Area</h4>
<p>The Seattle area encompasses the city of Seattle, two major satellite cities,
Bellevue and Renton, as well as a variety of different suburbs, including
Shoreline, Lynnwood, Bothell, Woodinville, Redmond, Kirkland, Kent, and Federal
Way, for instance. Here are some suggestions for things to do or places to go
when vacationing in the Seattle area:
</div>
```

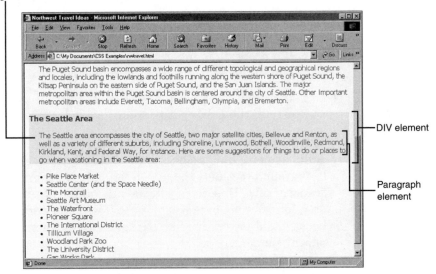

Figure 5.6: *The indicated paragraph element inherits its green color from the DIV element (its parent element), instead of inheriting a navy color from the BODY element (its grandparent element).*

✔ You haven't used the DIV element before in this book. It is a very handy HTML element designed specifically for use with styles. Because it has no default formatting, the DIV element is a perfect vehicle to which styles can be attached, since you don't have to be concerned with any other formatting other than that which you define for it using styles. To learn even more about using the DIV element with styles, see "Using the DIV Element," p. 205 (chapter 9).

You may have noticed that I've only mentioned the inheritance of foreground colors, but not of background colors. That's because, while foreground colors are inheritable, background colors aren't inheritable. Element backgrounds, however, are initially transparent, meaning that a background color assigned to a parent element shows through a child element's transparent background, rather than being inherited. You'll be learning all about using background colors and background images in your style sheets in the next chapter, Chapter 6, "Working with Colors and Backgrounds."

General Rules of Inheritance

Not all properties are inherited. In CSS, each property is defined as being either inheritable or not inheritable. Here's a brief sketch of what occurs to determine if a property is inherited or not:

- If the cascade results in a value, that value is used. For instance, if an author specifies that H1 is blue, that's what happens, as long as no contrary rules are expressed that have greater weight.

- If a property is inheritable, the element inherits the property from its parent element, in the form of its specific or computed value.

- If a property is not inheritable, the initial value assigned to the property in the CSS specifications is used.

The background of an element, for instance, is not inherited by a nested child element, but the background shines through the nested element's background (because the initial value for element backgrounds is set to transparent). This gives you the advantage of setting one background property, for example background-color, without worrying about whether other background properties like background-image might be inherited from the parent element.

Specified and Computed Values

Inherited values generally come in two variants: specified values and computed values. *Absolute values*, such as 10pt, red, or transparent, are inherited as specified. *Relative values*, however, are inherited as they are computed. For instance, here's an example of setting the BODY element's and the P element's font-size properties:

```
body { font-size: 16px; font-family: sans-serif; color: navy; background-color:
white; }
p { font-size: 1.5em; margin-left: 3%; }
```

Next, nest an EM (Emphasis) element inside of your page's first text paragraph (see Figure 5.7):

```
<h1>Northwest Travel Ideas</h1>
<p>You'll find here <em>all sorts of possibilities</em> for your next vacation
trip to the Pacific Northwest.</p>
```

EM (Emphasis) element   Font size = 1.5 ems

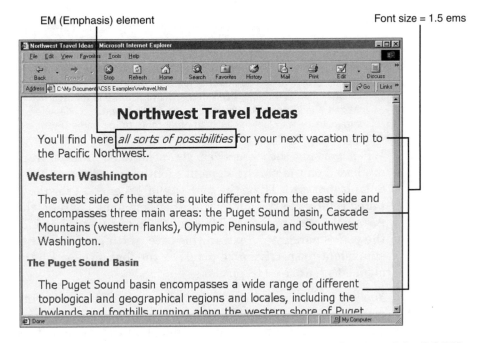

Figure 5.7: *The paragraph text is set at 1.5 times the size of the BODY element's font size.*

NOTE

The previous example includes another measuring unit you haven't used yet in this book, the em unit. The em unit is a traditional printer's measurement, deriving its name from its association with the size of the letter M in a particular font. In CSS, an em is equal to the size (or height) of a font. Therefore, if a font's size is 16 pixels, for instance, then one em is equal to 16 pixels. Likewise, if a font's size is 14 pixels, then one em is equal to 14 pixels.

By using relative measurements (ems for vertical measurements and percentages for horizontal measurements, for instance), you can create Web page designs that will scale relative to a user's own preferences.

You'll be learning much more about using ems, percentages, and other relative measuring units in Chapter 7, "Working with Fonts."

CAUTION

In the previous example, a font size of 16 pixels is set for the BODY element. This is done purely to provide a specific starting font-size value that can then be used to illustrate what a computed font-size value is. You should be aware that setting font sizes for the BODY or P elements should only be done with care, since doing so may cause problems relative to a user's default font size preference.

If you do decide to set font sizes for the BODY or P elements, using em measurements is generally better than using pixel measurements, since they will scale along with a user's default font-size settings.

You should, however, be very careful about decreasing the font size of the BODY or P elements using em measurements. That's because, doing so can result in the text being rendered in a size that makes it unreadable, depending upon a user's default font-size settings. If you choose to do this, you should reduce the size of the font only minimally—by setting .9em as the font size, for instance. Some Web designers like to minimally reduce the font size when specifying Verdana as their text font, since that font has a larger x-height (the size of the font's lowercase characters) than most other fonts, causing it to look larger than other fonts of the same height.

When working with font sizes, you need to be aware that relative font sizes are based on the parent element's font size and not on the current element's default font size. Thus, the font size of 1.5 ems set for the P element is computed relative to the font size of the P element's parent, the BODY element. As you'll notice in Figure 5.7, a font size of 1.5 ems has increased the size of the page's paragraph text. In this case, setting a font size of 1.5 ems is equivalent to specifying 24 pixels as the font size, or 1.5 times the BODY element's font size (16 pixels).

You'll also notice that the example's nested EM element inherits the P element's computed font-size value (24 pixels), since it is the same size as the surrounding P element's text, rather than the P element's specified font-size value (1.5 ems). If the EM element inherited the P element's specified font-size value, its font size would be 1.5 times that of the surrounding P element's text, which isn't the case.

To get an even clearer idea of the difference between computed and specified values, add a style rule to your style sheet specifying a font size of 1.2 ems for the EM element:

```
body { font-size: 16px; font-family: sans-serif; color: navy; background-color: white; }
p { font-size: 1.5em; margin-left: 3%; }
em { font-size: 1.2em; }
```

Next, nest an EM element within your page's H1 element, as shown here (see Figure 5.8):

```
<h1><em>Northwest</em> Travel Ideas</h1>
<p>You'll find here <em>all sorts of possibilities</em> for your next vacation
trip to the Pacific Northwest.</p>
```

EM elements

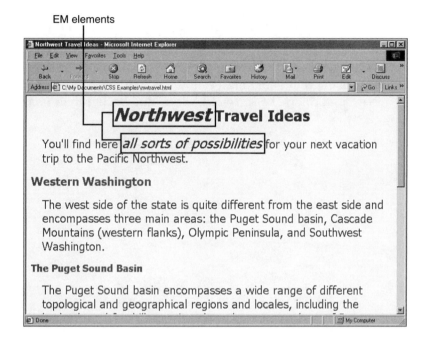

Figure 5.8: *The two EM elements are each 1.2 times their parent element's font size.*

As you'll notice in Figure 5.8, while the two EM elements have the same specified font-size value (1.2 ems), they have different computed values. That's because their computed font-size values are based on the font sizes of their parent elements, which are different in each case. The first EM element's font size is 1.2 times the font size of the H1 element, while the second EM element's font size is 1.2 times the font size of the P element.

What's Next?

In this chapter, you learned about three very important concepts in CSS: cascading, grouping, and inheritance. You should now be familiar with how properties from multiple style sheets cascade, how selectors can be grouped to make style sheets smaller and more efficient, and what inheritance is and how it works in CSS.

This is the end of Part II, "Understanding Basic Concepts." You should now have a good grounding in the basic concepts that underlie CSS and be ready to move onto learning about more specific aspects of CSS. In Part III, "Working with Colors, Fonts, and Text," you learn how to work with colors and backgrounds, set font and text properties, as well as control the look and feel of your hypertext links.

In the next chapter, "Working with Colors and Backgrounds," you learn all about using colors and backgrounds in your Web designs, including setting foreground colors, background colors, and background images.

Part III

Working with Colors, Fonts, and Text

Working with Colors and Backgrounds

Working with Fonts

Working with Text and Links

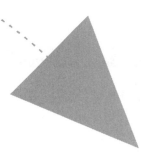

Working with Colors and Backgrounds

In this chapter, you review examples of using styles to control foreground colors, as well as background colors and background images. In HTML 4 and XHTML 1, all of the elements and attributes that control the presentation of foreground colors, background colors, and background images have been deprecated (p. 82) in favor of using styles to achieve the same or better results. CSS not only enables you to more efficiently achieve all of the color effects achievable through HTML, but also gives you many more options for controlling and adding colors and backgrounds in your pages.

In this chapter, you'll be covering the following ground:

- Setting foreground and background colors
- Using the 16 color names
- Using decimal and hexadecimal RGB color codes
- Setting colors using RGB percentages
- Using background images
- Repeating, positioning, and fixing background images
- Using the background shorthand property

Using the Example File

For this chapter's example file, you can just continue using the Northwest Travel Ideas example, nwtravel.html, you were working with in the previous chapter. You'll want to start fresh with a new style sheet, however, so first open it in your text editor and delete the styles from the page's STYLE element. You can also remove the two EM elements you added to the initial heading and paragraph. Then just resave your file as **nwtravel2.html** in your working folder. Here's a listing of what your file should look like starting out:

Listing 6.1 NWTRAVEL2.HTML—Northwest Travel Ideas

```
<!DOCTYPE HTML PUBLIC "-//W3C//DTD HTML 4.01 Transitional//EN"
"http://www.w3.org/TR/html4/loose.dtd">

<html>
<head>
<title>Northwest Travel Ideas</title>
<style type="text/css">

</style>
</head>
<body>

<h1>Northwest Travel Ideas</h1>
<p>You'll find here all sorts of possibilities for your next vacation trip to the
Pacific Northwest.</p>
<h2>Western Washington</h2>
<p>The west side of the state is quite different from the east side and
encompasses three main areas: the Puget Sound basin, Cascade Mountains (western
flanks), Olympic Peninsula, and Southwest Washington.
<h3>The Puget Sound Basin</h3>
<p>The Puget Sound basin encompasses a wide range of different topological and
geographical regions and locales, including the lowlands and foothills running
along the western shore of Puget Sound, the Kitsap Peninsula on the eastern side
of Puget Sound, and the San Juan Islands. The major metropolitan area within the
Puget Sound basin is centered around the city of Seattle. Other important
metropolitan areas include Everett, Tacoma, Bellingham, Olympia, and Bremerton.
<h4>The Seattle Area</h4>
<p>The Seattle area encompasses the city of Seattle, two major satellite cities,
Bellevue and Renton, as well as a variety of different suburbs, including
Shoreline, Lynnwood, Bothell, Woodinville, Redmond, Kirkland, Kent, and Federal
Way, for instance. Here are some suggestions for things to do or places to go
when vacationing in the Seattle area:

<ul>
<li>Pike Place Market
<li>Seattle Center (and the Space Needle)
<li>The Monorail
```

Listing 6.1 continued

```
<li>Seattle Art Museum
<li>The Waterfront
<li>Pioneer Square
<li>The International District
<li>Tillicum Village
<li>Woodland Park Zoo
<li>The University District
<li>Gas Works Park
</ul>

</body>
</html>
```

Setting Foreground and Background Colors

In previous chapters, you've already worked with several examples of using foreground and background colors. In this section, you'll be delving much deeper into the different ways in which you can set foreground and background colors in your pages.

> **NOTE**
>
> In HTML, you can set the foreground color for text using the FONT tag's COLOR attribute. You can use the BODY element's BACKGROUND, TEXT, LINK, VLINK, and ALINK attributes to set default background, text, and link colors for your page, as well as the BGCOLOR attribute to set background colors. All of these attributes have been deprecated in HTML 4 and XHTML 1, in favor of using styles instead.
>
> In this chapter, you learn how to set foreground colors, background colors, and background images using styles, rather than using deprecated HTML elements and attributes to achieve these effects. Later, in Chapter 8, "Working with Text and Links," you learn how to control the colors of your hypertext links.

In CSS, the `color` property is used to set the text color. You've had some experience with doing this in this book's examples, so you should already be somewhat familiar with how to do this. As long as no other color is set through an intervening style rule (in a user style sheet, for instance), elements that are nested inside of the BODY element should inherit the same color.

There are three ways to set colors in CSS styles: keyword color names, numerical RGB color values, and percentage RGB color values.

Using Color Names to Set Colors

A *keyword color name* specifies an RGB color based on a keyword specifying a particular color. Both HTML and CSS provide 16 standard color names that can be used to specify colors: black, white, aqua, blue, fuchsia, gray, green, lime, maroon, navy, olive, purple, red, silver, teal, and yellow.

NOTE

You can see examples of the colors produced by the 16 standard color names in the W3C's specification for HTML 4.01 at http://www.w3.org/TR/html4/types. html#h-6.5.

Here's an example of setting a red foreground color for the BODY element's font (see Figure 6.1):

```
<style type="text/css">
body { color: red; }
</style>
```

Red foreground color

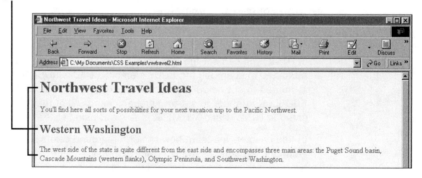

Figure 6.1: *The foreground text color is changed to red.*

NOTE

Be sure to check out this chapter's examples for yourself in your browser, rather than just relying on the figures to show you how the examples will be displayed. That's especially important in this chapter, since you're working with examples of setting background and foreground colors, while the figures are all printed in black and white.

In the absence of foreground colors being set for other elements, setting a foreground color for the BODY element will set the same color for all other elements that are nested inside the BODY element (such as headings, paragraphs, and lists, for instance), as well as for any inline elements that are nested inside those elements (such as emphasis, bolding, and italics, for instance).

You can use the background-color property to set an element's background color. Here's an example of setting the BODY element's foreground color to white and its background color to navy:

body { **color: white; background-color: navy;** }

As shown in Figure 6.2, all of the elements nested inside of the BODY element are now displayed in a white color against a navy blue background.

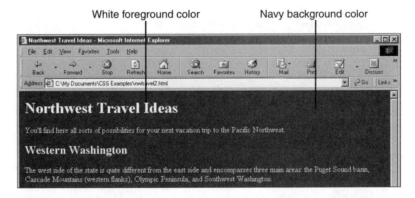

Figure 6.2: *A white foreground color is displayed against a dark navy blue background color.*

CAUTION

Whenever you set a foreground color, you should also set a background color. That's because you have no way of knowing if a user has set a background color for the BODY element in their browser preferences or for other elements through a user style sheet. A user might prefer to view white text against a black background, for instance. A person with a visual impairment might choose this, along with increasing the font size, to make the text more legible. You also can't depend upon a browser's default background color automatically being white—some browsers, such as Navigator 4 for the Macintosh, default to a gray background, for instance.

For instance, if a user has set a white foreground color and a purple background color in their browser preferences and you specify a purple foreground color, without specifying any background color, your text will end up displaying in that user's browser as purple on purple.

When setting a background color for the BODY element, always specify a specific color. For elements nested within the BODY element where you want to set a foreground color, but not a separate background color, you can specify a transparent background color (background-color: transparent) that will allow the BODY element's background color to shine through.

NOTE

A number of nonstandard color names that work in various browsers can be used. Notice, for instance, that there is no "orange" color name included in the 16 standard color names, but all recent browsers that I know of display something that at least resembles an orange color when color: orange is used. Another nonstandard color name that seems to work in recent browsers is the "violet" color name. There might be others that are also commonly supported. Generally, however, you're best off avoiding using these nonstandard color names, simply because there's no guarantee that they'll be supported in the future in any browser. Also, just because a particular nonstandard color name works in a couple browsers, doesn't mean that it works in any others. The only way to find out if it works in all current browsers is to test it out in all current browsers.

If you want to set colors other than those specified using the 16 standard color names, you should use numerical color values, which is covered in the next section, "Using Numerical RGB Values to Set Colors."

Using Numerical RGB Values to Set Colors

To gain access to an almost unlimited range of colors that can be used in your Web pages, you need to use numerical RGB (Red/Green/Blue) values. The three basic ways to set numerical RGB values are using decimal, hexa-decimal, and percentage values.

USING DECIMAL RGB VALUES

A *decimal RGB value* specifies the three components (red, green, and blue) of an RGB color according to their decimal values. You set decimal RGB color values by specifying a decimal value in a range from 0 to 255 that specifies the intensity of each component (red, green, blue) of the color. The general format for specifying decimal RGB color values is

```
color: rgb(rrr,ggg,bbb)
```

where *rrr*, *ggg*, and *bbb* correspond to decimal values for the red, green, and blue color components. For instance, here's an example of setting fore-ground and background colors using RGB decimal values for both the BODY and H1 elements (see Figure 6.3):

```
body { color: rgb(153,0,0); background-color: rgb(255,255,204); }
h1 { color: rgb(102,153,0); background-color: transparent; }
```

The result of this in a CSS-conforming browser is that the BODY element's foreground color is set to a dark red color and its background color is set to light yellow color.

By specifying red, green, and blue color values from 0 to 255, you can select from among 16.7 million possible RGB color combinations.

Green (102,153,0)   Light yellow (255,255,204)

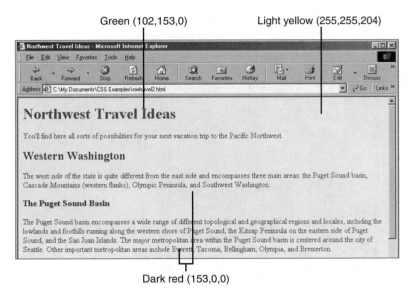

Dark red (153,0,0)

Figure 6.3: *Foreground and background colors are set for the BODY and H1 elements using RGB decimal values.*

TIP

Finding the color that you want, however, can be a bit of a challenge when you're using decimal RGB values. Unless you already have an intimate understanding of RGB color theory, your best bet is to use a color chart or picker from which you choose the color you want and that then provides the specific RGB decimal values for the color you've chosen.

Paint Shop Pro (for Windows) and Adobe Photoshop (for Windows and the Macintosh) are two graphics programs that display RGB decimal values for colors that you choose (see Figure 6.4). You can download evaluation versions of Paint Shop Pro from www.jasc.com and Adobe Photoshop from www.adobe.com. Other image editors or drawing programs also provide this information for different colors.

Many color charts and utilities are also available on the Web that let you choose a color and then provide you with the appropriate RGB color values. For links to where you can find these on the Web, visit this book's Web site at www.callihan.com/cssbook/.

In the previous example, you'll notice that the background color for the H1 element is set to be transparent. Element backgrounds are transparent by default, rather than being inherited—specifically declaring the background to be transparent in this case should trump any background color that might be set in a user style sheet for the H1 element, while still allowing the background color set for the BODY element to shine through.

Selected color

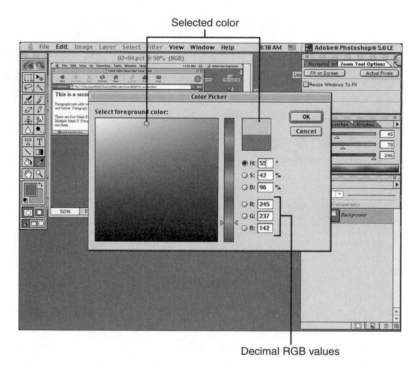

Decimal RGB values

Figure 6.4: Some graphics programs, such as Adobe Photoshop LE for the Macintosh shown here, provide color pickers that show decimal RGB values for any color.

USING HEXADECIMAL RGB VALUES

A *hexadecimal RGB value* specifies the three components (red, green, and blue) of an RGB color according to their hexadecimal values. The primary reason hexadecimal numbers are used with computers is that you can count from 0 to 255 in hexadecimal while only using two digits. For instance, the decimal number 255 corresponds to the hexadecimal number of FF. This is possible because the hexadecimal numbering system uses a base of 16 numbers (0, 1, 2, 3, 4, 5, 6, 7, 8, 9, A, B, C, D, E, and F) rather than 10 numbers, as with a decimal system.

Of course, in style sheets, using two-digit versus three-digit numbers really isn't an issue, so you might wonder why you should bother with hexadecimal numbers at all. One of the answers is that more online color charts, wheels, and utilities are available that generate hexadecimal RGB values than ones that generate decimal values. You might also already be familiar with using hexadecimal RGB values in HTML and, because they work almost exactly the same in CSS, you might want to stick with what you're comfortable with.

The general format for specifying hexadecimal RGB color values is

`color: #rrggbb`

where *rr*, *gg*, and *bb* correspond to hexadecimal values (from 00 to FF) for the red, green, and blue color components.

For instance, here's an example of using a group selector to apply the same foreground and background colors to the H2, H3, and H4 elements (see Figure 6.5):

```
h1 { color: rgb(102,153,0); background-color: transparent; }
h2, h3, h4 { color: #ffcc00; background-color: #000099; }
```

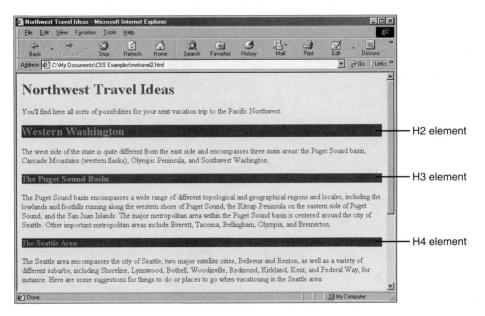

Figure 6.5: *Gold yellow and dark purple foreground and background colors are set for the H2, H3, and H4 elements using hexadecimal RGB color values.*

TIP

Some surfers of the Web are still using systems that are limited to displaying colors from a color palette of only 256 colors. Colors not included in their color palette are dithered. The results of this range from pretty good to just awful when it comes to the dithered color resembling the specified color. To insure that colors you select display as specified on 256-color displays, you can choose your colors from a 216-color palette, often called the browser-safe or Netscape palette (Netscape introduced it). As long as you stick to using only the hexadecimal values of 00, 33, 66, 99, CC, and FF (corresponding to the decimal values of 0, 51, 102, 153, 204, and 255), you select colors from only the browser-safe palette. Many color charts, wheels, and cubes are available on the Web that show the 216 browser-safe colors and their hexadecimal RGB values. Visit this book's Web site at `www.callihan.com/cssbook/` for links to some of these.

Besides using a six-digit code to denote a hexadecimal RGB value, you can also use a three-digit code that only uses a single hexadecimal digit for each red, green, and blue color component. The general format for doing this is:

```
color: #rgb
```

The single-digit hexadecimal value is actually shorthand for a two-digit value: 0 for 00, 3 for 33, C for CC, and so on. For instance, the hexadecimal color values, #ffcc00 and #000099, that were utilized in the previous example can also be stated using these three-digit values:

```
h2, h3, h4 { color: #fc0; background-color: #009; }
```

Using Percentage Values to Set Colors

The third way to set RGB color values is by using percentage values. A value of 100%, for instance, corresponds to a decimal RGB value of 255, and 0% corresponds to a decimal RGB value of 0. 50% corresponds to a decimal RGB value of 127. The general format for specifying percentage RGB values is very similar to that used for decimal RGB values, except that percentages are specified rather than integers for the red, green, and blue color components. For instance, edit your page's style sheet to add a style defining a lime green foreground color for your page's H2 element (see Figure 6.6):

```
h2, h3, h4 { color: #fc0; background-color: #009; }
h2 { color: rgb(80%,100%,40%); }
```

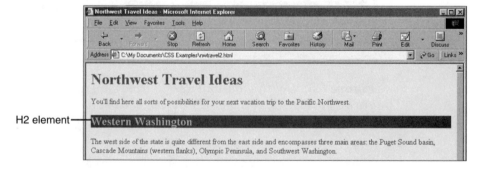

H2 element

Figure 6.6: *A lime green foreground color is set for the H2 element using percentage RGB values.*

The percentage values in the previous example correspond to decimal values of 204 (80%), 255 (100%), and 102 (40%). To find the percentage value, just add 1 to the decimal value (since the numbering of decimal values start from 0, not from 1) and then divide by 256 (the total number of decimal values). For instance, 102 + 1 / 256 = 40 percent (or just about).

NOTE

The examples included in this chapter of setting background colors for individual elements other than the BODY element are necessarily pretty simple. Later, in Chapter 9, "Formatting Block Elements," you'll learn how to combine backgrounds with borders, padding, and margins when formatting block elements.

Setting Background Images

In HTML, the BODY element's BACKGROUND attribute is used to set a background image for a page. That attribute has been deprecated in HTML 4 and XHTML 1 in favor of using styles to achieve the same or better results. In CSS, the background-image property is used to specify an element to be displayed in an element's background. I've included a background image, paper.gif, with the example files that you can use to try this out, although you can substitute any lighter colored background image you want to use. To apply a background image to your page, edit your style sheet codes as shown here (see Figure 6.7):

```
body { color: rgb(153,0,0); background-color: rgb(255,255,204); background-image:
url("paper.gif"); }
```

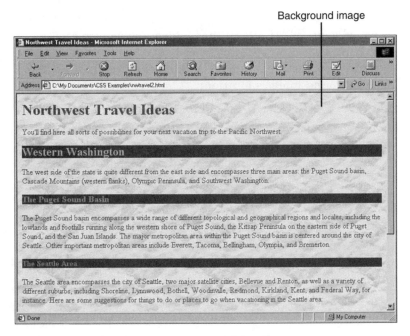

Figure 6.7: A "paper" texture background image is displayed.

If you downloaded the example files from this book's Web site, the background image used in the previous example is included with them. As long as you save your example HTML file in the same folder where the example files are located, the background image should display in your browser. If you haven't downloaded the example files, just substitute any background image (GIF, JPEG, or PNG format) you'd like to use. To do this, just copy to your working folder and specify the file name as the URL.

NOTE

Earlier in this chapter I cautioned you against setting a foreground color without also setting a background color, even if only declaring the background color to be transparent. There is a slight possibility, however, that a user might set their own background image in a user style sheet. One way of guarding against this is to set a `background-image: none` property for any element where you don't want this to happen.

You can also link to background images located in other folders in your site. For instance, here's an example of linking to a background image that's located in a subfolder, images, of the current folder:

```
background-image: url("images/paper.gif")
```

You might also want to link to a background image that is located in a different child folder of the current folder's parent folder. For instance, let's assume you've created a chap1 folder within your site's root folder and saved your HTML file in that folder. You've also created an "images" folder within your site's root folder and saved your background image in that folder. Here's an example of linking from the HTML file's location to the background image's location:

```
background-image: url("../images/paper.gif")
```

In this case, the `../` code steps back up one step on the folder tree and then the `images/` code steps back down one step to the "images" folder. You'd step back up two steps and then back down one this way:

```
background-image: url("../../images/paper.gif")
```

TIP

Whenever you set a background image, you should also specify a background color that closely matches the main color in your background image, in case the background image isn't available. Then, if someone is surfing with display of images turned off, your background color is displayed instead. This is especially important if you've set a light foreground text color to be displayed against a dark background image—otherwise, someone might end up viewing light yellow text against a white background.

If the background image is available, it is displayed on top of the background color.

Setting the Repeat Value

The background-repeat property controls how a background image is repeated (or tiled) in the background. It takes these values: repeat, repeat-x, repeat-y, and no-repeat. The repeat value is the default, which causes the background image to be repeated (or tiled) in the element's background along the x-axis and the y-axis. For instance, here's an example of using the repeat-y value to cause the background image to be tiled only along the y-axis (or along the left side of the page; see Figure 6.8):

```
body { color: rgb(153,0,0); background-color: rgb(255,255,255); background-image:
url("paper.gif"); background-repeat: repeat-y; }
```

Background image

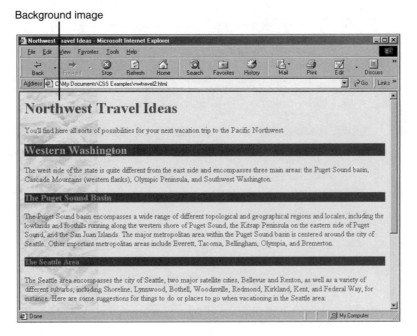

Figure 6.8: *The background image is repeated only along the y-axis.*

The no-repeat value causes the image to be displayed only once, in the element's upper-left corner. That, by itself, isn't very helpful, except that it enables you to position the background image in the page's background, as detailed in the next section.

Positioning a Background Image

The background-position property lets you position a background image within an element's background space. For this property to have affect, the background-repeat: no-repeat property value must also be set.

This can be effective for placing a *watermark* behind your page. A watermark is a light-toned low-contrast image that can be displayed behind text without interfering with the readability of the text. I've included an example watermark image of the letter "W" (for Washington state), wletter.gif, that you can use to try this out. Just edit the example page's style sheet so that it matches what is shown here (see Figure 6.9):

```
body { color: rgb(153,0,0); background-color: rgb(255,255,204); background-image:
url("wletter.gif"); background-repeat: no-repeat; background-position: center; }
```

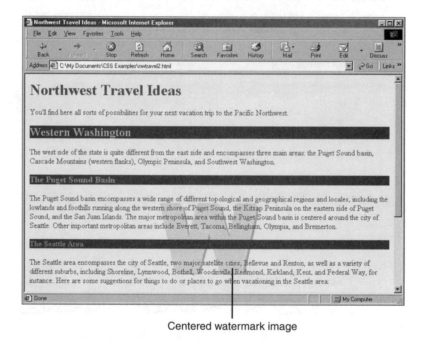

Centered watermark image

Figure 6.9: *A watermark image of the letter "W" is centered in the page's background.*

One to the problems with centering the watermark image in this fashion, however, is that the image is centered vertically relative to the full length of the page and not relative to the height of the browser window. To position the image more exactly relative to the top of the page's background, you can combine percentage and length measurements. To try this out, edit the background-position property to specify a 50 percent horizontal position (horizontally centering the image) and a vertical position ten ems down from the top of the page (see Figure 6.10):.

```
body { color: rgb(153,0,0); background-color: rgb(255,255,204); background-image:
url("wletter.gif"); background-repeat: no-repeat; background-position: 50% 10em;
}
```

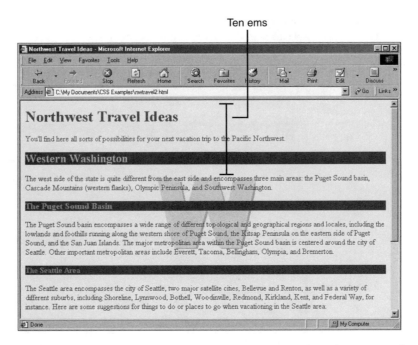

Figure 6.10: *The watermark image is centered and positioned vertically relative to the top of the page's background.*

This example vertically positions the watermark image so that it'll look close to being centered vertically within a maximized browser window running in an 800×600 screen resolution. To reposition the watermark higher or lower within the browser window, just decrease or increase the vertical positioning value in the background-position property. Besides the center keyword, you can also use the left and right keywords to horizontally position the background image and the top and bottom keywords to vertically position the background image (relative to the top or bottom of the page).

Setting a Fixed Background Image

One of the problems with positioning an unrepeated background image relative to the page is that the background image scrolls with the page. The background-attachment property allows you to specify whether a background image will remain fixed or scroll with the page. The fixed value causes the background image to be fixed relative to the browser window's background and the scroll value causes it to scroll (scroll is the default). To try this out, just add the following to your style sheet (see Figure 6.11):

```
body { color: rgb(153,0,0); background-color: rgb(255,255,204); background-image:
url("wletter.gif"); background-repeat: no-repeat; background-position: 50% 10em;
background-attachment: fixed; }
```

USING A TRANSPARENT WATERMARK IMAGE

If you save your background image with one of its colors set to be transparent, any background color that you also set shows through the transparent areas of the background image. In the example watermark image that you've been using, I've already set the background to be transparent, which allows the page's light yellow background color shine through the watermark image's transparent areas (see Figure 6.11).

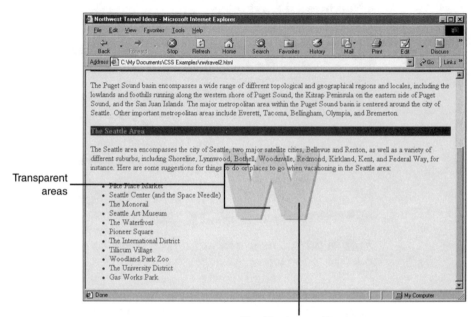

Figure 6.11: *A fixed background image remains fixed relative to the browser window's background and does not scroll along with the rest of the page.*

You can set GIF and PNG images as transparent; you can't set JPEG images to be transparent. All major image editors, such as Paint Shop Pro or Adobe Photoshop, can create transparent GIF and PNG images. Other graphics utilities can also be used to set transparency within GIF or PNG images, such as LView Pro for Windows and GraphicConverter, GIFConverer, and Transparency for the Macintosh. For links to where you can find out about downloading any of these programs or utilities, see this book's Web site at www.callihan.com/cssbook/.

NOTE

Earlier in this chapter, I cautioned you against specifying a foreground color without also specifying a background color. There is also a slight chance that a user will specify a background image. One way to foreclose this possibility is to set a `background-image: none` property wherever you want to make sure that a background image won't be displayed.

For a better solution to this problem, however, see the tip I've included in the next section, "Using the Background Shorthand Property."

Using the Background Shorthand Property

In CSS, the background shorthand property can be used to set any of the other background properties (background-color, background-image, background-repeat, background-attachment, and background-position). The background property first sets all of the background properties to their initial values and then assigns any explicit values stated in the declaration. For instance, the previous example of setting multiple background properties can be reduced to a single background property in this manner:

```
body { color: rgb(153,0,0); background: rgb(238,238,213) url("watermark.gif") no-repeat 50% 5em fixed; }
```

TIP

Because some earlier CSS-supporting browsers support the background property, but not the background-color property, it is often recommended that CSS designers exclusively use the background property to specify background colors, like this, for instance:

```
h2, h3, h4 { color: #fc0; background: #009; }
```

Because the background property resets all undeclared background properties to their initial values, doing this also has the side-benefit of turning off the display of any background image that a user may have set for these elements in a user style sheet. This saves you from having to insert background-image: none properties whenever you want to foreclose this possibility, since none is the initial value for background-image.

What's Next?

In this chapter, you experimented with setting foreground colors, background colors, and background images. You should now be familiar with setting the foreground and background colors for your page's body and elements, as well as with using and positioning background images. You should also know how to use the background shorthand property.

In the next chapter, you learn how to work with fonts in your Web pages, including setting font sizes, families, weights, and other font characteristics.

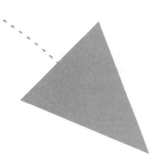

Working with Fonts

One of the benefits of using CSS is the flexibility it provides for working with fonts. With HTML, you're limited to working with only seven standard font sizes; with CSS, you can specify an unlimited range of font sizes. Besides specifying specific fonts that you want to display, you can also specify a generic font family as a fallback, in case none of your specified fonts are available. You can also change the font weight and set different font variants and styles (italic, oblique, and small caps, for instance).

As discussed previously, HTML's FONT tag is deprecated in HTML 4 in favor of using styles to achieve the same or better results. In this section, you review examples of how to exclusively use CSS styles to control the presentation of fonts in your HTML documents, without using any deprecated elements.

In this chapter, you learn how to use CSS styles to:

- Specify relative and absolute font sizes
- Assign generic and specific font typefaces
- Indicate font styles and variants
- Stretch (or condense) font widths
- Use the font shorthand property

Using the Example File

For creating the examples in this and the following chapter, you'll be working with a new example file, traveltips.html, a page of international travel tips. You'll find this file with the other example files for this book, if you've downloaded the example files from this book's web site and extracted them to your working folder. You can also type in the example HTML file yourself, if you wish:

Listing 7.1: TRAVELTIPS.HTML—International Travel Planning Tips

```
<!DOCTYPE HTML PUBLIC "-//W3C//DTD HTML 4.01 Transitional//EN"
"http://www.w3.org/TR/html4/loose.dtd">

<html>
<head>
<title>International Travel Planning Tips</title>
<style type="text/css">

</style>
</head>
<body>

<h1>International Travel Planning Tips</h1>
<p>Being prepared and anticipating needs and requirements can make all the
difference when it comes to ensuring that your trip abroad will be an enjoyable
one, instead of disappointing or unpleasant. The following are some tips to help
you plan your next trip abroad.</p>

<h2>Get Any Required Vaccinations and Immunizations</h2>
<p>You may be required to get various vaccinations or immunizations when
traveling to various parts of the world. You can find out about vaccinations or
immunizations that may be required for travel to or from different countries at
your county or state health department.</p>

<h2>Passport and Visas</h2>
<p>A visa may be required to gain entrance to many countries.
Many foreign countries require the obtaining of a visa to gain entry. It is your
responsibility to obtain any visas that may be required. Some foreign countries
waive the requirement for a visa for short stays by tourists, for instance; this
is the case in most Western European countries.</p>
<h3>Protect Your Passport</h3>
<p>Make a photocopy of your passport's page with your photo and identification
details, request a duplicate copy of your birth certificate, and have two
additional passport photos printed. Having these with you can help expedite
getting a replacement, in case your passport is lost or stolen.</p>

<h2>Check Your Coverages</h2>
<p>Check to see if your medical insurance policy will cover you while traveling
abroad. If not, medical insurance is available to cover you during your trip.
Also, you may want to consider getting insurance providing for emergency medical
```

Listing 7.1: continued

evacuation, if such should be necessary, especially if the area you'll be traveling to lacks top-flight medical facilities and personnel. Ask your travel agent for details.</p>

<p>If you take required medications, have your doctor write new prescriptions for you using generic drug names, since brand names for drugs may vary from country to country.</p>

<h2>Take Care of Your Money</h2>

<p>Don't risk having your passport, travelers' checks, credit cards, cash, and other important items lost or stolen. Carrying these in pockets or handbags is begging for them to be stolen. Get a good money belt so you can keep your valuables where thieves or pickpockets can't easily get to them.</p>

<p>Travelers' checks are better than cash, since they can be replaced, while cash can't. Also take your credit card, but check with your bank or provider to make sure it'll be accepted where you're going. Before leaving, learn what the current currency-exchange rate is, as well as what the usual currency-exchange fees are. Be sure to carry a small calculator.</p>

<h2>Don't Overpack!</h2>

<p>International flights may have more restrictive weight and different size allowances for baggage than is the case for domestic flights. If you can manage it, restrict yourself to one checked bag and one carry-on bag. For added versatility and ease in carrying, consider making your carry-on a backpack; you can also then use it for day excursions once you get to your destination. Especially if you'll have a long flight, make sure you've placed anything you'll need during your flight in your carry-on bag. Don't take more clothing than you'll realistically need—get laundry done at your hotel, rather than carry extra clothes. Remember, there are only two kinds of travelers: those who packed light and those who wish they had.</p>

<h2>Take the Right Converters and Adapters</h2>

<p>The electrical current used in Europe and many other countries is 220 volts, instead of 110 volts as in the United States. If you don't have the right converter or adapter, you won't be able to use your electric shaver or hair dryer, for instance. Most laptops have built in adapters, but be sure to check your documentation.</p>

<h2>Do Not Carry Packages for Others</h2>

<p>Do not carry packages, money, or messages for anyone else from one country to another, unless you've received specific authorization to do so from the countries involved. When at the airport, do not leave your bags unattended, even for a moment.</p>

<h2>Travel Resources</h2>

<p>Here are some travel resources that are available online:
<ul>
<li><a href="http://travel.state.gov/travel.cfm">Travel and Living Abroad</a> from the Bureau of Consular Affairs, U.S. Department of State. Passport and visa info, travel warnings, country background notes, and more.

<li><a href="http://www.x-rates.com/">Exchange Rates</a> for many foreign currencies, provided by the Federal Reserve Bank of New York.

<li><a href="http://travel.state.gov/olderamericans.html">Travel Tips for Older Americans</a> from the U.S. Department of State.

Listing 7.1:   continued

```
<li><a href="http://www.disabled-traveler.com/">Disabled-Traveler.com</a> -
Travel resources for the disabled traveler.
<li><a href="http://www.cdc.gov/travel/">Traveler's Health</a> from the CDC
(Centers for Disease Control and Prevention). Check here for health information
and required vaccinations/immunizations required for the country or area you'll
be visiting.
</ul>

<hr>
<address>
Priscilla Lewis<br>
E-Mail: <a
href="mailto:plewis@TheNewTraveler.com">plewis@TheNewTraveler.com</a><br>
URL: <a href="http://www.TheNewTraveler.com/">http://www.TheNewTraveler.com/</a>
</address>

</body>
</html>
```

Setting Font Sizes

In straight HTML, the deprecated FONT element is also used to set font sizes. It enables you to set only seven different font sizes, of which only four (sizes 4, 5, 6, and 7) correspond to font sizes that are larger than the normal font size. By using CSS styles, however, you can set an unlimited range of font sizes.

You've already had some experience setting font sizes earlier in this book. To illustrate how large you can go when setting font sizes using CSS, here's an example that sets the H1 element's font size to 10 ems, or ten times the font size of the H1 element's parent element (see Figure 7.1):

```
<style type="text/css">
h1 { font-size: 10em; color: rgb(200,140,40); }
</style>
```

In the previous example, a value of 10 ems sets the font size of the H1 element to 10 times the font size of that element's parent element. Remember, when using ems (as well as percentages and exes), the font size is computed relative to the parent element's font size, not relative to the current element's font size. Thus, for a P element nested directly inside of the BODY element (as is the case with all of the paragraphs in this example), a font size of 10 ems is equal to 10 times the font size of the BODY element (the H1 element's parent element) and not to 10 times the default font size of the H1 element.

Font size = 10 ems

Figure 7.1: *Using CSS, you can select as big a font size as you want.*

To reset the font size to a more readable size, you can reset it to something like 2.5 ems, for instance (see Figure 7.2):

h1 { **font-size: 2.5em;** color: rgb(200,140,40); }

Font size = 2.5 ems

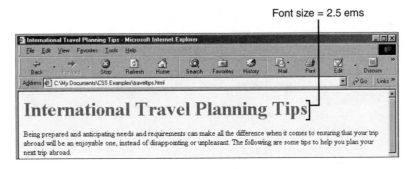

Figure 7.2: *The size of the H1 element is increased, to 2.5 ems.*

You can also just rely on the default sizing of an H1 heading (nothing says you have to change the default font sizing in an HTML document, because it is already sized for you).

You can set font sizes in a number of different ways in CSS. Here's a brief rundown on the options for setting font sizes:

- **Relative measurements**—em (ems), % (percentages), ex (x-height), and px (pixels)

- **Absolute measurements**—in (inches), cm (centimeters), mm (millimeters), pt (points), and pc (picas)

- **Absolute-size keywords**—xx-small, x-small, small, medium, large, x-large, xx-large

- **Relative-size keywords**—larger and smaller

Using Em or Percentage Units

When setting font sizes, em and percentage units work identically. They both set the font size relative to the font size of the parent element. Both of the following are equivalent:

```
p { font-size: 1.2em; }
```

and

```
p { font-size: 120%; }
```

The first example sets the font size to 1.2 times the font size of the P element's parent element, with one em being equivalent to that element's default font size. Thus, a setting of one em specifies a font size that is equal to the parent element's font size. For instance, if the user's browser is set to display the default proportional text font at 16 pixels, no font size is set for the BODY element, and the P element is nested directly inside of the BODY element, then a font size of 1.2 ems for that P element is equivalent in that case to a 19.2-pixel font size. Note, however, that someone else's browser might be set to display the default proportional font in an 18-pixel, or even a 20-pixel font, so you shouldn't necessarily assume that any particular font size in pixels will result when using ems to specify font sizes. The only real significance of using em or percentage values to determine font sizes is that they are relative to the parent element's font size, *whatever* that might be.

CAUTION

Think twice before resetting the font size of the BODY element. That's because a user might already have set their own optimum default font size either through browser preferences or a user style sheet. If you feel you must change it for reasons of design or emphasis, then increase it only marginally (to no more than 1.3 ems, for instance), but don't decrease it. That's because marginally increasing the default BODY font size will likely only make it larger, but decreasing it might make it unreadable (or at least less readable). If you feel that you *must* decrease the BODY font size, such as when specifying a default BODY font with a large x-height (such as Verdana), then only decrease it a sliver (by 0.9 ems, for instance).

Because ems and percentages work identically when used to set font sizes, you might want to stick to using ems when setting font sizes. Ems and percentages, however, do not work identically when setting horizontal measurements, such as margins, for instance.

✔ To learn more about how to set horizontal measurements and work with margins, padding, and borders, see Chapter 9, "Formatting Block Elements."

✔ As stressed earlier in this book in "Specified and Computed Values," p. 102 (chapter 5), relative font sizes are relative to the parent element's specific or computed font size.

Thus, two different P elements, both with the same specified font size, 1.2 ems, might have different computed font sizes due to being nested inside of different parent elements. To check this out for yourself, add styles for both the P and DIV elements to your style sheet, setting the font size for both to 1.2 ems:

```
h1 { font-size: 2.5em; color: rgb(200,140,40); }
p { font-size: 1.2em; }
div { font-size: 1.2em; color: black; background: #ccffff; }
```

Next, bracket a heading and following paragraph in your example file with the DIV element, as shown here:

```
<div>
<h3>Protect Your Passport</h3>
<p>Make a photocopy of your passport's page with your photo and identification
details, request a duplicate copy of your birth certificate, and have two
additional passport photos printed. Having these with you can help expedite
getting a replacement, in case your passport is lost or stolen.</p>
</div>
```

As shown in Figure 7.3, the P element that is nested inside the DIV element is larger than the P element that is nested inside the BODY element. That's because the font size of the first P element is 1.2 times the font size of the BODY element, while that of the second P element is 1.2 times the font size of the DIV element, which is, itself, 1.2 times the font size of the BODY element.

In many cases, you want a nested element to scale relative to its parent element. This is particularly true when nesting inline elements within block elements, such as nesting EM elements within an H1 element or a P element. You might want to set a slightly larger font-size, such as 1.1 ems, for your EM elements, just to add some additional emphasis; you want it to scale relative to the particular element in which it is nested. When nesting block elements within other block elements, however, you need to be cognizant that the effect of using em measurements in those instances might not be what you want.

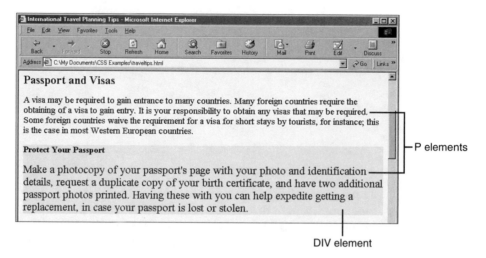

P elements

DIV element

Figure 7.3: *Both P elements are set to 1.2 ems, but the first is measured relative to the BODY element, while the second is measured relative to the DIV element.*

This is a case where understanding the structural import and function of an element can assist you in understanding how to apply styles that might affect that element. In HTML, the DIV element functions as a container that can contain other block elements. You shouldn't nest raw text directly within a DIV element, but should nest it inside of other block elements that are, in turn, nested inside of the DIV element.

SETTING A RELATIVE FONT SIZE USING A CONTEXTUAL SELECTOR

Another option is to use what is called a contextual selector. A *contextual selector* defines a style for an element *only* if it is nested within a specific element. As explained earlier in Chapter 4, "Using CSS with HTML," you specify a contextual selector in a similar fashion to a group selector, except that you leave out the commas. For an example of doing this, add the following contextual selector to your style sheet:

```
p { font-size: 1.2em; }
div { font-size: 1.2em; color: black; background: #ccffff; }
div p { font-size: 1em; }
```

As shown in Figure 7.4, while the font size of both the P and the DIV elements is still set to 1.2 ems, the contextual selector specifies that when a P element is nested inside of a DIV element, its font size will be one em (or one times the parent element's font size), not 1.2 ems. This has the effect of causing the font size of the two P elements (one nested inside the BODY element and the other nested inside of the DIV element) to be the same.

✔ To find more about using contextual selectors, see "Using Contextual Selectors," p. 77 (chapter 4).

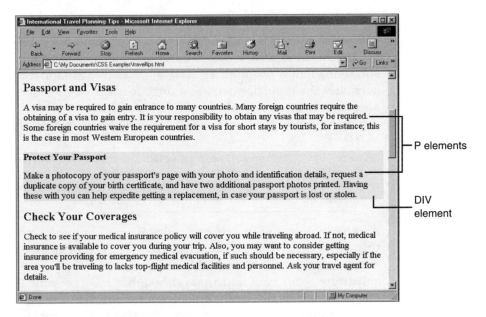

Figure 7.4: *Using a contextual style lets you specify that a nested element shares the same properties as the element in which it is nested.*

✔ To find more about using the DIV element, see "Using the DIV element," p. 205 (chapter 9).

Using Ex Units

Another option for setting relative font sizes is to use ex units. An *ex unit* corresponds to the x-height of the parent element's font. The term x-height refers to the height of the lowercase letter x, a measurement that is taken to correspond generally to the height of the lowercase glyphs in a particular font. Here's an example of using an inline style to set a font size using ex units:

```
<p style="font-size: 2ex">This is some example paragraph text.</p>
```

According to the CSS specifications, this should resize the font to twice the height of its x-height. In fonts with x-heights less than 50 percent of the font size, this should result in reducing the font size; in fonts with x-heights greater than 50 percent of the font size, this should result in increasing the font size. In reality, however, only two browsers that I know of actually do it this way: Internet Explorer 5 for the Macintosh and Netscape 6 (all platforms). Internet Explorer 5.5 for Windows and Opera 5 for Windows simply calculate the x-height as one half of the font size (or letter-height), or as equivalent to one half of an em.

If the implementation of the ex unit was uniform in otherwise CSS-conforming browsers, it might potentially be a useful unit to use in specifying font sizes or other vertical measurements in CSS. That's not currently the case, however, and until it is the case, you're best off just sticking to using em units instead of ex units.

NOTE

Some fonts don't have lowercase x characters or any lowercase characters at all. Those fonts still have x-heights; they just don't conform to the height of the letter x. The actual x-height in those cases is determined by the typographer who designed the typeface, the operating system, or a browser's CSS engine.

Another problem with using ex units, even in browsers that do implement this correctly, is that just because you specify a particular font, that doesn't mean that font will be available on a user's local system. A browser might substitute a different font that, although it has the same font size (or letter-height), has a significantly different x-height than the font you specified. CSS2 actually contains a potential solution to this problem, the `font-size-adjust` property, which will have the effect of adjusting the font sizes of elements based on their x-heights (or would, if it were implemented in current browsers). For a fuller explanation of the `font-size-adjust` property, see "Using the Font-Size-Adjust Property" later in this chapter.

Using Pixel Units

Another option for setting font sizes is the px unit. Using this unit, a measurement of `1px` should correspond on a computer display to one screen pixel. The primary virtue of using pixels for setting font sizes is that your fonts scale relative to the screen resolution in exactly the same fashion as any other text. Thus, if you increase the screen resolution (from 640×480 to 800×600, for instance) on the same monitor (a 17-inch monitor, for instance), the font-sizes for text shrink. That happens because in the first instance, a pixel corresponds to 1/480 of the screen height, and in the second instance it corresponds to 1/600 of the screen height. Here's an example of setting the font size using pixel units (see Figure 7.5):

```
div p { font-size: 1em; }
h2 { font-size: 28px; color: #339933; background: transparent; }
```

28-pixel font size

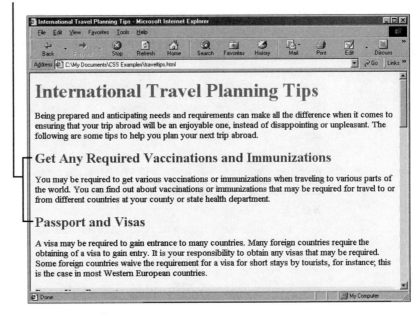

Figure 7.5: *The H2 element is set to a font size of 28 pixels.*

EMS OR PIXELS?

Whenever practicable, it is a good idea to try to use ems (or percentages) rather than pixels when setting font sizes. This will allow your font sizes to scale relative to whatever default font size is set in a system's configuration settings, a browser's preferences, or a user style sheet.

Some earlier browsers, however, have problems with em measurements. Internet Explorer 3 interprets one em as one pixel, for instance, meaning that elements set with em measurements in that browser will be rendered unreadable. Netscape Navigator 4 also has lots of problems with em measurements, primarily in the area of inheritance—child elements inherit the specified font-size, rather than the computed font-size, for instance. Not many users are still using Internet Explorer 3, but quite a few users are still using Netscape Navigator 4. So, if you're going to use em measurements in your style sheets, you need to implement some kind of strategy to shield your styles from browsers that don't handle em measurements properly. In Chapter 16, "Providing for Backward Compatibility," I cover a number of strategies you can use to shield earlier, less than fully CSS-compatible, browsers from stumbling over a style sheet containing em measurements.

There also can be problems with using em measurements when creating more sophisticated page layouts and designs. Many Web designers resort to using pixels to create

continues

continued

pixel-perfect layouts for their pages. Clients may also dictate that a page have a certain look and feel that can only be created using pixels, instead of ems and percentages. In other words, if you need to lock in a particular design and have it display invariably in all CSS-supporting browsers, the only way to do it is by using pixels instead of ems. Using ems, on the other hand, works best for creating *fluid* layouts that can dynamically scale relative to varying system, browser, or user settings.

In Chapter 14, "Creating Page Layouts and Site Designs," I show you examples of creating both pixel-perfect layouts (using pixels) and fluid layouts (using ems and percentages).

A third option exists: don't set font sizes at all. Allow the browser or the user to determine the appropriate size of the different HTML elements.

NOTE

One of the arguments against using pixels to set font sizes is that it can lead to accessibility problems for some users who've changed their system, browser, or user settings, resulting in font sizes that are less readable or too small to be readable. Most current browsers, however, now include facilities that enable users to easily zoom the display of text in their browsers. This feature was initially introduced by the Opera for Windows browser. Currently, Internet Explorer 5 for the Macintosh and Netscape 6 also offer this feature. Internet Explorer 5.5 for Windows, however, does not. Until Internet Explorer for Windows gets on board, at least, you might want to stick to using ems and lay off using pixels to set font sizes, since using pixels might be a disadvantage to some users.

Using Absolute Units

CSS provides a number of absolute measuring units that can be used to specify font sizes and other measurements. These include: in (inches), cm (centimeters), mm (millimeters), pt (points), and pc (picas). The CSS specifications, however, state that these measuring units "are only useful when the physical properties of the output medium are known." For instance, you might use them when setting measurements for a style sheet that is used when printing the document on an 8.5 by 11 inch page:

```
<style type="text/css" media="print">
body ( font-size: 13pt; }
h1 { font-size: 0.5in; }
h2 { font-size: 0.25in; }
</style>
```

When setting font sizes for display on the Web, however, don't use absolute measurements. Stick to using ems as your first choice for setting font sizes whenever possible, with pixels being your second choice when you need to set a more specific and invariable font size.

Using Absolute-Size Keywords

CSS also provides a set of seven absolute-size keywords that can be used with the `font-size` property to set font sizes: `xx-small`, `x-small`, `small`, `medium`, `large`, `x-large`, and `xx-large`.

Authors that are new to CSS often mistakenly presume that these seven absolute font sizes correspond to the seven font sizes that can be set using the FONT element in HTML. It might be nice if they were, but they aren't. The CSS specifications say that the `medium` absolute-size keyword should coincide with the default font size, which is the fourth out of seven among the absolute-size keywords; using the FONT element a font size of 3 corresponds to the default font size.

Internet Explorer 5.5 for Windows tries to kludge this by displaying fonts sized using the `small` keyword at the same size as the default font size. Opera 5 follows Internet Explorer 5.5's lead on this, also sizing a `small` font as equal to the default font size. Netscape 6 and even Internet Explorer 5 for the Macintosh get this right, however, displaying fonts sized using the `medium` keyword at the same size as the default font size. Figure 7.6 shows how this looks in both Internet Explorer 5.5 for Windows and Netscape 6.

Figure 7.6: *In Internet Explorer 5.5 for Windows, a* small *font size is equal to the default font size, while in Netscape 6 a* medium *font size is equal to the default font size.*

If you want to check this out in your own browser, be sure to eliminate any font sizes set for the BODY or P elements in your style sheet, because the fonts are sized relative to the browser's default font size (and not relative to any other font sizes set for the BODY or P elements).

That these keywords are termed as *absolute*-size keywords is a bit of a misnomer, because fonts sized using these keywords scale in relation to the default text font. For instance, if a visually impaired user sets the default text font at 24 pixels in browser preferences, in the browsers that do this the right way, a font sized using the medium keyword is displayed at the same size as the default text font (24 pixels, in this case), while fonts set using other absolute-size keywords are sized in relation to the medium size according to a scaling factor. CSS2 recommends, for instance, that browsers use a scaling factor of 1.2 to determine the size of fonts set using absolute-size keywords. Thus, if the default (or medium) font-size is set at 16 pixels, then one size larger (or large) would be displayed at 19.2 pixels (1.2 + 16 = 19.2).

This is actually an emendation of an earlier recommendation in CSS1 for a scaling factor of 1.5. However, user experience proved this factor to be too large, too easily resulting in illegible font sizes from the smaller absolute-sizes (xx-small, x-small, and small) or unreasonably large font sizes from the larger absolute-sizes (x-large and xx-large). Netscape 4 for the Macintosh, for example, applies the 1.5 scaling-factor, resulting in a small font being displayed at eight pixels high, which on the Macintosh is just shy of being legible. As long as there are widely used browsers still using the old 1.5 scaling factor, you should avoid using the three smaller absolute-size keywords to reduce the font size and should be aware when using the two larger absolute-size keywords that some users may end up seeing resulting font sizes that are much larger than you intended.

In the meantime, the Internet Explorer 5.5 for Windows kludge (sizing the small size as equal to the default font size) pretty much eliminates any usefulness of using these keywords to set font sizes. They might be useful in the future, after Internet Explorer 6 for Windows comes out, which undoubtedly will do it the right way. In the meantime, if you want to set font sizes relative to the default text size, you should use em units, instead.

Even once all current CSS-browsers apply the 1.2 scaling-factor, you should be very careful about using the three smaller absolute-size keywords when you've already reduced the font size—for instance, if you've reduced the font size of the BODY element to 0.9ems, any further reduction in the font size could result in an illegible font on some systems.

Using Relative-Size Keywords

Additionally, two relative-size keywords that can be used with the font-size property to set font sizes: larger and smaller. The CSS specifications say that these should be sized "relative to the table of font sizes and the font size of the parent element." That should mean that the font size should be based on the parent element's font size and then scaled according to the table of font sizes (at a 1.2 scaling factor between font sizes, according to the CSS2 specification).

In practice, however, current browsers are inconsistent in how they handle these keywords. Internet Explorer 5.5 for Windows, for instance, applies the same kludge here that it applies to the absolute-size keywords—it bases its font sizes on the small font size as the default, with a larger font size then resetting the font size to medium. Netscape 6 and Opera 6 both size a larger font as slightly larger than the default font size.

Current CSS-conforming browsers are much more consistent in how they treat the smaller keyword when resizing fonts. However, you should be aware that, if you use it to reduce the size of the default text font, in some browsers or platforms, the text might be rendered as illegible. That's close to the case in Internet Explorer 4 and Netscape 4 on the Macintosh platform, for instance, where the default text font is displayed in a much smaller font than is the case on the Windows platform.

The upshot of this is that you should probably just avoid using these keywords, at least until there is more consistent support for them by current browsers.

Using the Font-Size-Adjust Property

When a preferred font is not available on a local system, a browser substitutes another font for it. This might be the default text font that is set in the browser's preferences, a similar font (serif, sans-serif, or monospace, for instance), an alternative font specified by an author, and so on. Normally, the unavailable font is substituted by a font of the same font size.

The problem with this, however, is that different fonts of the same font size might have widely differing x-heights. Even in fonts that have an equal font size, the font with the larger x-height looks larger and takes up more horizontal space on a line.

CSS2 introduced the font-size-adjust property to address this situation. It allows authors to control the font size of a substituted font, ensuring that its x-height matches that of the font for which it is substituted. Unfortunately, no current browser at the time of this writing supports this property. When it is supported, it will be very handy, however.

To use this property, you just specify the aspect ratio of your preferred font as the value, and any substituted fonts are scaled up or down to match that aspect ratio. A font's *aspect ratio* is derived by dividing a font's x-height by its size (x-height/font-size). For instance, the Verdana font has one of the larger aspect ratios at 0.58, and Gil Sans has one of the smaller aspect ratios at 0.46. Fonts substituted for Verdana are likely to look too small, in other words, and fonts substituted for Gill Sans are likely to look too large. By specifying your preferred font's aspect ratio through a font-size-adjust value, you can lock in that aspect ratio for any substituted fonts. For instance:

```
body { font-family: verdana, sans-serif; font-size-adjust: 0.58; }
```

or

```
body { font-family: "gil sans", sans-serif; font-size-adjust: 0.46; }
```

Aspect ratios for some other common fonts are: Comic Sans MS (0.54), Trebuchet (0.53), Georgia (0.5), Myriad Web (0.48), Minion Web (0.47), Times New Roman (0.46), and Bernhard Modern (0.4). To find out the rough aspect ratio for other fonts, just print them out at a larger size and then get out your ruler and your calculator.

When measuring font sizes, however, you should keep in mind, according to the CSS2 specification, that the size of a font is "approximately equal to the distance from the bottom of the lowest letter with a descender to the top of the tallest letter with an ascender and (optionally) with a diacritical mark." This gets smudged a bit on the Macintosh, however, where in Internet Explorer 5 and Netscape 6 the height of the font is actually reduced to make room for a diacritical mark, if one is present.

Setting Font Families

In CSS, the term font family refers to either a specific font family—such as Times New Roman, Verdana, or Helvetica, for instance—or to a generic font family, such as serif, sans-serif, or monospace.

Font Realities

When specifying font families for display on your Web page, you need to realize that a font cannot be displayed if it is not installed on the user's system. You can't assume, in other words, that any one font is present and available. If the font you specify is not available and you've specified no additional alternative fonts, the default text font is displayed. If you specify additional alternative fonts, your first alternative font is displayed if it is available; if not, then your second alternative font is displayed, and so on.

Setting Specific Font Families

A *specific font family* refers to a specific font that may be installed on a local system. For instance, you might specify that Arial should be used for your page's headings, if available on the local system (see Figure 7.7):

```
h2 { font-size: 28px; color: #339933; background: transparent; }
h1, h2, h3 { font-family: Arial; }
```

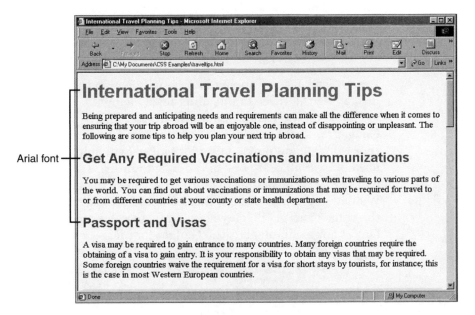

Arial font

Figure 7.7: The page's headings are displayed using an Arial font.

You'll notice in the previous example that the Arial font family is specified for a group selector that includes the top three heading-level elements (H1, H2, and H3). This is even though previous styles have already been declared for the H1 and H2 elements, specifying properties to be applied separately to each of them.

NOTE

CSS treats font family names as case-insensitive and no current browser that I know of cares about case in font family names. In fact, while the FACE attribute of the deprecated FONT element in HTML does require that font names match the actual font names exactly (including any uppercase characters), none of the current CSS-browsers care whether you specify "arial" or "Arial" when specifying a font family name.

The CSS2 specification, however, does leave open the possibility that some fonts on some platforms might still be case-sensitive. If you want to ensure that this will not be a problem, you can simply specify your font names with any uppercase characters in place.

Creating Font Lists

As mentioned previously, if a font is not available on a local system, it can't be displayed. If no other font is specified, the default text font is displayed, instead.

To help maximize the possibility of at least a similar font being present on a local system, you can specify a list of fonts that can be used. In a font list, the first font is used if it is available on a local system. If it is not available, the second font is used, and if it is not available, the third font is used, and so on. Here's an example of specifying a list of alternative fonts:

h1, h2, h3 { font-family: Tahoma, Gadget, Helvetica; }

In this case, if the Tahoma font is installed on the local system, it's used in displaying the three top heading-level elements. If the Tahoma font isn't available on the local system, the Gadget font is used, if available. If the Gadget font isn't available, the Helvetica font is used, if available. If neither the Tahoma nor the Gadget font is available, the Helvetica font is used, if available. If none of the listed fonts are available, the default text font is used. For instance, Figure 7.8 shows the example displayed on a Windows system on which the Tahoma font is available. Figure 7.9 shows the same example displayed on a Macintosh system on which the Tahoma font is not available, but the Gadget font is.

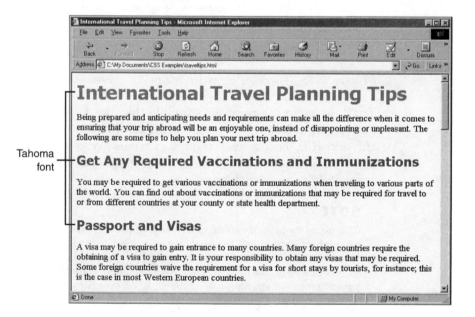

Figure 7.8: *The Tahoma font is displayed if it is available on a local system.*

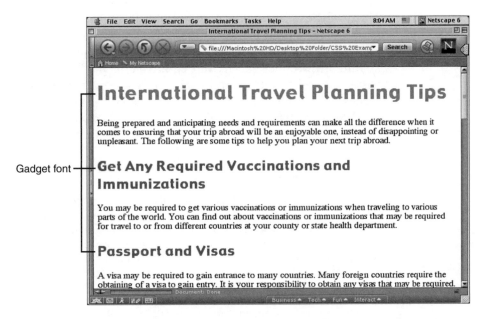

Gadget font

Figure 7.9: *If the Tahoma font is not available, the Gadget font is displayed.*

SOME COMMON FONTS

The fonts installed on a system are determined by the version of the operating system and the applications that are installed on it.

These TrueType fonts are included on Windows systems: Arial, Courier New, and Times New Roman. Other TrueType fonts are installed along with various versions of Internet Explorer, including: Arial Black, Comic Sans MS, Georgia, Impact, Monotype.com, Trebuchet MS, and Verdana.

Standard fonts included on the Macintosh (with OS 8.6) include: Capitals, Charcoal, Chicago, Courier, Gadget, Geneva, Helvetica, Monaco, New York, Palatino, Sand, Symbol, Techno, Textile, and Times. Other fonts, such as Arial, Arial Black, Comic Sans MS, Courier New, Espy Sans, Georgia, Impact, Minion Web, Times New Roman, Trebuchet MS, and Verdana may be installed along with Microsoft Office, Internet Explorer, or other applications.

Microsoft also has a collection of TrueType fonts, TrueType Core Fonts for the Web, that Windows, Macintosh, and Unix/Linux users can download and install on their systems. These include: Andale Mono (formerly Monotype.com), Arial, Comic Sans, Courier New, Impact, Georgia, Trebuchet MS, and Verdana.

Many of these fonts also include Bold, Italic, and Bold Italic versions (Courier New Bold Italic, for instance). However, since specifying these versions will only lesson the chance of making a successful font match, you should stick to just specifying regular versions (Times New Roman, for instance) and avoid specifying the more specific versions. If you want to add italics or bolding to a font, you can do so either through HTML (by using the EM, STRONG, I, or B elements) or CSS (by using the `font-style` property, covered a little later in this chapter, under "Setting Font Styles and Variants").

TIP

Adobe PostScript fonts are much more common on the Macintosh than they are on Windows or Unix/Linux systems. You should realize, however, that if Adobe Type Manager isn't installed on a Windows or Unix/Linux system, the user will see the bit-mapped version of a PostScript font, which will display a severe case of the "jaggies," especially in larger font sizes. For that reason, when creating font lists, you should always precede any PostScript fonts you list by one or more TrueType fonts:

```
h1, h2, h3 { font-family: Arial, Verdana, Helvetica; }
```

In this example, Arial and Verdana are TrueType fonts, while Helvetica is an Adobe PostScript font. The most common PostScript fonts that are included on Macintosh systems are: Courier, Times, and Palatino. Other PostScript fonts that might be included are: AvantGarde, Bookman, Helvetica-Narrow, New Century Schoolbook, and ZapfChancery.

Quoting Font Family Names

Font family names that include spaces, such as Arial Black, Comic Sans MS, Courier New, Minion Web, Times New Roman, and so on, should be quoted. Here's an example:

```
h1, h2, h3 { font-family: "Comic Sans MS", "Minion Web", Helvetica; }
```

Setting Generic Font Families

CSS specifies five generic font families that can be used as "catch-all" font categories. They are: `serif`, `sans-serif`, `monospace`, `cursive`, and `fantasy`.

The CSS specifications state that browsers "should provide reasonable default choices for the generic font families, which express the characteristics of each family as well as possible within the limits allowed by the underlying technology."

Generally, you can expect any level of uniformity only relative to the serif, sans-serif, and monospace font families. Browsers universally default to relatively similar fonts when one of these font families is specified. Usually some version of Times Roman is displayed as the default serif font, some version of Arial or Helvetica as the sans-serif font, and some version of Courier as the monospace font. If the cursive font family is specified, a script or calligraphic type font should be displayed; if a fantasy font-family is specified, a display or decorative font should be displayed.

In practice, however, it is anybody's guess which fonts will be displayed by which browsers when a cursive or fantasy font family is specified. For that reason, you should stick to specifying only the serif, sans-serif, and monospace generic font families, while avoiding using the cursive and fantasy font families.

For an example of doing this, first switch the group selector (h1, h2, h3) to an individual selector (h1), and then add selectors for the H2 and H3 elements using the sans-serif and monospace generic font families (see Figure 7.10):

```
h1 { font-family: "Comic Sans MS", "Minion Web", Helvetica; }
h2 { font-family: sans-serif; }
h3 { font-family: monospace; }
</style>
```

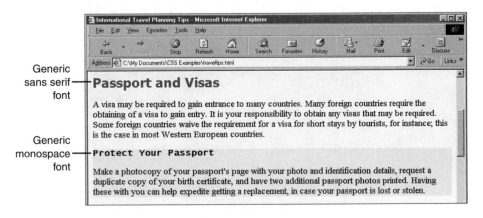

Generic sans serif font

Generic monospace font

Figure 7.10: *Generic sans-serif and monospace font families are specified for the H2 and H3 elements.*

Combining Specific and Generic Font Families

For the best of both worlds, you can combine both specific and generic font families when specifying fonts. This allows you to make specific font suggestions for displaying elements, while also suggesting a generic font family as a last resort, in case none of your specific suggested fonts are available. Here's an example:

```
h1 { font-family: Tahoma, Arial, Helvetica, sans-serif; }
```

This way, if neither Tahoma, Arial, or Helvetica is available, the browser's default sans-serif font is displayed. If the sans-serif font family is not specified, the browser defaults to displaying its default text font, which would likely be a serif font.

Setting Font Weights

CSS provides the font-weight property for setting different font weights. The heavier a font's weight, the bolder it is displayed. The font-weight property takes four keyword values, normal, bold, bolder, and lighter, and nine numeric values, 100, 200, 300, 400, 500, 600, 700, 800, and 900.

The CSS specifications say that normal is synonymous with 400 and bold is synonymous with 700, while bolder and lighter should select font weights that are relative to the font weight inherited from the parent element.

All CSS-supporting browsers should support the bold and normal keywords, as well as the 400 and 700 numeric values. For instance, here's an example of using inline styles to set bold and normal font weights (see Figure 7.11):

```
<h1 style="font-weight: normal">International <em style="font-weight:
bold">Travel Planning</em> Tips</h1>
```

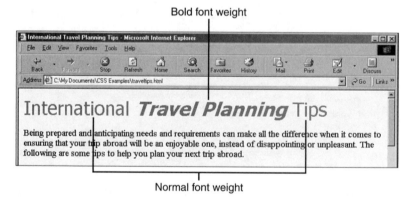

Bold font weight

Normal font weight

Figure 7.11: *The H1 heading is set using both normal and bold font weights.*

Using any of the other font-weight property values is problematic, however. Although both Internet Explorer 5 and Opera 5 support using the bolder and lighter relative weight values, Netscape 6 treats them indistinguishably from the bold and normal absolute weight values.

Current CSS-supporting browsers (see table 7.1) are also inconsistent in how they treat the numerical weight values:

Table 7.1: Browser Support for Font Weights

Weight	IE5/Mac	IE5.5/Win	Op5/Win	N6/Win	N6/Mac
100	Normal	Normal	Normal	Normal	Normal
200	Normal	Normal	Normal	Normal	Normal
300	Normal	Normal	Normal	Normal	Normal
400	Normal	Normal	Normal	Normal	Normal
500	Bold	Normal	Normal	Normal	Normal
600	Bold	Less Bold	Less Bold	Bold	Normal
700	Bold	Bold	Bold	Bold	Bold
800	Bold	Bold	Bold	Bold	Bold
900	Bold	Boldest	Boldest	Bold	Bold

The only commonalities in how these browsers treat the numerical weight values is that in all browsers a weight of 400 or less results in a normal weight font, and a weight of 700 or 800 results in a bold weight font. Any other numerical weight values yield inconsistent results from current browsers. In other words, you might as well stick to using the `bold` and `normal` weight values.

Setting Font Styles and Variants

The `font-style` property takes the values of `normal`, `italic`, and `oblique`. An `italic` value specifies a font that is classified within the browser's font database as an italic font, while an `oblique` value specifies a font that is classified within the browser's font database as an oblique font. Generally, an italic font was created separately from its corresponding non-italic roman typeface, and an oblique font was more likely created by simply slanting the normal roman typeface. When specifying a `font-style` of `italic`, a browser should display an "italic" font within the specified font family, if available. If an italic font is not available, it should display an "oblique" font instead. For an example of specifying an italic font style, edit your page's H1 element so it matches what is shown here (see Figure 7.12):

```
<h1 style="font-style: italic">International Travel Planning Tips</h1>
```

The `font-variant` property takes the values of `normal` and `small-caps`. Internet Explorer 5 (for Macintosh), Netscape 6 (for Windows and Macintosh), and Opera 5 all display small caps when the `small-caps` value is specified. Internet Explorer 5.5 (for Windows), however, displays the text in all caps, rather than in small caps. Here's an example of specifying a small-caps font variant:

```
<h1 style="font-variant: small-caps">International Travel Planning Tips</h1>
```

As shown in Figure 7.13, when small caps is set, the non-capped letters are displayed as uppercase letters, but in a reduced size.

Italic font style

Figure 7.12: *The H1 element is formatted in an italic font style.*

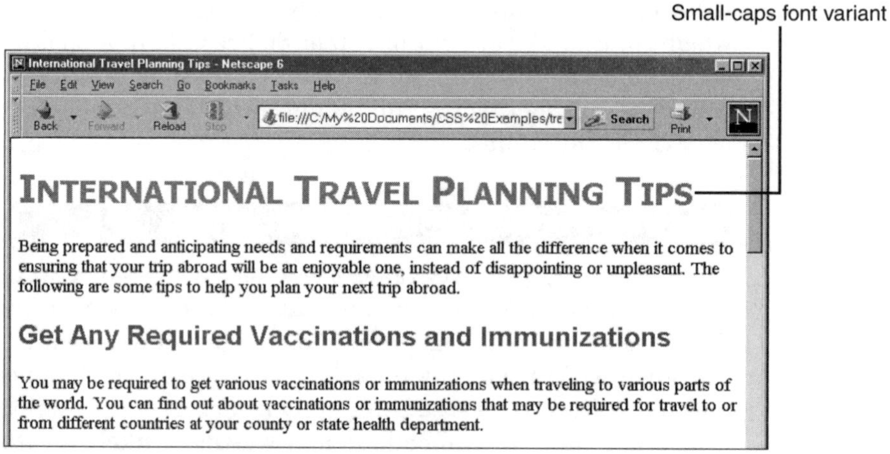

Small-caps font variant

Figure 7.13: *The H1 element is displayed in small-caps in Netscape 6.*

Using the Font Stretch Property

CSS2 includes the font-stretch property that can be used to stretch or condense a font's display. No current browser supports this, however. When supported, it will take these values: normal, wider, narrower, ultra-condensed, extra-condensed, condensed, semi-condensed, semi-expanded, expanded, extra-expanded, and ultra-expanded.

Using the Font Shorthand Property

In CSS, the font shorthand property can be used to set the other font properties. These include the font-size, font-family, font-weight, font-style, and font-variant properties, as well as the line-height property (which is covered in the next chapter, "Working with Text and Links"). Any font properties not declared in the font property are reset to their initial values. Two CSS2 properties, `font-stretch` and `font-size-adjust`, for the sake of backward compatibility with browsers that only support CSS1, can only be used to declare their default initial values (`normal` and `medium`, respectively). Other values for these properties should be set as individual properties.

Here's an example of setting a style rule for the P element that sets the font size, line height, and font family (see Figure 7.14):

```
p { font: 1.1em/1.3em "trebuchet ms", sans-serif; }
```

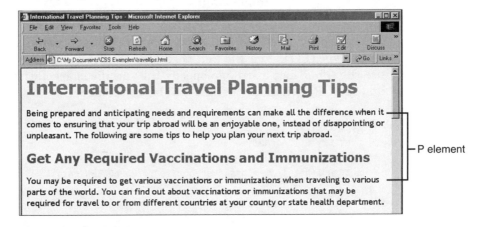

Figure 7.14: *The `font` shorthand property is used to declare the font size, line height, and font family of the P element.*

In the first declaration, `1.1em/1.3em`, the first part sets the font size, while the second part sets the line height. In the last declaration, `"trebuchet ms,"` `sans-serif`, a specific and generic font family is specified. The `line-height` property is discussed in more detail in the next chapter, "Working with Text and Links."

Font Matching and the `@font-face` At-Rule

CSS2 provides for more sophisticated font matching capabilities than are available in CSS1, providing for four different font matching methods:

- **Font name matching**—A browser uses an available font that has the same family name as the requested font. This is the only method provided for in CSS1.

- **Intelligent font matching**—A browser uses an available font that is the closest match in appearance to the requested font. The matching information includes the kind of font (text or symbol), nature of serifs, weight, cap-height, x-height, ascent, descent, slant, and so on. The font metrics need not match (meaning that a replacement font may have a smaller or larger font size than the requested font, based on the relative size of the replacement font's x-height, for instance).

- **Font synthesis**—A browser creates a font that is a close match in appearance to the requested font, matching the requested font's metrics (font size, for instance).

- **Font download**—The final option is to download the font from the Web. A Web designer can provide the URL of a specific font that is to display for a particular element or elements.

For Internet Explorer 4 and above, you must first create an Embedded Open Type (EOT) font file and post it to a folder on the Web. You can then use the @font-face at-rule to specify the specific characteristics of the font and the URL where its .eot file can be downloaded:

```
@font-face {
    font-family: Halloween;
    font-style:  normal;
    font-weight: bold;
    src: url(http://www.myserver.com/fonts/HALLOWEEN.eot);
  }
h1 { font-family: Halloween; }
```

This specifies a font family name of Halloween, a font style of normal, a font weight of bold, and the URL where the font's .eot file can be found. The font is then applied to the H1 element.

Microsoft provides a free tool, Microsoft WEFT (Web Embedding Fonts Tool) that you can use to create your own .eot files. It can scan fonts available on your local computer, for instance, and then create .eot files that can be made available over the Web. You can then specify the font name in a style property, just as though it was already available and present on the local computer. At present, however, .eot files can only be viewed in Internet Explorer 4 and above. To find out more about Microsoft WEFT, see http://www.microsoft.com/typography/web/embedding/weft/.

There are many additional font descriptors, other than the one shown in the previous example, that can be used to fine-tune the font characteristics being specified. For a full listing and descriptions, see the section on Font Selection in the CSS2 specification at http://www.w3.org/TR/REC-CSS2/fonts.html#font-selection.

Netscape Navigator 4 supports a competing form of downloadable fonts, the PFR format, that can be created using WebFont Maker, a tool from

BitStream. Netscape 6, however, does not support this font format. For that reason, if you want to experiment with using downloadable fonts in your Web pages, you should stick to using EOT files.

CAUTION

If you decide to experiment with using downloadable fonts in your Web pages, you should be aware that many typefaces available on your own local computer or over the Web are copyrighted. While you may have the legal right to use them on your own local computer (they came along with your operating system, for instance), that doesn't mean that the license extends to also using those same fonts as available for download from a remote Web server.

Before making any font available for download, you should make sure that the author of the font has released the font into the public domain or has otherwise provided permission for the font to be used and downloaded over the Web. If you're running a commercial site, you may want to get written permission before providing any downloadable fonts from your Web site.

What's Next?

In this chapter, you learned how to assign the different font characteristics to your page's elements, including setting the font size, family, weight, and other characteristics. You should now be comfortable with varying the font size of different elements, specifying specific and generic font families, as well as using the `font` shorthand property.

In the next chapter, you learn how to use styles to set text characteristics, such as aligning and indenting text, setting line heights, word and letter spacing, and other visual effects. You also learn how to create your own custom inline elements using the SPAN element in combination with styles, as well as how to control the appearance of hypertext links.

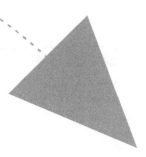

Working with Text and Links

So far, in Part III of the book, you've worked with examples of setting colors and backgrounds in Chapter 6 and setting font characteristics in Chapter 7. In this chapter, you work with examples of setting text characteristics, including:

- Horizontally aligning text, including left- and right-aligning, centering, and justifying text
- Indenting the first text line of an element
- Controlling the line height
- Controlling word and letter spacing
- Setting underlining, overlining, striking, and blinking
- Controlling capitalization
- Using the Text-Shadow property
- Using the SPAN element
- Controlling the appearance of links

Using the Example File

You'll be continuing to use the same example file, traveltips.html, that you used in the previous chapter. To save an example of your work from the previous chapter, open traveltips.html in your text editor and resave it as **traveltips1.html** in your working folder, and then resave it again as **traveltips2.html**. You'll be using traveltips2.html to do the examples in this chapter.

For this chapter's examples, just start fresh, deleting any of the styles in the traveltips2.html example file that you set in the previous chapter. The start of the example file should look like this (the remainder of the file, not shown here, should be identical to what is shown in Listing 7.1):

Listing 8.1: TRAVELTIPS2.HTML—International Travel Planning Tips

```
<!DOCTYPE HTML PUBLIC "-//W3C//DTD HTML 4.01 Transitional//EN"
"http://www.w3.org/TR/html4/loose.dtd">

<html>
<head>
<title>International Travel Planning Tips</title>
<style type="text/css">

</style>
</head>
<body>

<h1>International Travel Planning Tips</h1>
<p>Being prepared and anticipating needs and requirements can make all the
difference when it comes to ensuring that your trip abroad will be an enjoyable
one, instead of disappointing or unpleasant. The following are some tips to help
you plan your next trip abroad.</p>
```

Just to set some starting styles for your page's heading elements, add the following styles to your style sheet:

```
<style type="text/css">
h1, h2, h3 { font-family: Arial, Helvetica, sans-serif; }
h1 { font-size: 2.5em; color: rgb(200,140,40); }
</style>
```

This sets an Arial font family for the top three heading elements (H1, H2, and H3). The H1 element is also sized at 2.5 ems (2.5 times the BODY element's font size) and sports a gold colored foreground color.

Horizontally Aligning Text

In HTML, the CENTER tag and the ALIGN attribute are used to horizontally align text and other elements. In HTML 4.01, the CENTER tag is deprecated and all uses of the ALIGN attribute are also deprecated, except for use within tables.

In CSS, the `text-align` property is used to horizontally align or justify text within block elements. The values for this property include `left`, `right`, `center`, and `justify`.

Here's an example of centering the H1 element (see Figure 8.1):

```
h1, h2, h3 { font-family: Arial, Helvetica, sans-serif; }
h1 { text-align: center; font-size: 2.5em; color: rgb(200,140,40); }
```

H1 element (centered)

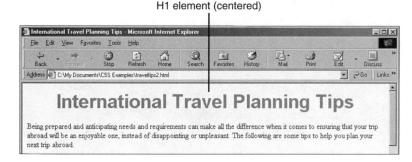

Figure 8.1: *The H1 element is centered using the* `text-align` *property.*

Next, here's an example of right-aligning the H2 and H3 elements (see Figure 8.2):

```
h1, h2, h3 { text-align: right; font-family: Arial, Helvetica, sans-serif; }
h1 { text-align: center; font-size: 2.5em; color: rgb(200,140,40); }
```

You'll notice in the previous example that the `text-align: right` property declaration is made for a group selector that includes the H1, H2, and H3 elements. However, a `text-align: center` property declaration is made in the following H1 style rule. Because the following instance of the `text-align` property takes precedence over any previous instances, the right-alignment is applied only to the H2 and H3 elements.

You could, of course, simply define individual selectors for each of the heading elements—it is a good idea, however, to always look for opportunities to use group selectors wherever several properties are shared by more than one element. It'll save you some typing, since you won't have to retype the same property value for each and every element, and your style sheets will be more efficient and consume less bandwidth (especially if your style sheet is at all involved).

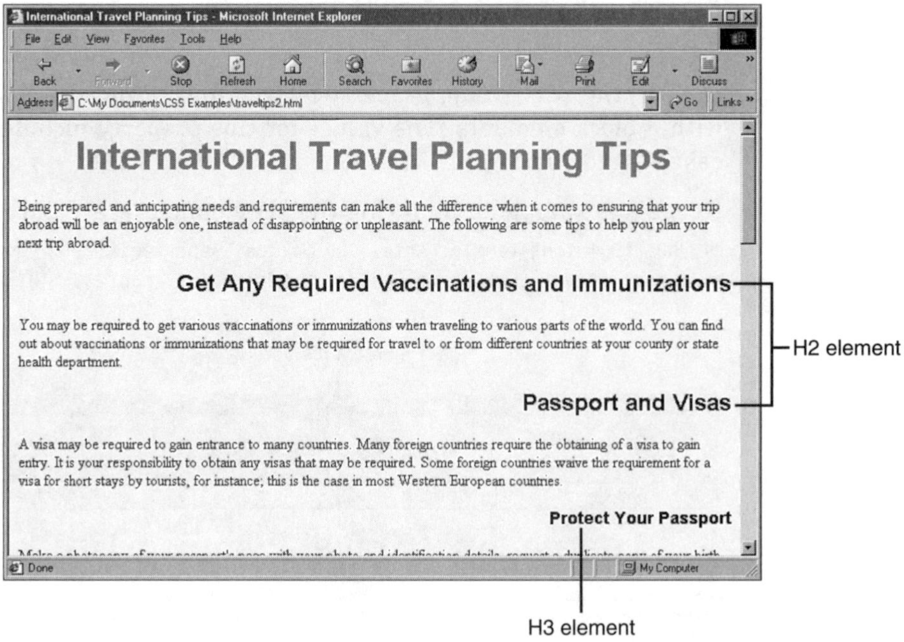

Figure 8.2: *The H2 and H3 elements are right-aligned using the* `text-align` *property.*

You can also justify text using the `text-align` property. When text is justified, it is aligned flush with both the left and right margins; a browser adjusts the amount of spacing inserted between letters and words to justify a line of text. By default, text is left aligned (with a ragged right margin).

To see how this works, first add some extra text to the P element in your HTML file, so you can see the justification effect, and then set the following style rule for the P element (see Figure 8.3):

```
h1 { text-align: center; font-size: 2.5em; color: rgb(200,140,40); }
p { text-align: justify; }
```

Left-alignment is the default for horizontally aligned text. You might use `text-align: left`, however, in an inline style—for instance, to reset a particular element from being centered to being left-aligned.

You might also want to create a class selector (p. 75), `p.left`, for instance, that resets left alignment for paragraphs included in that class, while all other paragraphs are set as justified. Without specifically setting left alignment in this case, all paragraphs included within the "left" class would also be justified, since they share any other formatting set for paragraphs in general.

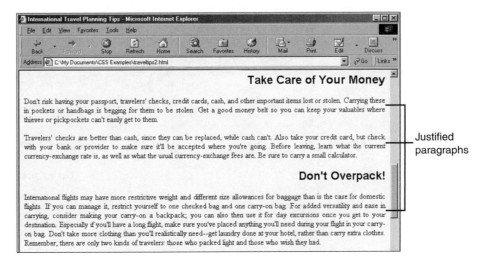

Justified paragraphs

Figure 8.3: *The P element is justified using the* `text-align` *property.*

Indenting the First Text Line

In HTML, vertical spacing is automatically inserted above and below text paragraphs to indicate paragraph breaks (or hard returns). Some organizations, however, have style conventions for their documents that require the use of text indents (or tabbed indents) to indicate the beginning of a new paragraph. A *text indent* indents the first line a specified distance from the element's left margin. Web designers might be compelled by the internal style czars within their organizations to enforce this rule in Web documents as well, even though this is largely a vestige of the typewriter era.

✔ Sometimes being able to easily set text indents can be very handy—when displaying paragraphs in columns, for instance, where you want to economize on the amount of vertical spacing occupied by the text. Later in this book, "Creating Multi-Column Layouts," p. 337 (chapter 14), you use text indents to create a layout using newspaper columns.

Another use for this property is to specify formatting to be used when printing a document, when using a style sheet with a "print" media descriptor (p. 69). If your document includes a large amount of text, for instance, using tabbed indents instead of vertical spacing can help to save some paper (and maybe some trees).

To see this in action, insert the following into your style sheet to set the text-indent to two ems and the top and bottom margins to zero for the P element (see Figure 8.4):

```
p { text-indent: 2em; margin-top: 0; margin-bottom: 0; text-align: justify; }
```

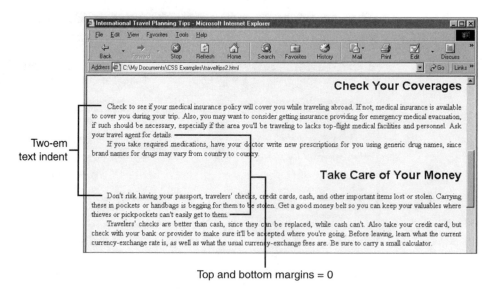

Two-em text indent

Top and bottom margins = 0

Figure 8.4: *The first line of the text paragraphs is indented by two ems.*

There should find a DIV element in the example file bracketing the H3 heading and following paragraph. If it's not present, just insert it, as shown here:

```
<div>
<h3>Protect Your Passport</h3>
<p>Make a photocopy of your passport's page with your photo and identification
details, request a duplicate copy of your birth certificate, and have two
additional passport photos printed. Having these with you can help expedite
getting a replacement, in case your passport is lost or stolen.</p>
</div>
```

The P element that is nested inside of the BLOCKQUOTE element (under the H2 element) also displays the text indent that you just set. By using a contextual style, however, you can cause the text indent to be turned off for paragraphs nested inside of block quotes. For instance (see Figure 8.5):

```
p { text-indent: 2em; margin-top: 0; margin-bottom: 0; text-align: justify; }
div p { text-indent: 0; color: black; background: aqua; }
```

✔ The preceding example isn't meant as a design example, but simply to illustrate how to use a contextual selector to turn off text indenting within a particular context. In "Using the DIV element," p. 205 (chapter 9), you work with using the DIV element as more of a design element, including setting margins, padding, and borders.

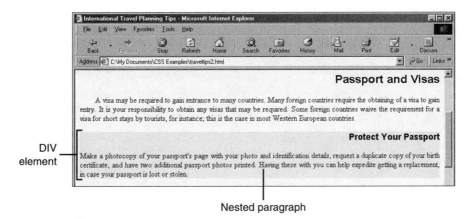

DIV element

Nested paragraph

Figure 8.5: *Using a contextual style, the first-line text indent is turned off just for paragraphs inside a document division (the DIV element).*

Controlling the Line Height

The line-height property is used to specify a line height for an element. The *line height* is the vertical distance separating the baselines of adjacent lines of text. The line-height property takes these kinds of values: length, percentage, and numerical values, as well as a normal value.

A length value sets the line height utilizing a relative measuring unit (em, ex, or px) or an absolute measuring unit (in, cm, mm, pt, or pc). Just like when setting font sizes, you're probably better off setting line heights using em units, with pixel units being a possible second choice. Here's an example of setting the line height of the P element to 1.5 ems (see Figure 8.6):

```
h1 { text-align: center; font-size: 2.5em; color: rgb(200,140,40); }
p { line-height: 1.5em; text-indent: 2em; margin-top: 0; margin-bottom: 0; text-
align: justify; }
```

NOTE

It is important to be aware that although a relative unit, such as an em, percentage, or numerical value, is equal to the parent element's font size when setting the font size, it is equal to the current element's font size when setting the line height. If fonts of varying sizes are used within an element, a browser should calculate the line height based on the largest font.

Using a percentage value to set the line height works exactly the same as using em values. For example, a percentage of 150% is equal to 1.5em.

Line height = 1.5 ems

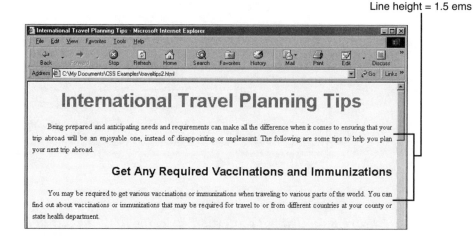

Figure 8.6: *The line height for paragraph elements is set to 1.5 ems.*

Numeric values are similar to em and percentage values, except that the specified value, and not the computed value, is inherited. For instance, let's say you set the following style rules (see Figure 8.7):

```
body { font-size: 1em; line-height: 1.5em; }
h1, h2, h3 { text-align: right; font-family: Arial, Helvetica, sans-serif; }
```

In this case, the line-height inherited by the H1 element is actually less than the H1 element's font size, because the computed value of the H1 element's inherited line-height (1.5 times the body text size) is less than its font size (two times the body text size). The same holds true if the line height was set using a percentage value (`150%`).

On the other hand, let's say you set the BODY element's line-height property using a numerical value (see Figure 8.8):

```
body { font-size: 1em; line-height: 1.5; }
```

In this case, the line-height inherited by the H1 element is 1.5 times the H1 element's font size (or 3 ems), because the actual numerical ratio, rather than the computed value, is inherited.

For this reason, you might want to stick to using numerical values when setting line heights, unless you specifically want the computed line height value to be inherited by child elements, rather than the actual numerical value (or ratio). This is also quite natural, in that a numerical value of 2 corresponds to a line height that is double-spaced.

Line height = 1.5em

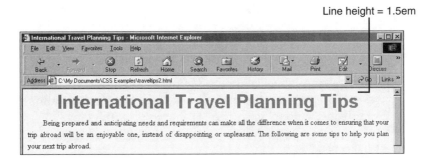

Figure 8.7: *An inherited line height set using em units gives you one result.*

Line height = 1.5

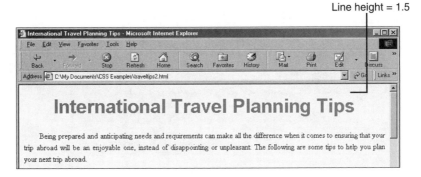

Figure 8.8: *An inherited line height set using numerical units gives you another result.*

CAUTION

Negative line height values (such as `line-height: -0.5em`) are illegal and should be ignored by browsers or treated as positive values.

Controlling Letter and Word Spacing

The `letter-spacing` and `word-spacing` properties let you control the amount of spacing that is inserted between characters and words, respectively.

Setting Letter Spacing

The `letter-spacing` property lets you control the spacing that is inserted between characters in a string or line of text. This property takes either a length value (em, pixel, or other measuring unit) or a value of `normal`.

The normal value is the default and allows a browser to increase or decrease the spacing between characters to justify a line of text (if the text-align property is set to justify). If a length value is set, a browser only adds spacing between words to justify a line.

When setting letter spacing, a length value indicates spacing in addition to the default spacing between characters. Here's an example of increasing the default letter spacing in the H1 element by 0.5 ems:

```
h1 { letter-spacing: 0.5em; text-align: center; font-size: 2.5em; color:
rgb(200,140,40); }
```

Figure 8.9 shows the H1 element with additional letter spacing of 0.5 ems inserted between the characters.

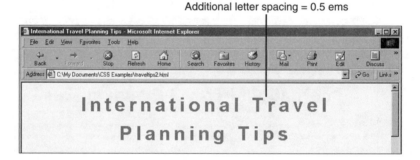

Figure 8.9: *An additional 0.5 ems of letter spacing is added between the characters in the H1 element.*

To see the difference, just compare the letter spacing for the H1 element shown in Figure 8.9 to that shown in Figure 8.8 (where the letter spacing for the H1 element is set to a default value of normal).

NOTE

Just as is the case when setting the line height, when setting letter spacing, an em unit is equal to the font size of the current element (unlike with when setting the font size, where an em is equal to the font size of the parent element). Percentage units can't be used to set letter spacing.

To decrease the amount of letter spacing inserted between characters, a negative length value can be used. Here's an example of decreasing the letter spacing by 0.2 ems (see Figure 8.10):

```
h1 { letter-spacing: -0.2em; text-align: center; font-size: 2.5em; color:
rgb(200,140,40); }
```

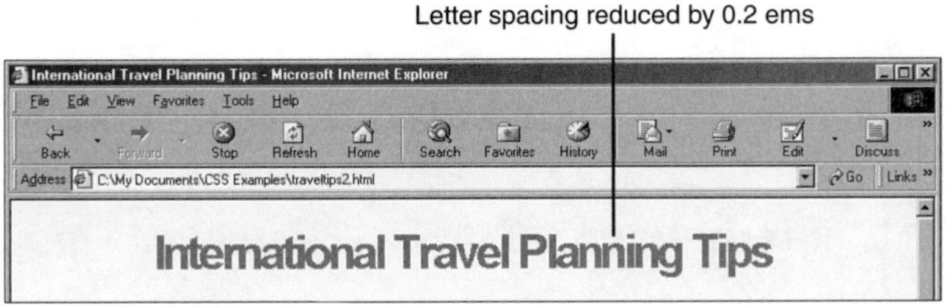

Letter spacing reduced by 0.2 ems

Figure 8.10: *The letter spacing between characters in the H1 elment is reduced by 0.2 ems.*

Setting Word Spacing

The word-spacing property lets you control the spacing inserted between words in a line or string of text. It works in the same fashion as the letter-spacing property, with a positive length value adding to and a negative length value subtracting from the default word spacing. The default value of normal allows browsers to increase or decrease the default spacing inserted between words to justify a line of text, while any length value (positive or negative) prohibits browsers from increasing or decreasing the resulting letter spacing in order to justify a line of text.

Here's an example of setting additional word spacing of 0.5 ems for the H1 element (replace the letter-spacing property you set earlier):

```
h1 { word-spacing: 0.5em; text-align: center; font-size: 2.5em; color:
rgb(200,140,40); }
```

Internet Explorer 5.5 doesn't support the word-spacing property, although Internet Explorer 6 does. Both Netscape 6 and Opera 5, however, do recognize positive or negative length values set for the word-spacing property. Figure 8.11 shows what the previous example looks like in a browser (Netscape 6) that recognizes length values set for the word-spacing property.

Additional word spacing of 0.5 ems

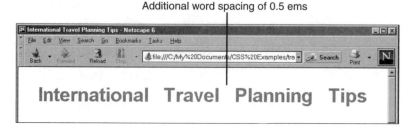

Figure 8.11: *Netscape 6 recognizes length values set for the word-spacing property.*

Setting Underlining, Overlining, and Other Highlighting

In HTML, the U element can be used to underline text, and the S or Strike elements can be used to strike through text. In HTML 4, all of these elements are deprecated in favor of using styles to achieve the same results. In CSS, the text-decoration property is used to set underlining and strikethrough, as well as overlining and blinking highlighting. The accepted values for the text-decoration property include none, underline, overline, line-through, and blink. Here's an example of setting overlining for the H1 element (see Figure 8.12):

```
h1 { text-decoration: overline; text-align: center; font-size: 2.5em; color:
rgb(200,140,40); }
```

Overlining

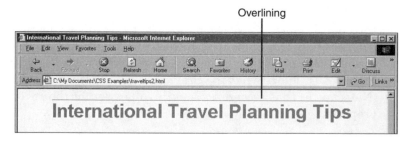

Figure 8.12: *Overlining is set here using the text-decoration property.*

Here's an example of setting underlining for the H1 element (see Figure 8.13):

✔ For an example of using the text-decoration property to turn off the default underlining of hypertext links, see "Turning Link Underlining Off," p. 177 (chapter 8).

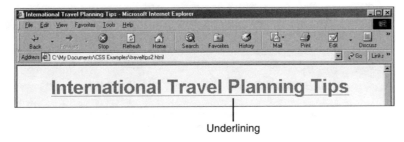

Underlining

Figure 8.13: *Underlining is set here using the* `text-decoration` *property.*

The `text-decoration: blink` property ostensibly replaces the BLINK element, which is a Netscape extension to HTML that's never been included in the official HTML specifications. The BLINK element is one of the least popular HTML elements, with many considering it to be highly irritating. You should be aware that many visitors to your page might feel exactly the same way in regard to blinking set using the `text-decoration` property. It's best to avoid it, in other words.

If an element has no text content (as with the IMG element, for instance), the `text-decoration` property is ignored.

Strikethrough text in HTML can also be set using the DEL element. The DEL element has not been deprecated in HTML 4.

Controlling Capitalization

The `text-transform` property lets you specify how you want an element's text to be capitalized. The values accepted by the `text-transform` property include `none`, `capitalize`, `uppercase`, and `lowercase`. The default value is `none`, which leaves any capitalization unchanged. The `capitalize` value capitalizes the initial letters in the text; the `uppercase` value capitalizes sets all letters to uppercase; and the `lowercase` value sets all letters to lowercase. Here's an example of setting all the letters in the H2 elements to uppercase (see Figure 8.14):

```
h1 { text-decoration: underline; text-align: center; font-size: 2.5em; color:
rgb(200,140,40); }
h2 { text-transform: uppercase; }
```

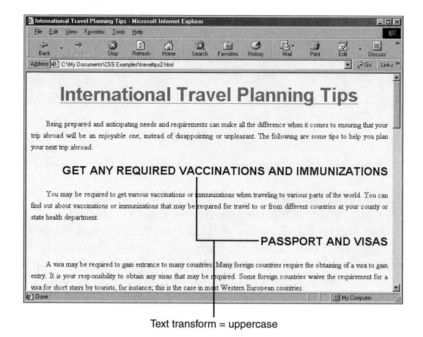

Text transform = uppercase

Figure 8.14: *The H2 elements are set in all uppercase.*

Setting Text Shadows

CSS2 also provides a `text-shadow` property that specifies that text be displayed with a shadow. No current browser (Internet Explorer 5/5.5, Netscape 6, or Opera 5) supports this property. When (and if) it is supported, you'll be able to set shadow effects for text, which might be handy, for instance, when creating callouts that need to be visible against both light and dark backgrounds.

For more information on how to set text shadows, once they are supported in current browsers, see the section, "Text shadows: the `'text-shadow'` property," in the W3C's CSS2 specification at http://www.w3.org/TR/REC-CSS2/text.html#text-shadow-props.

Using the SPAN Element

The SPAN element was first introduced as part of HTML 3.2 to enable Web authors to specify display characteristics for inline content (or "spans" of text). The SPAN element functions purely as a carrier of style information, possessing no display characteristics of its own.

The SPAN element provides a generic inline element in addition to the other specific inline elements (such as the I, B, EM, STRONG, SUP, and SUB elements, for instance).

For an example of using the SPAN element, add a style to your style sheet that applies overlining to any text nested inside of a SPAN element (delete the style for the P element, while you're at it):

```
p { line-height: 1.5em; text-indent: 2em; margin-top: 0; margin-bottom: 0; text-align: justify; }
div { color: black; background: #ccffff; }
div p { text-indent: 0; }
span { text-decoration: overline; }
```

Next, nest a SPAN element inside of your page's H1 element, like this:

```
<h1><span>International Travel Planning Tips</span></h1>
```

As shown in Figure 8.15, while underlining has already been set for the H1 element, the SPAN element is used here to also set overlining for text that is nested inside of the H1 element:

Figure 8.15: *The underlining is set for the H1 element, while the overlining is set for SPAN element (nested inside of the H1 element).*

If you just apply styles to the SPAN element, you're limited to creating only one set of properties you can apply to spanned text. The real versatility of the SPAN element, however, lies in its ability to be applied in multiple fashions and contexts within your page. For instance, as the example currently stands, any instance of the SPAN element inserted in your page will apply the same formatting, overlining, to text nested inside of the element. To limit the application of the overlining only to spanned text that is nested inside of the H1 element, just set the styling in the form of a contextual style, like this:

```
div p { text-indent: 0; }
```

h1 span { text-decoration: overline; }

This has the effect of limiting the application of overlining only to a SPAN element that is nested inside of the H1 element.

Another way of being able to specify different formatting for different SPAN elements is to use inline styles. For instance, here's an example of using an inline style in a SPAN element that italicizes nested text, sets underlining, and increases the font size to 1.1 ems:

```
<h2>Get Any <span style="font-style: italic; text-decoration: underline; font-size: 1.1em ">Required</span> Vaccinations and Immunizations</span></h2>
```

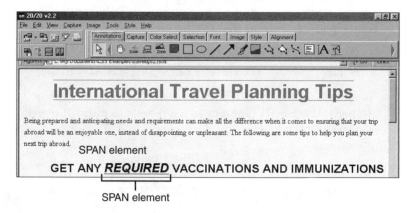

Figure 8.16: *An inline style is used to apply formatting to the SPAN element nested in the first H2 element.*

Another way to use the SPAN element to apply different formatting in different places is using a class selector. This allows you to apply different formatting to different SPAN elements, depending upon which class they belong to. For instance, here's an example of creating a class selector for the SPAN element:

```
h1 span { text-decoration: overline; }
span.standout { font-family: Tahoma, Helvetica, sans-serif; font-style: italic;
font-weight: bold; font-size: 1.1em; color: green; background: transparent; }
```

To have this take effect in a Web page, you just need to insert a SPAN element in your document body with a `class="standout"` attribute, like this (see Figure 8.17):

```
<h2>Don't Overpack!</h2>
<p>International flights may have more restrictive weight and different size
allowances for baggage than is the case for domestic flights. If you can manage
it, restrict yourself to one checked bag and one carry-on bag. For added
versatility and ease in carrying, consider making your carry-on a backpack; you
can also then use it for day excursions once you get to your destination.
Especially if you'll have a long flight, make sure you've placed anything you'll
need during your flight in your carry-on bag. Don't take more clothing than
```

you'll realistically need—get laundry done at your hotel, rather than carry extra clothes. **<span class="standout">**Remember, there are only two kinds of travelers: those who packed light and those who wish they had.**</span>**</p>

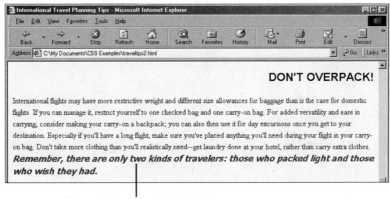

Class selector (span.standout)

Figure 8.17: *By using a class selector, you can create a custom span element that can be plugged in wherever you need it.*

By creating additional class selectors for the SPAN element, you can create many different custom variants of the SPAN element. In essence, the SPAN element lets you extend HTML with your own custom inline elements.

✔ Another HTML element, the DIV element works similarly to the SPAN element, except it lets you create your own custom block elements. You've already used some simple examples of using the DIV element; see "Using the DIV Element," p. 205 (chapter 9), for a more detailed explanation of using the DIV element.

Controlling the Appearance of Links

One of the most ubiquitous of inline elements is the hypertext link. If you change the color, font sizes, font families, and other characteristics, you'll also want to control the appearance of links within your document, so they're coordinated with the rest of your text.

In HTML, hypertext links are created using the A (or Anchor) tag. Following the "Travel Resources" heading, you can find a list of example hypertext links (and descriptive text), as shown here (see Figure 8.18):

```
<h2>Travel Resources</h2>
<p>Here are some travel resources that are available online:
<ul>
<li><a href="http://travel.state.gov/travel.cfm">Travel and Living Abroad</a>
from the Bureau of Consular Affairs, U.S. Department of State. Passport and visa
info, travel warnings, country background notes, and more.
```

```
<li><a href="http://www.x-rates.com/">Exchange Rates</a> for many foreign
currencies, provided by the Federal Reserve Bank of New York.
<li><a href="http://travel.state.gov/olderamericans.html">Travel Tips for Older
Americans</a> from the U.S. Department of State.
<li><a href="http://www.disabled-traveler.com/">Disabled-Traveler.com</a> -
Travel resources for the disabled traveler.
<li><a href="http://www.cdc.gov/travel/">Traveler's Health</a> from the CDC
(Centers for Disease Control and Prevention). Check here for health information
and required vaccinations/immunizations required for the country or area you'll
be visiting.
</ul>
```

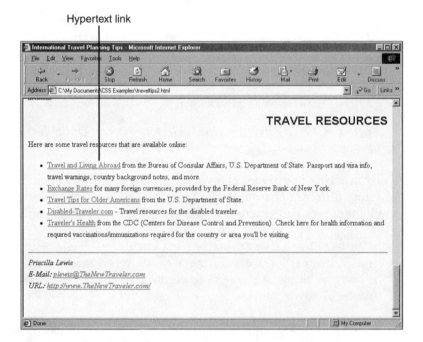

Figure 8.18: *By default, most browsers display hypertext links underlined and in blue.*

By defining properties for the A element, you can control the appearance of a hypertext link in your page. For instance, here's an example of specifying different display properties for hypertext links (see Figure 8.19):

```
span.standout { font-family: tahoma, helvetica, sans-serif; font-style: italic;
font-weight: bold; font-size: 1.1em; color: green; background: transparent; }
a { font-family: Arial, Helvetica, sans-serif; font-style: italic; font-weight:
bold; font-size: 1.1em; color: red; background: transparent; }
```

Hypertext link (A element)

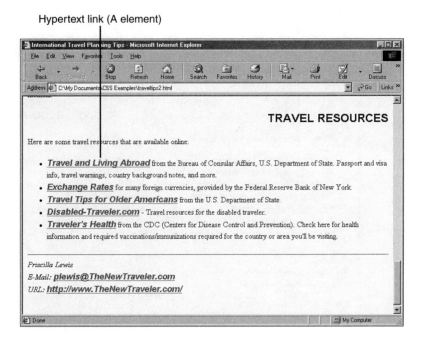

Figure 8.19: *You can change how hypertext links will appear in your page.*

Using a Contextual Selector to Control Links

Right now, any properties that are set for the A element are applied to any link within the page. You can use a contextual selector, however, to specify separate formatting that you want to be applied to links within a particular context. For instance, you can specify separate formatting for the links that are included within the page's ADDRESS element by using a contextual selector, like this (see Figure 8.20:

```
a { font-family: Arial, Helvetica, sans-serif; font-style: italic; font-weight:
bold; font-size: 1.1em; color: red; background: transparent; }
address a { font-size: 0.9em; font-style: normal; color: green; background:
transparent; font-family: serif;}
```

In this case, the links that are nested inside of the ADDRESS block are displayed in a green color, a serif font, and in a normal font style (no italics). The font size is also reduced to 0.9 ems. It is important to note here that any other properties set for the A element are also applied to the links within the ADDRESS element—for instance, the bold font weight specified for the A element is also applied to the A elements within the ADDRESS element.

Hypertext link (contextual selector)

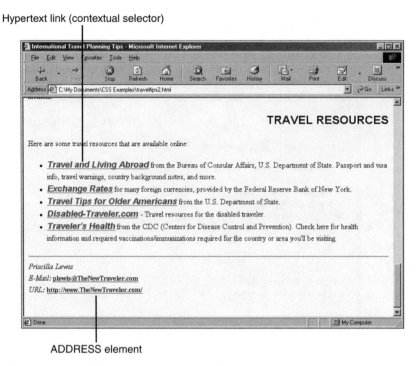

ADDRESS element

Figure 8.20: *Using a contextual selector, you can specify formatting for links that takes effect only within a particular context, such as within a page's address block (the ADDRESS element).*

Using Anchor Pseudo-Classes

In HTML, the BODY element's LINK, VLINK, and ALINK attributes can be used to set colors for unvisited, visited, and active links. These attributes, however, are deprecated in HTML 4, in favor of using styles to achieve the same or better results. In CSS, a special set of pseudo-classes, called *anchor pseudo-classes*, because they are applied to the A element) are used to set colors and other display characteristics for these different link states. The three anchor pseudo-classes that correspond to the BODY element's LINK, VLINK, and ALINK attributes are the a:link, a:visited, and a:active pseudo-classes. Because in CSS1 these pseudo-classes can only be applied to the A element, they can also be expressed as :link, :visited, and :active. Here's an example of using these anchor pseudo-classes to set different colors for unvisited, visited, and active links:

```
:link { color: navy; }
:visited { color: olive; }
:active { color: purple; }
```

In your browser, this should cause links that haven't been visited yet to be displayed in a navy color, and links that have been visited should be displayed in an olive color. When you hold the mouse button down on the link, the active link color should be displayed.

Using the `A:hover` Pseudo-Element

CSS2 provides an additional anchor pseudo-class, the `a:hover` pseudo-class, which lets you control how a link appears when the mouse cursor "hovers" over a link. Some earlier versions of Internet Explorer for Windows automatically set a red hover color that was displayed when the mouse hovered over a link.

Internet Explorer 5.5 for Windows does not automatically turn on the hover color, but does let the user assign a hover color and turn it on or off. Just click the Colors button in Internet Explorer 5.5's Internet Options dialog window to check this out for yourself if you're using that browser. Internet Explorer 5 for the Macintosh does not automatically display a hover color, nor does it let you turn it on or off.

The solution was provided by CSS, in the form of the `a:hover` pseudo-class. For example, here's an example of setting hypertext links to display a green hover color:

```
a:link { color: navy; }
a:visited { color: olive; }
a:active { color: purple; }
a:hover { color: green; }
```

In this case, when the mouse cursor hovers over the link, its color switches to green. When the mouse cursor passes off of the link, its color reverts back to its former state (as either an unvisited or visited link). All of the current CSS-supporting browsers (Internet Explorer 5.5 for Windows, Internet Explorer 5 for Macintosh, Netscape 6, and Opera 5) support setting the `:hover` pseudo-class.

TIP

Although in CSS1 the `a:link`, `a:visited`, and `a:active` pseudo-classes are the same as `:link`, `:visited`, and `:active`, because they can only be applied to the A element, in CSS2 the situation is a little different. In CSS2, properties defined by `:link` and `:visited` still can only be applied to the A element, but properties defined by `:active` and `:hover` can be applied to any element that is either active (such as a form text input field, for instance) or hovered over by the mouse cursor. The biggest concern here is `:hover`, which might cause not only a link to display the hover color, but any other element over which the cursor might hover. The only browser that actually does this right now, that I'm aware of anyway, is Netscape 6, which also colors any element with the hover color for which a foreground color has not been specified or inherited.

For that reason, you should stick to specifying active and hover colors using `a:active` and `a:hover`, rather than `:active` and `:hover`, when you want to set active and hover colors for hypertext links.

Creating CSS Roll-Over Links

You're not limited to only setting colors for the anchor pseudo-classes. You can set any other property that can be assigned to an inline element, such as background colors or images, fonts, weights, and so on. For instance, here's an example of creating a "roll-over" link using just CSS:

```
a { font-family: Arial, Helvetica, sans-serif; font-style: italic; font-weight:
bold; font-size: 1.1em; color: red; background: transparent; }
address a { font-size: 0.9em; font-style: normal; color: green; background:
transparent; font-family: serif;}
a:link { color: red; background: yellow; }
a:visited { color: red; background: yellow; }
a:active { color: yellow; background: yellow; }
a:hover { color: yellow; background: blue; }
```

In a browser that supports these pseudo-classes, the a:link, a:active, and a:visited pseudo-classes assign a red foreground color and a yellow background color to both unvisited and visited links. Browsers keep track of pages you've already accessed in their history lists and will display links to pages that you haven't visited recently (unvisited links) and links to pages that you have visited recently (visited links) in different colors to distinguish them (most browsers display unvisited links in a blue color, but visited links in a purple color, for instance).

The a:active pseudo-class is supposed to allow you to assign properties to an activated link. In many browsers, these properties are displayed when you hold the mouse button on a link. In Internet Explorer 5.5 for Windows, however, these properties are displayed after returning to the page (by clicking the Back button) after accessing the link's target. For that reason, it is probably a good idea to always set the same properties for the a:active pseudo-class that are set for the a:visited pseudo-class, as is done in the example (red foreground color and yellow background color).

The a:hover pseudo-class assigns properties to be displayed when the mouse hovers over the link. In the example, a yellow foreground color and a blue background color is assigned to the a:hover pseudo-class (as shown in Figure 8.21). The font (Arial), weight (bold), and padding for the link, whether in the non-hover or hover state, is set by the A element style rule.

CAUTION

In CSS1, the a:link, a:visited, and a:active pseudo-classes are mutually exclusive, which meant that you could insert them in any order. In CSS2, however, the a:link and a:visited pseudo-classes are still mutually exclusive, but the a:active and a:hover pseudo-classes are not. In CSS2, the same link element can display the active and hover properties at the same time. Properties defined in the later style rule in the sequence take precedence over ones defined in the earlier style rule; so, if you want to make sure that your hover and active properties will be displayed, you must always list the a:hover and a:active pseudo-classes like this:

```
a:link { color: yellow; background: blue; }
a:visited { color: white; background: blue; }
a:hover { color: red; background: aqua; }
a:active { color: lime; background: green; }
```

and *not* like this:

```
a:hover { color: red; background: aqua; }
a:active { color: lime; background: green; }
a:link { color: yellow; background: blue; }
a:visited { color: white; background: blue; }
```

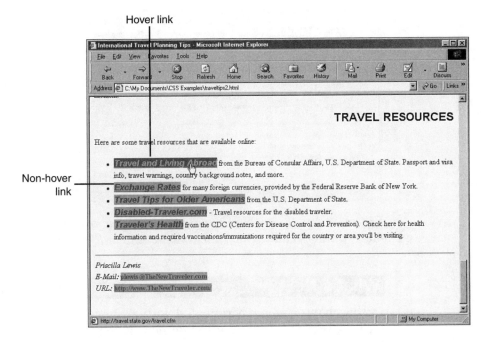

Figure 8.21: *When the mouse cursor hovers over a link, properties assigned to the a:hover pseudo-class are displayed.*

Turning Link Underlining Off

In most browsers, hypertext links are underlined by default. Users can also turn off underlining of hypertext links in most browsers, if they wish. Internet Explorer 5.5 for Windows, Internet Explorer 5 for the Macintosh, Netscape 6, and Opera 5 all allow users to turn off underlining of links.

Earlier in this chapter, you experimented with the text-decoration property to set underlining, overlining, and other highlighting. The same property, by using the none value, can be used by authors to turn off the underlining of hypertext links. Here's an example (see Figure 8.22):

a { **text-decoration: none;** font-family: Arial, Helvetica, sans-serif; font-style: italic; font-weight: bold; font-size: 1.1em; color: red; background: transparent; }

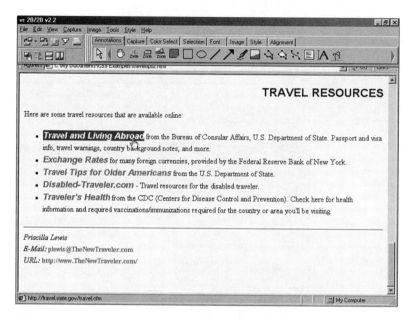

Figure 8.22: By setting the text-decoration property to none for the A element, authors can turn off the underlining of hypertext links.

What's Next?

In this chapter, you experimented with examples of setting style properties for your text and links. You should now be comfortable with controlling horizontal alignment, creating first line indents, setting the line height, controlling letter and word spacing, underlining or overlining, and capitalization. You should also know now how to create your own custom elements by applying styles to the SPAN element. In addition, you should be practiced in controlling the appearance of hypertext links.

Next, in Part IV, "Working with Block Elements and Objects," you learn how to apply style properties to block elements and objects. In Chapter 9, "Formatting Block Elements," you learn about the CSS formatting model and how to specify alignment, margins, padding, and other formatting characteristics to block elements.

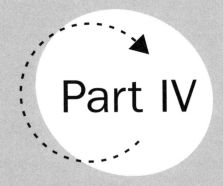

Part IV

Working with Block Elements and Objects

Formatting Block Elements

Aligning, Floating, and Positioning

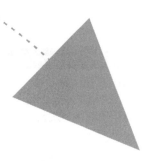

Formatting Block Elements

In Part III, you worked with examples of setting the font, text, and link characteristics for your HTML documents. In Part IV, you're working with examples of controlling how block elements and objects are displayed and formatted.

In this chapter, you focus on working with block elements, including reviewing and working with examples for the following:

- Understanding the CSS formatting model
- Setting margins and padding
- Setting borders
- Using the DIV element

Understanding the CSS Formatting Model

The CSS formatting model covered here applies to both inline and block elements. Most often, however, you have to take it into consideration when formatting block elements, so I've chosen to deal with this subject at this point, rather than in an earlier chapter.

Every CSS element forms a "box" composed of the following components:

- **Content**—This includes the actual content of the element, such as text, an image, and so on.

- **Padding**—This includes any padding that has been set around the content by the `padding-top`, `padding-bottom`, `padding-left`, `padding-right`, or `padding` properties.

- **Border**—This includes any border that has been set around the element's content and padding. Borders are set by the `border-top`, `border-bottom`, `border-left`, `border-right`, or `border` properties.

- **Margin**—This includes any margin that has been set around the element's content, padding, and border. Margins are set by the `margin-top`, `margin-bottom`, `margin-left`, `margin-right`, and `margin` properties.

See Figure 9.1 for an illustration of the relationships between these different components of the element box.

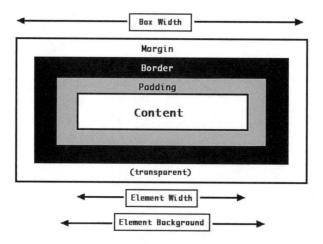

Figure 9.1: *The format model for CSS elements includes four basic elements: content, padding, border, and margin boxes.*

Don't worry if you don't yet understand everything illustrated in Figure 9.1. In this chapter's examples, you'll be working with actual examples of setting padding, borders, and margins for HTML elements, so some practical experience should help to make the conceptual relationships easier to grasp. As you do this chapter's examples, feel free to refer back to Figure 9.1 for a visual representation of how padding, borders, and margins function within an element.

Using the Example File

I've included an HTML file, perform-motive.html, with the example files that are downloadable from this book's Web site (http://www.callihan.com/cssbook/). If you've downloaded the example files and extracted them to your working folder, you should only need to open perform-motive.html in your text editor to get started. You can also type in the example file, if you wish:

Listing 9.1: PERFORM-MOTIVE.HTML—Performance Motivation Associates

```
<!DOCTYPE HTML PUBLIC "-//W3C//DTD HTML 4.01 Transitional//EN"
"http://www.w3.org/TR/html4/loose.dtd">

<html>
<head>
<title>Performance Motivation Associates</title>
<style type="text/css">

</style>
</head>
<body>

<h1>Performance Motivation Associates</h1>
<p>Are you living and working up to your potential? Do you wish to know how to
motivate yourself, family, associates, or employees to higher performance and
achievement? Are you spending more and more time seeking answers, but less and
less time activating solutions? We at Performance Motivation Associates make
providing solutions and activating success our primary business.</p>

<h2>The Performance Motivation Advantage</h2>
<p>We are industry leaders in performance motivation seminars, leadership style
assessments, interpersonal skills development courses, meta-goal planning
assistance, and other performance enhancement services. Our only job is the
liberation of performance potential for individuals, groups, and organizations.
</p>

<h3>The Performance Motivation Team</h3>
<p>Our highly skilled and experienced professional consultants have helped enable
thousands of clients to achieve success and maximize performance. Do you feel
you're falling short and going around in circles? Our experts, consultants, and
```

Listing 9.1: continued

```
coaches are experts in performance actualization, success achievement, and
leadership development. We can help you get where you want to go. Join the
Performance Motivation Team today!</p>

<h3>Performance Motivation Services</h3>
<p>We offer a wide range of seminars, consulting, and other services in the areas
of:</p>

<ul>
<li>Career and Job Success
<li>Youth and Adult Leadership Development
<li>Parenting and Family Skills
<li>Personal Achievement
<li>Goal and Success Visualization
<li>Meta-Goal Planning
</ul>

<hr>
<address>
Performance Motivation Associates<br>
E-Mail: <a href="mailto:contact@perform-motive.com">contact@perform-
motive.com</a><br>
Web Address: <a href="http://www.perform-
motive.com/welcome.html">http://www.perform-motive.com/welcome.html</a>
</address>

</body>
</html>
```

Setting Margins

The difference between margins and padding is that margins exist outside an element, and padding exists inside an element (surrounding the content). If the element has a background color or image assigned to it, the image is displayed in both the content and padding areas, but not in the margin area. Margin areas are always transparent, displaying the background of the parent element. The exception is if an element doesn't have a parent element to which display properties can be assigned, such as the BODY element, in which case any background color or image is displayed in both the margin and padding areas.

Another way to understand this is that the margin is the distance between the outer edge of an element (content and padding) and the inner edge of the parent element (the margin space). The padding is the distance between the margin and the content.

Margins can be set for every element, within and including the document body (the BODY element). Element margins are set by the `margin-left`, `margin-right`, `margin-top`, and `margin-bottom` properties.

Setting Horizontal Margins

The default initial value for the `margin-left` and `margin-right` properties is 0. A browser, however, sets its own default margins for the BODY element. Internet Explorer 5.5 for Windows, for instance, sets default horizontal margins of ten pixels, while Netscape 6 sets default horizontal margins of nine pixels. Most other browsers should set quite similar horizontal margin widths. There is nothing in the CSS or HTML specifications, however, dictating what the default margins for a page must be.

NOTE

Any horizontal margins set for the BODY element using CSS replace the default horizontal margins set by a browser. Therefore, if you set the left the BODY element's left margin to five pixels, that's what it'll be (not the default BODY margin plus five pixels). Setting it to zero eliminates the left margin entirely (regardless of what a browser's default left margin might be).

To see this more clearly in action, create a style sheet that justifies the P element's text (see Figure 9.2):

```
<head>
<title>Performance Motivation Associates</title>
<style type="text/css">
p { text-align: justify; }
</style>
</head>
```

For elements nested inside the BODY element, the left and right margins are initially set to zero. For instance, here's an example of setting the BODY element's left and right margins to zero, which also eliminates any horizontal margin spacing separating the nested heading and paragraph elements from the side of the page (see Figure 9.3):

```
<style type="text/css">
body { margin-left: 0; margin-right: 0; }
p { text-align: justify; }
</style>
```

Most block elements have their default left and right margins set to zero, so setting the BODY element's horizontal margins to zero causes those margins to be displayed flush with the left and right margins. There are a few exceptions to this, including the UL and OL elements (for creating bulleted and numbered lists) and the BLOCKQUOTE element (for creating block quotes).

Default BODY margins

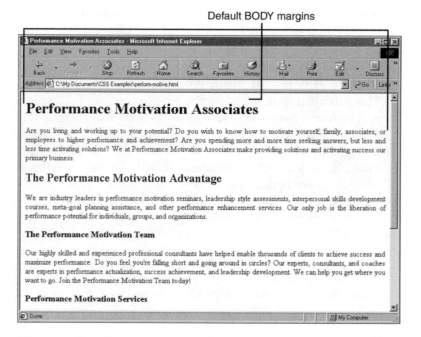

Figure 9.2: *A browser sets default margins for the BODY element.*

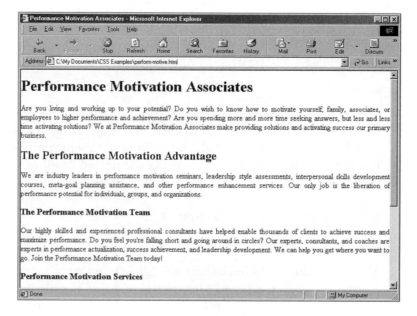

Figure 9.3: *Setting the BODY element's left and right margins to zero causes nested heading and paragraph elements to be displayed flush with the left and right margins of the page.*

You can increase the left and right margins that a browser normally displays for the BODY element, but you need to keep in mind that any measurement that you apply is based on initial horizontal margins for the BODY element being set to zero. For instance, here's an example of setting a margin of five percent for the BODY element's left and right margin (see Figure 9.4):

```
<style type="text/css">
body { margin-left: 5%; margin-right: 5%; }
p { text-align: justify; }
</style>
```

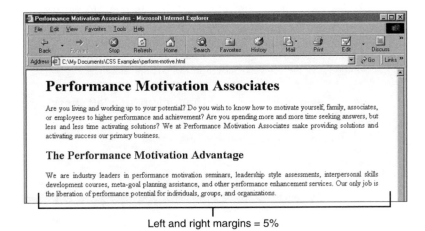

Left and right margins = 5%

Figure 9.4: *The BODY element's left and right margins are set to five percent.*

Of course, you might ask, "Five percent of what?" When you use a percentage value to specify a horizontal width, what you are setting is a percentage of the *containing block*. The width of the containing block is the sum of an element's margins, padding, and content. In the case of the BODY element, the containing block is the width of the whole page (or "canvas"); for a P element, for instance, the width of the containing block would run between any left or right margins set by its parent element (the BODY element, in this case).

Generally, in CSS, unless you specify otherwise, an element's text wraps dynamically within a browser's window. If you have set horizontal margin and padding widths for an element, but left the element's content width undefined, a browser automatically adjusts the element's content width to fit within a browser's window.

When setting vertical measurements, percentage and em values operate identically. That is not true, however, when setting horizontal measurements. Em values are based on an element's font size, not on a percentage of the containing block's width. If you don't want an element's margins to change relative to whatever browser width is employed, setting them using em values enables them to scale gracefully relative to any font sizes that might be set on a local system, through browser preferences, through a user style sheet, or even relative to inherited font size values that you've set in your own style sheet.

NOTE

A width of one em refers to what is called an *em square* in CSS. The measurement of one em, for instance, doesn't specifically refer to the height of a font, but rather to the size of that font's em square, which is a square of equal height and width, with the height equal to the height of the font. Thus, when setting a margin of one em, you're actually setting the margin to the width of one em square.

The traditional typesetting concepts of an em being equal to the width of the letter "M" in a font has no bearing in CSS, because CSS measurements may be applied to non-Roman fonts that don't include a letter "M," for instance.

Here's an example of setting the P element's left margin to one em (see Figure 9.5):

```
p { text-align: justify; margin-left: 1em; }
```

Left margin = 1em

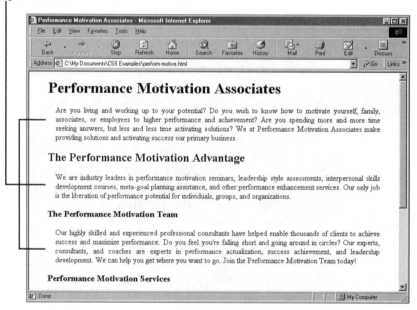

Figure 9.5: *The P element's left margin is set to one em.*

Because horizontal margins concatenate (adding onto each other), the actual horizontal distance between an element and the edge of the page is the sum of any horizontal margins set for it and for any of its parent elements. In this case, for instance, the P element's actual margin from the edge of the page is the sum of its and the BODY element's horizontal margins. In the case of the previous example, the distance of the P element from the left edge of the page would be the sum of its left margin (one em, or a width equal to the element's font size) and the BODY element's left margin (five percent of its containing block).

You can also set horizontal margins using pixel measurements. Pixel measurements don't scale relative to either the width of the containing block (normally determined by the browser window's width) or the font size, but relative to the screen resolution. On a system where the screen resolution is 800 pixels across, a margin measurement of eight pixels is equal to one percent of the screen width. On a system where the screen resolution is 1024 pixels across, however, a margin measurement of ten pixels is equal to about one percent of the screen width.

In some instances, pixel units can be handy—for instance, when setting margins, padding, or borders around images, which are dimensioned in pixels. In those cases, your measurements scale relative to the image and not relative to the containing block (as with percentages) or the font size (as with em values).

CAUTION

For Web pages, you should never use absolute measurements (such as inches, centimeters, points, or picas), because a Web page is always of uncertain dimensions. The only time you should use such measurements is when you know the exact dimensions of the output, such as an 8 × 11.5-inch piece of paper on which a document is printed. In that case, you could create a style sheet specifically for printing the document (by specifying a `media="print"` attribute in the STYLE element) that specifies absolute measurements.

Setting Negative Margins

You can also set a negative margin value. This can be handy, for instance, where you've set a left margin for your BODY element, but would like to set one element's left margin to less than the BODY element's left margin. You previously set the left margin for the BODY element to five percent. To test out how this works, first eliminate the left margin you set for the P element for the last example, and then set the left margin of the H1 element to a negative three percent (see Figure 9.6):

```
body { margin-left: 5%; margin-right: 5%; }
p { text-align: justify; }
h1 { margin-left: -3%; }
```

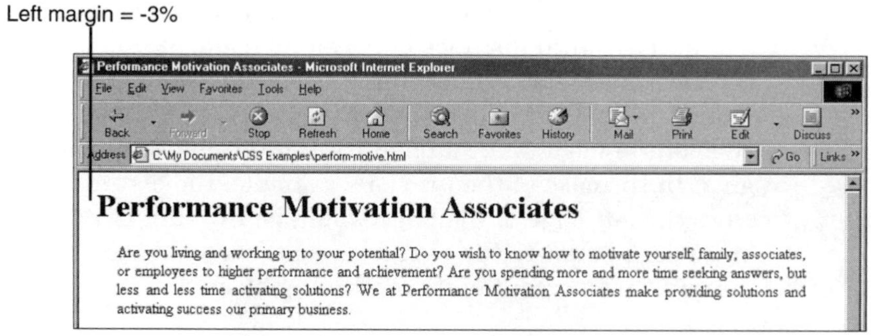

Left margin = -3%

Figure 9.6: _You can set a negative horizontal margin for an element._

Because the BODY element has a left margin of five percent, a negative left margin of three percent for the H1 element effectively results in its left margin amounting to two percent of the containing block.

Setting Vertical Margins

Unlike horizontal margins, which in CSS concatenate, abutting vertical margins collapse to the largest margin value. Thus, if one element has a bottom margin of two ems, for instance, but the following element has a top margin of one em, the amount of vertical margin space between the two elements is two ems (not three ems).

Browsers also set default top and bottom margins for elements, including the BODY element. Earlier, you set the left and right margins to zero, causing the heading and paragraph elements to be displayed flush with the left margin. That worked because browsers don't set left margins for those elements; they only set left margins for the BODY element. To display an H1 element at the top of your page flush with your page's top margin, however, you have to set the top margin for both it and the BODY element to zero. Here's an example of doing that (see Figure 9.7):

```
body { margin-left: 5%; margin-right: 5%; margin-top: 0; }
p { text-align: justify; }
h1 { margin-left: -3%; margin-top: 0; }
```

NOTE

This works the same in both Internet Explorer 5 and Netscape 6, but not in Opera 5. That's because in Opera 5 a margin-top property value set for the BODY element is measured relative to the default top margin that Opera sets, and not relative to the top edge of the page. Even when you set the top margin of your page to zero, you have to live with Opera 5 leaving its own default top margin in place.

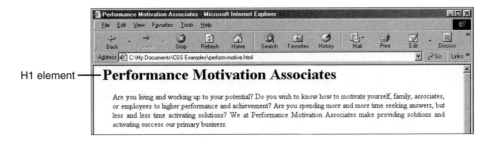

H1 element

Figure 9.7: To display the H1 element flush with the top of the page, you have to set the top margins for both the BODY element and the H1 element to zero.

In Figure 9.7, the top edge of the text in the H1 element isn't completely flush with the top of the page, even though its and the page's top margins have been set to zero. The reason for this is that a space above the letterforms is allocated within text fonts for accents and diacritical marks. You can see this in action by inserting an uppercase accented character in the H1 element's text (see Figure 9.8):

```
<h1>Performance Motivation Associates &Egrave;</h1>
```

Accent space

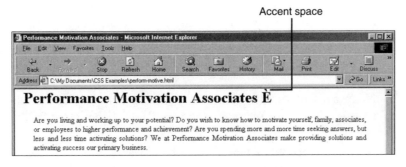

Figure 9.8: A letter's accent is inserted in the space above the letterforms that is reserved for displaying accents and diacritical marks.

You might think that you could just set a negative margin to roll the H1 element's text up so the top of its uppercase letterforms are flush with the top margin. Setting a -0.25em top margin for the H1 element in the previous example causes this to happen in the Windows versions of Internet Explorer 5.5 and Netscape 6.

Unfortunately, you can't rely on other browsers to necessarily follow suit. Even when rolling the H1 element back up a quarter of an em, Opera 5 still leaves a sliver of space at the top of the letterforms—it adds this additional vertical spacing for all block elements. Although Internet Explorer 5 and

Netscape 6 for the Macintosh allocate a sliver of space above a font's upper-case letterforms, they do not rely on it exclusively to display accents or diacritical marks, but reduce the vertical height of an uppercase character to make room for an accent or diacritical mark (see Figure 9.9). Thus, on the Macintosh platform, if you roll the H1 element back up a quarter of an em, part of uppercase letterforms are rolled beyond the top page margin.

Figure 9.9: *On the Macintosh, the height of an uppercase character is reduced to make room for displaying an accent.*

For Latin-based fonts, for instance, the character sequence of an uppercase "E" with a grave accent in combination with a lowercase "p" placed on adjacent lines where the top and bottom margins have been zeroed, should leave just enough vertical spacing between the grave accent on the one hand and the p descender on the other to ensure that the two don't clash. To try this out, first set the top and bottom margins of the H1 elements to zero:

```
h1 { margin-left: -3%; margin-top: 0; margin-bottom: 0; }
```

Next, copy and paste to create a second copy of your H1 element, editing the second line to transpose the position of the letter "p", as shown here (see Figure 9.10):

```
<h1>Performance Motivation Associates &Egrave;p</h1>
<h1>Performance Motivation Associates p&Egrave;</h1>
```

These examples aren't really intended as practical examples, because it isn't likely that you'll want your H1 element displayed absolutely flush with the page's top margin. They are helpful, however, in visualizing what is actually going on when you adjust an element's vertical margins.

For a more practical example of setting top and bottom margins, eliminate the margin-top: 0 property you set in the BODY element rule, and then set a negative bottom margin for the three top heading levels, as shown here:

```
body { margin-left: 5%; margin-right: 5%; }
p { text-align: justify; }
h1 { margin-left: -3%; }
h1, h2, h3 { margin-bottom: -0.5em; }
```

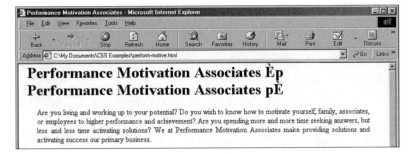

Figure 9.10: *With top and bottom margins zeroed, there should be just enough vertical spacing inserted between the E character's grave accent and the p character's descender to keep them from clashing.*

If you then delete the copy of the H1 element you created before, and delete the `&Eacute;p` sequence in your original H1 element, and then check what this looks like in your browser, what you see should be similar to what is shown in Figure 9.11.

Bottom margin = -0.5em

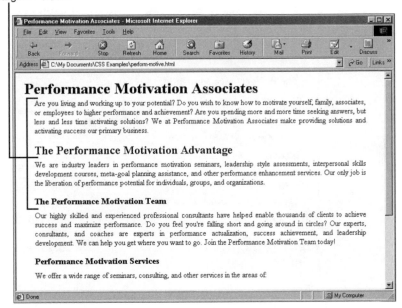

Figure 9.11: *The bottom margins of the three heading elements are reduced.*

You can even adjust the vertical margins for adjacent elements so that one overlaps the other. In the following example, the vertical margins of the two H1 elements, as well as the left margin for one of the elements, are set so that one element forms a shadow effect behind the other:

```
<style type="text/css">
body { margin-left: 5%; margin-right: 5%; }
p { text-align: justify; }
h1.shadow { font-size: 32px; font-family: "Arial Black", Arial, Helvetica, sans-
serif; color: #ffcc66; background: transparent; margin-top: 10px; margin-left:
3px; margin-bottom: 0; }
h1.top { font-size: 32px; font-family: "Arial Black", Arial, Helvetica, sans-
serif; color: red; background: transparent; margin-top: -48px; }
</style>
```

Then, make a copy of your H1 element, setting one as the "shadow" element and the other as the "top" element, as shown here (see Figure 9.12):

```
<h1 class="shadow">Performance Motivation Associates</h1>
<h1 class="top">Performance Motivation Associates</h1>
```

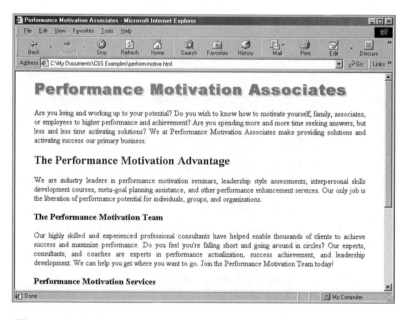

Figure 9.12: *By manipulating vertical margins, you can overlap one element with another.*

Of course, you wouldn't want this to display in a browser that doesn't support CSS, since a user using such a browser would simply see two H1 elements in that case, without any overlapping. Users of non-visual browsers, such as Braille or speech browsers, also wouldn't get that these two elements are meant to overlap each other.

For those reasons, this is more of a parlor trick, meant to illustrate how negative margins can cause adjacent elements to overlap, than a practical example. That doesn't mean that you couldn't do this, but you'd want to use some means to forewarn a user that their browser may not be up to snuff or to insure that user's using incompatible or non-visual browsers were rerouted to an alternative page, for instance.

NOTE

In the parlance of CSS, when the use of a CSS coding causes an undesirable result in a browser lacking support, or providing only partial support, for CSS, it is said to *degrade ungracefully*. Where a CSS coding doesn't cause an undesirable result in a non-supporting browser, it is said to *degrade gracefully*. Your goal should always be to utilize CSS code in your pages that degrades gracefully in non-supporting and partially supporting browsers.

✔ For guidance on using gateway pages, browser sniffing, DOM sniffing, and browser-upgrade alerts to help insure that users of non-compatible browsers aren't exposed to CSS code that degrades ungracefully, see "Using Gateway Pages and Browser Sniffers," p. 384 (chapter 16), and "Participating in the Web Standards Project," p.385 (chapter 16).

Using the Margin Shorthand Property

In CSS, the `margin` shorthand property can be used to set the other four margin properties. If four values are specified, they apply in sequence to the top, right, bottom, and left margins, respectively. If only one value is specified, it is applied to all four margins. If two values are specified, the first is applied to the top and bottom margins and the second to the right and left margins. If three values are specified, they are applied to the top, right, and bottom margins, with the second value also applied to the left margin.

This example specifies separate margin values for the top, right, bottom, and left margins, respectively:

```
body { margin: 2em 3% 1em 5% }
```

This example specifies two ems for the top and bottom margins and five percent for the right and left margins:

```
body { margin: 2em 5% }
```

This example specifies a value of five percent for all four margins:

```
body { margin: 5% }
```

Setting Padding

As noted in the previous section, margins specify vertical and horizontal spacing that is outside an element, and padding adds vertical and horizontal spacing within an element (between the element content and the margins around the element). The easiest way to visualize this is by setting a background for an element, because backgrounds are displayed behind both the content and padding areas for an element, but not behind the margin area.

If no padding is set for an element, then a background color, for instance, is only displayed behind the element's content area. Here's an example of setting a background color for the H1 element while not defining any padding:

```
<style type="text/css">
body { margin-left: 5%; margin-right: 5%; }
p { text-align: justify; }
h1 { margin-left: -3%; }
h1, h2, h3 { color: black; background: aqua; }
</style>
```

If you insert an Èp coding (to insert an E-grave character followed by a lowercase p character) at the end of the H1, H2, and H3 elements, as shown in Figure 9.13, you're able to see that the background color is only displayed behind those elements' content area (as shown by the grave accent at the top and p character's descender at the bottom).

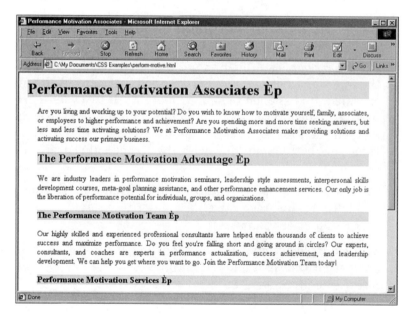

Figure 9.13: *If no padding is set for an element, a background color or image is only displayed behind the element's content area.*

However, if you set padding around an element, any background color that is set is displayed behind both the content and padding areas. Here's an example of setting horizontal padding of one percent (of the containing block) and vertical padding of 0.2 ems (two-tenths of the current font size):

```
h1, h2, h3 { color: black; background: aqua; padding-left: 1%; padding-right: 1%;
padding-top: 0.2em; padding-bottom: 0.2em; }
```

As shown in Figure 9.14, the background color is now displayed behind both the element's content and padding areas. You'll also notice that the amount of top and bottom padding for the three heading elements scales in relation to the font size, because em units are used to set the vertical padding. Using percentage units for setting the horizontal padding, on the other hand, ensures that elements sharing the same margins are aligned vertically, because percentage values are a ratio of an element's containing block.

Horizontal padding = 1%　　　　　　　　　　　　　Vertical padding = 0.2em

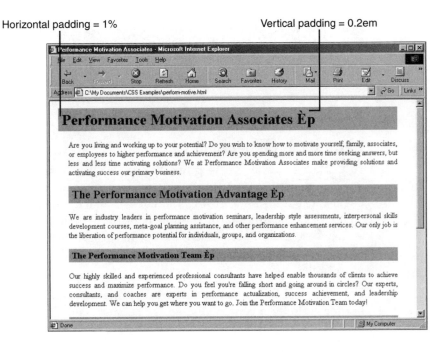

Figure 9.14: When padding is set for an element, a background color or image is displayed behind the element's content area and padding area.

Using the Padding Shorthand Property

In CSS, the `padding` shorthand property can be used to set the other four padding properties. If four values are specified, they apply in sequence to the top, right, bottom, and left padding, respectively. If only one value is specified, it is applied to all four padding areas. If two values are specified, the first is applied to the top and bottom padding areas and the second to the right and left padding areas. If three values are specified, they are applied to the top, right, and bottom padding areas, with the second value also applied to the left padding areas.

This example specifies separate padding values for the top, right, bottom, and left padding areas, respectively:

```
h1 { padding: 0.2em 1% 0.2em 1%; }
```

This example specifies 0.2 ems for the top and bottom padding and one percent for the right and left padding:

```
h1 { padding: 0.2em 1%; }
```

This example specifies a value of one percent for all four padding areas:

```
h1 { padding: 1%; }
```

Setting Borders

In CSS, you can easily set borders for block elements, including controlling their style, width, and color. You can control the appearance of the border around an element, as well as each individual border (top, right, bottom, and left).

Setting the Border Style

In CSS, the `border-style` property enables you to set various different border styles, using any of these values: none, `hidden`, `solid`, `double`, `dotted`, `dashed`, `groove`, `ridge`, `inset`, and `outset`. The default border style setting is none, which means that no border is initially displayed. All of these border styles were included in CSS1, except for `hidden`, which was included in CSS2. The none and `hidden` values operate the same, except when used with tables.

For instance, here is an example of setting margins, padding, and a solid border style for a center-aligned H1 element (see Figure 9.15):

```
<style type="text/css">
body { margin-left: 5%; margin-right: 5%; }
p { text-align: justify; }
h1 { color: navy; background: #ffffcc; text-align: center; margin: 0.15em 5%;
padding: 0.1em 5%; border-style: solid; }
</style>
```

In this example, the H1 element has been centered and vertical and horizontal margins have been set. In addition, vertical and horizontal padding has also been set for all three heading elements.

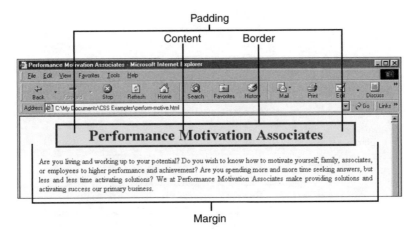

Figure 9.15: A solid border is drawn around the H1 element.

To see all of the border styles in action, except for none and hidden, enter the following example (see Figure 9.16):

```
<style type="text/css">
body { margin-left: 5%; margin-right: 5%; color: black; background: #dddddd; }
p { text-align: justify; }
h1 { color: navy; background: #ffffcc; text-align: center; margin: 0.15em 5%;
padding: 0.1em 5%; border-style: solid; border-width: 8px; }
</style>
</head>
<body>

<h1 style="border-style: double">Performance Motivation Associates</h1>
<h1 style="border-style: dotted">Performance Motivation Associates</h1>
<h1 style="border-style: dashed">Performance Motivation Associates</h1>
<h1 style="border-style: groove">Performance Motivation Associates</h1>
<h1 style="border-style: ridge">Performance Motivation Associates</h1>
<h1 style="border-style: inset">Performance Motivation Associates</h1>
<h1 style="border-style: outset">Performance Motivation Associates</h1>
```

The CSS specifications only give a very brief description of display characteristics for these border styles, so don't be surprised if individual browsers have their own ideas of what any of these border styles should look like, as shown in Figure 9.17.

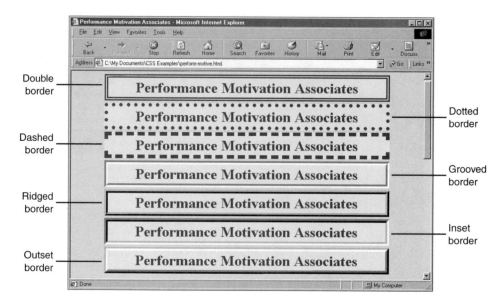

Figure 9.16: *As shown in Internet Explorer 5.5 for Windows, a variety of different border styles can be set.*

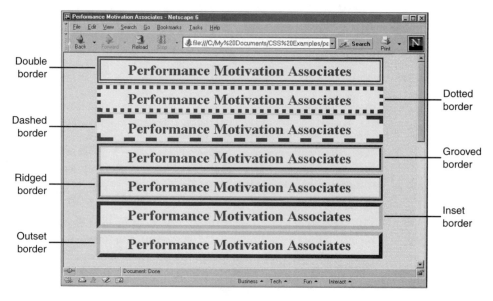

Figure 9.17: *The appearance of border styles may vary from browser to browser, as shown here in Netscape 6.*

Setting the Border Width

You can control the width of all four borders using the `border-top-width`, `border-right-width`, `border-bottom-width`, and `border-left-width` properties. Additionally, you can use the `border-width` shorthand property to set values for all four of these properties. When using the `border-width` shorthand property, width values are set for the top, right, bottom, and left borders, in that order. As with other similar shorthand properties, a single value is applied to all four borders and two values are applied to the top-bottom and right-left borders. When three values are stated, the left (or fourth) border takes the same value as the right (or second) border.

All of these properties take the following values: `thin`, `medium`, `thick`, or a numeric width value (ems, percentages, pixels, and so on). The default value is `medium`, although what that actually equates to is left for the browser to determine. For instance, Internet Explorer 5.5 for Windows draws a 4-pixel default (medium) border, and both Netscape 6 and Opera 5 draw a 3-pixel default (medium) border.

The following example includes examples of using the three border-width keywords, as well as a variety of different numeric width values (see Figure 9.18):

```
<h1 style="border-width: 1px">Performance Motivation Associates</h1>
<h1 style="border-width: thin">Performance Motivation Associates</h1>
<h1 style="border-width: medium">Performance Motivation Associates</h1>
<h1 style="border-width: thick">Performance Motivation Associates</h1>
<h1 style="border-width: 8px">Performance Motivation Associates</h1>
<h1 style="border-width: 10px">Performance Motivation Associates</h1>
<h1 style="border-width: 0.5em">Performance Motivation Associates</h1>
```

Setting the Border Color

You can control the color of all four borders using the `border-color` property. This property takes either keyword or numerical color values. If only one color value is stated, the color is applied to all four borders, if two color values are stated, the colors are applied to the top-bottom and right-left borders. If three color values are stated, the second stated color value is also used as the fourth.

Here's an example of setting a single color for all four element borders (see Figure 9.19):

```
<style type="text/css">
p { text-align: justify; }
h1 { color: navy; background: #ffffcc; text-align: center; margin: 0.15em 5%;
padding: 0.1em 5%; border-style: solid; border-width: 12px; border-color:
#ff9900; }
</style>
</head>
<body>

<h1>Performance Motivation Associates</h1>
```

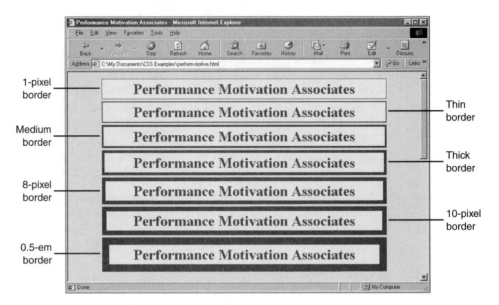

Figure 9.18: You can specify the border width for an element.

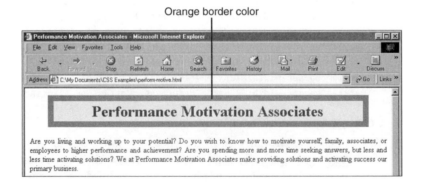

Figure 9.19: You can specify an element border's color.

Here's an example of setting different colors for the top, right, bottom, and left borders (see Figure 9.20):

```
h1 { color: navy; background: #ffffcc; text-align: center; margin: 0.15em 5%;
padding: 0.1em 5%; border-style: solid; border-width: 12px; border-color: red
aqua purple lime; }
```

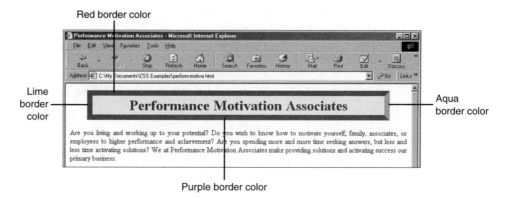

Red border color

Lime border color

Aqua border color

Purple border color

Figure 9.20: *You can set different colors for each border segment.*

NOTE

According to the CSS specifications, if no border color is specified, a browser should use the foreground color of an element when setting the default border color. Thus, if the foreground color of an element is set as blue, then the default border color for that element should also be blue. Opera 5, however, displays a black border color if no border color is set, regardless of what the element's foreground color is. Thus, if you want to make sure that your border color is displayed in all browsers, you should explicitly set it using the `border-color` property, and not rely on it being set by the element's `color` property.

Using the Other Border Shorthand Properties

You've already used one border shorthand property, the `border-width` property. In addition to that shorthand property, there are a number of other border shorthand properties that you can use.

The `border-top`, `border-right`, `border-bottom`, `border-left`, and border shorthand properties can be used to set the width, style, and color of an element's borders. For instance, here's an example of using the `border` shorthand property to set an element's border properties (see Figure 9.21):

```
h1 { color: navy; background: #ffffcc; text-align: center; margin: 0.15em 10%;
padding: 0.1em 5%; border: dotted 12px olive; }
```

The `border-top`, `border-right`, `border-bottom`, and `border-left` shorthand properties, work exactly the same way as the `border` shorthand property, except they set properties for only one border segment.

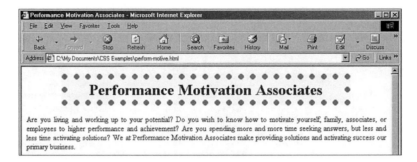

Figure 9.21: *A dotted, 12-pixel, olive border is set.*

Using Background Images with Borders

You've already worked with examples of combining background colors with borders. You can also combine background images with borders, which can be very effective (see Figure 9.22):

```
h1 { color: navy; background: #ffffcc url(paper.gif); text-align: center; margin:
0.15em 10%; padding: 0.1em 5%; border: dotted 12px olive; }
```

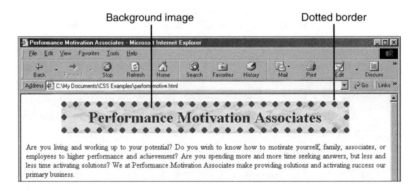

Figure 9.22: *Combining borders and background images can be effective.*

As you can see in Figure 9.22, in Internet Explorer 5.5 for Windows, "diamond-shape" dots are displayed, with the background image not only displayed behind the content and padding areas, but also behind the open areas in the border. You shouldn't depend, however, on this working exactly the same in other browsers. Internet Explorer 5 for the Macintosh displays round dots. Netscape 6 and Opera 5 display square dots, with Netscape 6 then displaying any background color assigned to the element behind the open areas between the dots.

Using the DIV Element

In HTML 4, the DIV element is a block element used to designate a division within a document. Otherwise, the DIV element has no formatting characteristics, although the deprecated ALIGN attribute can be used to center or right-align its content. From the start, the DIV element was intended to take any formatting characteristics from styles.

By nesting other elements within a DIV element, any styles applied to the DIV element also impact those nested elements. In the following example, a DIV rule is added to the style sheet, set to be displayed with a border, background image, and other formatting characteristics:

```
div { font-family: Verdana, Arial, sans-serif; font-size: 1.1em; color: #ffff99;
background: navy url(dark.jpg); border: solid 0.5em #ff9933; margin: 0.2em 3%;
padding: 0.2em 1%; }
div p { text-align: left; margin-left: 1%; margin-right: 1%; }
</style>
```

Next, insert the DIV element into the body of your HTML document, bracketing both the H1 element and the following P element, like this (see Figure 9.23):

```
<div>
<h1>Performance Motivation Associates</h1>
<p>Are you living and working up to your potential? Do you wish to know how to
motivate yourself, family, associates, or employees to higher performance and
achievement? Are you spending more and more time seeking answers, but less and
less time activating solutions? We at Performance Motivation Associates make
providing solutions and activating success our primary business.</p>
</div>
```

Applying a DIV Element to the Whole Page

By bracketing the whole page with your DIV element, you can apply the border, background, and other formatting characteristics to the whole page. For an example of doing that, first make these changes to your style sheet:

```
<style type="text/css">
body { margin: 0;   color: white; background: #660000; }
h1 { color: navy; background: #ffffcc url(paper.gif); text-align: center; margin:
0.15em 10%; padding: 0.1em 5%; border: dotted 12px olive; }
h2, h3 { color: #66ffcc; background: transparent; }
div { font-family: Verdana, Arial, sans-serif; font-size: 1.1em; color: #ffff99;
background: navy url(dark.jpg); border: solid 0.5em #ff9933; margin: 0.5%;
padding: 0.2em 1%; }
div p { text-align: left; margin-left: 1%; margin-right: 1%; }
a { color: lime; background: transparent; }
</style>
```

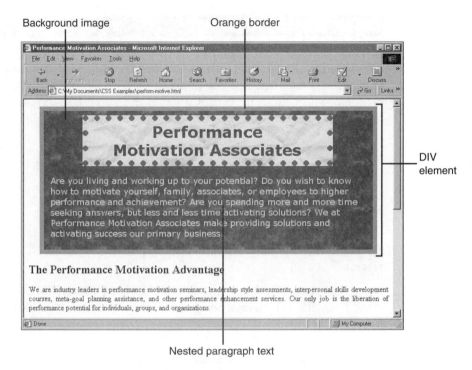

Background image

Orange border

DIV element

Nested paragraph text

Figure 9.23: *By using the DIV element, you can apply special formatting to a division within an HTML document.*

Then, just delete the `</div>` end tag you inserted previously and reinsert it at the bottom of your page, like this (see Figure 9.24):

```
</div>
</body>
```

Using the DIV Element to Create Custom Block Elements

The only problem with the previous examples is that they use only one DIV element. By using inline styles or class selectors, you can create as many custom block elements as you desire.

To try this out, first make the following changes to your style sheet:

```
<style type="text/css">
body { margin: 0;  color: white; background: #660000; }
h1 { color: navy; background: #ffffcc url(paper.gif); text-align: center; margin:
0.15em 10%; padding: 0.1em 5%; border: dotted 12px olive; }
h2, h3 { color: #66ffcc; }
div.body { font-family: Verdana, Arial, sans-serif; font-size: 1.1em; color:
#ffff99; background: navy url(dark.jpg); border: solid 0.5em #ff9933; margin:
0.5%; padding: 0.2em 1%; }
```

```
div.body p { text-align: left; margin-left: 1%; margin-right: 1%; }
div.inset { color: navy; background: url(clouds.jpg) aqua; border: inset 10px
aqua; font-family: Verdana, Arial, sans-serif; padding: 0.2em 4% 0 0; margin: 0
15% 1em; text-align: center; }
a { color: lime; background: transparent; }
```

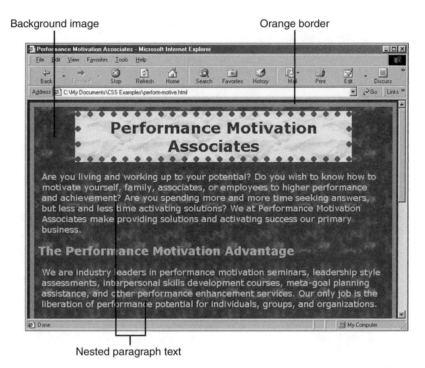

Background image   Orange border

Nested paragraph text

Figure 9.24: *You can use a DIV element to apply formatting to the body of your page.*

Notice in this example that the single style for the DIV element has been replaced with two styles for the `div.body` and `div.inset` class selectors. Also notice that the `div p` contextual selector has been changed to a `div.body p` contextual selector, so its formatting takes effect for paragraphs nested within the "body" DIV element.

Next, add a `class="body"` attribute to the previous DIV element you inserted, so it picks up the formatting characteristics you assigned to the `div.body` style rule:

```
<div class="body">
<h1>Performance Motivation Associates</h1>
```

You'll notice that "body" is specified as the value of the CLASS attribute. That's simply to indicate that this DIV element brackets everything else included within the document's BODY element.

Now, bracket the bulleted list near the bottom of your page with the new "inset" DIV element you just defined (see Figure 9.25):

```
<div class="inset">
<ul>
<li>Career and Job Success
<li>Youth and Adult Leadership Development
<li>Parenting and Family Skills
<li>Personal Achievement
<li>Goal and Success Visualization
<li>Meta-Goal Planning
</ul>
</div>
```

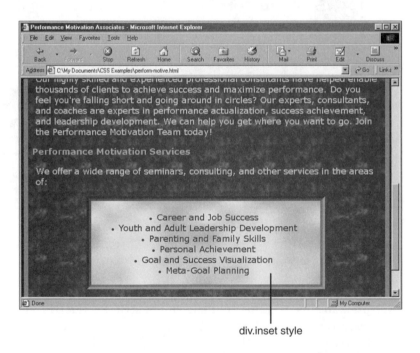

div.inset style

Figure 9.25: *Applying a background and borders to a DIV element can attractively set off the contents (here a list).*

Setting Padding, Borders, and Margins for Images and Other Objects

The IMG and OBJECT elements are used to insert an *inline image* and other *object* into a Web page. Inline images are inline elements that are displayed at the position where they are inserted on a line. An object in HTML might be an inline image, a Java applet window, or a streaming video console, for instance.

In HTML 4 (and XHTML) the BORDER attribute, used to control the display of a border around an inline image or object, is deprecated, in favor of using styles to achieve the same or better results.

To see an example of specifying a border for an IMG element, first insert the following inline image toward the bottom of your example page:

```
<div class="inset">
<ul>
<li>Career and Job Success
<li>Youth and Adult Leadership Development
<li>Parenting and Family Skills
<li>Personal Achievement
<li>Goal and Success Visualization
<li>Meta-Goal Planning
</ul>
</div>

<div class="ctr">
<img src="goals.gif" id="goals">
</div>

<hr>
```

You'll notice in this example that the DIV element, within which the IMG element is nested, is assigned to the "ctr" class, while the IMG element is given the ID of "goals." In the next step, you'll be using these to assign style properties to both of these elements.

Now, add the following two styles to your page's style sheet (see Figure 9.26):

```
a { color: lime; background: transparent; }
#goals { border: 10px yellow ridge; }
.ctr { text-align: center; }
</style>
```

In this example, the #goals ID selector applies a ten-pixel, yellow, ridged border to the image (with the id="goals" attribute), while the .ctr class selector center-aligns the content of the DIV element.

According to the CSS specifications, you should be able to also insert padding around the image, creating a space between the image and the surrounding border. Internet Explorer 5.5 for Windows, however, ignores any padding set around IMG elements.

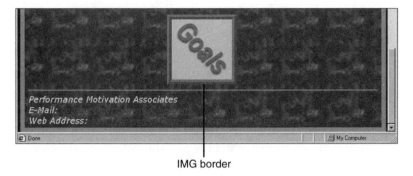

IMG border

Figure 9.26: *Using a style, you can draw a border around an inline image.*

There is a solution to this, although it is just a little complicated (due to a couple other bugs in Internet Explorer 5.5). It involves nesting the image inside of two DIV elements, assigning the padding and border to the inside DIV, while using the outside DIV to center the inside DIV.

To do this, first bracket the IMG element with another DIV element (with a class="ctrout" attribute), like this:

```
<div class="ctr">
<div class="border">
<img src="goals.gif" id="goals">
</div>
</div>
```

Next, edit your page's style sheet, like this:

```
#goals { vertical-align: bottom; }
.ctr { text-align: center; }
.border { border: 10px yellow ridge; padding: 10px; width: 125px; height: 125px;
margin-left: auto; margin-right: auto; }
```

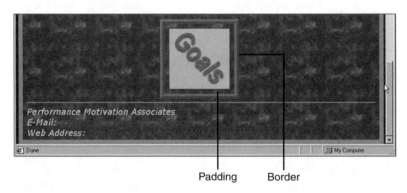

Padding   Border

Figure 9.27: *To apply padding between an image and a surrounding border in Internet Explorer 5.5, you have to apply the padding and border to a surrounding DIV element, rather than to the IMG element.*

The $\mathtt{vertical\text{-}align:\ bottom}$ property is necessary to position the image within the surrounding DIV element, so that it is equidistant from the surrounding borders

This example also uses a couple of properties, the $\mathtt{width}$ and $\mathtt{height}$ properties that haven't been discussed yet. You'll learn more about using these properties in the next chapter, "Aligning, Floating, and Positioning." For now, suffice it to say that they're used to set the dimensions of the DIV element in which the borders and padding are set.

The $\mathtt{margin\text{-}left:\ auto}$ and $\mathtt{margin\text{-}right:\ auto}$ properties, in combination with the $\mathtt{width}$ property, should center the "border" DIV element on the line. Due to another bug in Internet Explorer 5.5, however, this doesn't work in that browser. The trick to get Internet Explorer 5.5 to play along and also center the "border" DIV element is to nest that element inside of another DIV element (the "ctr" DIV element) with a $\mathtt{text\text{-}align:\ center}$ property set. This has the magical effect of causing Internet Explorer 5.5 to center the nested DIV—I say "magical" because this is an inexplicable, although also beneficial, behavior. You'll learn more in the next chapter about using this trick to center block elements with fixed widths in Internet Explorer 5.5.

What's Next?

In this chapter, you experimented with examples of setting style properties for block elements. You should now have a good understanding of the CSS block-formatting model and be comfortable with setting margins, borders, and padding for block elements. You should also know how to create your own custom block elements using the DIV element. You've also experimented with adding padding and borders around a centered inline image.

In Chapter 10, "Aligning, Floating, and Positioning," you learn how to horizontally align block elements relative to the page, flow text and other elements around floating elements, and use absolute and relative positioning to create dynamic layouts for your HTML documents.

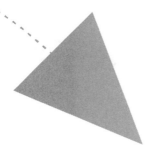

Aligning, Floating, and Positioning

In the previous chapter, "Formatting Block Elements," you worked with setting margins, borders, and padding for block elements and objects. In this chapter, you work with aligning, floating, and positioning block elements on the page.

In this chapter, you review and work with examples for the following:

- Horizontally aligning block elements
- Floating block elements around images and other objects
- Using relative and absolute positioning

Horizontally Aligning Block Elements

You also learned to create a centered box in the previous chapter by setting equal left and right margins outside of the box; you can also right-align the box by setting the right margin to zero. There are some limitations, however, in these two approaches:

- The text-align property doesn't actually horizontally align an element relative to the page, but only horizontally aligns text or other objects nested within an element relative to an element's content area.

- Setting equal left and right margins to center a boxed element only works if the width of the element's content area is unspecified or set to auto (the default).

✔ You've already worked with some examples in this book of horizontally aligning text and block elements. For instance, you've worked with using the text-align property to horizontally align text within an element—see "Horizontally Aligning Text," p. 156 (chapter 8) and "Setting Padding, Borders, and Margin for Images and Other Objects," p. 208 (chapter 9).

NOTE

The separate horizontal components (margins, padding, borders, and content area) included in an element must add up to 100 percent of the width of the element's containing block. The width of the containing block of a P element nested directly inside of the BODY element, for instance, is the width of the BODY element's content area. If no width is specified for the content area, a browser adjusts it so that it and any horizontal space occupied by margins, padding, or borders equal the width of the element's containing block.

For instance, if the width of an element's containing block is 400 pixels, then the sum of the widths of the element's margins, borders, padding, and content area must also equal 400 pixels. Likewise, if the width of an element's containing block is 15 ems, then the total width of the element (margins, borders, padding, and content area) must also equal 15 ems.

When it comes to widths, percentage widths are a bit easier to figure, in that they are based on the width of the element's containing block. In that case, the width of the containing block is assumed to be equal to 100 percent, with percentage values set for the element's margins, borders, padding, and content area needing to add up to 100 percent.

In most cases, however, one or more of these measurements will be set to auto, either specifically or as an initial value, which has the effect of automatically adjusting the width of the element so it is equal to the width of its containing block. You only have to be worried about getting everything to add up to 100 percent if you set all of the horizontal measurements to a value other than auto.

Using the Example HTML File

For this and the next section, you're using a continuation of the example, perform-motive.html, that you created in the previous chapter. To create the example for this section, just open that file in your text editor and then save it as perform-motive2.html. I've also included a finished copy of the perform-motive.html example with the example files as perform-motive_final.html—if you haven't done the example yet in the previous chapter, just open that HTML file in your text editor and save it as **perform-motive2.html**. Finally, if you'd like to type in the example file, here's a listing for perform-motive2.html:

Listing 10.1: PERFORM-MOTIVE2.HTML—Performance Motivation Associates

```
<!DOCTYPE HTML PUBLIC "-//W3C//DTD HTML 4.01 Transitional//EN"
"http://www.w3.org/TR/html4/loose.dtd">

<html>

<head>
<title>Performance Motivation Associates</title>
<style type="text/css">
body { margin: 0;  color: white; background: #660000; }
h1 { color: navy; background: #ffffcc url(paper.gif); text-align: center; margin:
0.15em 10%; padding: 0.1em 5%; border: dotted 12px olive; }
h2, h3 { color: #66ffcc; }
div.body { font-family: Verdana, Arial, sans-serif; font-size: 1.1em; color:
#ffff99; background: navy url(dark.jpg); border: solid 0.5em #ff9933; margin:
0.5%; padding: 0.2em 1%; }
div.body p { text-align: left; margin-left: 1%; margin-right: 1%; }
div.inset { color: navy; background: url(clouds.jpg) aqua; border: inset 10px
aqua; font-family: Verdana, Arial, sans-serif; padding: 0.2em 4% 0 0; margin: 0
15% 1em; text-align: center; }
a { color: lime; }
</style>
</head>
<body>

<div class="body">
<h1>Performance Motivation Associates</h1>
<p>Are you living and working up to your potential? Do you wish to know how to
motivate yourself, family, associates, or employees to higher performance and
achievement? Are you spending more and more time seeking answers, but less and
less time activating solutions? We at Performance Motivation Associates make
providing solutions and activating success our primary business.</p>

<h2>The Performance Motivation Advantage</h2>
<p>We are industry leaders in performance motivation seminars, leadership style
assessments, interpersonal skills development courses, meta-goal planning
```

Listing 10.1: continued

```
assistance, and other performance enhancement services. Our only job is the
liberation of performance potential for individuals, groups, and organizations.
</p>

<h3>The Performance Motivation Team</h3>
<p>Our highly skilled and experienced professional consultants have helped enable
thousands of clients to achieve success and maximize performance. Do you feel
you're falling short and going around in circles? Our experts, consultants, and
coaches are experts in performance actualization, success achievement, and
leadership development. We can help you get where you want to go. Join the
Performance Motivation Team today!</p>

<h3>Performance Motivation Services</h3>
<p>We offer a wide range of seminars, consulting, and other services in the areas
of:</p>

<div class="inset">
<ul>
<li>Career and Job Success
<li>Youth and Adult Leadership Development
<li>Parenting and Family Skills
<li>Personal Achievement
<li>Goal and Success Visualization
<li>Meta-Goal Planning
</ul>
</div>

<div class="ctr">
<div class="border">
<img src="goals.gif" id="goals">
</div>
</div>

<hr>

<address>
Performance Motivation Associates<br>
E-Mail: <a href="mailto:contact@perform-motive.com">contact@perform-
motive.com</a><br>
Web Address: <a href="http://www.perform-
motive.com/welcome.html">http://www.perform-motive.com/welcome.html</a>
</address>
</div>
</body>
</html>
```

Horizontally Aligning Specific-Width Elements

If you want to specify a value other than auto as the element's width, CSS provides a method that is supposed to center a block element on a page. This method sets both the left and right margins for the element to auto. CSS also provides a method that is supposed to right-align a specific-width block element on the page, by setting the right margin to zero and the left margin to auto.

Unfortunately, neither of these methods works in Internet Explorer 5.5 for Windows, which in both cases will display the specific-width element flush with the left margin, due to a bug in its implementation of CSS. To see how this works, just edit the section of the example file, starting with "The Performance Motivation Advantage" heading, so it matches what is shown here:

```
<div style="border: dashed aqua; width: 70%; margin-left: auto; margin-right:
auto; padding: 8px">
<h2 style="text-align: center; margin-top: 0">The Performance Motivation
Advantage</h2>
<p>We are industry leaders in performance motivation seminars, leadership style
assessments, interpersonal skills development courses, meta-goal planning
assistance, and other performance enhancement services. Our only job is the
liberation of performance potential for individuals, groups, and organizations.
</p>
</div>
```

Figure 10.1 shows what this looks like in Netscape 6 for Windows. It should look very similar in Netscape 6 for the Macintosh, Internet Explorer 5 for the Macintosh, and Opera 5 for Windows. Figure 10.2 shows what this looks like in Internet Explorer 5.5 for Windows.

This effectively means that you can't use this method. Happily, there is a neat little workaround that fixes this problem. It involves simply nesting the DIV element you want to center inside of another DIV element, but with text-align: center or text-align: right set. Here's an example of doing that:

```
<div style="text-align: center">
<div style="border: dashed aqua; width: 70%; margin-left: auto; margin-right:
auto; padding: 8px">
<h2 style="text-align: center; margin-top: 0">The Performance Motivation
Advantage</h2>
<p>We are industry leaders in performance motivation seminars, leadership style
assessments, interpersonal skills development courses, meta-goal planning
assistance, and other performance enhancement services. Our only job is the
liberation of performance potential for individuals, groups, and organizations.
</p>
</div>
</div>
```

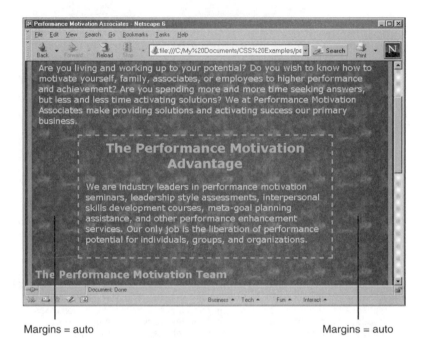

Margins = auto   Margins = auto

Figure 10.1: *In CSS, you are able to center a block element with a custom width by setting the left and right margins to auto.*

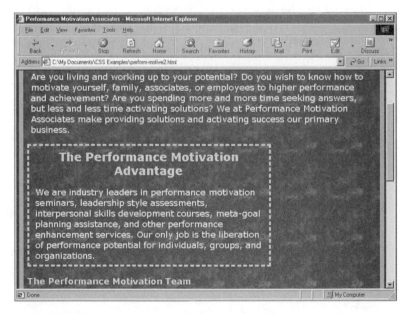

Figure 10.2: *Due to a bug, however, in Internet Explorer 5.5 for Windows, centering a block element with a custom width by setting the left and right margins to auto doesn't work.*

As shown in Figure 10.3, the nested DIV element with a width of 70% is now centered in Internet Explorer 5.5 for Windows.

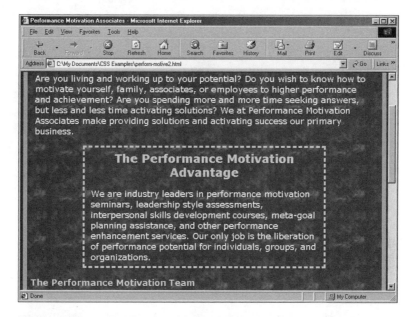

Figure 10.3: *To center a block element with a specific width in Internet Explorer 5.5 for Windows, just insert it inside of a DIV element with* `text-align: center` *set.*

Floating Elements

The `float` property allows an element to *float* relative to following elements. This means that following elements flow (or wrap) around the floating element.

For this section, just continue to use the example HTML file, `perform-motive2.html`, that you were using in the previous section.

Creating a Drop-Cap Effect

Here's an example of using the `float` property to create a drop-cap effect (see Figure 10.4):

```
<p><span style="color: lime; background: transparent; font-size: 2.6em; line-
height: 0.9em; float: left; width: 0.7em; padding-right: 2px">A</span>re you
living and working up to your potential? Do you wish to know how to motivate
yourself, family, associates, or employees to higher performance and achievement?
Are you spending more and more time seeking answers, but less and less time
activating solutions? We at Performance Motivation Associates make providing
solutions and activating success our primary business.</p>
```

Drop-cap letter

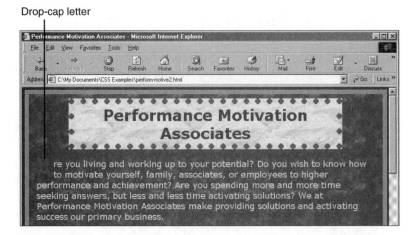

Figure 10.4: *You can use the float property to create a drop-cap letter effect.*

Flowing Text and Other Elements Around an Image

A more common use of the `float` property is to flow text and other elements around the left or right side of an image.

In HTML, the `align="left"` or `align="right"` attributes can be used in the IMG element to float an inline image (p. 208) to the left or right margin and cause following text or elements to flow around the image. These attributes, however, have been deprecated in HTML 4 and XHTML 1. You'll be happy to know that these same effects can easily be achieved through CSS alone, at least in the latest CSS1-supporting browsers.

✔ You've worked with one previous example of using an inline image, in "Setting Padding, Borders, and Margins for Images and Other Objects," p. 208 (chapter 9), where you set padding, borders, and margins for an inline image, as well as centering it on the page.

FLOWING TEXT AND OTHER ELEMENTS AROUND THE RIGHT SIDE OF AN IMAGE

Here's an example of using the `float` property to flow text and other elements around the right side of an image (see Figure 10.5):

```
<h3><img src="goals.gif" alt="Goals image" style="float: left; width: 125px;
height: 125px; margin: 0 1.5% 0">The Performance Motivation Team</h3>
<p>Our highly skilled and experienced professional consultants have helped enable
thousands of clients to achieve success and maximize performance. Do you feel
you're falling short and going around in circles? Our experts, consultants, and
coaches are experts in performance actualization, success achievement, and
leadership development. We can help you get where you want to go. Join the
Performance Motivation Team today!</p>
```

TIP

You'll notice that an ALT attribute is included in the IMG element used in the previous example. The purpose of that attribute is to provide alternative text that can be displayed if the image can't be displayed, such as might be the case if someone is using a text browser, a non-visual browser (such as a speech or Braille browser), or has turned display of graphics off in their browser. To assist these users in navigating and perusing the content of your page, it is a good idea to always include ALT attributes in your IMG elements.

Float = left

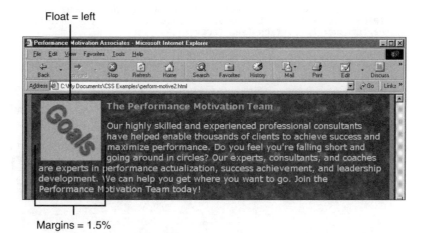

Margins = 1.5%

Figure 10.5: *Using the* `float` *property, you can flow text and other elements around the right side of an image.*

NOTE

If on your system there isn't enough example text to flow entirely around the right side of the image in this and the following examples, go ahead and copy and paste to add more example text until you can see it flow to the left margin in your browser's window.

A few comments on the previous example are in order:

- The IMG element is an inline element and is nested inside of the H2 element. This ensures that the top margins of these two elements are the same.

- The `width` and `height` properties express the actual dimensions of the image in pixels.

- The margin shorthand property sets left and right margins of 1.5 percent for the image, while zeroing out the top and bottom margins.

FLOWING TEXT AND OTHER ELEMENTS AROUND THE LEFT SIDE OF AN IMAGE

You can also flow text around the left side of a right-aligned floating image. To do this example, just copy the previous example you created and paste in an additional copy, and then edit the copied example so it matches what is shown here (see Figure 10.6):

```
<h3><img src="results.gif" alt="Results image" style="float: right; width: 125px;
height: 125px; margin: 0 1.5% 0">The Performance Motivation Team</h3>
```

```
<p>Our highly skilled and experienced professional consultants have helped enable
thousands of clients to achieve success and maximize performance. Do you feel
you're falling short and going around in circles? Our experts, consultants, and
coaches are experts in performance actualization, success achievement, and
leadership development. We can help you get where you want to go. Join the
Performance Motivation Team today!</p>
```

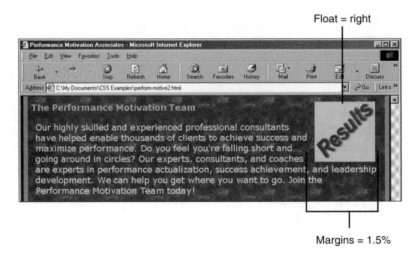

Float = right

Margins = 1.5%

Figure 10.6: *Using the* float *property, you can flow text and other elements around the left side of a right-aligned image.*

FLOWING TEXT AND OTHER ELEMENTS BETWEEN IMAGES

You can also use the float property to flow text and other elements between two images. To do this, copy either of the two previous examples you created and then edit it so it matches what is shown here (see Figure 10.7):

```
<h3><img src="goals.gif" alt="Goals image" style="float: left; width: 125px;
height: 125px; margin: 0 1.5% 0"><img src="results.gif" alt="Results image"
style="float: right; width: 125px; height: 125px; margin: 0 1.5% 0">The
Performance Motivation Team</h3>
```

```
<p>Our highly skilled and experienced professional consultants have helped enable
thousands of clients to achieve success and maximize performance. Do you feel
you're falling short and going around in circles? Our experts, consultants, and
coaches are experts in performance actualization, success achievement, and
leadership development. We can help you get where you want to go. Join the
Performance Motivation Team today!</p>
```

Float = left   Float = right

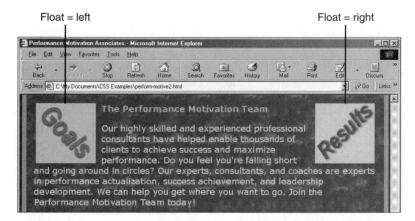

Figure 10.7: *Using the left and right* float *properties, you can also flow text and other elements between two images.*

Using the Clear Property

One of the problems with floating an image can be that everything that follows the image flows around the image until the bottom of the image has been reached. In many cases, this is what you want, but in other cases, it might not be what you want.

You also need to be mindful that the amount of text or other content required to flow all the way around a particular image (or other object) might differ radically from one system to another, depending on such factors as the default font-size, screen resolution, browser width, and so on. In other words, the amount of text required to flow around a particular image on your system might not be the same amount required to achieve the same result on someone else's system.

In HTML, the BR element inserts a line break within an HTML file. By inserting a CLEAR attribute, in conjunction with the values of "left," "right," and "all," you can cause any following text or elements to be moved down until the margin is clear (not blocked by an intervening left-aligned or right-aligned image). This attribute, however, has been deprecated in HTML 4 in favor of using styles to achieve the same result.

In CSS, the clear property can be assigned to any element, in conjunction with the values of left, right, and both. This property causes the element to be moved down until the left, right, or both margins are clear (not blocked by an intervening floated image or other object).

Using the example you previously created for using the float: left property, here's an example of using the clear: left property to cause following text or elements to be moved down until the left margin is clear (see Figure 10.8):

```
<h3><img src="goals.gif" alt="Goals image" style="float: left; width: 125px;
height: 125px; margin: 0 1.5% 0">The Performance Motivation Team</h3>
```

```
<p>Our highly skilled and experienced professional consultants have helped enable
thousands of clients to achieve success and maximize performance.<br
style="clear: left">Do you feel you're falling short and going around in circles?
Our experts, consultants, and coaches are experts in performance actualization,
success achievement, and leadership development. We can help you get where you
want to go. Join the Performance Motivation Team today!</p>
```

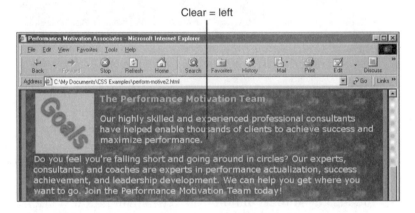

Figure 10.8: *Using a* clear: left *property, you can cause any following text or other elements to be moved down until the left margin is clear.*

Using the example you previously created for using the float: right property, here's an example of using the clear: right property to cause following text or elements to be moved down until the right margin is clear (see Figure 10.9):

```
<h3><img src="results.gif" alt="Results image" style="float: right; width: 125px;
height: 125px; margin: 0 1.5% 0">The Performance Motivation Team</h3>
```

```
<p>Our highly skilled and experienced professional consultants have helped enable
thousands of clients to achieve success and maximize performance.<br
style="clear: right">Do you feel you're falling short and going around in
circles? Our experts, consultants, and coaches are experts in performance
actualization, success achievement, and leadership development. We can help you
get where you want to go. Join the Performance Motivation Team today!</p>
```

Using the example you previously created for flowing text or other elements between two images, here's an example of using the clear: both property, this time in a paragraph element, to cause following text or elements to be moved down until both the left and right margins are clear (see Figure 10.10):

```
<h3><img src="goals.gif" alt="Goals image" style="float: left; width: 125px;
height: 125px; margin: 0 1.5% 0"><img src="results.gif" alt="Results image"
style="float: right; width: 125px; height: 125px; margin: 0 1.5% 0">The
Performance Motivation Team</h3>
<p>Our highly skilled and experienced professional consultants have helped enable
thousands of clients to achieve success and maximize performance.</p><p
style="clear: both">Do you feel you're falling short and going around in circles?
Our experts, consultants, and coaches are experts in performance actualization,
success achievement, and leadership development. We can help you get where you
want to go. Join the Performance Motivation Team today!</p>
```

Clear = right

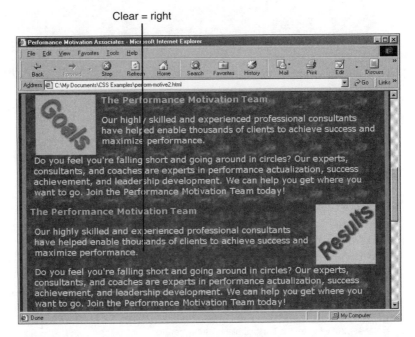

Figure 10.9: *Using a* clear: right *property, you can cause any following text or other elements to be moved down until the right margin is clear.*

Unlike in HTML, where the CLEAR attribute can only be used with the BR element, as shown in the previous example, in CSS you can use the clear property with any element to cause following text or elements to break past a floating image or other element. Remember that although some users might be viewing your page in a maximized browser window at 640×480 screen-resolution, others might be viewing it in a maximized browser window at 1024×768 or even larger screen resolution. In other words, you should always apply the clear property to any element that you want to make sure will break past a floating image or other element.

Clear = both

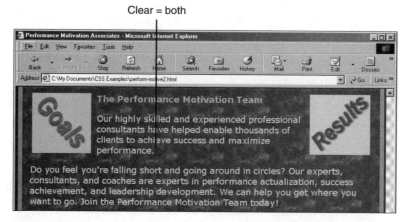

Figure 10.10: *Using a* `clear:` *both property, you can cause any following text or other elements to be moved down until both the right and left margins are clear.*

Floating Elements Around Elements

Images are only one kind of element to which the `float` property can be applied. For instance, you can flow text in one paragraph around the text included in another paragraph. For an example of doing that, edit the initial heading and paragraph in the example HTML file so it matches what is shown here (see Figure 10.11):

```
<h1>Performance Motivation Associates</h1>
```

**<p style="float: left; margin: 17px 10px 0 10px; padding: 5px 10px 5px; border: solid 5px aqua; font-family: Verdana, sans-serif; font-size: 24px; font-weight: bold; color: white; background: fuchsia">Success
Secrets!</p>**

```
<p><span style="color: lime; background: transparent; font-size: 2.6em; line-
height: 0.9em; float: left; width: 0.7em; padding-right: 2px">A</span>re you
living and working up to your potential? Do you wish to know how to motivate
yourself, family, associates, or employees to higher performance and achievement?
Are you spending more and more time seeking answers, but less and less time
activating solutions? We at Performance Motivation Associates make providing
solutions and activating success our primary business.</p>
```

In this example, a line break (BR element) is used to determine the width of the floating paragraph element. CSS includes a `width` property that would be nice to use in this instance to specify the width of the floating P element, instead of using a line break (or line breaks) to foreshorten its width. Unfortunately, Internet Explorer 5.5 for Windows, due to a bug in its implementation of the CSS box formatting model, mistakenly takes the value of the `width` property to be equal to the sum of the widths of the content area, padding, and borders, instead of just being equal to the width of the content area. To test this out, first delete the BR element included in the previous example (replacing it with a space) and then use the `width` property to set the width of the floating element to 150 pixels, as shown here:

```
<p style="float: left; width: 125px; margin: 17px 10px 0 10px; padding: 5px 10px
5px; border: solid 5px aqua; font-family: Verdana, sans-serif; font-size: 24px;
font-weight: bold; color: white; background: fuchsia">Success Secrets!</p>
```

Float = left

Figure 10.11: *You can flow text or other elements around another element.*

The result is that if you set the element width, you get a smaller total box width in Internet Explorer 5.5 than in the other current CSS-supporting Web browsers, because it calculates that value as also including any padding or border widths you've set. Figure 10.12 shows what a floating text box, using the same padding and borders as the previous example and with a width: 125px property also set, looks like in both Netscape 6 and Internet Explorer 5.5 for Windows.

One workaround for this problem is to use nested DIV elements, with width, padding, and border values set for the parent DIV element, but only the width value set for the nested DIV element, like this (see Figure 10.13):

```
<div style="float: left; width: 125px; margin: 17px 10px 0 10px; padding: 5px
10px 5px; border: solid 5px aqua; color: white; background: fuchsia">
<div style="width: 125px; font-family: Verdana, sans-serif; font-size: 24px;
font-weight: bold">Success Secrets!</div>
</div>
<p><span style="color: lime; font-size: 2.6em; line-height: 0.9em; float: left;
width: 0.7em; padding-right: 2px">A</span>re you living and working up to your
potential? Do you wish to know how to motivate yourself, family, associates, or
employees to higher performance and achievement? Are you spending more and more
time seeking answers, but less and less time activating solutions? We at
Performance Motivation Associates make providing solutions and activating success
our primary business.</p>
```

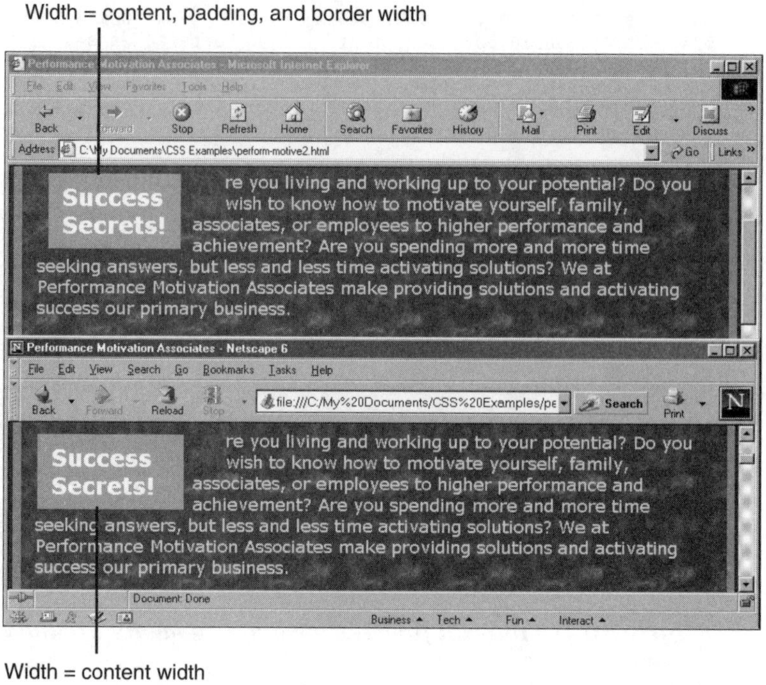

Width = content, padding, and border width

Width = content width

Figure 10.12: Internet Explorer incorrectly calculates the element width as also including padding and border widths.

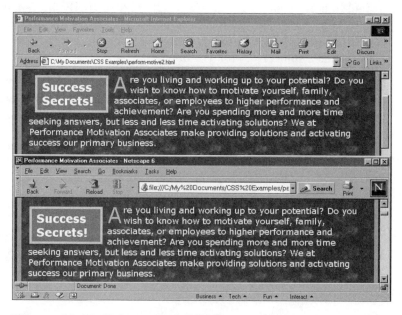

Figure 10.13: Using nested DIV elements causes Internet Explorer 5.5 for Windows to set the same element width as Netscape 6.

This works because the nested DIV element is the only content of the parent DIV element, causing Internet Explorer 5.5 for Windows to reduce the parent DIV element's width to that of the nested DIV element.

CAUTION

In the example shown in Figure 10.13, the left margins for the floating element are treated differently in Internet Explorer 5.5 for Windows and Netscape 6. That's because different interpretations of what the margin is being measured from are used by those browsers. Unfortunately, there is no easy work around for this, although it only shows up when you're working with a floating element with a margin set between it and the side of the page. This is a good example of why you should always test your page in several CSS1-supporting browsers, rather than simply relying on a single browser to verify your results.

Another more complex workaround is what is generally referred to on the Web as the *box model hack*. This involves taking advantage of an error in Internet Explorer 5.5 for Window's parsing model to trick it into displaying the correct element width. For more information on how to use the box model hack, see the explanation of the person who came up with it, Tantek Çelik, at `http://www.tantek.com/CSS/Examples/`.

Creating an Online Picture Gallery

There are many ways in which you can use the `float` and `clear` properties in Web pages to flow text and other elements around floating images and other elements. A particularly good use for this is in creating an online picture gallery, in which image captions and descriptions flow alternatively around the right and left sides of floating photos. I've included an example file, gallery.html, with the other example files for this book; just open it in your text editor and then edit it as shown here to create the example online picture gallery, and then save it as **mygallery.html** (see Figures 10.14 and 10.15):

Listing 10.2: MYGALLERY.HTML—An online picture gallery

```
<!DOCTYPE HTML PUBLIC "-//W3C//DTD HTML 4.01 Transitional//EN"
"http://www.w3.org/TR/html4/loose.dtd">

<html>
<head>
<title>My Online Picture Gallery</TITLE>

<style type="text/css">
<!--
body {
    margin-top: 5px;
```

Listing 10.2: continued

```
    color: white;
    background: black url(dark.jpg);
    }
    /* Body display settings */
span.pictitle {
    color: aqua;
    background: transparent;
    font-family: Verdana, Arial, sans-serif;
    font-size: 2em;
    }
    /* Picture title display settings */
img.left {
    float: left;
    border-width: 0;
    margin-right: 10px;
    }
    /* Left image float settings */
img.right {
    float: right;
    border-width: 0;
    margin-left: 10px;
    }
    /* Right image float settings */
-->
</style>
</head>
<body>
<div style="text-align: center"><img src="gallery.gif" alt="Online Gallery Banner
Image" style="width: 500px; height: 75px;">
</div>
<hr>

<p><a href="picture1.jpg"><img src="picture1_sm.jpg" class="left" alt="View of
Elliott Bay" style="width: 300px; height: 203px"></a>
<span class="pictitle">View of Elliott Bay</span><br>from the west side of Queen
Anne Hill, Seattle, Washington.<br style="clear: left"></p>
<hr>

<p><a href="picture2.jpg"><img src="picture2_sm.jpg" class="right" alt="View of
Elliott Bay & Alki" style="width: 300px; height: 203px"></a>
<span class="pictitle">View of Elliott Bay and Alki</span><br>from the west side
of Queen Anne Hill, Seattle, Washington.<br style="clear: right"></p>
<hr>

<p><a href="picture3.jpg"><img src="picture3_sm.jpg" class="left" alt="View of
Elliott Bay/Alki" style="width: 300px; height: 203px"></a>
<span class="pictitle">Another View of Elliott Bay</span><br>from the west side
```

Listing 10.2: continued

```
of Queen Anne Hill, Seattle, Washington.<br style="clear: left"></p>
<hr>

<address>
John Richards<br>
E-Mail: <a href="mailto:johnr@goforit.com">johnr@goforit.com</a><br>
Web Address: <a
href="http://www.goforit.com/johnr/">http://www.goforit.com/johnr/</a>
</address>

</body>
</html>
```

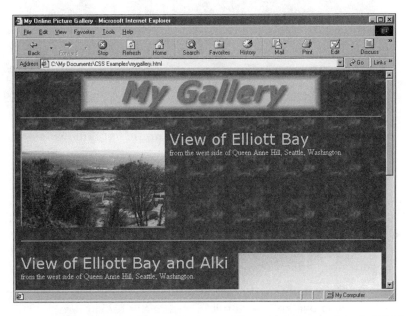

Figure 10.14: *An online picture gallery is only one kind of Web page you can create using floating image elements.*

TIP

You'll notice in Listing 10.2 that the style rules are formatted differently than in the other code examples. You're free to format and arrange your style rules and property declarations in any fashion you like. Many CSS authors favor the arrangement shown in Listing 10.2, since it makes it easy to scan the content of, and add comments to, a style sheet. In this book, I've stuck to listing style rules and their property declarations on a single line, to save space and cut down on some of the typing you have to do.

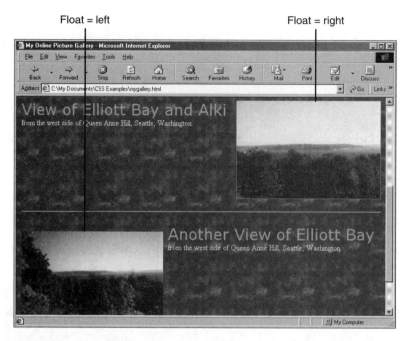

Figure 10.15: *The online gallery example alternates floating images on the left and right sides of the page.*

This online gallery example utilizes smaller-sized images, or *thumbnail images*, that link to larger-sized images. A thumbnail image is a version of an image that has been reduced in size and then linked to the full-sized version of the image. This lets you display a larger number of pictures on your initial gallery page while helping to conserve bandwidth. To create your own gallery images follow these steps:

1. Scan a photo at a higher resolution (300 dpi, for instance). You can also use an image taken with a digital camera.

2. Resize your scanned image (or digital photo) in your image editor to a width of not more than 600 pixels (while preserving the aspect ratio). Save it as a JPEG image (as picture1.jpg, picture2.jpg, and so on).

3. Resize the image further to a width of not more than 300 pixels (while preserving the aspect ratio) to create your thumbnail image. Save it with a filename that designates it as a thumbnail image (as picture1_sm.jpg, picture2_sm.jpg, and so on).

In the example code, the height and width of the linked picture images is specified through a STYLE attribute in the IMG tags. Be sure to specify the actual dimensions of your images in pixels—otherwise, your pictures might appear distorted when you view them in your browser. These need to be the dimensions of the thumbnail images, and not of the larger-sized images to which the thumbnail images link.

Positioning Elements

In CSS2, the position property enables you to position elements on the page. It takes the following values: static, absolute, relative, and fixed. The static value corresponds to the normal flow and is the default. The absolute value positions an element relative to the containing block. The relative value positions an element relative to its current position. The fixed value "fixes" an element's position relative to the browser window, so that it remains fixed when the page is scrolled. The fixed value is currently only supported by Opera 5 (with some bugs).

Using Absolute Positioning

The position: absolute property specifies that an element is to be positioned relative to the containing block. If the element is nested inside the BODY element, then the document body is the containing block. If it is nested inside some other element, that element is the containing block.

The top, bottom, left, and right properties are used to position the element. These properties can take length or percentage values, as well as an auto value. In addition, you can use the width and height properties to specify specific dimensions for a positioned element.

An example file, perform-news.html, is included with the other example files for this book—just open it in your text editor and then edit it as shown here to create the example newsletter layout (see Figure 10.16):

Listing 10.3: PERFORM-NEWS.HTML—An online newsletter layout

```
<!DOCTYPE HTML PUBLIC "-//W3C//DTD HTML 4.01 Transitional//EN"
"http://www.w3.org/TR/html4/loose.dtd">

<html>
<head>
<title>Performance News!</title>
<style type="text/css">
<!--
body { margin: 0; }
div.masthead { position: absolute; top: 0; height: 90px; width: 100%; text-align:
center; }
div.runner { position: absolute; top: 90px; height: 30px; width: 100%; text-
align: center; }
div.sidebar { position: absolute; top: 120px; width: 150px; height: 45em; }
div.main { position: absolute; top: 120px; left: 150px; height: 45em; }
```

Listing 10.3: continued

```
p.banner { margin: 0; padding: 0; }
p.runner { font-size: 0.95em; font-weight: bold; margin-top: 5px; }
-->
</style>
</head>
<body>

<div class="masthead">
<p><img src="perform-bann.gif" alt="Top Banner"></p>
</div>

<div class="runner">
<p>Vol. 1 No. 1   -   Jan. 1, 2002</p>
</div>

<div class="sidebar">
<h3>Contents:</h3>
<p><a href="#lead">Results Commitment</a></p>
<p><a href="#story2">Meta-Goal Planning</a></p>
<p><a href="#story3">Personality<br>Types</a></p>
<p><a href="#story4">Activate<br>Success</a></p>
<p><a href="archive.html">Back<br>Issues</a></p>
<p><a href="contact">Contact<br>Us</a></p>
</div>

<div class="main">

<h1><a name="lead"></a>Committing to Results</h1>
<p>The secret of life success is continuity of effort and commitment to results.
Our latest seminar series, Committing to Results, can put you on the fast-track
to enjoying the fruits of your endeavors. (<a href="story1.html">Read
More</a>...)</p>

<h2><a name="story2"></a>Meta-Goal Planning Secrets</h2>
<p>What is your true aim in life? Success not in line with what you really want
out of life is hollow. Learn how Meta-Goal Planning can help you be both
successful and happy. (<a href="story2.html">Read More</a>...)
<p>Return to <a href="perform-news.html" class="top">Top</a>.</p>

<h2><a name="story3"></a>What Is Your Personality Type?</h2>
<p>Do you know your personality type? Your personality type determines the
leadership style that will lead to your success. Stop fighting yourself! Learn
how to maximize your potential for achievement by liberating your own personal
traits for success. (<a href="story3.html">Read More</a>...)
<p>Return to <a href="perform-news.html" class="top">Top</a>.</p>

<h2><a name="story4"></a>Activating Performance Motivation</h2>
<p>Learn how to activate strength, continuity, commitment, imagination,
```

Listing 10.3: continued

```
sacrifice, and infinite learning in your life. Start applying the PMA's result-
oriented methods and techniques today! (<a href="story4.html">Read More</a>...)
<p>Return to <a href="perform-news.html" class="top">Top</a>.</p>

<hr>

<address>
Performance Motivation Associates<br>
E-Mail: <a href="mailto:contact@perform-motive.com">contact@perform-
motive.com</a><br>
Web Address: <a href="http://www.perform-
motive.com/welcome.html">http://www.perform-motive.com/welcome.html</a>
</address>

</div>

</body>
</html>
```

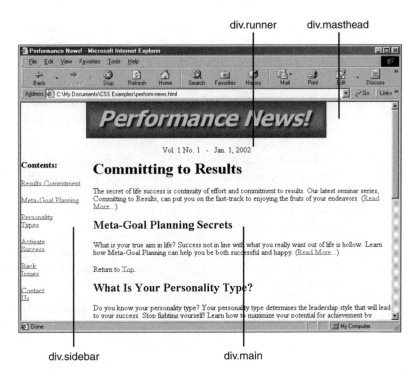

Figure 10.16: *The "masthead," "runner," "sidebar," and "main" document divisions are positioned on the page.*

After creating this example in your text editor, save it as **newsletter.html** in your working folder. As long as the example files are located in that folder, the example graphics used in this example show up when you preview it in your browser.

If you save the file under a different filename, be sure to edit the "Return to Top" links to match. The current example links to four files—story1.html, story2.html, story3.html, and story4.html—that are intended for holding the actual article documents. These files aren't included with the example files; you need to supply them yourself. If you want to save your article documents using different file names, just edit the "Read More" links to match.

Don't worry if this looks a little funky right now. You'll shortly be adding margins, some colors and backgrounds, and other styling, which should help improve the appearance. Here are some comments on this example:

- The **body** rule eliminates margins around the body of the document.

- The **div.masthead** rule positions the masthead division at the top of the page, with a height of 90 pixels and a width of 100 percent.

- The **div.runner** rule positions the runner division 90 pixels down from the top of the page (the same as the height of the masthead division), with a height of 30 pixels and a width of 100 percent.

- The **div.sidebar** rule positions the "sidebar" division 120 pixels down from the top of the page (the same as the combined heights of the masthead and runner divisions), with a width of 150 pixels and a height of 45 ems.

- The **div.main** rule positions the main division 120 pixels down from the top of the page and 150 pixels from the left of the page (the same as the width of the sidebar division), with a height of 45 ems. The width is left undefined, which allows it to expand or contract relative to the width of the browser window.

- The **p.banner** rule turns off any margins or padding for the banner paragraph. This ensures that browsers position the banner graphic vertically in the same position on the page.

- The **p.runner** rule reduces the size of the font for the runner paragraph, as well as eliminating its top margin. This is necessary to ensure that the paragraph fits within the runner division.

TIP

Setting a one-pixel border for your positioned divisions can help you to visualize their position. Just add `border-style: solid; border-width: 1px;` to your division rules to do this (see Figure 10.17).

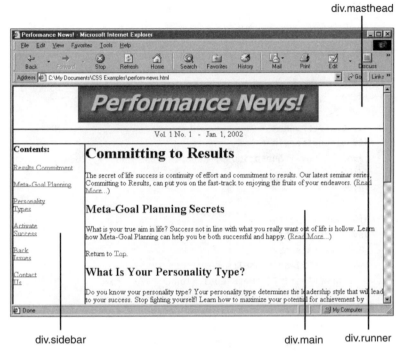

Figure 10.17: Turning on the borders of your positioned divisions can help you visualize their relative positions.

SETTING INTERNAL MARGINS

No margins or padding have been set for the positioned divisions. Margins aren't set because they'd be applied outside of the divisions, messing up their positioning. Padding isn't set because of the box model bug that afflicts Internet Explorer 5.5 for Windows (causing it to include both any padding or borders within an element's specified width or height). One way to deal with this situation is to create a separate class selector, div.margin, that can then be used to set margins inside of the positioned elements. While you're at it, you might also eliminate the top margin for the H1 element. To make those changes, just edit your document's code, like this:

```
p.banner { margin: 0; padding: 0; }
p.runner { font-size: 0.95em; font-weight: bold; margin-top: 5px; }
div.margin { margin: 5px 10px; }
h1 { margin-top: 0; }
```

Next, nest the margin division inside of the positioned elements (except for the runner division), like this (see Figure 10.18):

```html
<body>

<div class="masthead">
<div class="margin">
<p><img src="perform-bann.gif"></p>
</div>
</div>

<div class="runner">
<div class="margin">
<p>Vol. 1 No. 1   -   Jan. 1, 2002</p>
</div>
</div>

<div class="sidebar">
<div class="margin">
<h3>Contents:</h3>
<p><a href="#lead">Results Commitment</a></p>
<p><a href="#story2">Meta-Goal Planning</a></p>
<p><a href="#story3">Personality<br>Types</a></p>
<p><a href="#story4">Activate<br>Success</a></p>
<p><a href="archive.html">Back<br>Issues</a></p>
<p><a href="contact">Contact<br>Us</a></p>
</div>
</div>

<div class="main">
<div class="margin">
<h1><a name="lead"></a>Committing to Results</h1>

<p>The secret of life success is continuity of effort and commitment to results.
Our latest seminar series, Committing to Results, can put you on the fast-track
to enjoying the fruits of your endeavors. (<a href="story1.html">Read
More</a>...)</p>

<h2><a name="story2"></a>Meta-Goal Planning Secrets</h2>
<p>What is your true aim in life? Success not in line with what you really want
out of life is hollow. Learn how Meta-Goal Planning can help you be both
successful and happy. (<a href="story2.html">Read More</a>...)
<p>Return to <a href="perform-news.html" class="top">Top</a>.</p>

<h2><a name="story3"></a>What Is Your Personality Type?</h2>
<p>Do you know your personality type? Your personality type determines the
leadership style that will lead to your success. Stop fighting yourself! Learn
how to maximize your potential for achievement by liberating your own personal
traits for success. (<a href="story3.html">Read More</a>...)
<p>Return to <a href="perform-news.html" class="top">Top</a>.</p>
```

```
<h2><a name="story4"></a>Activating Performance Motivation</h2>
```

```
<p>Learn how to activate strength, continuity, commitment, imagination,
sacrifice, and infinite learning in your life. Start applying the PMA's result-
oriented methods and techniques today! (<a href="story4.html">Read More</a>...)
```

```
<p>Return to <a href="perform-news.html" class="top">Top</a>.</p>
```

```
<hr>
```

```
<address>
```

```
Performance Motivation Associates<br>
```

```
E-Mail: <a href="mailto:contact@perform-motive.com">contact@perform-
motive.com</a><br>
```

```
Web Address: <a href="http://www.perform-
motive.com/welcome.html">http://www.perform-motive.com/welcome.html</a>
```

```
</address>
```

```
</div>
```

```
</div>
```

```
</body>
```

5-pixel margin   5-pixel margin   5-pixel margin

10-pixel margin

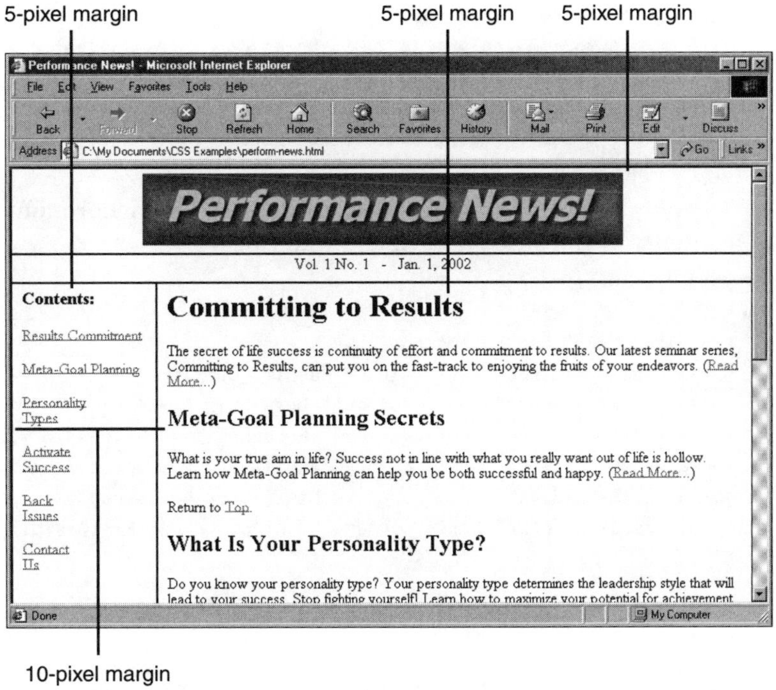

Figure 10.18: *Margins are inserted for the masthead, sidebar, and main divisions.*

DRESSING IT UP

You've now created the "superstructure" for your newsletter page. You can now dress it up, adding colors, backgrounds, and fonts. Also, get rid of the borders you set earlier. Here's one example (using background images included with the example files downloaded from this book's Web site):

```css
body { margin: 0; }
div.masthead { position: absolute; top: 0; height: 90px; width: 100%; text-align:
center; color: black; background: aqua url(clouds.jpg); }
div.runner { position: absolute; top: 90px; height: 30px; width: 100%; text-
align: center; color: #ffffcc; background: #336699; font-family: Arial, sans-
serif; }
div.sidebar { position: absolute; top: 120px; width: 150px; height: 45em; color:
white; background: navy url(dark.jpg); }
div.main { position: absolute; top: 120px; left: 150px; height: 45em; color:
black; background: white url(paper.gif); }
p { font-family: Verdana, Arial, sans-serif; font-size: 1.05em; }
p.banner { margin: 0; padding: 0; }
p.runner { font-size: 0.95em; font-weight: bold; margin-top: 0; color: #ffffcc;
background: #336699; }
div.margin { margin: 5px 10px; }
h1 { margin-top: 0; color: #ff6600; background: transparent; }
h2 { color: #009933; background: transparent; }
h3.toc { margin-top: 0.5em; font-size: 1.5em; }
a.sidebar { color: yellow; font-weight: bold; font-size: 0.9em; background: navy
url(dark.jpg); }
```

To apply the color you assigned to the sidebar anchor elements, edit the contents of the sidebar division, like this:

```html
<div class="sidebar">
<div class="margin">
<h3 class="toc">Contents:</h3>
<p><a class="sidebar" href="#lead">Results Commitment</a></p>
<p><a class="sidebar" href="#story2">Meta-Goal Planning</a></p>
<p><a class="sidebar" href="#story3">Personality<br>Types</a></p>
<p><a class="sidebar" href="#story4">Activate<br>Success</a></p>
<p><a class="sidebar" href="archive.html">Back<br>Issues</a></p>
<p><a class="sidebar" href="contact">Contact<br>Us</a></p></div>
</div>
```

Figure 10.19 shows what this should look like in a CSS-supporting Web browser.

Feel free, of course, to experiment with different colors and backgrounds.

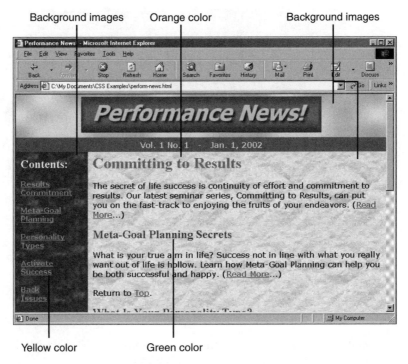

Background images   Orange color   Background images

Yellow color   Green color

Figure 10.19: *After building the "superstructure," you can dress it up.*

Using Relative Positioning

The position: relative property is used to specify that an element is positioned relative to its current (or original) position. Here's an example of positioning the H2 element 50 percent in from the left of its current position (see Figure 10.20):

```
h2 { color: #009933; background: transparent; position: relative; left: 25%; top:
0.7em; width: 70%; text-align: right; border-style: solid; border-width: 2px 0 0;
}
```

In this example, the width is also set to 50 percent. The amount of space the element is positioned in from the left and the width of the element must equal 100 percent, otherwise it extends beyond the right edge of the browser window, causing a horizontal scroll bar to be displayed. You might also have to adjust these values, depending on the actual length of your story headlines.

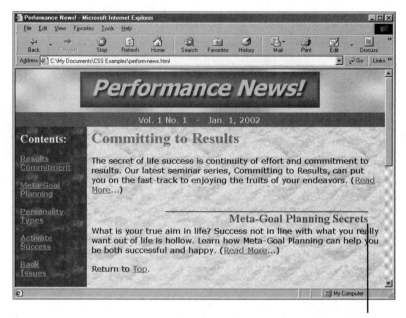

H2 element

Figure 10.20: *The H2 element is repositioned 50 percent to the left and 0.7 ems down relative to its current position.*

What's Next?

In this chapter, you learned about aligning, floating, and positioning elements. You should now know how to horizontally align an element on the page, flow text and other elements around images (and around other elements), and create fancy layouts using absolute and relative positioning.

In the next chapter, "Working with Lists," you learn all about creating styles lists, including controlling the bullet character for bulleted lists, specifying bullet images, and creating a multilevel outline.

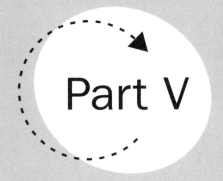

Part V

Working with Lists and Tables

Working with Lists

Working with Tables

Working with Lists

Only paragraphs and headings are used more frequently on the Web than lists. Lists, especially bulleted lists, are everywhere on the Web. The most common use for a bulleted list, for instance, is to present hypertext links. If you're like me, you've spent lots of time on the Web just jumping from one list of links to another. If you want to get serious about Web publishing, in other words, you've got to learn about making lists!

In HTML, the UL (Unordered List) and OL (Ordered List) elements, when combined with the LI (List Item) element, enable you to specify a list of bulleted or numbered items. A third kind of list, a glossary list, can also be created using the DL (Definition List) element. This chapter covers the following:

- Creating bulleted lists
- Creating numbered lists
- Creating glossary lists

Creating Bulleted Lists

Bulleted lists are used frequently on the Web. You can find them anywhere the creator wants to call attention to a list of particulars, be it a list of services, products, or qualifications.

Using the Example HTML File

You can find the example HTML file, perform-motive3.html, that is used in this chapter included with the other example files you downloaded and extracted to your working folder. You can also type in the example file, if you wish (see Figure 11.1):

Listing 11.1: PERFORM-MOTIVE3.HTML—Performance Motivation Associates

```
<!DOCTYPE HTML PUBLIC "-//W3C//DTD HTML 4.01 Transitional//EN"
"http://www.w3.org/TR/html4/loose.dtd">

<html>

<head>
<title>Performance Motivation Associates</title>
<style type="text/css">
body { margin: 3.5%; color: navy; background: #fcc; }
h1 { color: #c00; background: #fcc; margin-left: -2%; font-family: Arial, sans-
serif; }
h2 { color: #606; background: #fcc; font-family: Arial, sans-serif; }
</style>
</head>
<body>

<h1>Performance Motivation Associates</h1>

<p>Are you living and working up to your potential? Do you wish to know how to
motivate yourself, family, associates, or employees to higher performance and
achievement? Are you spending more and more time seeking answers, but less and
less time activating solutions? We at Performance Motivation Associates make
providing solutions and activating success our primary business.</p>

<h2>Performance Motivation Services</h2>
<p>We offer a wide range of seminars, consulting, and other services in the areas
of:</p>

<ul>
<li>Career and Job Success
<li>Youth and Adult Leadership Development
<li>Parenting and Family Skills
<li>Personal Achievement
<li>Goal and Success Visualization
```

Listing 11.1: continued

```
<li>Meta-Goal Planning
</ul>

<hr>

<address>
Performance Motivation Associates<br>
E-Mail: <a href="mailto:contact@perform-motive.com">contact@perform-
motive.com</a><br>
Web Address: <a href="http://www.perform-
motive.com/welcome.html">http://www.perform-motive.com/welcome.html</a>
</address>

</body>
</html>
```

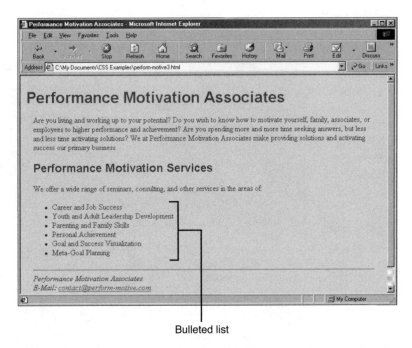

Bulleted list

Figure 11.1: *Straight HTML bulleted lists are displayed indented from the left margin without any spacing between the list items.*

Controlling Nested Bulleted Lists

When you nest bulleted lists to create a multi-level bulleted list, browsers automatically vary the bullet type for the different nested list levels. For instance, edit your example HTML file to create a multi-level bulleted list (see Figure 11.2):

```
<ul>
<li>Career and Job Success
    <ul>
    <li>Interpersonal Skills Seminars
        <ul>
        <li>Being a Team Member
        <li>Negotiating for Success
        </ul>
    <li>Employee Conflict Mediation Courses
    </ul>
<li>Youth and Adult Leadership Development
<li>Parenting and Family Skills
<li>Personal Achievement
<li>Goal and Success Visualization
<li>Meta-Goal Planning
</ul>
```

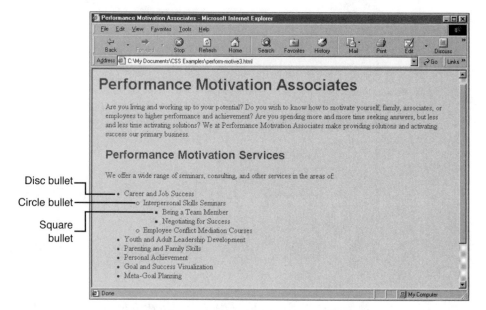

Figure 11.2: *Browsers automatically vary the bullet type for nested bullet lists.*

In this example, the initial bullet level is displayed using a solid disc, but the nested bullet levels use a hollow circle and a filled square, respectively.

Specifying the Bullet Type

The list-style-type property lets you change the type of bullet that is displayed in a list. The values that are used with bulleted lists are disc, circle, square, and none.

For instance, here's an example of setting styles to specify that your nested bulleted lists display a hollow circle, a filled square, and a solid disc, in that order (see Figure 11.3):

```
h2 { color: #606; background: #fcc; font-family: Arial, sans-serif;
}
ul { list-style-type: circle; }
ul ul { list-style-type: square; }
ul ul ul { list-style-type: disc; }
```

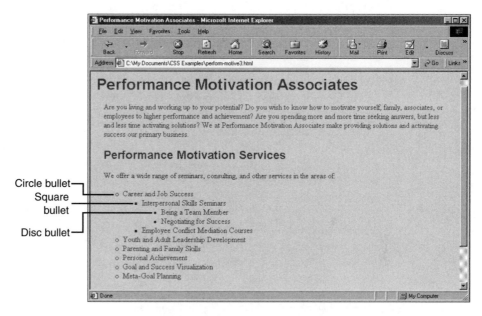

Figure 11.3: *Using styles, you can vary the type of bullet used for different nested bullet levels.*

This example works by specifying contextual styles for the different nested bullet levels. The first style (the ul rule) is applied to any bulleted list on the page, in the absence of other styles specifying differently. The second style (the ul ul rule) is applied only to bulleted lists that are nested inside of another bulleted list (to UL elements nested inside of another UL element). The third style (the ul ul ul rule) is applied only to bulleted lists that are nested inside bulleted lists that are nested inside of another bulleted list (nested two levels deep, in other words).

This can also be achieved by using class selectors, setting "first," "second," and "third" classes for the different list levels, but using contextual styles doesn't require making any changes to the HTML elements.

The sequence of the contextual styles is important here. Reverse the order of the styles, and all three levels of the bulleted list are displayed with a circle bullet. That's because each following declaration of the `list-style-type` property (for the `ul ul` and `ul ul ul` styles) supercedes the previous declaration for the contextual situation for which it is targeted.

Controlling List Positioning

The `list-style-position` property specifies the position of the bullet character relative to the following list item text. Two values are allowed: `outside` and `inside`. The first, `outside`, is the default and displays the bullet outside its corresponding list item block (the bullet is actually positioned inside of the list item's margin space). The second, `inside`, displays the bullet inside its corresponding list item block.

To best see how this works, the bullet list items have to be long enough to wrap. Go ahead and add some additional text to a few of the list items. Here's an example (but feel free to devise your own or copy and paste to create the additional text):

```
<ul>
<li>Career and Job Success - Our seminars, courses, and other services can be
key for unlocking the achievement potential of managers and employees.
    <ul>
    <li>Interpersonal Skills Seminars - Nothing drains productivity out of an
organization, enterprise, department, or team faster than interpersonal conflicts
and friction.
        <ul>
        <li>Being a Team Member
        <li>Negotiating for Success
        </ul>
    <li>Employee Conflict Mediation Courses
    </ul>
<li>Youth and Adult Leadership Development
<li>Parenting and Family Skills
<li>Personal Achievement
<li>Goal and Success Visualization
<li>Meta-Goal Planning
</ul>
```

As Figure 11.4 shows, long text included in list items wraps indented under the bullet. In other words, by default, list bullets are located outside of the list block.

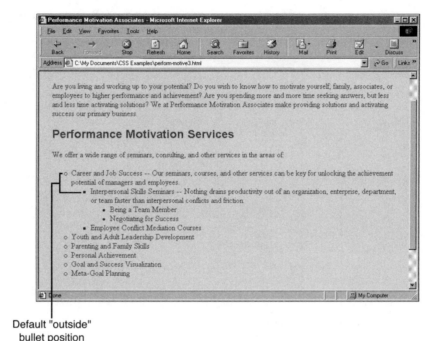

Default "outside"
bullet position

Figure 11.4: Long text included in a bulleted list item wraps under the bullet.

You can change this by specifying that the list bullet be positioned inside of the list block. For instance, make the following change to your style sheet to see how this works (see Figure 11.5):

```
ul { list-style-type: circle; }
ul ul { list-style-type: square; list-style-position: inside; }
ul ul ul { list-style-type: disc; }
```

To get a graphic look at how this works, add a style for the LI element that draws a one-pixel border around the list item block (see Figure 11.6):

```
ul ul ul { list-style-type: disc; }
li { border-style: solid; border-width: 1px; }
```

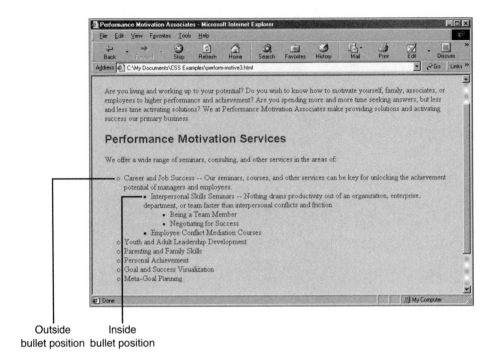

Outside   Inside
bullet position   bullet position

Figure 11.5: *Using styles, you can vary the bullet position.*

Specifying a Bullet Image

The list-style-image property enables you to specify a bullet image to be displayed as a list's bullet. The property takes as its value either a URL or none. If you downloaded and extracted the example files to your working folder, a bullet image, goldball.gif, will be available in your working folder that you can use for this example (otherwise, substitute a bullet image of your choosing).

The following example not only specifies a URL value, url(goldball.gif), to specify a bullet image to be displayed for the bulleted list items, but also sets a none value to turn off display of the bullet image for the two nested bulleted lists:

```
ul { list-style-type: circle; list-style-image: url(goldball.gif); }
ul ul { list-style-type: square; list-style-image: none; }
ul ul ul { list-style-type: disc; }
</style>
```

Outside bullet position

List item block border

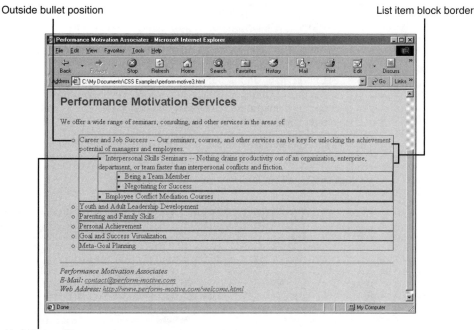

Inside bullet position

Figure 11.6: *Drawing a border around the list item blocks visually helps to show the difference between outside and inside bullet positioning.*

Be sure to delete the LI rule you created earlier to draw a border around the list item block. In this example, `list-style-image: none` is only specified for the first nested bulleted list and not for the second. That's because the second nested bulleted list inherits the same value from the first nested bulleted list, because it is nested inside it. Figure 11.7 shows what this looks like in a CSS1-supporting browser.

TIP

To use only the filename of the bullet image as the URL, the image must be located in the same folder where your style sheet's HTML file (or your external style sheet) is saved. If you want to use the same bullet image for multiple pages stored in separate folders, however, you need to specify a relative URL. A relative URL states the position of the linked object relative to the position of the linking file. For instance, if the bullet image is stored in an images folder within your working folder, and files for two projects are saved in separate folders, proj1 and proj2, for instance, within your working folder, then a style sheet located within the proj1 or proj2 folders links to the bullet image in the images folder like this:

continues

continued

    url(../images/goldball.gif)

This example tells the browser to look in the current page's parent folder (`../`) of the linking file's folder for an images folder (`images/`), and then to look within that folder for `goldball.gif`. On the other hand, you may want to consolidate all of your images within their own folder within your working folder (the root folder for your site). In that case, you'd link to the bullet image in that folder from a page in your working folder in this manner:

    url(images/goldball.gif)

Bullet Image (goldball.gif)

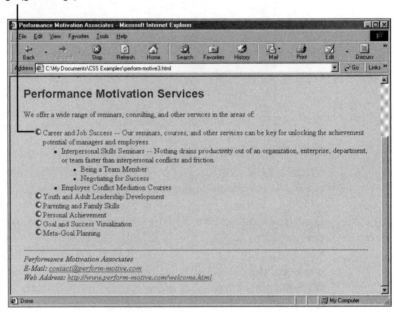

Figure 11.7: *You can specify that a bullet image be used for a bulleted list.*

Controlling List Margins

You can control the relative position on the page of your bulleted list by specifying margins or for the UL and LI elements (see Figure 11.8):

```
ul { list-style-type: circle; list-style-image: url(goldball.gif); margin-top:
-0.95em; }
ul ul { list-style-type: square; list-style-image: none; margin-top: 0; }
ul ul ul { list-style-type: disc; }
ul li { margin-right: 2em; }
```

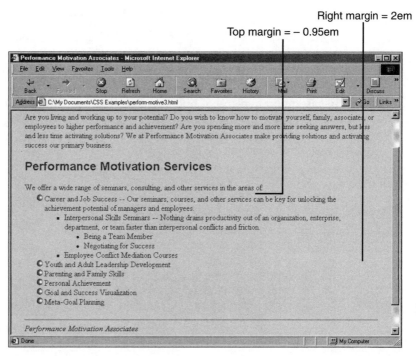

Figure 11.8: *The top margin of the first-level bulleted list is decreased, and the right margin for the bullet list items is increased.*

✔ For more guidance on setting margins, see "Setting Margins," p. 184 (chapter 9).

The styling for the bulleted list items is set using a contextual style, ul li, rather than simply for the LI element. This has the effect of setting the styling only for LI elements that are nested inside of UL elements. Otherwise, the same styling would be applied to the list items of any numbered lists (created with the OL element) you might want to include.

TIP

In the previous example, a vertical margin is set for the UL element, and a horizontal margin is set for the LI element. That's because CSS1-supporting browsers handle setting horizontal margins for UL elements inconsistently. For that reason, you should always specify horizontal margin spacing for a list's LI elements, but not for the list element itself (UL or OL).

Another way to set horizontal margins for a list is to nest it inside of a DIV element and then set horizontal margins for the DIV element.

Controlling List Item Vertical Margins

By default, no additional vertical spacing is inserted between list items. You can easily space out your list items, however, by specifying a positive top margin. To try this out, first delete the previous margin settings you inserted for your lists, and then set the top margin of the UL element's list items to a value of one em, like this (see Figure 11.9):

```
ul { list-style-type: circle; list-style-image: url(goldball.gif); }
ul ul { list-style-type: square; list-style-image: none; }
ul ul ul { list-style-type: disc; }
ul li { margin-right: 2em; margin-top: 1em; }
```

This example also resets the UL element's top margin to one em. For what this looks like in a browser, see Figure 11.9.

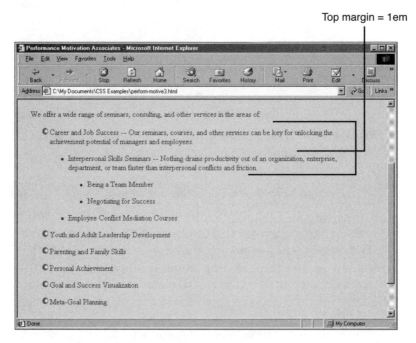

Top margin = 1em

Figure 11.9: A top margin of one em is applied to the list items.

Controlling the Bullet Separation

Especially when setting a bullet image for your bulleted list items, the amount of horizontal spacing separating the bullet from the list item text might seem a bit sparse. To add additional horizontal spacing between the list's bullets and the following list item text, just set some left padding for the list item. For instance, here's an example of setting left padding of 1.5 percent for the list's list items (see Figure 11.10):

```
ul { list-style-type: circle; list-style-image: url(goldball.gif); }
ul ul { list-style-type: square; list-style-image: none; }
ul ul ul { list-style-type: disc; }
ul li { margin-right: 2em; margin-top: 1em; padding-left: 1.5%; }
```

Left padding = 1.5%

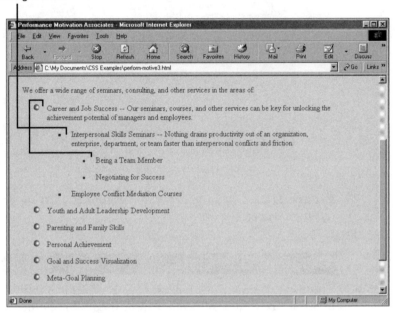

Figure 11.10: *Padding of 1.5 percent is set between the bullet and the following list item text.*

✔ For more guidance on setting padding, see "Setting Padding," p. 195 (chapter 9).

As is the case when setting bullet positioning, drawing a one-pixel border around the list items visually helps show what the padding is actually doing in this situation (see Figure 11.11):

```
ul li { margin-right: 2em; margin-top: 1em; padding-left: 1.5%; border-style:
solid; border-width: 1px; }
```

Left padding = 1.5%

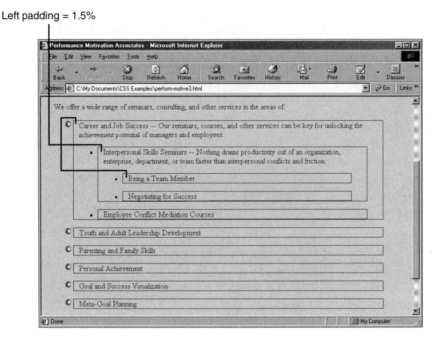

Figure 11.11: *Drawing a border around the list items emphasizes what the left padding in the list is doing.*

Creating Link Lists

The most common use for lists on the Web is simply listing hypertext links, or what are commonly called "link lists." To test out an example of controlling the appearance of link lists, first make the following changes to your style sheet:

```
ul li { margin-right: 2em; margin-top: 1em; padding-left: 1.5%; font-style:
italic; }
ul a { font-family: Verdana, Arial, sans-serif; font-weight: bold; color: red;
background: transparent; text-decoration: none; font-style: normal; }
```

This causes the UL element's list item text to be displayed in an italic font; the ul a contextual style sets the display characteristics for hypertext links (the A element) that are nested inside of the UL element. Hypertext links that aren't nested inside of the UL element are not affected.

To have this actually show up in your example page, you need to add some hypertext links to your page, as well as some descriptive text (to provide list item text outside of the links). Just edit the content of your page, so it matches what is shown here (see Figure 11.12):

```
<ul>
<li><a href="career.html">Career and Job Success</a> — Our seminars, courses,
and other services can be key for unlocking the achievement potential of managers
and employees.
<li><a href="leader.html">Youth and Adult Leadership Development</a> — We've got
the programs guaranteed to give you a step up!
<li><a href="family.html">Parenting and Family Skills</a> — Learn how to get
your family on your side!
<li><a href="achieve.html">Personal Achievement</a> — Methods and techniques for
achieving what you really want to get out of life.
<li><a href="success.html">Goal and Success Visualization</a> — Before you can
achieve it, you have to see it!
<li><a href="goals.html">Meta-Goal Planning</a> — Learn how to put your
priorities in order!
</ul>
```

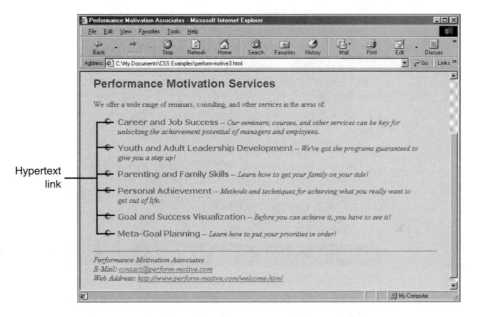

Figure 11.12: One of the most common uses for lists on the Web is listing hypertext links.

The links in this example jump to pages that are located in the same folder as the linking page. These are fictional pages, so if you want to check out the actual links, just save some sample HTML files in your working folder using the filenames given in the links.

There are numerous ways in which hypertext links can be employed in HTML files. To link to Web pages out on the Web that are not part of your own site, just specify the full Web address as the URL (the HREF attribute value). href="http://www.callihan.com/cssbook/" links to the page I've set up for this book, for instance.

You can also link to pages located in other parts of your site by using what is commonly referred to as a "relative URL" (or the location of the linked object stated relative to the linking file). For example, if the linking page is located in your site's root folder and the linked page is located in a myproject folder, then the relative URL is stated something like this: href="myproject/plans.html", for instance. A page located in your myproject folder, on the other hand, might link back to a page located in your root folder like this: href="../welcome.html", for instance.

Another common use for hypertext links is to jump to a locations within a page. These links can either jump to locations within the same page or a different page. You can create a menu this way, or you can link index references to a page of index entries. In the previous chapter, the newsletter example used hypertext links to create a menu in that page's sidebar window that jumped to locations within the page's main window. These sorts of links require two A tags, one forming the jump point and the other the landing spot. To see how those are formed, see the perform-news.html example you created in the previous chapter.

NOTE

The discussion provided here on this subject is admittedly somewhat brief, because creating hypertext links is part of HTML, not CSS. For more detailed information and instructions, see the W3C's page on creating hypertext links at http://www.w3.org/TR/html4/struct/links.html.

Creating Numbered Lists

Numbered lists are less common on the Web than bulleted lists, but they are useful when you want to present an ordered set of instructions, for instance, or any other numbered list of items.

Using the Example HTML File

The example HTML file, counterfeit.html, should already be available, if you downloaded and extracted the example files to your working folder. You can also type in the example file, if you wish (see Figure 11.13):

Listing 11.2: COUNTERFEIT.HTML—Is It Genuine Or Is It Counterfeit?

```
<!DOCTYPE HTML PUBLIC "-//W3C//DTD HTML 4.01 Transitional//EN"
"http://www.w3.org/TR/html4/loose.dtd">

<html>
```

Listing 11.2: continued

```
<head>
<title>Telling Real from Counterfeit</title>
<style type="text/css">
body { margin: 3.5%; color: #030; background: #ffc; font-family: Verdana, Arial,
sans-serif; font-size: 1.05em;}
body div { border-style: groove; border-width: 8px; border-color: green; }
body div div { margin: 0.25em; padding: 0 1em 0.5em; border-style: double;
border-width: 8px; border-color: olive; background: transparent; }
h1 { color: green; background-color: #ffc; font-family: Verdana, Arial, sans-
serif; font-size: 1.75em; text-align: center; border-top: 0; }
h2 { color: #606; background: #ffc; font-family: Arial, sans-serif;
}
address { font-family: Garamond, serif; text-align: center; }
</style>
</head>
<body>

<div>
<div>
<h1>Is It Genuine Or Is It Counterfeit?</h1>

<p>Telling the difference between genuine and counterfeit currency can be a
challenge. Here are some steps you can follow to help insure you don't get
burned:</p>

<ol>
<li>Compare the face of the bill in question with one you know to be genuine,
checking closely the workmanship and clarity of the engraving.
<li>Compare the paper of the bill in question with that of a bill you know to be
genuine.
<li>If still in doubt, show the bill in question to an experienced money-handler,
such as a bank teller, for example.
</ol>

<hr>

<address>
Abraham Randolph<br>
E-Mail: <a href="mailto:arand@mypage.com">arand@mypage.com</a><br>
Web Address: <a
href="http://www.mypage.com/arand/">http://www.mypage.com/arand/</a>
</address>
</div>
</div>
</body>
</html>
```

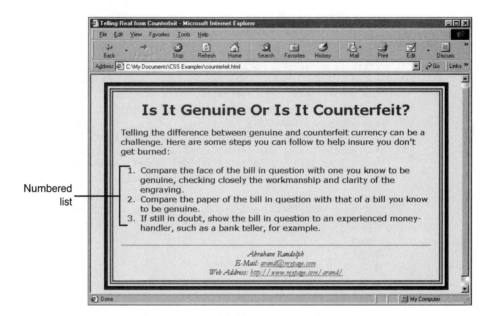

Numbered list

Figure 11.13: *A browser automatically numbers a numbered list for you.*

Specifying the Number Type

The `list-style-type` property is used to specify the number type to be used in your list. The values that can be used include:

Value	Result
decimal	1, 2, 3, 4, etc.
upper-roman	I, II, III, IV, etc.
lower-roman	i, ii, iii, iv, etc.
upper-alpha	A, B, C, D, etc.
lower-alpha	a, b, c, d, etc.
none	No numbering

To try this out, edit the example file, but specifying uppercase alphabetic letters for numbering the OL element, like this (see Figure 11.14):

```
address { font-family: Garamond, serif; text-align: center; }
ol { list-style-type: upper-alpha; }
</style>
```

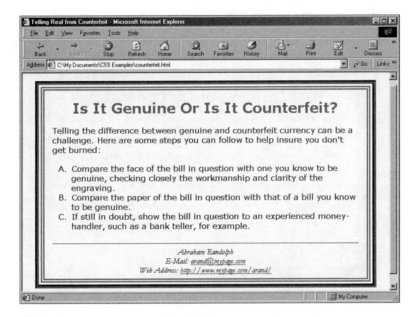

Figure 11.14: *The numbered list is formatted using uppercase alphabetic numbering.*

CSS2 specifies a number of additional list-style-type values that can be used with numbered lists, but of current Web browsers, only Netscape 6 supports them. These include the following values: decimal-leading-zero, lower-greek, lower-latin, upper-latin, hebrew, armenian, georgian, cjk-ideographic, hiragana, katakana, hiragana-iroha, and katakana-iroha. Of these, decimal-leading-zero is similar to decimal, except that the numbers display a leading zero (01, 02, 03, and so on, up to 09 for two-digit numbers); lower-latin and upper-latin have the same result as lower-alpha and upper-alpha; and the remaining correspond to numbering systems for non-Latin or non-Western languages. Figure 11.15 shows a numbered list using lowercase Greek numbers displayed in Netscape 6:

Creating a Multilevel Outline

By using nested numbered lists, with different number types assigned to them, you can create a multilevel outline. A handy way to do this is to create contextual styles for the different levels of the outline. To do that, edit your style sheet, making the following changes:

```
ol { list-style-type: upper-roman; font-weight: bold; }
ol ol { list-style-type: upper-alpha; font-weight: normal; font-style: italic; }
ol ol ol { list-style-type: decimal; font-style: normal; }
</style>
```

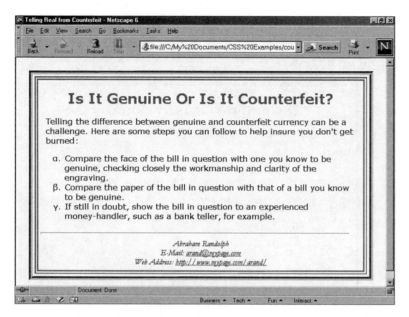

Figure 11.15: CSS2 supports the display of alternative number styles, such as using lowercase Greek numbers, as shown here in Netscape 6 (currently the only browser to support this).

Next, add the following HTML code to your document's body to create the multilevel outline (see Figure 11.16):

```
<ol>
<li>Compare the face of the bill in question with one you know to be genuine,
checking closely the workmanship and clarity of the engraving.
    <ol>
    <li>Check the Portrait.
        <ol>
        <li>Genuine: Sharply delineated from background; lifelike eyes; regular,
unbroken lines in background.
        <li>Counterfeit: Smudgy delineation with background; eyes dull and
un-lifelike; smudgy, broken lines in background.
        </ol>
    <li>Check the Seal.
        <ol>
        <li>Genuine: Saw-tooth points sharp and distinct.
        <li>Counterfeit: Saw-tooth points broken, blunted, or uneven.
        </ol>
    <li>Check the Scroll Work.
        <ol>
        <li>Genuine: Lines are fine, sharp, and unbroken.
        <li>Counterfeit: Lines are crude, smudgy, and broken.
        </ol>
```

```
    </ol>
<li>Compare the paper of the bill in question with that of a bill you know to be
genuine.
    <ol>
    <li>Genuine: High quality paper; imbedded red and blue threads.
    <li>Counterfeit: Cheaper paper; printed red and blue threads.
    </ol>
<li>If still in doubt, show the bill in question to an experienced money-handler,
such as a bank teller, for example.
</ol>
```

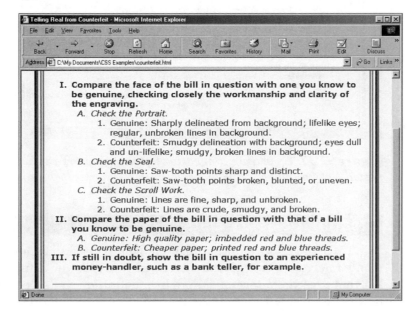

Figure 11.16: *By setting number styles using contextual styles, you can easily create a multilevel outline.*

Controlling Horizontal Positioning

By default, browsers indent nested list levels so that the nested number (or letter) is spaced in from and not vertically aligned with the preceding list item block. To cause nested list levels to be vertically aligned with the preceding list item block, just set a negative left margin for the list items, like this (see Figure 11.17):

```
ol ol ol { list-style-type: decimal; font-style: normal; }
ol li { margin-left: -0.7em; }
```

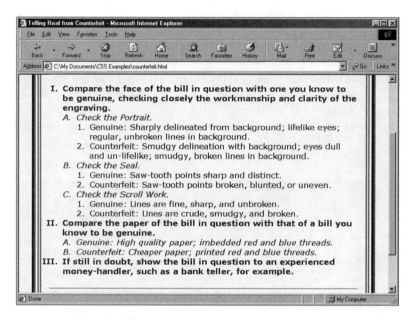

Figure 11.17: *By setting a negative left margin, you can vertically align a nested list's numbers with the preceding list item block.*

Creating Glossary Lists

In HTML, the DL (Definition List) element is used to create what is commonly referred to as a *glossary list*. A glossary list (or definition list) is a list that presents a term, followed by a definition that is positioned one line down and indented in from the margin. The term is formatted using a DT (Definition Term) element, and the definition is formatted by a DD (Definition Description) element.

Unlike for bulleted and numbered lists, there aren't any specific CSS properties that are used to format glossary lists. Style properties, however, can be defined for the DL, DT, and DD elements to alter the appearance of a glossary list.

I've created an example file, investment.html, included with the other example files for this book, that you can use to create the example for this section. You can also type the example in yourself (see Figure 11.18):

Listing 11.3: INVESTMENT.HTML—Glossary of Investment Terms

```
<!DOCTYPE HTML PUBLIC "-//W3C//DTD HTML 4.01 Transitional//EN"
"http://www.w3.org/TR/html4/loose.dtd">
```

Listing 11.3: continued

```html
<html>
<head>
<title>Glossary of Investment Terms</title>
<style type="text/css">

</style>
</head>
<body>
<h1>Glossary of Investment Terms</h1>

<dl>

<dt>Bear
<dd>Someone who believes the market will fall. A market that is falling is often
referred to as a "bear market."

<dt>Bull
<dd>Someone who believe the market will rise. A market that is rising is often
referred to as a "bull market."

<dt>Growth stock
<dd>Stock in a company that is projected to have rapidly increasing revenues and
profits.

<dt>Limit order
<dd>An order to buy or sell a stock at a specified or better price. For instance,
while the current bid for a stock may be $10.50/share, an investor may put in a
limit order to purchase the stock at $9.00/share, hoping that the price will fall
to or below that level.

<dt>Long
<dd>Refers to a position where a stock has been purchased (usually to be held).
This is often referred to as "going long." Being long in a stock means that you
believe that its value will rise.

<dt>Option
<dd>The right to purchase or sell a stock (or commodity) at a fixed price within
a specific time frame. An option to purchase is called a "call," while an option
to sell is called a "put."

<dt>Short
<dd>Refers to a position where a stock has been borrowed from a brokerage and
then sold, in hopes of being able to repurchase (or cover) the stock at a lower
price. The profit (or loss) is the difference between the price at which the
stock was borrowed and the price at which it was repurchased (or covered). This
is often referred to as "going short."
```

Listing 11.3: continued

```
<dt>Stop Order
<dd>An order to purchase a stock at a price above the current market price or to
sell a stock at a price below the current market price. A "stop buy," for
instance, is often used to limit losses from a short position, while a "stop
sell" may be used to limit losses from a long position.

</dl>

<hr>

<address>
Jorgenson Investment Advisors<br>
E-Mail: <a href="mailto:advice@jorgenson-invest.com">advice@jorgenson-
invest.com</a><br>
Web Address: <a href="http://www.jorgenson-invest.com/">http://www.jorgenson-
invest.com/</a>
</address>

</body>
</html>
```

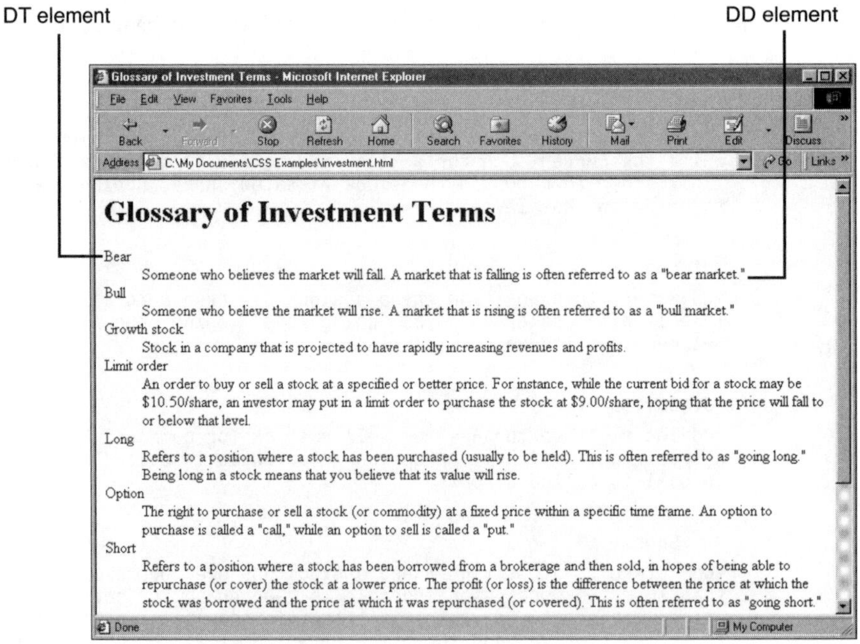

DT element   DD element

Figure 11.18: A glossary list, by itself, is a bit bland.

To make the appearance of the glossary list a bit more appealing, add the following styles to the example page (see Figure 11.19):

```
<style type="text/css">
dt { font-family: Arial, sans-serif; font-weight: bold; margin-left: 1em; color:
red; background: transparent; }
dd { position: relative; left: 7.25em; top: -1.25em; width: 75%; }
</style>
```

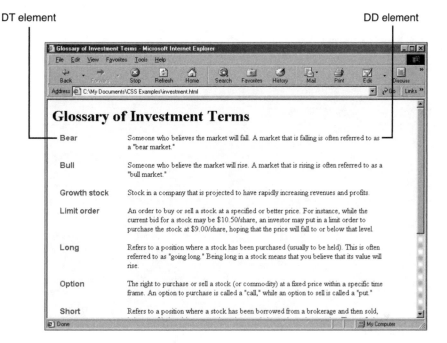

Figure 11.19: *Styles can make a glossary list much more readable.*

The main feature in this example is that relative positioning is used to reposition the content of the DD element so it is moved over to the right and horizontally aligned with the content of the DT element.

✔ For more guidance on using relative positioning, see "Using Relative Positioning," p. 241 (chapter 10).

NOTE

If your glossary list includes terms that need more horizontal spacing provided for in this example, just increase the distance specified in the dd selector's `left` property—you could specify 8em instead of 7.25em, for instance.

What's Next?

In this chapter, you learned about applying styles to bulleted, numbered, and glossary lists. You should now have a firm grasp on styling any kind of list, including link lists, outlines, and glossaries that you might want to use in your pages.

In the next chapter, "Working with Tables," you learn all about using styles to control the appearance of tables in your pages.

12

Working with Tables

In HTML, tables enable you to present information arranged in rows, columns, and cells. In Web pages, there are many uses for tables, from presenting facts and figures in an orderly and organized fashion, to more specific uses, such as creating product catalogs, price lists, agendas, calendars, and much more.

In this chapter, you learn how to apply the following table features using CSS:

- Controlling spacing, padding, and borders
- Aligning table cell contents
- Setting row and column colors and backgrounds
- Controlling column widths
- Creating horizontal and vertical borders

Using the Example HTML File

The example you use in this chapter is a table that compares the effects of various down-payment sizes when purchasing a home. The example HTML file, downpayment.html, should already be available, if you downloaded and extracted the example files to your working folder. You can also type in the example file, if you wish (see Figure 12.1):

Listing 12.1: DOWNPAYMENT.HTML—Down-payment Size Effects

```
<!DOCTYPE HTML PUBLIC "-//W3C//DTD HTML 4.01 Transitional//EN"
"http://www.w3.org/TR/html4/loose.dtd">

<html>

<head>
<title>Down-Payment Size Effects</title>
<style type="text/css">

</style>
</head>
<body>

<table border="1">
<caption>Table I. Down-Payment Size Effects ($200,000 home at 8 percent interest)

<colgroup id="cgroup1">
    <col id="col1">
</colgroup>
<colgroup id="cgroup2">
    <col id="col2">
    <col id="col3">
    <col id="col4">
</colgroup>
<colgroup id="cgroup3">
    <col id="col5">
    <col id="col6">
    <col id="col7">
</colgroup>

<thead>
<tr>
<th> </th><th colspan="3">Monthly Payment<br>(principal & interest)</th><th
colspan="3">Total Interest</th>
</tr>

<tr>
<th>Down-<br>Payment</th><th>20 Years</th><th>25 Years</th><th>30
```

Listing 12.1:   continued

```
Years</th><th>20 Years</th><th>25 Years</th><th>30 Years</th>
</tr>
</thead>

<tbody>
<tr>
<td>$0</td><td>$1,670</td><td>$1,540</td><td>$1,470</td><td>$201,100</td><td>$262
,800</td><td>$327,800</td>
</tr>

<tr>
<td>$10,000</td><td>$1,590</td><td>$1,470</td><td>$1,390</td><td>$191,110</td><td
>$249,700</td><td>$311,400</td>
</tr>

<tr>
<td>$20,000</td><td>$1,511</td><td>$1,390</td><td>$1,320</td><td>$181,100</td><td
>$236,500</td><td>$295,500</td>
</tr>

<tr>
<td>$30,000</td><td>$1,420</td><td>$1,310</td><td>$1,250</td><td>$170,900</td><td
>$223,400</td><td>$278,600</td>
</tr>

<tr>
<td>$40,000</td><td>$1,340</td><td>$1,240</td><td>$1,170</td><td>$160,900</td><td
>$210,800</td><td>$262,200</td>
</tr>

<tr>
<td>$50,000</td><td>$1,260</td><td>$1,160</td><td>$1,100</td><td>$150,800</td><td
>$197,100</td><td>$245,800</td>
</tr>
</tbody>

<tfoot>
<tr>
<td colspan="7">Note: The monthly payment is rounded off to the nearest $10; the
total interest payment is rounded off to the nearest $100.</td>
</tr>
</tfoot>

</table>

</body>
</html>
```

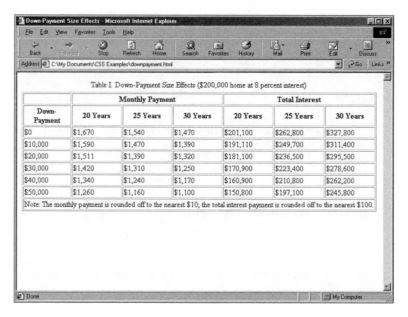

Figure 12.1: *An HTML table lets you arrange information in rows, columns, and cells.*

NOTE

Because the focus of this book is on CSS, and not on HTML, the various HTML table elements and attributes are not explained in any depth in this chapter. For more detailed explanations for creating HTML tables, see the W3C's page on tables at `http://www.w3.org/TR/html4/struct/tables.html`.

CSS and Tables

A number of table element attributes have been deprecated in HTML 4 and XHTML 1, in favor of using styles to achieve the same or better results. The focus of this book is on creating Web pages without using deprecated HTML elements or attributes. The examples included in this chapter show you how to use CSS styles to control the presentation of HTML tables. See Table 12.1 for a listing of HTML attributes used in tables that have been deprecated, along with their CSS alternatives.

Table 12.1: *Deprecated Table Element Attributes*

HTML Attribute	Where Deprecated	CSS Alternative
align	table, caption	text-align
bgcolor	table, tr,	background or td, th background-color

Table 12.1: continued

height	td, th	height
nowrap	td, th	white-space: nowrap
width	td, th	width

There are also a number of additional HTML table attributes for which CSS provides alternatives, even though those attributes aren't deprecated in HTML 4. In the spirit of depending upon CSS to determine presentation wherever possible, the examples in this chapter use the CSS alternatives for these un-deprecated table attributes. Table 12.2 shows the HTML table attributes for which CSS alternatives exist.

Table 12.2: Un-Deprecated Attributes with CSS Alternatives

HTML Attribute	Where Used	CSS Alternative
border	table	border properties
cellpadding	table	padding properties
cellspacing	table	border-spacing (CSS2) (Note)
frame	table	border properties
rules	table	border properties
valign	tr, td, th,	vertical-align tbody, thead, tfoot, col, colgroup
width	table	width

Note: Sets spacing between cell borders when `border-collapse: separate` is set. Supported only by Opera 5 at this time.

A word should also be provided on the frequent use of tables on the Web for creating multi-column layouts. One of the objectives of CSS is to eliminate the need to use tables to create Web page layouts, in line with the overall objective of separating appearance from structure in Web pages. When HTML elements and attributes are used to specify both appearance and structure, it can be confusing to non-visual user agents, such as Braille or speech browsers. They are unable to distinguish between tables used for formatting purposes and tables used (as they are supposed to be) for the presentation of information and data in a tabular format (in rows, columns, and cells). By relying as much as possible on CSS, and not on tables, to create your Web page layouts, you can do your part to help ensure that the Web will be accessible to all in the future. All of the Web page layouts presented in this book rely entirely on CSS, and not on tables.

✔ For examples of using CSS, and not tables, to create multi-column layouts, see "Positioning Elements," p. 233 (Chapter 10), as well as Chapter 13, "Creating Menus and Interfaces," and Chapter 14, "Creating Page Layouts and Site Designs."

Many Web authors and designers, however, continue to use tables to create Web page layouts, due to incomplete or non-existent support for CSS in all but the more recent browsers. Deprecated elements are perfectly legal elements; their use is discouraged, but not forbidden.

However, with all current major browsers now fully supporting CSS1, and as older legacy browsers fall more and more into disuse, the need for and use of such hybrid design solutions (part CSS, part deprecated HTML) should diminish significantly in the future.

Controlling Table Width and Horizontal Alignment

Although the WIDTH attribute is not deprecated in the TABLE element, CSS provides an alternative (the `width` property) that can be used to control the width of a table. For an example of doing this, just add the following style rule to your example file:

```
<style type="text/css">
table { width: 90%; }
</style>
```

CSS also provides an alternative to using the ALIGN attribute to center or right-align tables and table captions. In CSS, this is done by setting the left and right margins to `auto`, like this:

```
table { width: 90%; margin-left: auto; margin-right: auto; }
```

However, as discussed in Chapter 10, "Aligning, Floating, and Positioning," this just doesn't work in Internet Explorer 5.5 for Windows, due to a bug in that browser; in Internet Explorer 5.5 for Windows, the table remains left-aligned. There is a fairly simply workaround for that, however, involving nesting the table inside of a DIV element with the `text-align` property set. To do that, first insert the following DIV start tag at the start of the table, in this case using an inline style to set centered text-alignment (see Figure 12.2):

```
<div style="text-align: center">
<table border="1">
<caption>Table I. Down-Payment Size Effects ($200,000 home at 8 percent interest)
```

Next, insert a DIV end tag at the end of the table, like this:

```
</table>
</div>
```

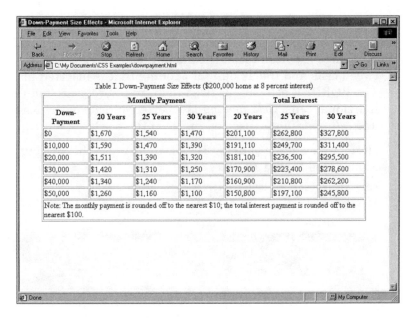

Figure 12.2: *The table's width is set to 90 percent and it is centered on the page.*

This works well in all of the current-generation CSS-supporting browsers, except for one. In Netscape 6, the table's TD cells inherit the center-alignment from the DIV element that is being used to center the table on the page. This causes the content of all of the TD cells to be center-aligned. TH elements are centered by default, so they're not a problem. To reset the table's TD cells to their default left-alignment in Netscape 6, just insert the following line in your style sheet:

```
table { width: 90%; margin-left: auto; margin-right: auto; }
td { text-align: left; }
```

It should be noted here, of course, that this is only necessary when using the DIV centering trick to get around the centering bug in Internet Explorer 5.5 for Windows.

Controlling Spacing, Padding, and Borders

In the example HTML file for this chapter, a `border="1"` attribute is set in the TABLE element, causing a one-pixel border to be drawn around the table and its cells. This is included to help you visualize how cell spacing and padding is controlled in HTML and CSS. By default, browsers do not draw borders for tables, but they do insert spacing between cells (usually two pixels) and padding within cells (usually one pixel).

Controlling Spacing, Padding, and Borders with HTML

In HTML, the TABLE element's CELLSPACING and CELLPADDING attributes are used to set the amount of spacing that is displayed between cells and the amount of padding that is inserted inside of cells. The BORDER attribute is used to draw a border around the table and its individual cells. *Cell spacing* is inserted outside of the border of a cell, and *cell padding* is inserted inside of the border of a cell.

Here's an example of using HTML to increase the spacing and padding for a table (see Figure 12.3):

```
<div style="text-align: center">
<table border="1" cellpadding="5" cellspacing="5">
```

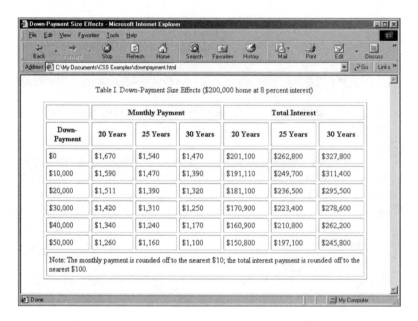

Figure 12.3: *Cell padding and spacing is increased to five pixels using HTML.*

On the other hand, you can reduce the amount of spacing between the cells to zero, resulting in a single border being drawn between the cells, like this (see Figure 12.4):

```
<div style="text-align: center">
<table border="1" cellpadding="5" cellspacing="0">
```

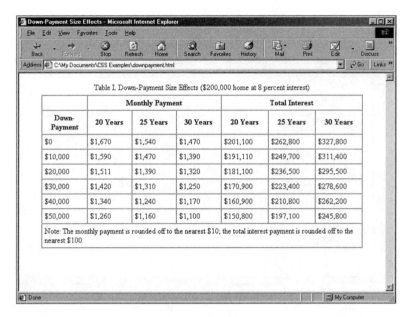

Figure 12.4: *Cell spacing is reduced to zero using HTML.*

Controlling Cell Padding with CSS

The padding property is used to control cell padding within tables. Because this is actually a CSS1 property, all current-generation browsers support it. To set the cell padding for the table by using only CSS, first delete the CELLPADDING attribute that you inserted in the TABLE element earlier:

```
<div style="text-align: center">
<table border="1" cellpadding="5" cellspacing="0">
```

Setting the cell padding for your table to zero is handy when you want to use less space to display a table with a lot of rows or columns. In HTML you can do this by inserting a cellpadding="0" attribute in the TABLE element. To do this in CSS, just set padding for the TH and TD elements to zero, like this (see Figure 12.5):

```
table { width: 90%; margin-left: auto; margin-right: auto; }
th { padding: 0; }
td { text-align: left; padding: 0; }
```

In most cases, however, it is preferable to have some padding set for your table cells to make them more readable. Edit your style sheet to set four pixels of vertical padding and six pixels of horizontal padding for the table's TH and TD cells (see Figure 12.6):

```
table { width: 90%; margin-left: auto; margin-right: auto; }
th { padding: 4px 6px; }
td { text-align: left; padding: 4px 6px; }
```

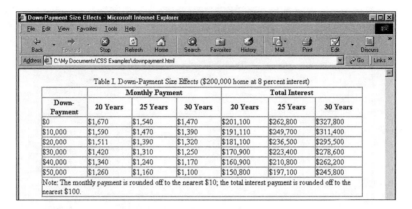

Figure 12.5: *Cell padding within the TH and TD table cells is set to zero using CSS.*

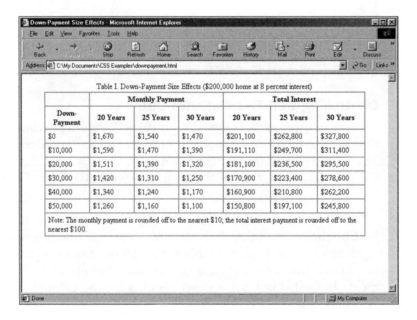

Figure 12.6: *Four pixels of vertical and six pixels of horizontal cell padding is set using CSS.*

Controlling Cell Spacing and Borders with CSS

While setting single borders between table cells is not a problem in CSS, controlling cell spacing between cells (and their borders) is a more uncertain proposition. That's because the method for doing this is part of CSS2 and current browsers are only required to support CSS1 to be considered to be CSS-compliant.

First, so you can be sure that the effects you're producing are a result of using CSS and not HTML, remove the BORDER and CELLSPACING attributes from your table's TABLE element (if you're a Macintosh user, however, just remove the BORDER attribute):

```
<table border="1" cellspacing="0">
```

To reduce cell spacing to zero and draw a single-line (one-pixel wide) border around the table and its cells, insert the following in your style sheet (see Figure 12.7):

```
table { border-collapse: collapse; border: 1px solid black; border-spacing: 0;
width: 90%; margin-left: auto; margin-right: auto; }
th { padding: 4px 6px; border: 1px solid black; }
td { text-align: left; padding: 4px 6px; border: 1px solid black; }
```

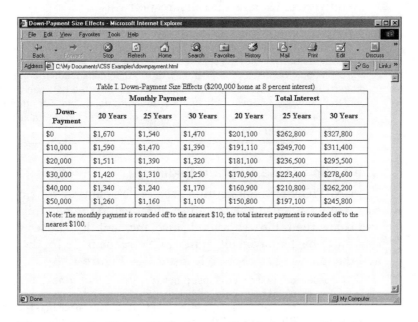

Figure 12.7: *Using CSS alone, cell spacing is reduced to zero and a single-line (one-pixel) border is drawn around the table and its cells.*

TIP

The reason I had Macintosh users leave the `cellspacing="0"` attribute in the TABLE element is that Internet Explorer 5 for the Macintosh and Netscape 6 for the Macintosh do not support reducing cell spacing to zero using CSS.

For that reason, when you want to reduce cell spacing to zero, you should also set an equivalent `cellspacing="0"` attribute in the TABLE element and not just rely on CSS to achieve this effect. Otherwise, Macintosh users will still see the default cell spacing between table cells. Remember, the CELLSPACING attribute (as well as the CELLPADDING attribute) is not a deprecated element, so it is perfectly okay to use it.

A few things in this example deserve some explanation:

- The border-collapse: collapse property is used in CSS to reduce the spacing between borders (the cell spacing) to zero.

- Netscape 6 doesn't actually recognize the border-collapse property, but does recognize the border-spacing: 0 property that is set for the table selector, which in that browser reduces spacing between borders to zero. This is a quirk, however, and shouldn't be expected to have an effect in any other browsers.

- A one-pixel solid border (border: 1px solid black) is set separately for the table, th, and td selectors. The first draws the border around the outside of the table; the other two draw the border around the individual TH and TD cells, respectively.

NOTE

In CSS2, the border-collapse: separate property is used to specify that a table's borders should be displayed separately, rather than collapsed. The border-spacing property is then used to control the spacing to be inserted between the separated cell borders. Currently, however, only Opera 5 supports doing this. For other browsers, a CELLSPACING attribute value other than zero must be set in the table's TABLE element to display separated table borders.

Controlling Table Caption Padding

The CAPTION element contains the table's caption. Setting cell padding to zero using CSS also has the effect of reducing the padding inserted above and below the table's caption. It also, incidentally, causes the table caption's content to be displayed off-center in Netscape 6. To fix these problems, just add the following to your style sheet (see Figure 12.8):

```
table { border-collapse: collapse; border: 1px solid black; border-spacing: 0;
width: 90%; margin-left: auto; margin-right: auto; }
caption { caption-side: top; padding-bottom: 1.5em; padding-top: 1.5em; margin-
left: auto; margin-right: auto; }
th { padding: 4px 6px; border: 1px solid black; }
td { text-align: left; padding: 4px 6px; border: 1px solid black; }
```

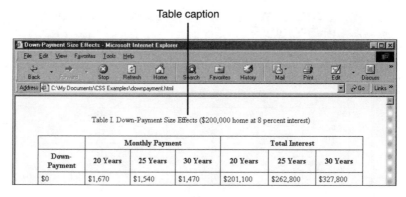

Figure 12.8: *Padding is added above and below the table caption.*

Aligning Table Cell Contents

By default, the content of TH cells is centered and the content of TD cells is left-aligned.

HTML 4 includes three table elements, the THEAD, TBODY, and TFOOT elements, that can be used to create groups of row groups. These let you, for instance, apply different formatting to header, body, and footer sections within a table.

In the following example, you style the TBODY element to set left-alignment for table rows nested within that element. You also style the THEAD element to set bottom-alignment for the table rows nested within that element. Just edit your style sheet, as shown here (see Figure 12.9):

```
th { padding: 4px 6px; border: 1px solid black; }
td { text-align: left; padding: 4px 6px; border: 1px solid black; }
thead tr th { vertical-align: bottom; }
tbody tr td { text-align: right; }
```

To better align the table's numbers (in the TD cells nested in the TBODY element), set some additional left-padding, like this (see Figure 12.10):

```
tbody tr td { text-align: right; padding-right: 1.5em; }
```

Ideally, using percentages to set this padding is preferable, in that it allows the padding to shrink or expand along with the width of the containing block. Internet Explorer 5.5 for Windows, however, flubs this up, adding the padding to the left, rather than to the right, of the right-aligned numbers.

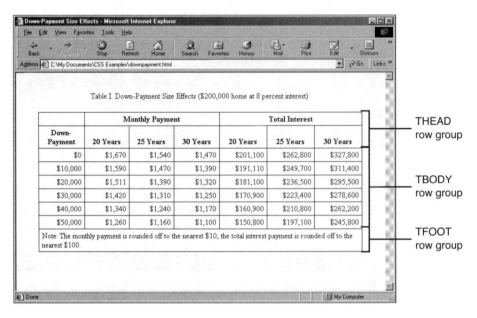

Figure 12.9: *The table rows nested inside of the THEAD element are bottom-aligned and the table cells nested inside of the TBODY element are right-aligned.*

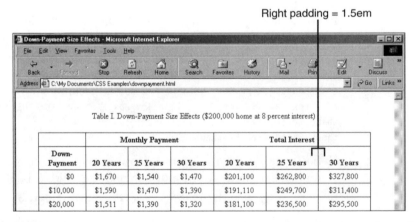

Figure 12.10: *1.5 ems of padding is set on the right side of the TD cells within the TBODY row group.*

Working with Rows and Columns

Using CSS, you can assign different colors and backgrounds to highlight row groups and column groups within your table. This not only makes your table more visually appealing, but it also helps to make your table more readable, by more clearly highlighting its different areas.

Setting Colors and Backgrounds for Row Groups

By assigning colors and backgrounds for the THEAD, TABLE, and TFOOT elements, you can distinguish your table's header, body, and footer sections by formatting them using different color schemes. For instance, here's an example of setting different colors for these three areas of the table (see Figure 12.11:

```
table { border-collapse: collapse; border: 1px solid black; border-spacing: 0;
width: 90%; margin-left: auto; margin-right: auto; background: #ffc; }
caption { caption-side: top; padding-bottom: 1.5em; padding-top: 1.5em; margin-
left: auto; margin-right: auto; }
th { padding: 4px 6px; border: 1px solid black; }
td { text-align: left; padding: 4px 6px; border: 1px solid black; }
thead tr th { vertical-align: bottom; color: navy; background: #fc9; }
tbody tr td { text-align: right; padding-right: 1.5em; color: #c00; background:
transparent; }
tfoot tr td { color: #030; background: #fcc; }
```

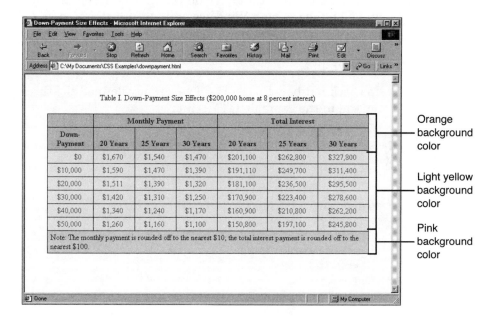

Figure 12.11: *The header, body, and footer sections of the table are distinguished using different color schemes.*

In this example, a background color is set for the TABLE element, and the corresponding foreground color is set for the TD elements that are nested inside of the TBODY row group. You could just as easily set the background color for the respective TD elements that you want to affect. However, in the next section, I show you how to vary the background colors of your table's data columns—to do that, the background colors for the individual TD cells must remain undeclared (and transparent, as is the default).

The reason for this is that a table is composed of layers, ordered in the following sequence from back to front: table, column groups, columns, row groups, rows, and cells. Thus, a background color set in an individual cell, for instance, blocks out any other background color set in one of the underlying layers. On the other hand, a background color set for the table, itself, is blocked out by any other background color set in any of the other layers.

Setting Colors and Backgrounds for Column Groups

The columns in the example table form three column groups, encompassing the first column, second through fourth columns, and fifth through seventh columns, respectively. It would be nice if you could assign background colors to column groups; and in fact, you can–at least this works fine in Internet Explorer 5.5 for Windows, Internet Explorer 5 for the Macintosh, and Netscape 6 (both Windows and Macintosh). Alas, it doesn't work in Opera 5. In that browser, the only way to assign different background colors for column groups is to assign them to the individual table cells within those groups.

To check out how this works, I've already defined the three column groups for you in the example HTML file:

```
<table cellspacing="0">
<caption>Table I. Down-Payment Size Effects ($200,000 home at 8 percent interest)

<colgroup id="cgroup1">
    <col id="col1">
</colgroup>
<colgroup id="cgroup2">
    <col id="col2">
    <col id="col3">
    <col id="col4">
</colgroup>
<colgroup id="cgroup3">
    <col id="col5">
    <col id="col6">
    <col id="col7">
</colgroup>
```

Now, to assign different background colors to the second column group (id="cgroup2") and the third column group (id="cgroup3"), just edit your example style sheet to add two id selectors pointing to those groups (see Figure 12.12):

```
tfoot tr td { color: #030; background: #fcc; }
colgroup#cgroup2 { color: black; background: #cff; }
colgroup#cgroup3 { color: black; background: #cfc; }
```

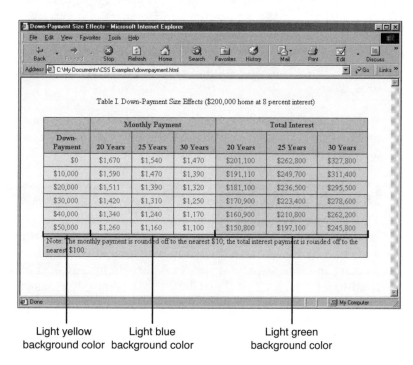

Light yellow background color   Light blue background color   Light green background color

Figure 12.12: *The three column groups are highlighted with different background colors.*

Controlling Column Widths

You can also vary the widths of the columns in the three column groups. For instance, edit your style sheet as follows to set a width of 16 percent for the first column, 13 percent for the second through fourth columns, and 15 percent for the fifth through seventh columns (see Figure 12.13):

```
colgroup#cgroup2 { color: black; background: #cff; }
colgroup#cgroup3 { color: black; background: #cfc; }
col#col1 { width: 16%; }
col#col2 { width: 13%; }
col#col5 { width: 15%; }
```

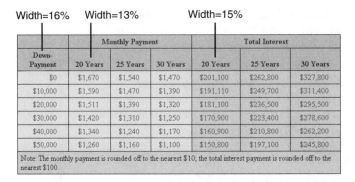

Figure 12.13: Varying column widths are set for the different column groups.

You can set the width explicitly for all seven columns, but I've found in practice that setting the width for the first column in a column group sets it for the rest.

Putting On the Finishing Touches

There's quite a bit more you can do to embellish the table. In the following sections, you set horizontal and vertical borders, turn off internal borders, and set a border around the outside of your table, in addition to setting background images in your table. Before doing any of that, however, you need to add some CLASS attributes (class="top", class="none", and class="left") to your example code, so you can then attach specific style properties to them:

```
<thead>
<tr>
<th> </th><th colspan="3">Monthly Payment</th><th colspan="3">Total
Interest</th>
</tr>

<tr class="top">
<th class="none">Down-<br>Payment</th><th class="left">20 Years</th><th>25
Years</th><th>30 Years</th><th class="left">20 Years</th><th>25 Years</th><th>30
Years</th>
</tr>
</thead>

<tbody>
<tr class="top">
<td>$0</td><td class="left">$1,670</td><td>$1,540</td><td>$1,470</td><td
class="left">$201,100</td><td>$262,800</td><td>$327,800</td>
</tr>
```

```
<tr>
<td>$10,000</td><td class="left">$1,590</td><td>$1,470</td><td>$1,390</td><td
class="left">$191,110</td><td>$249,700</td><td>$311,400</td>
</tr>

<tr>
<td>$20,000</td><td class="left">$1,511</td><td>$1,390</td><td>$1,320</td><td
class="left">$181,100</td><td>$236,500</td><td>$295,500</td>
</tr>

<tr>
<td>$30,000</td><td class="left">$1,420</td><td>$1,310</td><td>$1,250</td><td
class="left">$170,900</td><td>$223,400</td><td>$278,600</td>
</tr>

<tr>
<td>$40,000</td><td class="left">$1,340</td><td>$1,240</td><td>$1,170</td><td
class="left">$160,900</td><td>$210,800</td><td>$262,200</td>
</tr>

<tr>
<td>$50,000</td><td class="left">$1,260</td><td>$1,160</td><td>$1,100</td><td
class="left">$150,800</td><td>$197,100</td><td>$245,800</td>
</tr>
</tbody>

<tfoot>
<tr class="top">
<td colspan="7">Note: The monthly payment is rounded off to the nearest $10; the
total interest payment is rounded off to the nearest $100.</td>
</tr>
</tfoot>
```

Adding Horizontal Borders

You can add horizontal borders to your table to help highlight different areas. For instance, edit your style sheet to match what is shown here (see Figure 12.14):

```
col#col1 { width: 16%; }
col#col2 { width: 13%; }
col#col5 { width: 15%; }
tr.top th { border-top: 8px ridge yellow; color: #c03; }
tr.top th.none { border-top: 0px; }
tbody tr.top td { border-top: 8px ridge aqua; }
tfoot tr.top td { border-top: 8px ridge lime; }
```

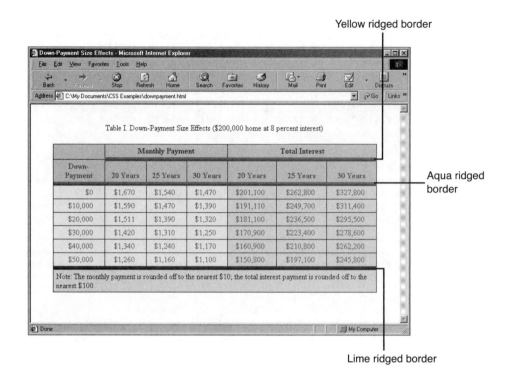

Figure 12.14: *Using CSS, you can set horizontal borders in a table.*

A few comments are in order for this example:

- **The first style (`tr.top th`) draws the top horizontal border**—It draws the border above TH cells nested inside a TR element with a "top" class set.

- **The second style (`tr.top th.none`) turns off the border above the Down-Payment cell**—It turns off the border above the TH cell with a "none" class set.

- **The third style (`tbody tr.top td`) draws a horizontal border that takes effect only in the TBODY row group**—It draws the border above the TD cells in the TR row with a "top" class set.

- **The third style (`tbody tr.top td`) draws a horizontal border that takes effect only in the TFOOT row group**—It draws the border above the TD cells in the TR row with a "top" class set.

NOTE

It would be nice to just use a row span (rowspan="2") to eliminate the border drawn above the Down-Payment cell, rather than setting a null border. Opera 5, however, flubs this up, displaying a gap that can't be removed between the lower spanned cell and the other cells in its row.

Adding Vertical Borders

You can also add vertical borders to help further highlight the important areas in your table (see Figure 12.15):

```
tr.top th { border-top: 8px ridge yellow; color: #c03; }
tr.top th.none { border-top: 0px; }
tbody tr.top td { border-top: 8px ridge aqua; }
tfoot tr.top td { border-top: 8px ridge lime; }
th.left { border-left: 8px ridge yellow; }
td.left { border-left: 8px ridge yellow; }
```

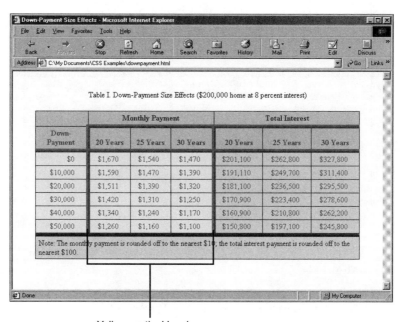

Yellow vertical borders

Figure 12.15: *Using CSS, you can set vertical borders in a table.*

This example uses the "left" class that you set earlier for some of the TH and TD elements, allowing you to use a class selectors (td.left and th.left) to assign a border to the left side of those elements. In the example, both of these styles are set to create the same border (an 8-pixel, ridged, yellow border), but you can just as easily set different colors, for instance, for these two styles.

Turning Off the Internal Borders

Right now, the internal borders between cells within the table are still being displayed. For a cleaner look, you can easily eliminate them. To do that, just edit your style sheet to delete the one-pixel borders that are set for the TH and TD elements, like this (see Figure 12.16):

```
th { padding: 4px 6px; border: 1px solid black; }
td { text-align: left; padding: 4px 6px; border: 1px solid black; }
```

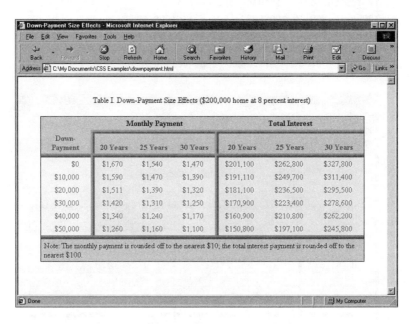

Figure 12.16: *The one-pixel internal borders within the table are eliminated.*

Adding a Border Around the Table

You can also add a fancier border around the outside of the table. Edit your style sheet to set a border around the outside of your table (see Figure 12.17):

```
table { border-collapse: collapse; border: 8px groove #f90; border-spacing: 0;
width: 90%; margin-left: auto; margin-right: auto; background: #ffc; }
```

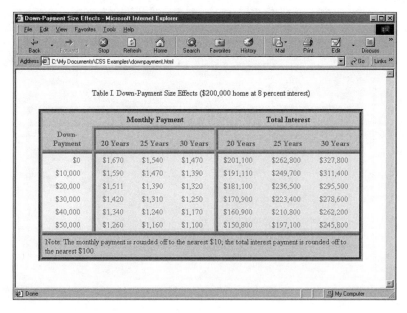

Figure 12.17: *You can add a fancier border around the outside of your table, too.*

You need to realize, however, that adding a border wider than a single pixel, in conjunction with setting border-collapse: collapse, causes Opera 5 to mess up displaying the border around the table. It doesn't cause the table to be unreadable or unusable in Opera 5, so you might decide you can live with this. A better alternative, however, is to simply delete the border-collapse: collapse property, relying on the CELLPADDING attribute to collapse the space between borders to zero, if you decide you want to set a border more than one-pixel wide around your table.

Using Background Images

You can add more visual appeal to your tables by using background images. Here's an example of displaying background images behind the THEAD and TFOOT row groups (see Figure 12.18):

```
thead tr th { vertical-align: bottom; color: navy; background: #fc9
url(mottle.gif); }
tbody tr td { text-align: right; padding-right: 1.5em; color: #c00; background:
transparent; }
tfoot tr td { color: #030; background: #fce url(tanback.jpg); }
```

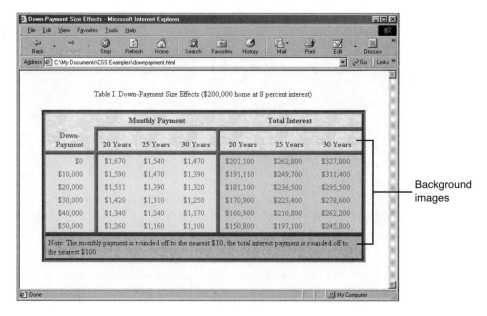

Figure 12.18: *Using background images in a table can add to its visual appeal.*

What's Next?

In this chapter, you learned about applying styles to HTML tables. You should now have a good understanding of how to control spacing, padding, and borders. You should also understand how to control the colors and backgrounds of row groups and column groups, as well as how to apply horizontal and vertical borders to your table.

In the next part, Part VI, "Getting Deeper Into Using Styles," you apply much of what you've learned so far, as well as new features not yet covered, in developing and designing some actual, real-world Web projects. In the next chapter, "Creating Menus and Interfaces," you create a variety of different menus and interfaces, including interactive boxed, floating, sidebar, and ribbon menus.

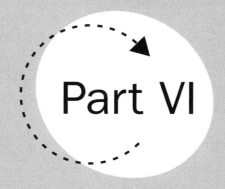

Part VI

Getting Deeper into Using Styles

Creating Menus and Interfaces

Creating Page Layouts and Site Designs

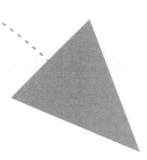

13

Creating Menus and Interfaces

With CSS you can design visually rich and interactive menu systems and user interfaces that can otherwise only be achieved through HTML in combination with the liberal use of tables and scripting or other programming technologies.

In this chapter, you learn to do the following:

- Create interactive menus
- Set up floating menus
- Create interactive sidebar menus
- Create ribbon menus

Using the Example HTML File

The example you use in this chapter is for a fictional computer consulting firm, Cramer Computer Consultants. The example HTML file, cramer-consult.html, should already be available, if you downloaded and extracted the example files to your working folder. You can also type in the example file, if you wish (see Figure 13.1):

Listing 13.1: CRAMER-CONSULT.HTML—Cramer Computer Consultants

```
<!DOCTYPE HTML PUBLIC "-//W3C//DTD HTML 4.01 Transitional//EN"
"http://www.w3.org/TR/html4/loose.dtd">

<html>
<head>
<title>Cramer Computer Consultants</title>
<style type="text/css">
body { color: black; background: #fc9; font-family: Arial, sans-serif; }
p { margin-left: 2em; margin-right: 2em; }
h1 { color: #fc0; background: #306; padding-left: 0.2em; padding-bottom: 0.1em;
margin-top: 0; border-bottom: 2px solid red; }
h2 { color: #306; background: #fc0; padding-left: 0.2em; padding-bottom: 0.1em;
border-bottom: 2px solid red; }
ul { position: relative; left: 8%; margin-top: 0; margin-bottom: 0; padding-top:
1em; padding-bottom: 1em; }
li { margin-top: 0; margin-bottom: 0; text-align: left; }
a { color: blue; background: transparent; }
</style>
</head>

<body>

<h1>Cramer Computer Consultants</h1>
<p>Beginning in 1984, CCC has provided comprehensive computer consulting services
unmatched by any of its competitors to government, educational, and business
customers, including hardware and software sales, after-sales support, network
design and installation, database application design, and data conversion
services.</p>

<ul><a name="menu"></a>
<li><a href="#part1">Hardware Sales & Support</a>
<li><a href="#part2">Software Sales & Support</a>
<li><a href="#part3">Network Sales & Support</a>
<li><a href="#part4">Custom Database Programming</a>
<li><a href="#part5">Data Conversion</a>
</ul>

<h2><a name="part1"></a>Hardware Sales & Support</h2>
<p>The size of our customer base and the diversity of their needs ensures that we
```

Listing 13.1: continued

```
can offer a breadth and depth of hardware sales and support services unmatched by
any competitors, all at discount prices! Our professional consultants can also
assist you making the correct hardware purchasing and upgrading decisions. We
make sure that you get the tools to do the job you want to do! With our own in-
house service department, we back up what we sell, with plans available for
onsite or offsite maintenance, troubleshooting, and repair.</p>

<p>Return to <a href="#menu">Menu</a>.</p>

<h2><a name="part2"></a>Software Sales, Training & Support</h2>
<p>Get ahead of the technology curve! Do you feel you're spending more time
chasing down gremlins than getting actual work done. The biggest software costs
aren't for what's inside the box, but for what comes after you've opened the box.
We first help you select the software that matches your needs, provide
professional on-site installation and configuration, provide training sessions
and materials, as well as providing ongoing after-sales support. We make sure
your employees have the right tools to do the job and that they know how to use
them!</p>

<p>Return to <a href="#menu">Menu</a>.</p>

<h2><a name="part3"></a>Network Design & Sales</h2>
<p>No other companies in the region have the professional expertise and
experience that CCC has in network and intranet design, sales, training, and
support. Don't get stuck with a network system that you'll outgrow and have to
scrap before you're through paying for it! Our professional consultants make sure
that you have network systems that fit your current needs and that can grow and
scale along with your organization or enterprise.</p>

<p>Return to <a href="#menu">Menu</a>.</p>

<h2><a name="part4"></a>Custom Database Application Design</h2>
<p>We specialize in Access, FoxPro, and SQL database application design,
installation, training, and support. Don't make an expensive mistake and hire
amateurs or college kids to do a job that requires real professional expertise
and experience. We make understanding our customers needs and providing timely
and finished solutions our very top priority.</p>

<p>Return to <a href="#menu">Menu</a>.</p>

<h2><a name="part5"></a>Data Conversion Services</h2>
<p>The computer world moves on, but data is forever, or at least it should be. Do
you need to move data from legacy archives so your personnel and/or customers can
access it through your PC network? Do you have stacks of mainframe tapes that
need to be converted to CD-R format? Do you need to transfer data from a legacy
database system to more modern systems, such as Access or FoxPro? Whatever your
needs, we've got the equipment and the expertise to provide solutions.</p>

<p>Return to <a href="#menu">Menu</a>.</p>

<hr>
<address>
```

Listing 13.1 continued

```
Cramer Computer Consultants<br>
E-Mail: <a href="mailto:contact@cramer-
consult.com">contact@yourdomain.com</a><br>
Web Address: <a href="http://www.cramer-consult.com/">http://www.cramer-
consult.com/</a>
</address>
</div>
</div>
</body>
</html>
```

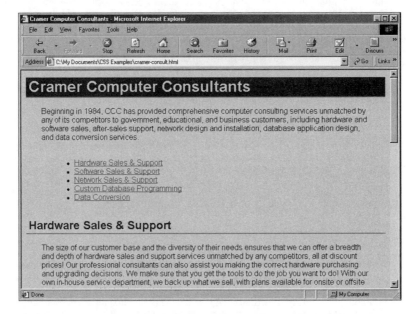

Figure 13.1: *The example file includes an ordinary link menu.*

I've already set some styles for you in the example file. For instance, a background color is set for the page and the paragraphs are indented in from the margins. Foreground colors, background colors, and bottom borders are set for the heading elements.

You're going to re-use this same example file for several different examples of creating menus and interfaces. For each example, I prompt you to resave the example file under a new name.

Creating Interactive Menus

In this section, you create three kinds of interactive menus, a simple interactive menu using roll-over links (p. 176), a more complex box menu, and a floating menu.

Creating a Simple Interactive Menu

The example file includes a link menu that jumps to the different sections of the page. It isn't particularly colorful, just the stock link blue, nor is it at all interactive.

Because you're reusing the example file for this chapter, go ahead and resave it in your working folder under another name (**cramer-consult1.html**, for instance).

A good deal can be done to jazz up this menu. Let's start by setting up roll-over links:

```
a { color: blue; ; background: transparent; font-weight: bold; }
a:link { color: red; background: transparent; }
a:visited { color: red; background: transparent; }
a:active { color: blue; background: lime; }
a:hover { color: #fc0; background: red; text-decoration: none; }
```

When you now open cramer-consult1.html in your browser, the foreground and background colors for the links change when you pass the mouse over the links, as shown in Figure 13.2.

CAUTION

Remember to always specify a:active next to last and a:hover last in the sequence of anchor pseudo-classes. Otherwise, your roll-over hover effect may not work.

✔ To review the reasons for this, see the caution in "Creating CSS Roll-Over Links," p. 176 (chapter 8).

Creating a Boxed Menu

Adding interactive and visually appealing menus and navigation bars to your pages helps make your site more accessible and more enjoyable to use. The easier and more fun your site is to use, the more likely visitors will want to stick around or return for more.

For this example, just continue working with the same example file, cramer-consult1.html, that you created in the previous section.

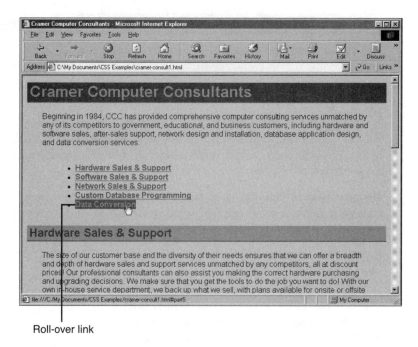

Roll-over link

Figure 13.2: *Just adding roll-over links to a menu adds interactivity and helps to liven up a page.*

To make your interactive menu more visually appealing, you can nest it inside of a bordered box, as well as adjust the colors of the interactive menu links to better set them off against the box's background color. To do that, just insert the following styles into your style sheet:

```
a { color: blue; background: transparent; font-weight: bold; }
a:link { color: red; background: transparent; }
a:visited { color: red; background: transparent; }
a:active { color: blue; background: lime; }
a:hover { color: #fc0; background: red; text-decoration: none; }
div.menu { color: #fc0; background: #306; width: 50%; margin-right: auto; margin-left: auto; margin-top: 0; border: 6px #fc0 ridge; }
div a { font-weight: bold; font-family: Arial, sans-serif; }
div a:link { color: #ffc; background: transparent; }
div a:visited { color: #ffc; background: transparent; }
div a:active { color: blue; background: lime; }
div a:hover { color: red; background: #fc0; text-decoration: none; }
```

Next, in the body of your document, bracket the menu codes with the div.menu style you just created:

```
<div class="menu">
<ul><a name="menu"></a>
<li><a href="#part1">Hardware Sales & Support</a>
```

```
<li><a href="#part2">Software Sales & Support</a>
<li><a href="#part3">Network Sales & Support</a>
<li><a href="#part4">Custom Database Programming</a>
<li><a href="#part5">Data Conversion</a>
</ul>
</div>
```

✔ This produces a centered menu in Netscape 6 and Opera 5, but not in Internet Explorer 5.5 for Windows, which displays the menu box flush with the left margin. As covered earlier the in "Horizontally Aligning Block Elements," p. 214 (chapter 10), the fix for this is to insert the menu's DIV element inside of another, but center-aligned, DIV element, like this (see Figure 13.3):

```
<div style="text-align: center">
<div class="menu">
<ul><a name="menu"></a>
<li><a href="#part1">Hardware Sales & Support</a>
<li><a href="#part2">Software Sales & Support</a>
<li><a href="#part3">Network Sales & Support</a>
<li><a href="#part4">Custom Database Programming</a>
<li><a href="#part5">Data Conversion</a>
</ul>
</div>
</div>
```

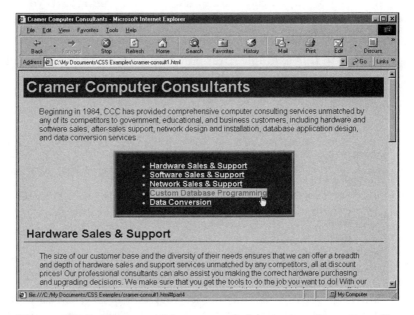

Figure 13.3: *For something more elaborate, set the menu off against a bordered box and background, and then center it.*

The main things to notice about this example are

- **The "menu" division is centered.** In the div.menu style, the margin-left: auto and margin-right: auto properties center the box, except in Internet Explorer 5.5 for Windows, which due to a bug needs to have the box nested inside of an additional, center-aligned, DIV element.

- **Links nested inside of a DIV element are assigned a different appearance from other links on the page.** Contextual styles (div a, div a:link, etc.) specify display settings only for hypertext links that are nested inside of a DIV element. Other links, such as displayed in the ADDRESS element, which is nested inside of the BODY element, retain the display settings previously specified for links (through the a, a:link, and other styles).

✔ To review previous coverage of creating boxes using borders and backgrounds, see "Setting Borders," p. 198 (chapter 9).

Creating a Floating Menu

For a variation, you can create a menu that floats at the right margin, with the initial paragraph flowing around the left side of the menu.

For this example, continue to use the example HTML you've been creating, but save it in your working folder under a new name (**cramer-consult2.html**, for instance).

To create this example, first edit the p, h1, and dir.menu styles, setting the top margin for each to one em, as shown here:

```
<style type="text/css">
body { color: black; background: #fc9; font-family: Arial, sans-serif; }
p { margin-left: 2em; margin-right: 2em; margin-top: 1em; }
h1 { color: #fc0; background: #306; padding-left: 0.2em; padding-bottom: 0.1em;
margin-top: 1em; margin-bottom: 0; border-bottom: 2px solid red; }
h2 { color: #306; background: #fc0; padding-left: 0.2em; padding-bottom: 0.1em;
border-bottom: 2px solid red; }
ul { position: relative; left: 8%; margin-top: 0; margin-bottom: 0; padding-top:
1em; padding-bottom: 1em; }
li { margin-top: 0; margin-bottom: 0; text-align: left; }
a { color: blue; background: transparent; font-weight: bold; }
a:link { color: red; background: transparent; }
a:visited { color: red; background: transparent; }
a:active { color: blue; background: lime; }
a:hover { color: #fc0; background: red; text-decoration: none; }
div.menu { float: right; color: #fc0; background: #306; width: 50%; margin-top:
1em; border: 6px #fc0 ridge; }
```

```
div a { font-weight: bold; font-family: Arial, sans-serif; }
div a:link { color: #ffc; background: transparent; }
div a:visited { color: #ffc; background: transparent; }
div a:active { color: blue; background-color: lime; background: transparent; }
div a:hover { color: red; background: #fc0; text-decoration: none; }
</style>
```

Next, highlight and cut the menu codes from their previous position (following the first text paragraph), and then paste them at the location shown in the following example:

```
<h1>Cramer Computer Consultants</h1>

<div style="text-align: center">
<div class="menu">
<ul><a name="menu"></a>
<li><a href="#part1">Hardware Sales & Support</a>
<li><a href="#part2">Software Sales & Support</a>
<li><a href="#part3">Network Sales & Support</a>
<li><a href="#part4">Custom Database Programming</a>
<li><a href="#part5">Data Conversion</a>
</ul>
</div>
</div>

<p>Beginning in 1984, CCC has provided comprehensive computer consulting services
unmatched by any of its competitors to government, educational, and business
customers, including hardware and software sales, after-sales support, network
design and installation, database application design, and data conversion
services.</p>
```

Finally, edit the following H2 element, to keep it from also flowing around the floating menu and to make sure that sufficient vertical spacing is inserted above it, like this (see Figure 13.4):

```
Beginning in 1984, CCC has provided comprehensive computer consulting services
unmatched by any of its competitors to government, educational, and business
customers, including hardware and software sales, after-sales support, network
design and installation, database application design, and data conversion
services.</p>

<h2 style="clear: right; margin-top: 1.5em"><a name="part1"></a>Hardware Sales &
Support</h2>
```

Now, when you click any of the menu links, you jump to the link's corresponding target anchor. For instance, the second link (`<a href="#part2">Software Sales & Support</a>`) jumps to the location marked by the target anchor (`<a name="part2"></a>`), as shown in Figure 13.5.

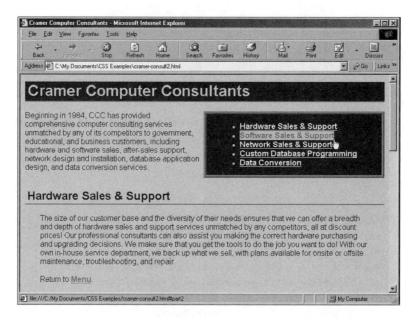

Figure 13.4: *The menu box is floated at the right margin.*

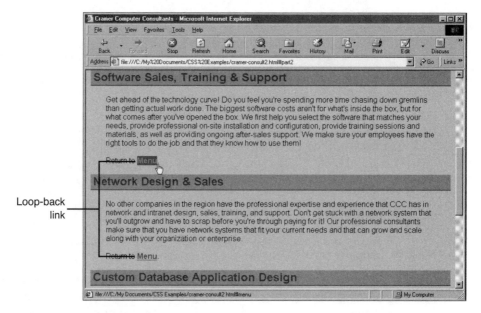

Figure 13.5: *Each menu link jumps to a corresponding location in the HTML document.*

The callout for Figure 13.5 points out what is referred to as a *loop-back link*. This link loops back to another target anchor, but this time it's located at the start of the menu box codes. Including loop-back links at the end of any subsections in your document is a good idea, if only to cue a visitor that he or she can easily return to the menu to select additional options.

✔ To review previous coverage of floating elements and object on your page, see "Floating Elements," p. 219 (chapter 10).

Creating an Interactive Sidebar Menu

For this example, you create an interactive sidebar menu. To create this example, reopen cramer-consult.html from your working folder and resave it as **cramer-consult3.html**.

To get started, add the following codes at the top of your example file:

```
<body>

<a name="menu"></a>
<h1>Cramer Computer Consultants</h1>

<div class="side">

<p>
<a href="#part1">Hardware</a>
<a href="#part2">Software</a>
<a href="#part3">Networking</a>
<a href="#part4">Databases</a>
<a href="#part5">Conversion</a>
</p>

</div>

<div class="main">

<p>Beginning in 1984, CCC has provided comprehensive computer consulting services
unmatched by any of its competitors to government, educational, and business
customers, including hardware and software sales, after-sales support, network
design and installation, database application design, and data conversion
services.</p>
```

Now, add the end tag for the "main" DIV start tag you inserted just above your H1 heading:

```
<address>
Cramer Computer Consultants<br>
E-Mail: <a href="mailto:contact@cramer-
consult.com">contact@yourdomain.com</a><br>
```

```
Web Address: <a href="http://www.cramer-consult.com/">http://www.cramer-
consult.com/</a>
</address>

</div>

</body>
```

You've now created two document divisions (the "side" and "main" DIV elements). You now just need to create styles to position these divisions side-by-side, with the first division functioning as a sidebar menu and the second containing the main content of your page (see Figure 13.6):

```
<style type="text/css">
body { color: black; background: #fc9; font-family: Arial, sans-serif; }
p { margin-left: 2em; margin-right: 2em; }
h1 { color: #fc0; background: #306; padding-left: 0.2em; padding-bottom: 0.1em;
margin-top: 0; border-bottom: 2px solid red; }
h2 { color: #306; background: #fc0; padding-left: 0.2em; padding-bottom: 0.1em;
border-bottom: 2px solid red; }
ul { position: relative; left: 8%; margin-top: 0; margin-bottom: 0; padding-top:
1em; padding-bottom: 1em; }
li { margin-top: 0; margin-bottom: 0; text-align: left; }
a { color: blue; background: transparent; }

div.side { position: absolute; top: 4em; left: 0; width: 145px; height: 90em;
padding: 0.5em 0 0; margin-left: 0.6em; background: #099; }

div.main { position: absolute; top: 4em; left: 155px; height: 90em; margin: 0
0.5em 0 0; padding: 0.5em; background: #fec; }
div.side p { margin: 0 0 0 12px; }

</style>
```

Although the sidebar menu isn't created yet, the basic layout for the page has been. The key things to note so far are

- **The two document divisions ("side" and "main") are positioned on the page using absolute positioning.** Both document divisions are positioned four ems from the top of the document, with the div.side division positioned flush with the left margin and the div.main division positioned 155 pixels in from the left margin.

- **The width of the sidebar division (`div.side`) is set at 145 pixels.** This leaves a vertical gutter of ten pixels between it and the main division (`div.main`).

- **A left margin is set for the sidebar division and left and right margins are set for the main division.** A left margin of 0.6 ems is set for the sidebar division, and left and right margins of 0.5 ems are set for the main division.

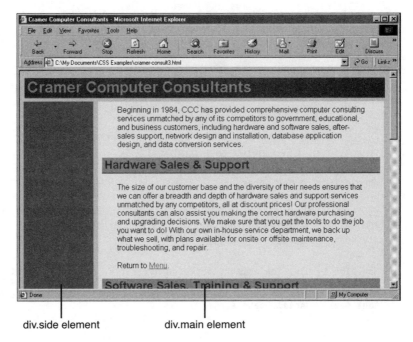

div.side element   div.main element

Figure 13.6: *The sidebar layout is created, but the sidebar menu styles still need to be created.*

- **Background colors are set for the sidebar and main divisions.** This set them off from the document background.

- **Heights of 315 percent are set for the sidebar and main divisions.** This helps ensure that both divisions extend to the bottom of the page. This works reasonably well for the length of the example page, with some margin for variability in document length added at the bottom. The actual percentages that you need to set depend on the length of the main division's content. The only possibly negative impact here is simply that the sidebar division's height doesn't match that of the main division, because the height setting is a minimum (not a maximum) setting.

- **Top padding is set for the sidebar division and padding all the way around for the main division.** Top padding of 0.5 ems is set for the sidebar division, and padding all the way around of 0.5 ems is set for the main division. No left or right padding is set for the sidebar division, partly to allow as much space as possible for content, but also to avoid Internet Explorer 5.5 for Window's box model bug.

- **Left and right margins and top padding is set for the main division.** Left and right margins of 0.5 ems, as well as a top padding of 0.5 ems, are set for the main division.

- **A left margin is set for paragraphs nested inside of the sidebar division.** The div.side p contextual style sets a 12-pixel left margin for paragraphs nested inside the sidebar division.

Lastly, add the styles to your style sheet to create roll-over menu buttons in your document's sidebar (see Figure 13.7):

```
div.side { position: absolute; top: 4em; left: 0; width: 9em; height: 315%;
margin-left: 0.5em; background: #099; }

div.main { position: absolute; top: 4em; left: 155px; height: 315%; padding-top:
1em; margin: 0.5em; padding: 0.5em; background: #fec; }
div.side p { margin: 0 0 0 12px; }

div.side a, div.side a:link, div.side a:visited, div.side a:active { display:
block; padding: 5px; border: 3px #fc0 outset; margin-bottom: 0.5em; margin-top:
0.5em; color: #cf6; background: #066; font-weight: bold; text-decoration: none;
font-family: Arial, sans-serif; }

/* Box model hack */

div.side a, div.side a:link, div.side a:visited, div.side a:active { width:
116px; voice-family: "\"}\""; voice-family: inherit; width: 100px; }
html>body div.side a { width: 100px }

/* End of box model hack */

div.side a:hover { color: red; background: #fc0; border: 3px #09f outset; }
a { color: blue; font-weight: bold; }
a:link { color: red; }
a:visited { color: red; }
a:active { color: blue; background: lime; }
a:hover { color: #fc0; background: red; text-decoration: none; }
```

Here are some things to note about this example:

- **The display property is used to set the A elements (links) as block elements**. The display: block property set for the div.side a, div.side a:link, div.side a:visited, and div.side a.active contextual selectors has the effect of specifying that the A element, normally an inline element, is treated in this case as a block element. Not only does this display each link on its own line, but it also lets you assign a width for the element, which can't be done for an inline element.

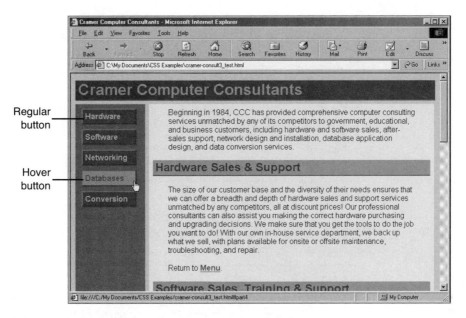

Regular button

Hover button

Figure 13.7: *A sidebar button menu is added.*

- **The "box model hack" is used to overcome Internet Explorer's 5.5 for Windows' problems with the CSS box formatting model.** This has the effect of tricking that browser to not include any padding or borders within the width of the element. Unlike other situations, where nested DIV elements can be used to separate the width setting from any padding or border settings, in this situation there really is no other recourse, if you want to have menu buttons display at the same width in Internet Explorer 5.5 for Windows and other CSS1-supporting browsers, such as Netscape 6 or Opera 5, for instance.

NOTE

For more information on how to use the box model hack, see the explanation of the person who came up with it, Tantek Çelik, at `http://www.tantek.com/CSS/Examples/`.

- **Different color, background, and border properties are set for a link's hover state (a:hover) than are set for its other states (a:link; a:visited; and a:active).** Thus when the mouse hovers over the button link, its appearance changes to that specified for its hover state.

- **Underlining of hover links is turned off.** The `text-decoration: none` property turns off the underlining for hover links, and a bold font-weight is set to give more weight to the button labels.

- **Separate properties are set for links in the sidebar and in other parts of the document.** The a, a:link, a:visited, a:active, and a:hover styles set display characteristics for links located in other parts of the document (not located in the sidebar).

NOTE

It won't matter how snazzy your menu is if your site is poorly organized. Plan the structure of your site, in other words, before working on its appearance. Often, the simpler the structure the better—you don't want 30 top-level menu options running down the side of your page, for instance. At the same time, you want important information and resources to never be more than a click or two away—don't bury that price list six levels deep!

✔ To review previous coverage of using relative and absolute positioning, see "Positioning Elements," p. 233 (chapter 10).

CAUTION

Relative and absolute positioning are CSS features that are guaranteed to mess up the display of your page in any browser that either doesn't support these features or supports them poorly. For that reason, whenever including these features in your page, you should use one of the methods or techniques discussed in Chapter 16, "Providing for Backward Compatibility," to shield partially compliant and non-compliant browsers from accessing your style sheet.

Remember that the position property is part of CSS2, not CSS1. That all current major browsers do support both relative and absolute positioning is a bonus—they aren't currently required to support these features to be considered CSS-compliant.

Creating a Ribbon Menu

You can also create interactive menus and navigation bars that run horizontally across the page. In this section, I show you how to create a type of navigation bar that is sometimes referred to as a *ribbon menu*. It is called that because it runs across the page like a ribbon, taking up a minimum of vertical space on the page. This type of menu is often used as a *navigation bar*; a navigation bar is a horizontal menu running across the top or bottom of a Web page that enables you to navigate through the different parts of a Web site.

For this example, continue using the same example you created for the sidebar menu example. Just resave it as **cramer-consult4.html**, so you can separately refer back to this example, as well as the others you created in this chapter.

First, edit the top of the body of your document, to set it up for creating your ribbon menu (leave the remainder as it is):

```
<body>

<a name="menu"></a>

<div class="ribbonwide">
<div class="ribbon">
<div class="ribbonpad">
<p>
<a href="home.html"><span>Home</span></a>
<a href="home.html"><span>Products</span></a>
<a href="home.html"><span>Services</span></a>
<a href="home.html"><span>Support</span></a>
<a href="home.html"><span>Contact</span></a>
</p>
</div>
</div>
</div>

<div class="bannerwide">
<div class="banner">
<h1>Cramer Computer Consultants</h1>
</div>
</div>
```

Now, create the styles for the your ribbon menu. Edit your style sheet so it matches what is shown here (see Figure 13.8):

```
<style type="text/css">
body { color: black; background: #fc9; font-family: Arial, sans-serif; }
p { margin-left: 2em; margin-right: 2em; }
h1 { color: #fc6; background: #306; padding-top: 0.5em; padding-bottom: 0.2em;
margin: 0; }
h2 { color: #306; background: #fc0; padding-left: 0.2em; padding-bottom: 0.1em;
border-bottom: 2px solid red; }
ul { position: relative; left: 8%; margin-top: 0; margin-bottom: 0; padding-top:
1em; padding-bottom: 1em; }
li { margin-top: 0; margin-bottom: 0; text-align: left; }
a { color: blue; background: transparent; }

div.side { position: absolute; top: 6.5em; left: 0; width: 145px; height: 90em;
padding-top: 0.5em 0 0; margin-left: 0.6em; background: #099; }
div.main { position: absolute; top: 6.5em; left: 155px; height: 90em; margin: 0
0.5em 0 0; padding: 0.5em; background: #fec; }

div.side p { margin: 0 0 0 12px; }
div.side a, div.side a:link, div.side a:visited, div.side a:active { display:
block; padding: 5px; border: 3px #fc0 outset; margin-bottom: 0.5em; margin-top:
```

```
0.5em; color: #cf6; background: #066; font-weight: bold; text-decoration: none;
font-family: Arial, sans-serif; }

/* Box model hack */

div.side a, div.side a:link, div.side a:visited, div.side a:active { width:
116px; voice-family: "\"}\""; voice-family: inherit; width: 100px; }
html>body div.side a { width: 100px }

/* End of box model hack */

div.side a:hover { color: red; background: #fc0; border: 3px #09f outset; }
a { color: blue; background: transparent; font-weight: bold; }
a:link { color: red; background: transparent; }
a:visited { color: red; background: transparent; }
a:active { color: blue; background: lime; }
a:hover { color: #fc0; background: red; text-decoration: none; }

div.bannerwide { color: lime; background: #306; text-align: center; width: 100%;
border-bottom: 2px solid red; }
div.banner { color: #fc6; background: #306; text-align: center; width: 750px;
margin-left: 0; margin-right: auto; }

div.ribbonwide { background: #900; text-align: center; width: 100%; }
div.ribbon { background: #900; text-align: center; width: 750px; margin-left:
auto; margin-right: auto; }
div.ribbonpad { padding: 0.2em 0; }

div.ribbon p { margin: -2px 5px 0 5px; font-family: Arial, sans-serif; font-size:
14px; text-align: center; font-weight: bold; }
div.ribbon a { margin: 0 6px; text-decoration: none; }
div.ribbon span { padding: 0 30px; margin: 0; }
div.ribbon a:link, div.ribbon a:visited, div.ribbon a:active { color: white;
background: #900; }
div.ribbon a:hover { color: red; background: #ffce63; }

</style>
```

One of the primary features of this example is that the width of the page is
protected against contracting to less than 750 pixels across. This is to allow
the ribbon menu sufficient horizontal space for its display. It also generally
displays in a maximized browser window on a system running at 800×600
screen resolution without displaying horizontal scroll bars. If a browser is
running at a lower screen resolution or has a non-maximized window that
is less than 800 pixels across, the banner doesn't collapse to less than a
750-pixel width, although the text in the main window area does.

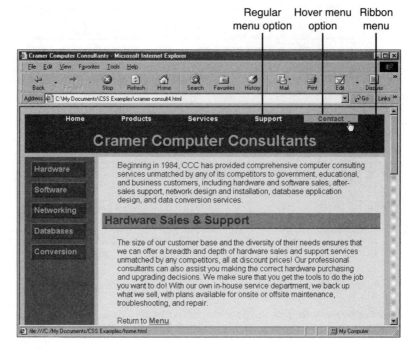

Figure 13.8: A ribbon menu is added to the top of the banner heading.

On the other hand, if a browser window is maximized on a system running at a 1024×768 screen resolution, for instance, or in a non-maximized browser window that is wider than 800 pixels across, this example scales upward to fill the additional horizontal spacing (see Figure 13.9).

To create this feature, two styles are created for both the ribbon menu (ribbonwide and ribbon) and the banner (bannerwide and banner). The first (the "wide" styles) set the width at 100 percent, and the second set the width at 750 pixels.

Some other things to take note of in this example are

- **Both the ribbon menu and the banner headline are centered.** This is done by setting left-margin: auto and right-margin: auto in the div.banner and div.ribbon styles, and setting text-align: center in the div.bannerwide and div.ribbonwide style. As noted previously, the text-align: center property assigned to the bracketing division is necessary to trick Internet Explorer 5.5 for Windows into centering the nested division.

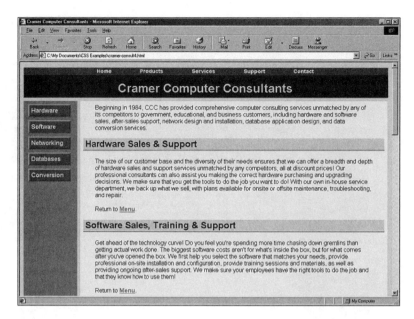

Figure 13.9: *The ribbon menu example scales up to fill the width of a browser window running maximized at a 1024×768 screen resolution.*

- **The div.ribbonpad style controls the amount of vertical padding that is added above and below the ribbon menu options.** It is currently set at 0.2 ems of vertical padding. Just increase or decrease this value to expand or contract the amount of vertical padding.

- **The div.ribbon a style sets the horizontal margins that separate the ribbon menu options.** You might notice this separation when you turn on the hover style by passing the mouse over an option. Just increase or decrease this value to expand or contract the horizontal margin spacing of the menu options.

- **The div.ribbon span style sets the internal horizontal padding for the ribbon menu options.** You might also notice this when you pass the mouse over the options. Without this padding being set, the background color displayed when the mouse hovers over an option is only as wide as the option text.

- The link styles that create the interactive hover effect work exactly the same as the other examples in this chapter.

What's Next?

In this chapter, you learned how to create a variety of different menus and navigation bars, including interactive roll-over menus, sidebar menus, and ribbon menus.

In Chapter 14, "Creating Page Layouts and Site Designs," you learn more about creating a total look for your page or site, including understanding the virtue of simplicity, using fixed sidebar backgrounds, creating a newspaper-column layout, creating a three-column page layout, and using an external style sheet to control the look and feel of a whole site.

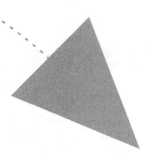

14

Creating Page Layouts and Site Designs

Although you've already worked with a number of different examples of laying out pages, you haven't focused specifically on page layout and site design up to this point. You should now have learned all of the key features of CSS and gained the confidence to start putting all the pieces together in creating your own page layouts and site designs. In this chapter, you learn about the following:

- Keeping it simple
- Creating scrolling sidebar designs
- Creating multi-column page layouts
- Creating site designs

Using the Example HTML Files

In this chapter, you use several different example files. If you've downloaded the example files from this book's site and extracted them to your working folder, all of the example files used in this chapter should already be available to you. Just follow the instructions provided in the example sections to open and resave the starting example files used in those sections. Listings are also provided, in case you prefer to type the starting examples in for yourself.

Keeping It Simple

Often, the best design for a page or site is a simple one. The critical decisions about how your site should be designed should be functional ones, such as how best to facilitate a visitor's access to the information that you're presenting. This involves trying to insure that a visitor can navigate and move throughout your pages and site without a lot of extra clicks, windows, or scrolling. Preferably, all of the key areas in a page or site should be a click away, without the need for extra windows or undue scrolling. Although the visual appeal of a site can be part of what makes a site enjoyable for a visitor, it is the ease and facility with which a visitor can move around and access the different parts of your page or site that play the largest role in whether someone visiting your page or site has an enjoyable or frustrating experience. The most whiz-bang front page design means very little if visitors can't find what they're looking for or have to jump through a bunch of hoops to get to it.

Another consideration is that with simpler page and site designs, you're liable to run into fewer compatibility problems and issues, whether due to flawed or incomplete CSS support by earlier first-generation CSS-browsers or the remaining bugs and quirks of the current second-generation of CSS-browsers. Getting a fully functional CSS-formatted page or site up and running is much easier when you start out relatively simple, rather than planning an elaborate or grand design right out of the gate. In other words, get used to riding with the training wheels on first, before trying to ride with no hands.

To show you just how simple a page layout can be while still being both attractive and effective, I'm going to have you create a simple layout using the Declaration of Independence. This is an example of creating a page layout suitable for a text-intensive page or site. To make it easier for you to create this example, I've created a starting example file, independence.html, that you can use to get started creating this example. You can use Listing 14.1 to type in the starting example yourself, if you wish (see Figure 14.1).

NOTE

If you're typing in the following example text, feel free to copy and paste paragraph and list elements, rather than type them all in. The main thing is that you have a good amount of text to work with, with at least one list of bullet items. You'll be reusing this example a little further on, when you learn how to create a newspaper-column layout.

Listing 14.1: INDEPENDENCE.HTML—The Declaration of Independence

```html
<!DOCTYPE HTML PUBLIC "-//W3C//DTD HTML 4.01 Transitional//EN"
"http://www.w3.org/TR/html4/loose.dtd">
<html>

<head>
<title>U.S. History: Declaration of Independence</title>
<style type="text/css">

</style>
</head>
<body>

<h1>The Declaration of Independence</h1>
<h2>In Congress, July 4, 1776</h2>

<a name="top"></a>
<p>When in the Course of human events, it becomes necessary for one people to
dissolve the political bands which have connected them with another, and to
assume among the powers of the earth, the separate and equal station to which the
Laws of Nature and of Nature's God entitle them, a decent respect to the opinions
of mankind requires that they should declare the causes which impel them to the
separation.</p>

<p>We hold these truths to be self-evident, that all men are created equal, that
they are endowed by their Creator with certain unalienable Rights, that among
these are Life, Liberty, and the pursuit of Happiness. That to secure these
rights, Governments are instituted among Men, deriving their just powers from the
consent of the governed. That whenever any Form of Government becomes destructive
of these ends, it is the Right of the People to alter or to abolish it, and to
institute new Government, laying its foundation on such principles and organizing
its powers in such form, as to them shall seem most likely to effect their Safety
and Happiness.</p>

<p>Prudence, indeed, will dictate that Governments long established should not be
changed for light and transient causes; and accordingly all experience hath
shewn, that mankind are more disposed to suffer, while evils are sufferable, than
to right themselves by abolishing the forms to which they are accustomed.</p>

<p>But when a long train of abuses and usurpations, pursuing invariably the same
object evinces a design to reduce them under absolute Despotism, it is their
right, it is their duty, to throw off such Government, and to provide new Guards
for their future security.</p>
```

Listing 14.1: continued

```
<p>Such has been the patient sufferance of these Colonies; and such is now the
necessity which constrains them to alter their former Systems of Government. The
history of the present King of Great Britain is a history of repeated injuries
and usurpations, all having in direct object the establishment of an absolute
Tyranny over these States. To prove this, let Facts be submitted to a candid
world.</p>


<p>He has refused his Assent to Laws, the most wholesome and necessary for the
public good.</p>


<p>He has forbidden his Governors to pass Laws of immediate and pressing
importance, unless suspended in their operation till his Assent should be
obtained, and when so suspended, he has utterly neglected to attend to them.</p>

<p>He has refused to pass other Laws for the accommodation of large districts of
people, unless those people would relinquish the right of Representation in the
Legislature, a right inestimable to them and formidable to tyrants only.</p>

<p>He has called together legislative bodies at places unusual, uncomfortable,
and distant from the depository of their public Records, for the sole purpose of
fatiguing them into compliance with his measures.</p>

<p>He has dissolved Representative Houses repeatedly, for opposing with manly
firmness his invasions on the rights of the people.</p>

<p>He has refused for a long time, after such dissolutions, to cause others to be
elected; whereby the Legislative powers, incapable of Annihilation, have returned
to the People at large for their exercise; the State remaining in the meantime
exposed to all the dangers of invasion from without, and convulsions within.</p>


<p>He has endeavoured to prevent the population of these States; for that purpose
obstructing the Laws for Naturalization of Foreigners; refusing to pass others to
encourage their migrations hither, and raising the conditions of new
Appropriations of Lands.</p>

<p>He has obstructed the Administration of Justice, by refusing his Assent to
Laws for establishing Judiciary powers.</p>

<p>He has made Judges dependent on his Will alone, for the tenure of their
offices, and the amount and payment of their salaries.</p>

<p>He has erected a multitude of New Offices, and sent hither swarms of Officers
to harass our people, and eat out their substance.</p>

<p>He has kept among us, in times of peace, Standing Armies, without the consent
of our legislatures.</p>

<p>He has affected to render the Military independent of and superior to the
Civil power.</p>
```

Listing 14.1: continued

```
<p>He has combined with others to subject us to a jurisdiction foreign to our
constitution and unacknowledged by our laws; giving his Assent to their Acts of
pretended Legislation:</p>

<ul>
<li>For protecting them by a mock Trial from punishment for any Murders which
they should commit on the Inhabitants of these States:
<li>For cutting off our Trade with all parts of the world:
<li>For imposing Taxes on us without our Consent:
<li>For depriving us in many cases of the benefits of Trial by Jury:
<li>For transporting us beyond Seas to be tried for pretended offences:
<li>For abolishing the free System of English Laws in a neighbouring Province,
establishing therein an arbitrary government, and enlarging its Boundaries so as
to render it at once an example and fit instrument for introducing the same
absolute rule into these Colonies:
<li>For taking away our Charters, abolishing our most valuable Laws and altering
fundamentally the Forms of our Governments:
<li>For suspending our own Legislatures, and declaring themselves invested with
power to legislate for us in all cases whatsoever.
</ul>

<p>He has abdicated Government here by declaring us out of his Protection and
waging War against us.</p>

<p>He has plundered our seas, ravaged our Coasts, burnt our towns, and destroyed
the lives of our people.</p>

<p>He is at this time transporting large Armies of foreign Mercenaries to
complete the works of death, desolation and tyranny, already begun with
circumstances of cruelty and perfidy scarcely paralleled in the most barbarous
ages, and totally unworthy the Head of a civilized nation.</p>

<p>He has constrained our fellow Citizens taken Captive on the high Seas to bear
Arms against their Country, to become the executioners of their friends and
Brethren, or to fall themselves by their Hands.</p>

<p>He has excited domestic insurrections amongst us, and has endeavoured to bring
on the inhabitants of our frontiers, the merciless Indian Savages, whose known
rule of warfare is an undistinguished destruction of all ages, sexes and
conditions.</p>

<p>In every stage of these Oppressions We have Petitioned for Redress in the most
humble terms. Our repeated Petitions have been answered only by repeated injury.
A Prince, whose character is thus marked by every act which may define a Tyrant,
is unfit to be the ruler of a free people.</p>

<p>Nor have We been wanting in attentions to our British brethren.</p>

<ul>
<li>We have warned them from time to time of attempts by their legislature to
```

Listing 14.1: continued

```
extend an unwarrantable jurisdiction over us. We have reminded them of the
circumstances of our emigration
and settlement here.
<li>We have appealed to their native justice and magnanimity, and we have
conjured them by the ties of our common kindred to disavow these usurpations,
which would inevitably interrupt our connections and correspondence.
</ul>

<p>They too have been deaf to the voice of justice and of consanguinity. We must,
therefore, acquiesce in the necessity, which denounces our Separation, and hold
them, as we hold the rest of mankind, Enemies in War, in Peace Friends.</p>

<p>We, therefore, the Representatives of the United States of America, in General
Congress, Assembled, appealing to the Supreme Judge of the world for the
rectitude of our intentions, do, in the Name, and by the authority of the good
People of these Colonies, solemnly publish and declare.</p>

<p>That these United Colonies are, and of Right ought to be Free and Independent
States; that they are Absolved from all Allegiance to the British Crown, and that
all political connection between them and the State of Great Britain is  and
ought to be totally dissolved; and that as Free and Independent States, they have
full Power to levy War, conclude Peace, contract Alliances, establish Commerce,
and to do all other Acts and Things which Independent States may of right do.</p>

<p>And for the support of this Declaration, with a firm reliance on the
protection of Divine Providence, we mutually pledge to each other our Lives, our
Fortunes, and our sacred Honor.</p>

<p>Return to <a href="home.html">Home</a>.</p>

<address>
John Smith<br>
E-Mail: <a href="mailto:jsmith@us-history.com">jsmith@us-history.com</a><br>
Web Address: <a href="http://www.us-history.com/">http://www.us-history.com/</a>
</address>

</body>
</html>
```

You'll be reusing this example file later, so go ahead and resave it now in your working folder as **independence1.html**.

Right now, there are no display characteristics specified for this page, other than the default display characteristics that are determined by the HTML coding. To get started creating a more appealing and effective layout for the information in this page, use document divisions to highlight the different areas of the page. First, mark up the HTML code with the document divisions you're using. To do that, edit the top of your page's body to add the following codes:

```
<div class="top">
<div class="padtop"
<h1>The Declaration of Independence</h1>
<h2>In Congress, July 4, 1776</h2>
</div>
</div>

<div class="main">
<div class="padmain">
<a name="top"></a>
<p class="first"><span class="drop">W</span>hen in the Course of human events,
it becomes necessary for one people to dissolve the political bands which have
connected them with another, and to assume among the powers of the earth, the
separate and equal station to which the Laws of Nature and of Nature's God
entitle them, a decent respect to the opinions of mankind requires that they
should declare the causes which impel them to the separation.</p>
```

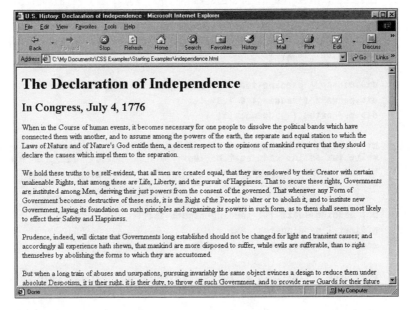

Figure 14.1: *Starting out, the example file contains only structural elements defined using HTML, without any display characteristics yet specified using CSS.*

Next, edit the code at the bottom of your page's body, like this:

```
<p>Return to <a href="home.html">Home</a>.</p>
</div>
</div>

<div class="bottom">
<div class="padbottom">
```

```
<address>
John Smith<br>
E-Mail: <a href="mailto:jsmith@us-history.com">jsmith@us-history.com</a><br>
Web Address: <a href="http://www.us-history.com/">http://www.us-history.com/</a>
</address>
</div>
</div>
```

You now need to create the styles to specify the display characteristics you want applied to the document divisions you just added to your HTML file. Edit your file to add the following styles (see Figure 14.2):

```
<style type="text/css">

body { background: #fc9; color: black; margin: 10px; }

div.top { background: url(blackmarb.jpg) #039; color: black; padding-left: 15px;
padding-right: 15px; margin-bottom: 0; }
div.main { background: url(paper2.gif) #ffc; color: black; margin-top: 15px; }
div.bottom { background: url(tanback.jpg) #cfc; color: navy; text-align: center;
margin-top: 10px; }

div.padtop { padding-top: 0; padding-bottom: 5px; }
div.padmain { padding: 0 1.5% 1%; }
div.padbottom { padding: 1%; }

h1 { color: #fc0; background: transparent; text-align: center; border-bottom:
white 1px solid; padding-top: 10px; padding-bottom: 10px; margin-top: 0;}
h2 { color: #cf9; background: transparent; text-align: center;  padding-bottom:
0; }

p { padding-left: 1%; padding-right: 1%; }
p.first { padding-top: 2%; }
address { padding-top: 1%; padding-bottom: 1%; }

span.drop { float: left; font-size: 40px; font-weight: bold; color: maroon;
background: transparent; margin-top: -3px; margin-bottom: -5px; }

</style>
```

NOTE

This example utilizes three background images that are included with the example files that can be downloaded from this book's Web site (http://www.callihan.com/cssbook/). If you want you can substitute background images of your own choosing—just substitute a darker background image for blackmarb.jpg and lighter background images for paper2.gif and tanback.jpg.

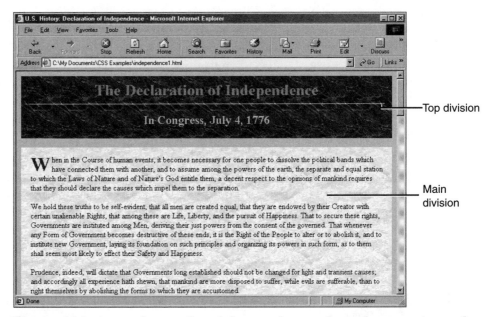

Top division

Main division

Figure 14.2: A page layout doesn't have to be complex to be attractive and effective.

Here are some points of interest relative to the previous example codes:

- **Class selectors (`div.top`, `div.main`, and `div.bottom`) apply style properties to the document's three divisions.** Background images, along with foreground and background colors, are set for each of the divisions.

- **Class selectors (`div.padtop`, `div.padmain`, and `div.padbottom`) apply padding to the document's divisions.** This is necessary to by-pass the box model bug in Internet Explorer 5.5 for Windows (otherwise, the padding could just be applied using the div.top, div.main, and div.bottom selectors).

- **Style properties are applied to the H1, H2, P, and ADDRESS elements.** Various formatting is applied to these elements, including foreground and background colors, margins, padding, borders, and text alignment.

- **Additional class selectors (`p.first` and `span.drop`) format the first paragraph and the first letter in that paragraph.** Additional top padding is added to the first paragraph, while the first letter in that paragraph is set up as a drop-cap.

Using a Fixed Sidebar Background

The next example is also a relatively simple layout design, but it's one that makes use of a special feature of CSS, a fixed background, to good effect. A fixed background image stays fixed relative the canvas (the background of the page), instead of scrolling with the page's content when it is scrolled.

For this example, you're creating a page that uses a fixed background to create the look of a ring-binding running down the side of the page. The page you create is a list of gasoline conservation tips.

You use a different example file, savegas.html, to create this example. Just open it from your working folder. You can also type it in, if you wish, as shown in Listing 14.2 (see Figure 14.3).

Listing 14.2: SAVEGAS.HTML—Gasoline Conservation Tips

```
<!DOCTYPE HTML PUBLIC "-//W3C//DTD HTML 4.01 Transitional//EN"
"http://www.w3.org/TR/html4/loose.dtd">

<html>
<head>
<title>Gasoline Conservation Tips</title>
<style type="text/css">

</style>
</head>
<body>

<h1>Gasoline Conservation Tips</h1>

<p>With the increasing cost of gasoline in a world of diminishing supply and
expanding demand, the need to economize on the consumption of gasoline is
becoming more and more important. The simplest solution in this situation is
simply to purchase a vehicle that consumes less gasoline per mile driven. Those
who don't have the option of trading in their current vehicle for a new one with
lower fuel consumption can still do many things to decrease their consumption of
gasoline. Here are some tips for doing that:</p>

<ul>
<li>Drive at a lower speed. The optimum speed for getting the best mileage while
driving on the highway varies for different vehicle models, but if you keep your
speed between 50 and 55 miles per hour, you'll consume less gasoline than you
would if driving at a higher speed.

<li>Drive smoothly, without speeding up or slowing down too rapidly. Sudden
spurts, stops, or other changes in speed cause your vehicle's engine to consume
additional fuel.

<li>Gradually accelerate up to speed. The more gradual your rate of acceleration,
the less fuel your engine will need to consume to get up to speed. Anticipate
```

Listing 14.2: continued

```
 stops, turns, hills, traffic, and so on, so you can gradually vary your speed to
a suitable rate before hand, rather than suddenly having to speed up or slow
down.

<li>When your car is not moving, avoid pumping the gas pedal or racing the
engine. When stopped on an incline, use your breaks, not the gas pedal to hold
your vehicle in place.

<li>Don't needlessly idle the engine. If you're waiting for a friend, a bridge to
close, or a train to go by, don't continue to idle your engine while waiting.
Turn it off.

<li>Check your tire pressure. Tires that are underinflated place extra drag on
the engine, causing it to consume more fuel. Check your owner's manual for the
recommended tire pressure and make sure your tires are inflated to match.

<li>Keep your vehicle's engine tuned according to the specification provided in
the owner's manual. An out-of-tune vehicle will likely consume more gasoline.

<li>If you have more than one car in your family, use the care with the best fuel
economy as often as possible, especially for short trips. Use the other vehicle
(or vehicles) only if the car with the best fuel economy isn't available or if it
isn't practical to use it instead.

<li>Don't carry unnecessary weight. Check your vehicle's trunk or other storage
areas to see how you can slim your vehicle down. If it is the middle of the
summer, store your tire chains in the garage, not in your trunk, for instance. If
storing tools in your car, store only those you think you might need, rather than
every tool that you have.

<li>Make sure that your wheels are properly aligned. Misaligned wheels cause your
engine to consume additional fuel to overcome the rolling resistance of the
tires.

<li>Operate the air conditioner only if you really need it. Running it causes a
drop in your fuel mileage of a mile or two per gallon of gasoline. If possible,
run it only enough, about once a week, to keep it functioning properly.
</ul>
<hr>

<address>
Bradley Bogart<br>
E-Mail: <a href="mailto:bbogart@bucksavers.com">bbogart@bucksavers.com</a><br>
Web Address: <a href="http://www.bucksavers.com/">http://www.bucksavers.com/</a>
</address>

</body>

</html>
```

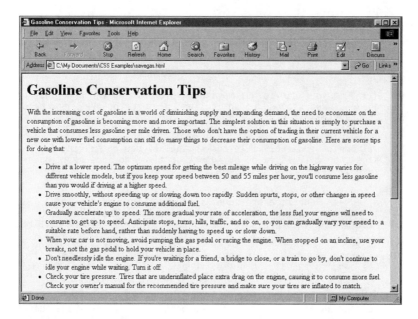

Figure 14.3: This example uses an unordered list (bulleted list) to display a list of gasoline conservation tips.

To prepare the example file for the application of the styles you're creating, you only have to add one document division to your page. To do that, first edit the top of your page's body codes, like this:

```
<div class="body">
<h1>Gasoline Conservation Tips</h1>
```

And then edit the bottom of your page's body codes, like this:

```
<address>
Bradley Bogart<br>
E-Mail: <a href="mailto:bbogart@bucksavers.com">bbogart@bucksavers.com</a><br>
Web Address: <a href="http://www.bucksavers.com/">http://www.bucksavers.com/</a>
</address>
</div>
```

Now, you're ready to create the styles that transform the look of your page of gas saver tips. Just add the following style sheet to your page, like this (see Figure 14.4):

```
<style type="text/css">

body { color: black; background: white url(rings3.jpg); background-repeat:
repeat-y; background-attachment: fixed; font-size: 1.1em; padding-left: 75px;
```

```
margin: 0; padding-top: 0; padding-right: 0; }
div.body { color: black; background: #fef2f2; padding: 0.5em; margin-top: 0; }
li { margin-bottom: 0.5em; }
```

```
</style>
```

Fixed sidebar
background image

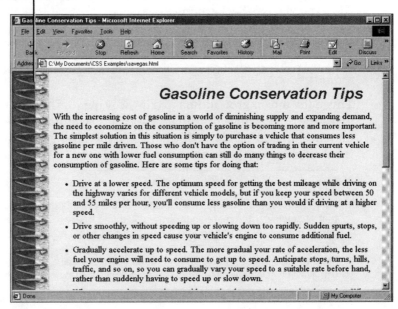

Figure 14.4: *The page is transformed using a fixed sidebar background and other effects.*

NOTE

This example utilizes two background images that I've specially created for this example and which are included with the example files that can be downloaded from this book's Web site. While you can use other background images, just to see how using a fixed sidebar background image works, your results will look quite different from what's shown in the figures.

Take note of these main features in this example:

- The background-repeat: repeat-y property causes the background image (rings3.jpg) to run down the left side of the page. The background-attachment: fixed property causes the background image to be fixed (non-scrolling) relative to the page's background (the canvas).

- The `padding-top: 0` and `padding-right: 0` properties defined for the `div.body` selector are required in order to cause Opera 5 to display the page flush with top and right margins.

Adding the Finishing Touches

To add the finishing touches to your page of gas conservation tips, add a background image to the `div.body` division that matches and merges with the fixed sidebar background:

```
body { color: black; background: white url(rings3.jpg); background-repeat:
repeat-y; background-attachment: fixed; font-size: 1.1em; padding-left: 75px;
margin: 0; padding-top: 0; padding-right: 0; }
div.body { color: black; background: #fef2f2 url(ringscov.jpg); padding: 0.5em;
margin-top: 0; }
```

This adds a background image, ringscov.jpg, to the `div.body` element that gives the appearance of being a cover. I also created this image so that it matches up and melds with the rings3.jpg image that is used to create the fixed sidebar background.

TIP

Paint Shop Pro, one of the better image editors available for Windows, has a feature that enables you to create your own background images. Just select the area of your image that you want to turn into a background image, and then select Selections, Convert to Seamless Pattern. The image you use must be a 24-bit image. You might need to experiment a bit to get the result you really want, but when you do get a result you like, it'll give your page its own unique look used by no-one else on the Web.

You can find out more about Paint Shop Pro, as well as download an evaluation version of the software, at `http://www.jasc.com/`.

While you're at it, go ahead and gussy up your paragraph and list text. Set up some special display characteristics for the first lines and letters of your paragraphs. To set that up, first edit the code in your page's body, like this:

```
<h1>Gasoline Conservation Tips</h1>

<p><span class="first">W</span>ith the increasing cost of gasoline in a world of
diminishing supply and expanding demand, the need to economize on the consumption
of gasoline is becoming more and more important. The simplest solution in this
situation is simply to purchase a vehicle that consumes less gasoline per mile
driven. Those who don't have the option of trading in their current vehicle for
a new one with lower fuel consumption can still do many things to decrease their
consumption of gasoline. Here are some tips for doing that:</p>

<ul>
<li><span class="first">D</span>rive at a lower speed. The optimum speed for
getting the best mileage while driving on the highway varies for different
vehicle models, but if you keep your speed between 50 and 55 miles per hour,
you'll consume less gasoline than you would if driving at a higher speed.
```

```
<li><span class="first">D</span>rive smoothly, without speeding up or slowing
down too rapidly. Sudden spurts, stops, or other changes in speed cause your
vehicle's engine to consume additional fuel.

<li><span class="first">G</span>radually accelerate up to speed. The more gradual
your rate of acceleration, the less fuel your engine will need to consume to get
up to speed. Anticipate stops, turns, hills, traffic, and so on, so you can
gradually vary your speed to a suitable rate before hand, rather than suddenly
having to speed up or slow down.

<li><span class="first">W</span>hen your car is not moving, avoid pumping the gas
pedal or racing the engine. When stopped on an incline, use your breaks, not the
gas pedal to hold your vehicle in place.

<li><span class="first">D</span>on't needlessly idle the engine. If you're
waiting for a friend, a bridge to close, or a train to go by, don't continue to
idle your engine while waiting. Turn it off.

<li><span class="first">C</span>heck your tire pressure. Tires that are
underinflated place extra drag on the engine, causing it to consume more fuel.
Check your owner's manual for the recommended tire pressure and make sure your
tires are inflated to match.

<li><span class="first">K</span>eep your vehicle's engine tuned according to the
specification provided in the owner's manual. An out-of-tune vehicle will likely
consume more gasoline.

<li><span class="first">I</span>f you have more than one car in your family, use
the care with the best fuel economy as often as possible, especially for short
trips. Use the other vehicle (or vehicles) only if the car with the best fuel
economy isn't available or if it isn't practical to use it instead.

<li><span class="first">D</span>on't carry unnecessary weight. Check your
vehicle's trunk or other storage areas to see how you can slim your vehicle down.
If it is the middle of the summer, store your tire chains in the garage, not in
your trunk, for instance. If storing tools in your car, store only those you
think you might need, rather than every tool that you have.

<li><span class="first">M</span>ake sure that your wheels are properly aligned.
Misaligned wheels cause your engine to consume additional fuel to overcome the
rolling resistance of the tires.

<li><span class="first">O</span>perate the air conditioner only if you really
need it. Running it causes a drop in your fuel mileage of a mile or two per
gallon of gasoline. If possible, run it only enough, about once a week, to keep
it functioning properly.
</ul>
```

Next, add the following codes to your style sheet, as shown here (see Figure 14.5).

```
li { margin-bottom: 0.5em; }
p:first-line, li:first-line { font-style: italic; font-weight: bold;  line-
height: 1; }
span.first { font-family: arial, sans-serif; font-size: 1.8em; color: maroon;
font-style: italic; font-weight: bold; }
```

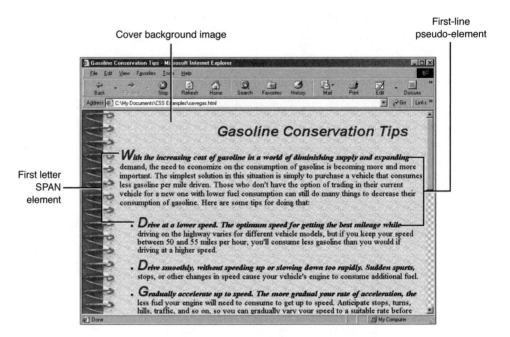

Figure 14.5: *The finishing touches are added to the Gas Conservation Tips page.*

Here are some of the key points about the previous code example:

- The background: white url(ringscov.jpg) property added for the div.body selector displays a background image in the "body" division that melds with the vertical background running down the left side of the page (or a white background, if display of images is turned off in a browser). The overall look is that of a ring-bound notebook cover.

- The :first-line pseudo-element is used to cause the first lines of the P and LI elements to be bold and italicized.

- The span.first selector is used to apply display characteristics to the first letter of the page's P and LI elements to set it apart from the following text.

In CSS, a *pseudo-element* is utilized in a style selector to indicate the presentation of typographical elements, rather than structural elements. CSS1 includes two pseudo-elements, with the :first-line pseudo-element indicating the presentation of the first line in an element and the :first-letter pseudo-element indicating the presentation of the first letter in an element.

Because of some problems with how current second-generation CSS-browsers (p. 175) display the :first-letter pseudo-element, I've substituted using a SPAN element to achieve the same ends. Opera 5 also doesn't apply the :first-line formatting to the first line of the LI elements, but at least that doesn't otherwise disrupt the layout or interfere with users gaining access to the information that's being presented.

Creating Multi-Column Layouts

Multi-column layouts are the key to creating more complex page layouts. The point of a multi-column layout is that by breaking up the horizontal span of the page, it allows more significant information to be located within the browser window. Although with a single-column layout, a user might have to scroll down through the page to find important information (because the different sections of the page are stacked vertically), with a multi-column layout sections (or stories) can be aligned horizontally.

The idea, in other words is to bring as many significant headings, links, and other objects as possible up to the top of the page, so they're visible and available to the user without scrolling.

A multi-column layout can also be handy when you are presenting a lot of text to be read. Newspapers, for instance, present information in columns because it is easier to track and less tiring to read shorter, as opposed, to long, text lines. The same effect can be created on a Web page to break up long text lines and make them easier to track and read.

Creating Newspaper Columns

In this example, you use the Declaration of Independence example you worked with before, but this time you set the text of the declaration in three evenly spaced newspaper-type columns. I've included the final version of the previous example, as indendence_final.html, with the example files. Just open it and then resave it as **independence2.html**.

To create this example, you need to first edit the body of your document, adding "main," "left," "center," and "right" divisions. You'll later attach styles to these divisions to set the width and other formatting for the containing page and the three newspaper columns.

For starters, at the top of your document's body, insert start tags for the "main" and "left" divisions, as well as for a "pad" division (that sets the padding for the left newspaper column):

```
<body>

<div class="main">
```

```
<div class="top">
<div class="padtop">
<h1>The Declaration of Independence</h1>
<h2>In Congress, July 4, 1776</h2>
</div>
</div>

<div class="left">
<div class="pad">
<a name="top"></a>
<p class="first"><span class="drop">W</span>hen in the Course of human events, it
becomes necessary for one people to dissolve the political bands which have
connected them with another, and to assume among the powers of the earth, the
separate and equal station to which the Laws of Nature and of Nature's God
entitle them, a decent respect to the opinions of mankind requires that they
should declare the causes which impel them to the separation.</p>
```

Now, you need to add the codes to close off the left column and start the center column. First, insert two </div> end tags to close off the "left" and "pad" divisions you started at the top of the document's body. Next, add a new division for specifying the format and positioning of a loop-back link at the bottom of the column. Lastly, insert start tags for the "center" division and for another "pad" division. To do these three things, just scroll down through your document's text and then insert the following codes:

```
<p>He has called together legislative bodies at places unusual, uncomfortable,
and distant from the depository of their public Records, for the sole purpose of
fatiguing them into compliance with his measures.</p>
</div>
</div>

<div id="leftlink">
<p>Return to <a href="#top">Top</a>.</p>
</div>

<div class="center">
<div class="pad">
<p>He has dissolved Representative Houses repeatedly, for opposing with manly
firmness his invasions on the rights of the people.</p>
```

Now, you need to add the codes to close off the center column and start the right column. Just scroll down through your document's text and insert the following codes:

```
<p>He has plundered our seas, ravaged our Coasts, burnt our towns, and destroyed
the lives of our people.</p>
</div>
</div>
```

```
<div id="ctrlink">
<p>Return to <a href="#top">Top</a>.</p>
</div>
```

```
<div class="right">
<div class="pad">
<p>He is at this time transporting large Armies of foreign Mercenaries to
complete the works of death, desolation and tyranny, already begun with
circumstances of cruelty and perfidy scarcely paralleled in the most barbarous
ages, and totally unworthy the Head of a civilized nation.</p>
```

Now, you need to add the codes to close off the right column, as well as add a division ("bottompos") to help position the "bottom" division. Also, add one final </div> end tag at the bottom of your document's body (just above the </body> end tag) to close off the "main" division you started at the top of the document body. Just scroll down through your document's text and insert the following codes:

```
<p>And for the support of this Declaration, with a firm reliance on the
protection of Divine Providence, we mutually pledge to each other our Lives, our
Fortunes, and our sacred Honor.</p>
</div>
</div>
```

```
<div id="rightlink">
<p>Return to <a href="home.html">Home</a>.</p>
</div>
```

```
<div class="bottompos">
<div class="bottom">
<address>
John Smith<br>
E-Mail: <a href="mailto:jsmith@us-history.com">jsmith@us-history.com</a><br>
Web Address: <a href="http://www.us-history.com/">http://www.us-history.com/</a>
</address>
</div>
</div>
```

```
</div>
</body>
</html>
```

Finally, create a style sheet to control the formatting of the document divisions you've added to your document, as well as of other elements within your document (see Figure 14.6):

```
<style type="text/css">

body, p, li, address { font-family: "Times New Roman", Times, serif; font-size:
16px; }
```

```css
body { background: #fc9; color: black; margin: 10px; padding: 0 0 10px 0; }
/*  Margin setting above required for Opera 5 */

div.top { background: url(blackmarb.jpg) #039; color: black; padding-left: 15px;
padding-right: 15px; margin-bottom: 0; }

div.main { width: 750px; }

div.left { position: absolute; left: 15px; top: 152px; background:
url(paper2.gif) #ffc; color: black; width: 240px; height: 1665px; text-align:
left; padding: 5px 0; text-align: left; margin-right: 1.5%; }

div.center { position: absolute; top: 152px; left: 15px; background:
url(paper2.gif) #ffc; color: black; width: 240px; height: 1665px; padding: 5px 0;
text-align: left; margin-left: 250px; margin-right: auto; }

div.right { position: absolute; left: 500px; top: 152px; background:
url(paper2.gif) #ffc; color: black; width: 240px; height: 1665px; padding: 5px 0;
text-align: left; margin-left: 2%; margin-right: 0; }

div.bottompos { position: absolute; left: 15px; top: 1840px; }

div.bottom { position: relative; bottom: 10px; width: 740px; background:
url(tanback.jpg) #cfc; color: navy; text-align: center; margin-top: 10px;
padding-bottom: 5px; }

div.pad { padding: 0 5px 0 10px}

div.padtop { padding-top: 0; padding-bottom: 5px; }

div#leftlink { position: absolute; top: 1785px; left: 25px; }
div#leftlink p { text-indent: 0; }

div#ctrlink { position: absolute; top: 1785px; left: 275px; }
div#ctrlink p { text-indent: 0; }

div#rightlink { position: absolute; top: 1785px; left: 525px; }
div#rightlink p { text-indent: 0; }

a { color: blue; background: transparent; }

h1 { color: #fc0; background: transparent; text-align: center; border-bottom:
white 1px solid; padding-top: 10px; padding-bottom: 10px; margin-top: 0;}
h2 { color: #cf9; background: transparent; text-align: center;  padding-bottom:
0; }

p { margin-top: 0; margin-bottom: 0; text-indent: 1.5em; }
p.first { text-indent: 0; }
```

```
ul { margin-top: 0; margin-bottom: 0; }
li { margin-left: -2em; list-style-position: inside; text-indent: 1em;}

address { padding-top: 1%; padding-bottom: 1%; }

span.drop { float: left; font-size: 40px; font-weight: bold; color: maroon;
background: transparent; margin-top: -3px; margin-bottom: -5px; }

</style>
```

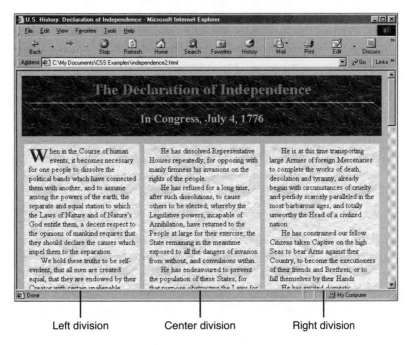

Left division   Center division   Right division

Figure 14.6: *A newspaper-column layout can make text in text-intensive pages easier to track and read.*

Take note of the following main features in this example:

- **The layout in this example uses pixels.** That's the only way in which to be able to determine the length of the columns, which would vary if ems or percentages were used. If pixels were not used, the text in the columns might overflow the bottoms of the columns.

- **The width of the page is set at 740 pixels.** This is the maximum width for a page that doesn't turn on horizontal scroll bars in most browsers running maximized at a 800×600 screen resolution.

- **The three newspaper columns are absolutely positioned on the page.** Each of the divisions bracketing the columns is positioned relative to the upper-left corner of the page.

- **Tabbed indents are used to indicate the start of new paragraphs.** The top and bottom margins of the text paragraphs and bulleted lists are set to zero. The `text-indent` property is used to create a "tabbed" indent at the start of the paragraphs (see Figure 14.7).

- **ID selectors (`div#leftlink`, `div#ctrlink`, and `div#rightlink`) are used to position loop-back links at the bottoms of the columns to make it easier to navigate the page.** The first two loop-back links jump back up to the top of the columns, so the reader can continue reading without having to scroll back up to the top; the third jumps to a fictional home page, so that a reader could return to the main page for the site without having to click the Back button, for instance. (See Figure 14.8.)

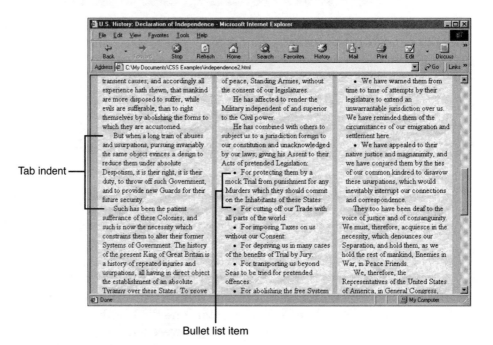

Figure 14.7: In newspaper columns, tabbed paragraphs are easier to read.

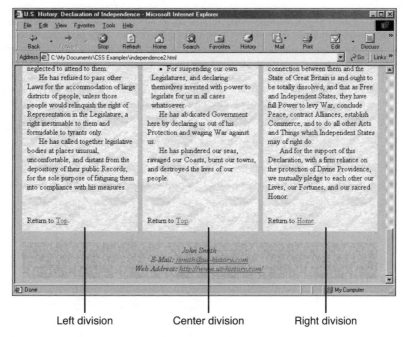

Left division　　　　Center division　　　　Right division

Figure 14.8: *Loop-back links are positioned at the bottom of the columns to make navigating easier.*

Creating a Three-Column Layout

Many of the more involved pages that you've visited on the Web are designed using three, four, or more columns. The vast majority of those layouts, however, was created using tables to control the positioning and dimensions of the columns. This section's example shows you how to create a more-complex three-column layout that features a menu in the left column, the main content of the page in the middle column, and a list of links to related resources in the right column.

For this example, you create a page of Christmas safety tips. I've created an example file, xmastips.html, that you can use to create this example. Just open it from your working folder and edit it as shown in Listing 14.3 (see Figure 14.9).

TIP

Up until now you worked with simpler examples, assembling the building blocks, so to speak, that you'll be able to combine later to assemble more complicated edifices. The example shown in Listing 14.3 is the most complex example shown in this book, and takes advantage of many of the features that you worked with previously in this book.

Previously, for the less complicated examples in this book, the property declarations for a particular style rule were presented all on the same line, primarily to conserve space, since many of the example code lines are shown multiple times to provide context. In this example, however, the property declarations are presented as a list below the style rule's selector, spaced in a couple of spaces from the margin. For more complicated style sheets, this can help make your style sheet more readable and easier to decipher. It can also make it easier to spot typing errors, such a colon typed in place of semicolon, a missing right squiggly bracket, and so on.

You're free to format your style sheets however you wish. In HTML files, however, you should avoid using tabs, but you can freely use hard returns and spaces to arrange your style sheets in whatever format works best for you.

Listing 14.3: XMASTIPS.HTML—Christmas Safety Tips

```
<!DOCTYPE HTML PUBLIC "-//W3C//DTD HTML 4.01 Transitional//EN"
"http://www.w3.org/TR/html4/loose.dtd">

<html>
<head>
<title>Christmas Safety Tips</title>
<style type="text/css">

body {
  color: white; background: #050;
  font-family: "Times New Roman", Times, serif;
  font-size: 16px; margin: 0; padding: 0;
}

/* Top banner bar formatting */
div.top {
  position: absolute; top: 10px; left: 10px; z-index: 2;
  width: 630px; height: 55px;
  color: #063; background: #fc0;
  border: 3px lime outset;
/* Start box model hack */
  voice-family: "\"}\""; voice-family: inherit; width: 624px; height: 49px;
}
html>body div.top {
  width: 624px; height: 49px;
}
/* End box model hack */

/* Formatting for side, main, and right column divisions. */
div.side {
  position: absolute; top: 0; left: 0; z-index; 1;
  width: 135px; height: 900px;
  color: black; background: #c00 url(holly2.gif); background-repeat: repeat-y;
  padding-bottom: 10px;
```

Listing 14.3: continued

```
}
div.main {
  position: absolute; top: 0; left: 135px; z-index: 1;
  width: 515px; height: 900px;
  padding-top: 0; padding-bottom: 10px; margin-top: 0;
  color: black; background: white url(paper2.gif);
}
div.right {
  position: absolute; top: 0; left: 650px;
  width: 125px; height: 900px;
  color: white; background: #050;
  padding-bottom: 10px;
}

/* Nested padding for side, main, and right column divisions. */
div.sidepad {
  padding-top: 65px; padding-left: 10px;
}
div.mainpad {
  padding: 60px 10px 5px 10px;
}
div.rightpad {
  padding: 3px;
}

/* Settings for the side division. */

div.side p {
  margin: 0 10px;
}

div.side a, div.side a:link, div.side a:visited, div.side a:active {
  display: block;
  padding: 5px;
  margin-top: 16px; margin-bottom: 16px;
  border: 3px #fc0 outset;
  color: #cf6; background: #066;
  font-weight: bold; text-decoration: none;
  font-family: Arial, sans-serif; }

div.side a, div.side a:link, div.side a:visited, div.side a:active {
/* Start box model hack */
  width: 106px; voice-family: "\"}\""; voice-family: inherit; width: 90px;
}
html>body div.side a {
```

Listing 14.3: continued

```
  width: 90px
}
/* End box model hack */

div.side a:hover {
  color: red; background: #fc0;
  border: 3px #09f outset;
}

div.side a:hover {
  color: #036; background: #fc0;
  border: 3px #cf0 outset;
  margin-bottom: 16px; margin-top: 16px;
}

/* Settings for the main division */

div.main img {
  type: block; float: left;
  margin: 0 10px 15px 5px;
}

div.main p {
  font-size: 18px;
  color: #060; background: transparent;
  clear: left;
}

div.main h2 {
  font-family: Arial, Helvetica, sans-serif;
  color: navy; background: transparent;
  text-align: center;
  padding-top: 0; padding-bottom: 5px;
}

/* Settings for the right division */

div.right h2 {
  color: #f90; background: transparent;
  border-bottom: lime 3px groove;
  margin-top: 10px;
  padding-bottom: 3px;
}
```

Listing 14.3: continued

```
div.right h3 {
  font-size: 16px;
  margin-bottom: 0;
  color: aqua; background: transparent;
}

div.right p {
  margin-bottom: 0; margin-top: 0; margin-left: 5px;
  font-family: Arial, Helvetica, sans-serif;
  font-size: 11px;
  text-indent: -5px;
}

div.right a, div.right a:link, div.right a:visited, div.right a:active {
  color: yellow; background: transparent;
}

div.right a:hover {
  color: lime; background: #c00;
  text-decoration: none;
}

/* General settings */

h1 {
  font-family: Arial, Helvetica, sans-serif;
  font-size: 41px;
  color: #c00; background: transparent;
  text-align: center;
  margin-top: 0; margin-bottom: 0;
}

a {
  color: blue; background: transparent;
  font-weight: bold;
}
a:link {
  color: red; background: transparent;
}
a:visited {
  color: red; background: transparent;
}
a:active {
  color: blue; background: lime; }
```

Listing 14.3: continued

```
a:hover {
  color: #fc0; background: red;
  text-decoration: none;
}

</style>
</head>

<body>

<div class="top">
<a name="menu"></a>
<h1>Christmas Safety Tips</h1>
</div>

<div class="side">
<div class="sidepad">
<p>
<a href="xmastips2.html">Lights</a>
<a href="xmastips3.html">Candles</a>
<a href="xmastips4.html">Trimming</a>
<a href="xmastips5.html">Fires</a>
<a href="xmastips6.html">Paper</a>
<a href="xmastips7.html">Trees</a>
<a href="xmastips8.html">Snow</a>
</p>
</div>
</div>

<div class="main">
<div class="mainpad">
<h2>General Tips:</h2>

<p><img src="glass2.gif">Keep matches, lighters, and candles out of the reach of
children.</p>
<p><img src="glass2.gif">Don't smoke cigarettes or pipes near flamable
decorations or wrappings.</p>
<p><img src="glass2.gif">Create an emergency exit plan in case a fire should
start in your house or apartment. Make sure all family members know the plan and
what they need to do in case of a fire.</p>
<p><img src="glass2.gif">Don't wear loose and flowing clothes, especially with
long and open sleeves, in the vicinity of a fireplace fire, lit candles, or other
open flames.</p>
```

Listing 14.3: continued

```
<p><img src="glass2.gif">Never burn evergreen trimmings or branches in the
fireplace. When dry, they can easily flare out of control, sending sparks into
the room.</p>
<p><img src="glass2.gif">Don't burn Christmas wrappings in the fireplace, since
they can produce embers that can float up your chimney and then land on your (or
a neighbor's) roof.</p>
<p><img src="glass2.gif">Carefully examine any Christmas light or extension cords
for fraying or other damage, using only electrical cords that are in new
condition.</p>

<p>Return to <a href="#menu">Top</a>.</p>

<hr>
<address>
The Safety-First Association<br>
E-Mail: <a href="mailto:info@be-safe-first.com">info@be-safe-first.com</a><br>
Web Address: <a href="http://www.be-safe-first.com/">http://www.be-safe-
first.com/</a>
</address>
</div>
</div>

<div class="right">
<div class="rightpad">
<h2>X-Mas Resources:</h2>
<h3>X-Mas Links</h3>
<p><a href="http://www.christmas.com/">Christmas.com</a></p>
<p><a href="http://www.holidays.net/christmas/">X-Mas on the Net</a>
<p><a href="http://www.merry-christmas.com/">Merry-Christmas<br>.com</a></p>
<h3>X-Mas Recipes</h3>
<p><a href="http://www.christmasrecipe.com/">ChristmasRecipe<br>.com</p>
<p><a href="http://www.christmas-joy.com/recipes/">Fav X-Mas Recipes</a></p>
<h3>Traditions</h3>
<p><a href="http://www.howstuffworks.com/christmas.htm">How X-Mas Works</a></p>
<h3>Publications</h3>
<p><a href="http://www.christmasmagazine.com/">Christmas Magazine</a></p>
<p><a href="http://christmas.readersdigest.com/">Reader's Digest X-Mas</a></p>
<h3>Free X-Mas Stuff</h3>
<p><a href="http://www.christmasfreebies.com/">ChristmasFreebies<br>.com</a></p>
<p><a href="http://christmas-software.com/default.htm">Christmas-
Software<br>.com</a></p>
</div>
</div>

</body>
</html>
```

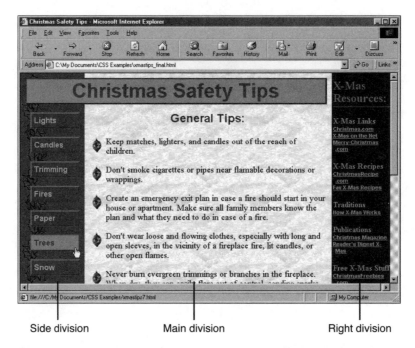

Side division   Main division   Right division

Figure 14.9: *A three-column layout is an effective way to present a more complex page.*

Take note of these key features in this example:

- **This layout is created using only pixel measurements.** Although three-column layouts can be created using em and percentage units, it is generally easier to create complex three-column layouts using pixels. This also ensures a minimum width for your page that won't be collapsed along with the width of the browser window. Feel free, however, to experiment with creating three-column layouts using em and percentage units, since in many ways they are preferable, if practicable.

- **The "top" division creates the banner box which overlays the left and main columns.** It contains the H1 banner text and is absolutely positioned relative to the top and left sides of the page. The `z-index:2` property causes the top division to overlap the following side and main columns, which are set to a lower value, `z-index:1`.

- **The box model hack is used to set box widths where necessary.** This causes Internet Explorer 5.5 for Windows to display the correct height and width for the top division, as well as the correct widths for the roll-over buttons in the side division.

- **The three column divisions (side, main, and right) are absolutely positioned on the page.** Three separate divisions (`div.sidepad`, `div.mainpad`, and `div.rightpad`) are used to set padding for the three column divisions (otherwise, the box model hack would have to be used with them, as well).

- **A vertical string of holly leaves is displayed behind the roll-over buttons in the side column division.** A `background-repeat: repeat-y` property causes the background image (holly2.gif) to run down the left side of the side division.

- **Roll-over button links are used in the side column division to add interactivity and dynamism to the page.** The box model hack is used to make sure the button widths will be the same in Internet Explorer 5.5 and other CSS-supporting browsers. Anchor pseudo-classes are used to create the roll-over effect.

- **A decorative Christmas bulb is used as the bullet icon for the list of tips.** The `div.main img` rule causes the image of the Christmas bulb decoration to float at the left margin of the main division, causing the following text to flow around it. The `margin` shorthand property sets the horizontal spacing that separates the floating image from the flowing text, as well as additional vertical spacing below the image (to keep following lines from wrapping to the left margin). Margins, and not padding, must be used to set horizontal and vertical spacing around images in Internet Explorer 5.5 for Windows.

Creating Site Designs

So far, you've been working with single-page layouts and designs. One of the benefits of using CSS, however, is to standardize the look-and-feel of an entire site, not just a single page. To demonstrate this, you use the preceding example you created of Christmas safety tips, expanded to encompass more than just the front page of general tips.

I've already created example files for the different pages of the Christmas safety tips site. These files are with the other example files, named xmastips2.html, xmastips3.html, and so on.

Creating an External Style Sheet

First, you need to create your external style sheet. An external style sheet contains exactly the same codes you nest inside of a page's STYLE element, but in this case the codes are contained within a file. To create and save your external style sheet follow these steps:

1. Open the Christmas safety tips example file you created (xmastips.html) in your text editor.

2. Highlight and copy all of the codes nested inside of the STYLE element. Do not copy the STYLE start or end tags.

3. In your text editor, open a blank window and paste in the style codes you just copied. Save this file in your working folder as **xmastips.css**.

4. Open xmastips2.html (I've already created this example for you) in your text editor. Delete the style codes that are nested inside the STYLE element and then insert the following LINK element above the style element, like this:

   ```
   <link rel="stylesheet" type="text/css" href="xmastips.css">
   <style type="text/css">

   </style>
   ```

   Save **xmastips2.html** in your working folder.

5. In your browser, open xmastips.html from your working folder. Click the **Lights** button in the sidebar to display xmastips2.html. (See Figure 14.10.)

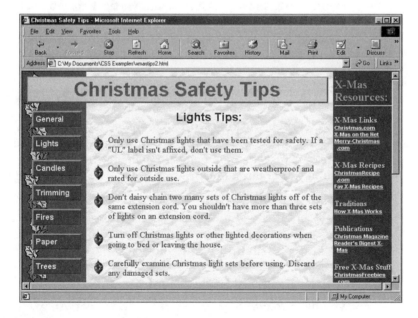

Figure 14.10: *The display characteristics of the Lights Tips page are entirely determined by an external style sheet.*

6. In turn, open xmastips.html, xmastips3.html, xmastips4.html, xmastips5.html, xmastips6.html, xmastips7.html, and xmastips8. html in your text editor, repeating step 4.

The formatting of your Christmas safety tips site should now be entirely controlled by the styles included in the xmastips.css external style sheet. You can now make global changes to the appearance of your site by editing the external style sheet that is linked to its pages.

CAUTION

If your external style sheet contains a reference to a background image using a relative URL, you need to be aware that Netscape Navigator 4 incorrectly interprets a relative URL (such as ../bgimages/backimg.jpg, for instance) as being relative to the location of the HTML file, rather than to location of the style sheet file. Unless you're using a technique to block access to Navigator 4 (such as using the @import at-rule to import an external style sheet), the only way to overcome this problem is to use an absolute URL. Thus if the address of your remote site is http://www.yoursite.com/ and you've saved your background image, backimg.jpg, in a bgimages folder located in your site's root folder, you would need to use the URL, http://www.yoursite.com/bgimages/backimg.jpg to reference it in your external style sheet. To test this out on your own local machine, you'd need to transfer the background image up to your remote bgimages folder (since the absolute URL is pointing to there, and not to a bgimages folder located on your local machine).

✔ For more information on using external styles sheets, see "Linking and Importing Style Sheets," p. 73 (chapter 4) and "Using the @import At-Rule," p. 390 (chapter 16)

What's Next?

You should now have a good understanding of how to create a variety of different page layouts and designs, including creating layouts using fixed sidebar backgrounds, newspaper columns, multiple-columns, and more. You also have had hands-on experience creating and applying an external style sheet to multiple pages within a Web site.

In Chapter 15, "Validating Your Style Sheet," you learn how to validate your style sheets and HTML files, so you can make sure that your work conforms to the current recommended specifications.

Part VII

Validation and Compatibility

Validating Your Style Sheet

Providing for Backward Compatibility

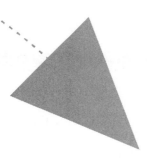

Validating Your Style Sheet

There are lots of ins and outs to creating correct and valid CSS style sheets. It is best to discover errors that might be hiding in your style sheet or HTML file *before* you announce your site on the Web to the rest of the world.

In this chapter, you learn about the following:

- Why validate?
- Using the W3C CSS and HTML validators
- Using the Web Design Group's CSS and HTML validators

Why Validate?

As much as you try to pay attention to details, it is easy for small errors to sneak into your style sheet. *Validating* your style sheet and HTML file can serve as a form of proofreading, catching small errors and typos in your code that are otherwise difficult to see or notice. A common example of a CSS error, for instance, is forgetting to specify a measuring unit. This is easy to do, because in HTML, numerical measures specify pixels by default, while in CSS you have to specifically identify which measuring system you're referencing (pixels, ems, percentages, centimeters, and so on). Other very common errors include using a regular parenthesis when you need to use a squiggly parenthesis or using a colon when you need to use a semi-colon. Validating your style sheet also catches any property/value mismatches—you might think that a property takes a particular value, for instance, but it doesn't.

Validating your style sheet can also help make sure that you're following best practices when creating your style sheets. For instance, just specifying a foreground color for elements, without also specifying a background color, doesn't generate any errors, but does generate warnings when you validate your style sheet. That's because a user might be using a user style sheet that specifies foreground and background colors for certain elements—if you only specify a foreground color, you might end up with dark blue text against a black background, for instance. At minimum, you should declare a transparent background color (background: transparent), which lets any underlying background color that you've set for the parent element shine through.

Because CSS style sheets are used in conjunction with HTML, you should also validate your HTML files to discover if there are any errors in your page's HTML code. The same holds true if you're using CSS with XHTML or XML pages.

Another issue to be concerned with is forward-compatibility. Just because something displays in current browsers doesn't mean that it will display the same or at all in future browsers. There is no guarantee that non-standard tags and attributes will be supported in future browsers. However, as long as your page is coded correctly using only standard tags and attributes, you can be assured that it will be displayed at least similarly in future browsers. Validating your page's HTML and CSS code can help insure that your pages will remain accessible for many, many years to come.

Internet Explorer 5 also includes error-correction routines that will actually correct your HTML for you. Just because your page displays fine in

Internet Explorer 5 doesn't mean that it will display at all in other browsers, in other words. Netscape Navigator, on the other hand, will often refuse to display a page with errors in its HTML or CSS code. If you care about everyone having an equal chance to access your page, test it out in several browsers (Internet Explorer 5, Netscape 6, and Opera 5, at minimum) and validate its HTML and CSS code.

Validation Options

The two main options for validating your CSS style sheets and HTML files are

- The W3C's CSS Validator and HTML Validator
- The Web Design Group's (WDG) CSSCheck and HTML Validator

The W3C's CSS and HTML Validators

The W3C (World Wide Web Consortium) hosts online CSS and HTML validators that you can use to validate your CSS style sheets and HTML files.

Using the W3C CSS Validator

To use the W3C CSS Validator, just go to the W3C's home page at `http://www.w3.org/` and click the CSS Validator link in the sidebar menu. You can also access the W3C CSS Validator directly at `http://jigsaw.w3.org/css-validator/` (see Figure 15.1).

As you'll notice in Figure 15.1, you can also download the W3C's CSS Validator and run it from your own local computer. In this section, however, I'll just be focusing on options available for using W3C's CSS Validator as an online utility. Just scroll down to see the three online options you have for using the W3C's CSS Validator:

- By specifying the Web address (URI) of an HTML file containing a CSS style sheet or of a standalone CSS style sheet file
- By pasting in your style sheet codes into a text area box
- By uploading a CSS style sheet file

NOTE

What is normally called a URL (Uniform Resource Locator) is referred to by the W3C as a URI (Uniform Resource Indentifier). A URI is actually a larger category. A URI can be either a URL or a URN (Uniform Resource Name). A URN is supposed to remain globally unique and persistent even when the resource ceases to exist or becomes unavailable. For practical purposes, however, all current URIs are URLs—URNs are something for the future.

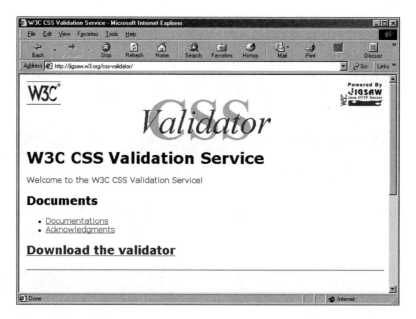

Figure 15.1: *You can use the W3C's CSS Validator to check the validity of your CSS style sheets.*

To use the first option, you need to transfer your HTML or CSS file to the Web. You can then use the CSS Validator's first option to specify the Web address of the source file you want validated (see Figure 15.2). If you don't yet have a Web hosting account or access to a folder on the Web in which you can publish your HTML files, you aren't able to use this option.

If you can't transfer your page to the Web, you can use the second option. Just open your HTML or CSS file in your text editor and then highlight and copy the style codes (see Figure 15.3). Don't copy the STYLE start or end tags, or any HTML comment tags you're using to shield your CSS styles, however—just copy the style rules themselves. You then just need to paste the CSS codes into the text area box provided by the W3C for that purpose.

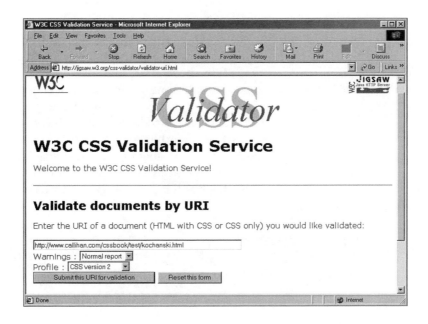

Figure 15.2: You can ask the W3C CSS Validator to validate a style sheet you've already transferred to the Web.

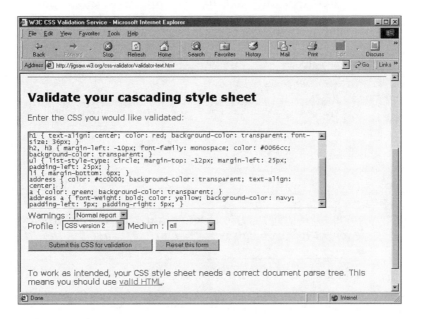

Figure 15.3: You can paste in the style sheet you want validated in the text area box provided for that purpose in the W3C's CSS Validator.

If you want to test out how this works for yourself, just open the kochanski.html example file you saved at the end of Chapter 3, "Setting Your Page's Other Styles," highlight and copy the style codes from the second style sheet (the "screen" style sheet), and then paste those style codes into the W3C's text area box. I'm not going to provide a listing here for you to type in, because it is best that you check the codes that you actually created, to catch any typos or incorrect code you might have added. You can also check the codes of any of the other example style sheets you've created in this book. After pasting the style sheet codes in the text area box, just click the button (Submit this style sheet for validation) to validate your style sheet. If your style sheet validates, you get a result similar to what is shown in Figure 15.4.

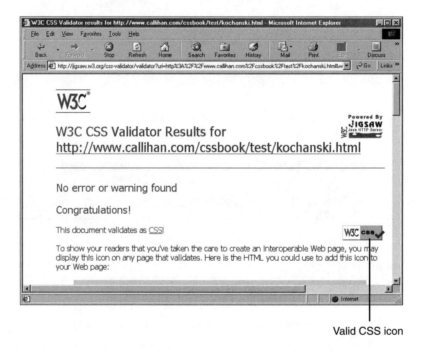

Valid CSS icon

Figure 15.4: *If your style sheet validates, the W3C provides you with the code for an icon you can post on your page showing that it uses valid CSS.*

NOTE

When getting your validation response using the W3C's CSS Validator, you'll notice the following message: "To work as intended, your CSS style sheet needs a correct document parse tree. This means you should use valid HTML." This doesn't mean that there is anything wrong with your HTML, but is meant to remind you that problems in your HTML (such as overlapping rather than nesting elements) can be the cause of errors and warnings received when validating your CSS. In the next section, "Using the W3C's HTML Validator," you learn about how to use the W3C's HTML Validator.

You can also upload a CSS style sheet to be validated. For this to work, you have to upload a standalone CSS style sheet (with a .css extension). If your styles are embedded, rather than linked or imported, you need to copy and paste the style codes into a separate blank text file and then save it as your upload file (in that case, however, you might as well use the second option).

You can select a number of options when validating your style sheet. The Warnings list menu enables you to set the level of warnings you want reported, with All being the highest level of warning reports; No warnings returns errors, but no warnings. The default is Normal report, which is sufficient in most cases.

The Profiles list enables you to set the level of CSS support you want to validate. In most cases, you should just stick with the default selection, CSS version 2. If you choose the second option, CSS version 1, any CSS2 properties or selectors in your style sheet will generate errors. The other options are No special profile and Mobile, with the latter testing for conformance to the W3C's CSS Mobile Profile, a subset of CSS2 that is tailored for mobile devices (cell phones or other wireless devices).

When using either of the last two validation options (copying and pasting or uploading the CSS style sheet), the Medium option enables you to specify the style sheet's target medium. The default, All, is what you should use in most cases. The other options enable you to select a specific target medium for which you want to test your style sheet.

Figure 15.5 shows an example of an error and a series of warnings issued by the W3C's CSS Validator. In this case, in the "screen" style sheet for kochanski.html I changed one semi-colon to a colon and deleted all of the `background-color: transparent` properties, before resaving the file as kochanski_error.html and transferring it to the Web.

If you want to try this out for yourself, first resave kochanski.html as **kochanski_error.html**. In the P style, just switch the ending semi-colon for the `margin-top` property to a colon, changing `margin-top: 20px;` to `margin-top: 20px:` and delete the `background-color: transparent;` properties for the three heading elements (H1, H2, and H3), as shown here:

```
body { background-color: #ffffcc; color: teal; font-family: verdana, arial,
helvetica, sans-serif; margin-top: 25px; margin-bottom: 25px; margin-left: 25px;
margin-right: 25px; }
p { margin-top: 20px: margin-bottom: 20px;  margin-left: 20px; margin-right:
20px; }
```

```
.first { font-style: italic; font-weight: bold; }
h1 { text-align: center; color: red; background-color: transparent; font-size:
36px; }
h2, h3 { margin-left: -10px; font-family: monospace; color: #0066cc; background-
color: transparent; }
.special { font-family: sans-serif; text-decoration: underline; }
ul { list-style-type: circle; margin-top: -12px; margin-left: 25px; padding-left:
25px; }
li { margin-bottom: 6px; }
address { color: #cc0000; background-color: transparent; text-align: center; }
a { color: green; background: transparent; }
address a { font-weight: bold; color: yellow; background-color: navy; padding-
left: 5px; padding-right: 5px; }
```

Next, just highlight and copy these styles, paste them into the W3C HTML
Validator's text area box (as shown in Figure 15.3), and then click the button to upload and validate your style sheet. As you'll notice in Figure 15.5,
the W3C CSS Validator responds by flagging the line (20) where the colon
was improperly substituted for a semi-colon, as well as issuing a series of
warnings about the missing background-color properties for elements for
which color properties had been declared.

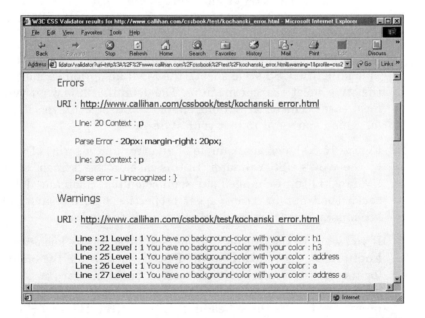

Figure 15.5: *The CSS Validator reports any errors it finds in your style
sheet, as well as giving warnings about parts of your style sheet that might
cause problems.*

A *CSS validation error* signifies that there is something in your style sheet that doesn't conform to the CSS1 or CSS2 specifications. A *CSS validation warning*, on the other hand, signifies a condition in your style sheet that might affect its accessibility or usability, for instance, even though there might not be anything in your style sheet that is specifically invalid. For instance, you aren't required to specify a background color (even if set as transparent) whenever you specify a foreground color for an element in order for your style sheet to be valid, but you should, because to do otherwise might result in your page being unreadable to some users.

Using the W3C's HTML Validator

An *HTML validator* checks your page for compatibility with the latest versions of HTML. By inserting a Document Type Declaration (or DocType Declaration) at the top of your document, you declare which version (HTML 4, for instance) and which flavor (strict, transitional, or frameset) of HTML your page should be compXatible with.

An HTML validator actually checks your page for conformance with the official Document Type Definition (DTD) for the version and flavor of HTML you've declared it to be compatible with. An official HTML specification is really just a description and elaboration of that HTML version's DTD. For a look at the "transitional" HTML 4.01 DTD, for instance, see http://www.w3.org/TR/html4/sgml/loosedtd.html. To see the "strict" XHTML 1.0 DTD, see http://www.w3.org/TR/xhtml1/DTD/xhtml1-strict.dtd.

✔ For guidance on using the right Document Type Declaration for your HTML or XHTML file, see "The Three Flavors of HTML," p. 84 (Chapter 4).

NOTE

When using CSS in your pages, you should always declare your pages as being HTML 4-compliant using one of the HTML 4 Document Type Declarations. HTML 3.2 supports neither the SPAN tag nor the STYLE, CLASS, OR ID attributes, for instance, so any use of them in your HTML file will be flagged as errors if you declare your page to be only HTML 3.2-compliant.

Since the W3C is in charge of deciding what is and what is not valid HTML, the W3C's HTML Validator should be your first stop when you want to check to see that your page contains valid HTML. The W3C's HTML Validator can check the validity of both HTML and XHTML documents.

To find the W3C's HTML Validator, just go to the W3C's home page at http://www.w3.org/ and click the HTML Validator link in the left sidebar, or you can go to it directly at http://validator.w3.org/. To use the HTML Validator, you can either provide a Web address for the page you want to check or you can upload the page to be checked.

To use the first option, you need to have already transferred the page you want to check up onto the Web. If you've done that, just type the Web address of your page in the Address box. Figure 15.6 shows a Web address for the kochanski.html example file typed in the Address box, so it can be validated.

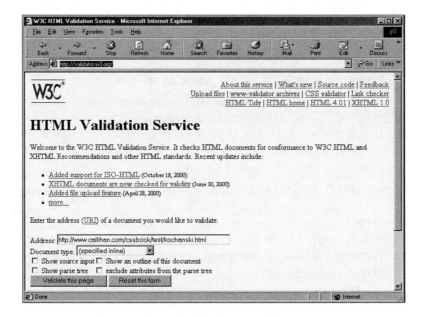

Figure 15.6: *The Web address of the kochanski.html example file is typed in the HTML Validator's Address box, so it can be validated.*

You just need to click the Validate this page button to validate the page.

You can also upload an HTML file to be validated. Just scroll down below the current form and click the "upload files" link. To select the file to be uploaded, just click the Browse button, open the folder where the document you want to check is stored, and then double-click it. Figure 15.7 shows the local location of kochanski.html inserted in the File box, ready for uploading. To upload the document to be validated, you just need then to click the Validate this document button.

As shown in Figure 15.8, the kochanski.html example file passed with flying colors. If your document passes, the W3C provides you with the codes to include an icon on your page to show that it is coded using valid HTML.

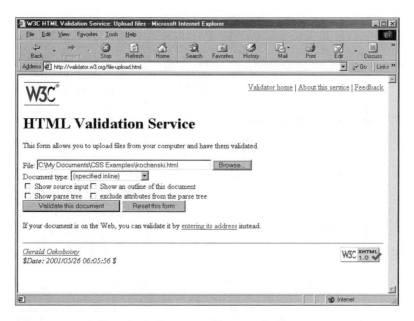

Figure 15.7: You can also upload an HTML file to be validated.

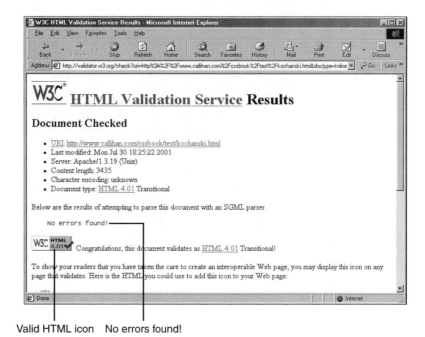

Valid HTML icon　No errors found!

Figure 15.8: If your page passes, you get the message "No errors found!"

If there are errors in your HTML, the W3C's HTML Validator flags the line and column where the error is found. It doesn't necessarily tell you the reason for the error, but likely provides enough information so you can figure it out for yourself. To give you an example of this, I purposefully inserted some errors into the kochanski.html example file by causing a number of the elements to overlap, rather than be nested inside of each other. If you want to try this out for yourself, just open kochanski.html in your text editor, resave it as **kochanski_error2.html**, and then make the following changes to the file's HTML code:

```
<h1><em>The Kochanski Family Page</h1></em>
<p class="first">Welcome to the Kochanski Family page! Look here for information
on birthdays, anniversaries, milestones, graduations, family gatherings, and
other stuff related to our immediate and extended family.</p>
<p>George and I will also be presenting the latest information and details about
our own lives and careers, as well as the latest info on our two wonderful kids,
Joe and Sue (or at least what we've been able to wring out of them!).</p>

<h2 class="special">The Kochanski Family Gathering</h2>
<p class="first">You'll all be pleased to know that the annual Kochanski family
gathering has been scheduled for next July 1st. It will be held at Ford Park at
Stove #24 starting at 12 noon. Back by popular demand, George will be handling
the barbecue (ribs and hot dogs), but others are encouraged to contribute other
dishes and items to eat or drink.</p>
<p>Please, however, follow safe food preparation practices — we don't want any
more outbreaks like we had last year! Remember, if bringing food to the
gathering, it is important to keep cold food cold and hot food hot. If in doubt,
see the Department of Agriculture's <a
href="http://www.fsis.usda.gov/OA/pubs/facts_barbecue.htm">Barbecue Food
Safety</a> tips.</p></a>
```

If you now validate the HTML code using any of the methods discussed previously, you should get the same result shown in Figure 15.9 (unless, of course, you've created any additional errors or problems in your HTML code).

You can also get errors and warnings when you validate your HTML if you've declared an incorrect Document Type Declaration. For instance, if you've declared your document to be compatible with the strict DTD for HTML 4.01, any deprecated elements and attributes included in your page will be flagged as errors.

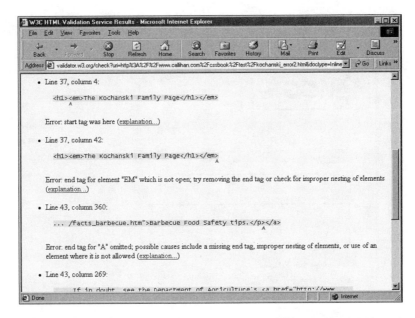

Figure 15.9: *If your page doesn't pass, the W3C's HTML Validator flags the exact places, by line and column coordinates, where errors can be found.*

Using the WDG's CSS and HTML Validators

The Web Design Group (WDG) hosts online CSS and HTML validators that you can use to validate your CSS style sheets and HTML files.

Using the WDG CSSCheck Validator

The WDG has another online validator, CSSCheck, that you can use to validate your CSS style sheets. You can find the WDG CSSCheck program at http://www.htmlhelp.com/tools/csscheck/ (see Figure 15.10).

To use the WDG CSSCheck program, you need to either specify a link to a CSS style sheet file (with a .css extension) or paste your style sheet's codes into the provided text box. Unlike with the W3C CSS Validator, you can't just specify the URL of an HTML file containing a style sheet. Figure 15.11 shows the codes from the style sheet for kochanski.html pasted into the CSSCheck program's text area box.

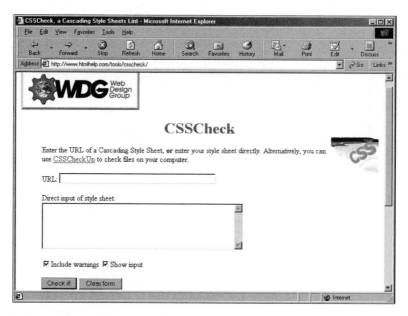

Figure 15.10: You can also use the WDG CSSCheck online validator to check your CSS style sheet.

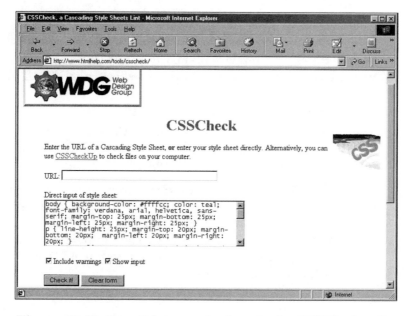

Figure 15.11: To validate a style sheet in the CSSCheck online utility, you need to paste in the codes from your style sheet.

The WDG CSSCheck program is a little more stringent and will likely provide more warnings than the W3C CSS Validator. For instance, Figure 15.12 shows some warnings produced by the CSSCheck program for the style sheet that you created for the kochanski.html example. You'll notice two types of warnings, one about a missing background-image property and another about the use of the background-color property rather than the background shorthand property, because some earlier CSS-browsers support the latter, but not the former.

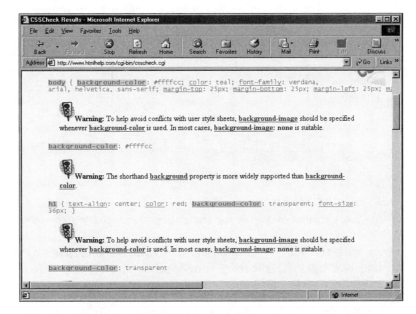

Figure 15.12: *The CSSCheck program might produce warnings that the W3C's CSS Validator doesn't.*

However, if you replace all of the background-color properties with background properties, all of the warnings are taken care of, as shown in Figure 15.13. Using the background shorthand includes the implication of setting a background-image: none property, because the initial values for all of the background properties are assumed, unless they are otherwise stated.

Using the WDG HTML Validator

The WDG also provides an online utility, the HTML Validator, that you can use to validate your HTML files. To find it, just go to the WDG site at http://www.htmlhelp.com/ and scroll down and click the "HTML Validator" link in the Tools section. You can also go directly to it at http://www. htmlhelp.com/tools/validator/.

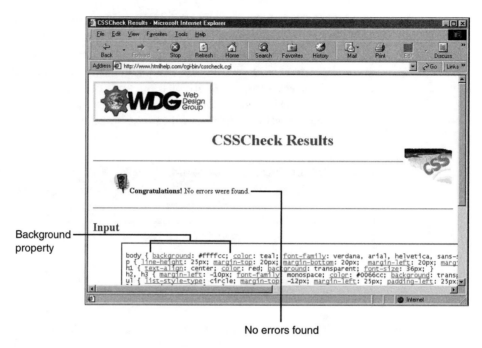

Background property

No errors found

Figure 15.13: *All of the CSSCheck warnings are resolved by substituting the* background *property for the* background-color *property.*

As with the W3C's version, you can validate your page by providing its Web address, uploading it from your local computer, or pasting your HTML codes into a text area box.

To use the first method, you need to first transfer your page up onto the Web. You then type your page's Web address in the HTML Validator's URL box. Figure 15.14 shows a Web address for the kochanski.html example file typed in the URL box.

You can also use the second method, copying and pasting all of the codes in your page and uploading them to be validated.

To validate the page, just click the Validate It! button. Figure 15.15 shows the result of validating the kochanski.html example file.

To test out the error reporting and warnings provided by the WDG's HTML Validator, purposefully introduce some HTML errors into your HTML file. Just reuse the HTML codes from the kochanski_error2.html file you created previously, if you'd like to check this out for yourself. Figure 15.16 shows the result of validating a page where some HTML elements are overlapping each other, rather than being nested.

Web address

Figure 15.14: To validate a page already located on the Web, you just need to provide the page's Web address.

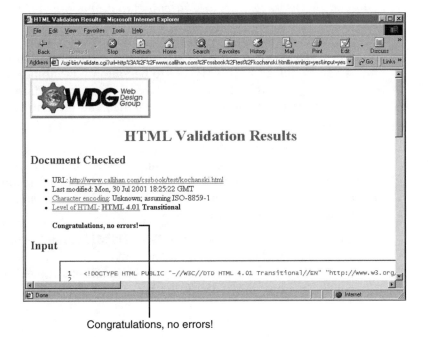

Congratulations, no errors!

Figure 15.15: The kochanski.html example page passes the WDG HTML validation test with flying colors.

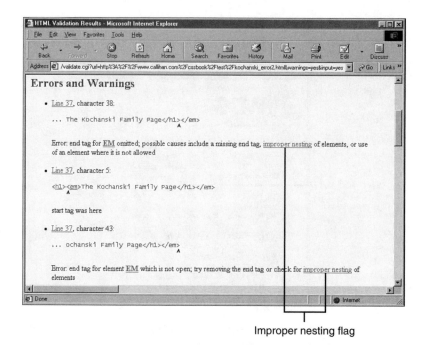

Improper nesting flag

Figure 15.16: *The WDG's HTML Validator reports the location (line and character) of errors it finds and attempts to diagnose what the problems might be.*

In the first paragraph of the HTML Validator's front page, are links that enable you to upload an HTML file to be validated (validate files on your computer) or paste in the HTML codes you want to validate into a text area box (enter your HTML directly). You can also validate multiple URLs using batch mode.

You also have the option of validating all of the pages in a site. The checkbox for this, Validate entire site, is unchecked by default. If you check it, the HTML Validator also validates any pages that are internal to your site and are linked to from the page being validated. If your site has lots of pages, that can be real handy.

The WDG HTML Validator and the W3C HTML Validator produce very similar validation checks, so which one you choose to use is pretty much a matter of which one you feel gives you the most useful feedback. Nothing says, of course, that you can't use both.

Using Other HTML Validators and Page Checkers

The W3C and WDG HTML validators check your page against the official DTD ("strict," "transitional," or "frameset") for the version of HTML used in your page. Other so-called "validators" do not check your page directly against the DTD for your page's HTML version and flavor, but may do additional checks and provide additional feedback on your page. These services or software might more accurately be described as "page checkers." They might provide more profuse advice on your page's coding, warning of current or earlier browsers either not supporting or inconsistently supporting a particular feature, for instance. Other page checkers might test out all your links, reporting back to you which ones are dead or not responding.

Dr. Watson, an online page checker, for instance, will check your HTML, verify your regular and image links, do a spell-check, estimate your page's download speed, and check your page for search engine compatibility. You can access Dr. Watson at `http://watson.addy.com/`.

Another interesting page checker is Bobby, a freeware Java-based "web site validator" that will check your site for its accessibility to individuals with disabilities. You can find out more about Bobby at `http://www.cast.org/bobby/`.

Additional listings of HTML validators and other page checkers are available for the Windows and Macintosh platforms at TuCows at `http://www.tucows.com/`.

What's Next?

You should now have a good understanding of why you should validate your CSS style sheets and HTML (or XHTML) documents. You should also now know how to use the online CSS and HTML validators that are available from the W3C and the WDG, as well as know where to find other validation and page checker utilities.

In Chapter 16, "Providing for Backward Compatibility," you learn how to ensure that your CSS-powered HTML files don't produce adverse results when displayed in Web browsers that lack support, or provide imperfect support, for CSS.

Providing for Backward Compatibility

All of the CSS examples presented in this book work reliably in current CSS-supporting browsers, including Internet Explorer 5.5 for Windows, Internet Explorer 5 for the Macintosh, Netscape 6, and Opera 5. You can't expect, however, that visitors to your site won't use earlier versions of these browsers, which either don't support CSS at all or support it imperfectly.

In this chapter, you learn about the following:

- Non-conforming browsers

- Using gateway pages and browser sniffers

- Participating in the Web Standards Project

- Using the @import At-Rule

- Using the LINK element with a MEDIA attribute

- Understanding how DocType switching works

Using the Example File

For this chapter, you use the Performance Motivation Associates example page you created in Chapter 9, "Formatting Block Elements." Just open in your text editor the perform-motive.html that you created and saved in your working folder; you can also find this file available as perform-motive_final.html. Just resave it in your working folder as perform-motive4.html. You can also type in the codes and text for this file, as shown here:

Listing 16.1: PERFORM-MOTIVE4.HTML—Performance Motivation Associates

```
<!DOCTYPE HTML PUBLIC "-//W3C//DTD HTML 4.01 Transitional//EN"
"http://www.w3.org/TR/html4/loose.dtd">

<html>

<head>
<title>Performance Motivation Associates</title>
<style type="text/css">
body { margin: 0;  color: white; background: #660000; }
h1 { color: navy; background: #ffffcc url(paper.gif); text-align: center; margin:
0.15em 10%; padding: 0.1em 5%; border: dotted 12px olive; }
h2, h3 { color: #66ffcc; background: transparent; }
div.body { font-family: Verdana, Arial, sans-serif; font-size: 1.1em; color:
#ffff99; background: navy url(dark.jpg); border: solid 0.5em #ff9933; margin:
0.5%; padding: 0.2em 1%; }
div.body p { text-align: left; margin-left: 1%; margin-right: 1%; }
div.inset { color: navy; background: url(clouds.jpg) aqua; border: inset 10px
aqua; font-family: Verdana, Arial, sans-serif; padding: 0.2em 4% 0 0; margin: 0
15% 1em; text-align: center; }
a { color: lime; background: transparent; }
#goals { vertical-align: bottom; }
.ctr { text-align: center; }
.border { border: 10px yellow ridge; padding: 10px; width: 125px; height: 125px;
margin-left: auto; margin-right: auto; }
</style>
</head>
<body>

<div class="body">
<h1>Performance Motivation Associates</h1>

<p>Are you living and working up to your potential? Do you wish to know how to
motivate yourself, family, associates, or employees to higher performance and
achievement? Are you spending more and more time seeking answers, but less and
less time activating solutions? We at Performance Motivation Associates make
providing solutions and activating success our primary business.</p>
```

Listing 16.1: continued

```
<h2>The Performance Motivation Advantage</h2>
<p>We are industry leaders in performance motivation seminars, leadership style
assessments, interpersonal skills development courses, meta-goal planning
assistance, and other performance enhancement services. Our only job is the
liberation of performance potential for individuals, groups, and
organizations.</p>

<h3>The Performance Motivation Team</h3>
<p>Our highly skilled and experienced professional consultants have helped enable
thousands of clients to achieve success and maximize performance. Do you feel
you're falling short and going around in circles? Our experts, consultants, and
coaches are experts in performance actualization, success achievement, and
leadership development. We can help you get where you want to go. Join the
Performance Motivation Team today!</p>

<h3>Performance Motivation Services</h3>
<p>We offer a wide range of seminars, consulting, and other services in the areas
of:</p>

<div class="inset">
<ul>
<li>Career and Job Success
<li>Youth and Adult Leadership Development
<li>Parenting and Family Skills
<li>Personal Achievement
<li>Goal and Success Visualization
<li>Meta-Goal Planning
</ul>
</div>

<div class="ctr">
<div class="border">
<img src="goals.gif" id="goals">
</div>
</div>

<hr>

<address>
Performance Motivation Associates<br>
E-Mail: <a href="mailto:contact@perform-motive.com">contact@perform-
motive.com</a><br>
Web Address: <a href="http://www.perform-
motive.com/welcome.html">http://www.perform-motive.com/welcome.html</a>
</address>
</div>
</body>
</html>
```

What About Non-Conforming Browsers?

You can expect that visitors to your site use a variety of different browsers. Some of these browsers do not support CSS at all and totally ignore any styles that you set, but some imperfectly support CSS. Earlier, I characterized browsers that imperfectly support CSS1 as first-generation CSS-browsers, and characterized browsers that support most (at least 90 percent) of CSS1 as second-generation CSS-browsers.

✔ If you want to review the earlier discussion of first-, second-, and third-generation CSS-browsers, see "Implementation of CSS in Browsers," p. 17 (chapter 1).

Non-Supporting Browsers

Of the major browsers, these versions don't support CSS at all: Opera 3.5 and earlier versions, Netscape Navigator 3.x and earlier versions, and Internet Explorer 2.x and earlier versions. In these browsers, any CSS styling you include in your page is completely ignored.

You probably don't want to download and install an older browser version that doesn't support CSS, just to see that CSS doesn't work in it, right? If you have a version of Netscape Navigator 4 on your computer, however, you can turn it into a non-CSS-supporting browser by turning off either style sheets or JavaScript. Just select Edit, Preferences, double-click Advanced in the Category panel, and then uncheck the Enable style sheets check box.

Figure 16.1 shows perform-motive4.html displayed in Internet Explorer 5.5, as well as in a copy of Netscape Navigator 4.7 with display of style sheets turned off. With styles turned off, Netscape Navigator 4.7 displays only the raw HTML codes, which include no particular display formatting other than that the display defaults of the browser.

You can also turn off display of styles in Internet Explorer 5.5 for Windows. Just select Tools, Internet Options, click the Accessibility button, and then check the second check box (Ignore font styles specified on Web pages). In Internet Explorer 5 for the Macintosh, select File, Preferences, click Web Content in the side panel, and then uncheck the Show style sheets check box.

In Opera 5 for Windows, to turn off display of styles, just select File, Preferences, click Documents in the side panel, and then uncheck the Document check box on the Document CSS line.

Internet Explorer 5.5

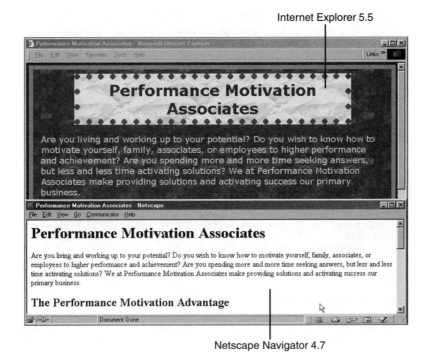

Netscape Navigator 4.7

Figure 16.1: *The top browser (Internet Explorer 5.5) recognizes styles, but the bottom browser (Netscape Navigator 4.7, with style sheets turned off) ignores them.*

CAUTION

If you do choose to turn off display of styles in your browser to check this out, don't forget to turn display of styles back on!

Combining Styles and Deprecated Elements and Attributes

A way to provide more than just an entirely vanilla Web page to users of browsers that don't support CSS is to combine styles with the use of deprecated elements and attributes. Users of non-supporting browsers see the effect of the deprecated elements and attributes; but, depending on how they're inserted in your page, users of browsers that support CSS see the appearance specified through styles.

For instance, you could insert TEXT, LINK, VLINK, BGCOLOR, and BACKGROUND attributes in your page's BODY tag to specify text, link, and background colors, as well as a background image, to be displayed in a browser that doesn't display CSS styles.

You can also use the FONT element, as well as other HTML elements, to insert formatting for non-supporting browsers or browsers in which styles have been turned off.

For an example of doing this, just edit your example file, making additions and deletions as shown here (see Figure 16.2):

```
<body text="#ffff99" link="lime" vlink="lime" bgcolor="#660000"
background="dark.jpg">

<font face="Verdana, Arial" size="4">
<div class="body">
<font color="#66ffcc"><h1 align="center">Performance Motivation
Associates</h1></font>

<p>Are you living and working up to your potential? Do you wish to know how to
motivate yourself, family, associates, or employees to higher performance and
achievement? Are you spending more and more time seeking answers, but less and
less time activating solutions? We at Performance Motivation Associates make
providing solutions and activating success our primary business.</p>

<font color="#66ffcc"><h2>The Performance Motivation Advantage</h2></font>
<p>We are industry leaders in performance motivation seminars, leadership style
assessments, interpersonal skills development courses, meta-goal planning
assistance, and other performance enhancement services. Our only job is the
liberation of performance potential for individuals, groups, and
organizations.</p>

<font color="#66ffcc"><h3>The Performance Motivation Team</h3></font>
<p>Our highly skilled and experienced professional consultants have helped enable
thousands of clients to achieve success and maximize performance. Do you feel
you're falling short and going around in circles? Our experts, consultants, and
coaches are experts in performance actualization, success achievement, and
leadership development. We can help you get where you want to go. Join the
Performance Motivation Team today!</p>

<font color="#66ffcc"><h3>Performance Motivation Services</h3></font>
<p>We offer a wide range of seminars, consulting, and other services in the areas
of:</p>

<div class="inset">
<ul>
<li>Career and Job Success
<li>Youth and Adult Leadership Development
<li>Parenting and Family Skills
<li>Personal Achievement
<li>Goal and Success Visualization
<li>Meta-Goal Planning
</ul>
</div>
```

```
<div class="ctr">
<div class="border">
<img src="goals.gif" id="goals">
</div>
</div>

<hr>

<address>
Performance Motivation Associates<br>
E-Mail: <a href="mailto:contact@perform-motive.com">contact@perform-
motive.com</a><br>
Web Address: <a href="http://www.perform-
motive.com/welcome.html">http://www.perform-motive.com/welcome.html</a>
</address>
</div>
</font>
</body>
```

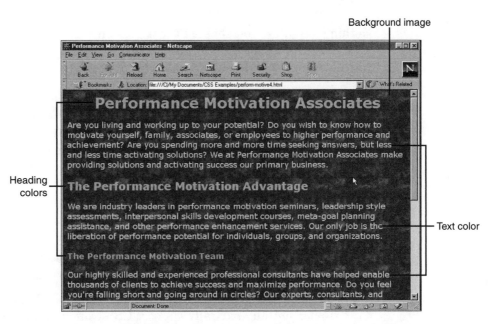

Figure 16.2: *In Netscape Navigator 4.7 (with styles turned off), you can use HTML to set text, link, and other font colors, as well as to specify a background image.*

In Figure 16.2, notice the FONT elements bracket the heading elements (H1, H2, and H3), instead of being nested inside of them. If the FONT elements are nested inside the heading elements, the color specified by the FONT element is displayed, even in a CSS-supporting browser.

✔ For tables showing all elements and attributes that have been deprecated in HTML 4.01, see "CSS and Deprecated Elements and Attributes," p. 82 (chapter 4).

You might not want to spend too much time trying to dress up your pages for browsers that don't support CSS. That's because a relatively small proportion of users use browsers that don't support CSS or have turned off display of style sheets in their browsers. As time goes by, such users will only become fewer and fewer.

NOTE

BrowserWatch.com recently reported, of all the visitors to Internet.com, only 0.22 percent were using Netscape 3.x, and 0.20 percent were using Internet Explorer 2.x. This amounts to approximately one out of every 238 users using one of these browsers. For the latest statistics, see `http://browserwatch.internet.com/stats/icst ats.html`.

Nothing says that you shouldn't just present the raw HTML formatting to these users—they're able to view and read the structural content of your page, even if the styles controlling appearance are invisible to them.

Using Gateway Pages and Browser Sniffers

You can also use a *gateway page* to forewarn users of the browser requirements for viewing your page, or to provide a link to an alternative page that doesn't use styles. A gateway page is a page that provides an entrance to your site. The main problem with this approach is that you have to maintain three pages instead of one: the gateway page, the page using styles, and the page not using styles.

Another problem with this is that you can't compel users to only enter your page through your gateway page. Someone might post a link to your page using styles, which entirely bypasses your gateway page.

A similar approach is to use a *browser sniffer* to shield earlier browsers that don't support or only partially support CSS from accessing your page. A browser sniffer is a script that tests for which browser (and version) is accessing a page and routes the users to an appropriate page for the browser they're using. Browser sniffers are most commonly JavaScript scripts, but server-side browser sniffers, written in Perl, for instance, can also be used.

A browser sniffer, for instance, might try to shield browsers earlier than Internet Explorer 5.5 for Windows, Internet Explorer 5 for the Macintosh,

Netscape 6, or Opera 5 from accessing your CSS-styled Web page. If detected, users of earlier browser versions than these would see a version of your page that doesn't use CSS styles.

There are also problems with this. For one thing, just like with a gateway page, you have to create separate pages that use and do not use CSS. Browser sniffers also tend to be somewhat inconsistent and unreliable in identifying browsers. They also have to be constantly updated as new browsers become available. Browser sniffers created using JavaScript also require that users haven't disabled JavaScript in their browsers. Perl or other scripts that run on the server can also be used, but they are somewhat harder to find.

You can find a selection of browser sniffers, as well as guidance for creating your own browser sniffer, at WebReference.com's site at `http://www.webreference.com/tools/browser/`. For an in-depth explanation of how browser sniffers work, see `http://hotwired.lycos.com/webmonkey/99/02/index2a.html`.

NOTE

Some of the figures in this chapter show examples of the example HTML files that you create in this chapter displayed in Netscape Navigator 4.x. If you have a version of that browser installed on your computer, feel free to check these examples out for yourself in that browser. On the other hand, if you want to rely on the figures to show you what should happen in Netscape Navigator 4.x, that's fine too.

However, if you're planning on using any of the methods specified in this chapter for shielding Netscape Navigator 4.x from displaying styles that are problematic in that browser, you might want to consider downloading and installing one of the later versions of Netscape Navigator 4.x, if you don't already have one installed. You can then use it to personally test out CSS properties or features included in your style sheets that might be problematic in that browser. To download and install Netscape Navigator 4.7, for instance, just go to `http://home.netscape.com/download/archive.html`.

Participating in the Web Standards Project

Another option for dealing with both browsers that don't support CSS and those that only partially support it is to join the Web Standards Project.

The Web Standards Project (WaSP) is a coalition of Web developers and users formed to persuade browser makers of the importance of standards and to encourage users to upgrade to the latest standards-compliant Web browsers. Of particular interest to CSS-authors is the WaSP's Browser Upgrade Initiative (see `http://www.webstandards.org/upgrade/what.html`), which provides two methods that CSS-authors can use to deal with earlier non-standards-compliant browsers that either don't support or only partially and imperfectly support the current CSS standards. The following two sections cover these methods.

The DOM Sniff Method

This more radical method redirects all users of non-compliant browsers to an upgrade page, either your own or one provided by the Web Standards Project. All you have to do is insert JavaScript scripts provided by WaSP that handle the redirection. Users using non-compliant Web browsers are then automatically redirected to a page that recommends that they upgrade their browser, with links to where they can download and install the latest browsers. If you create your own upgrade page, you can also include a link enabling the user to view your page, as is, or to view an alternative page that you've created for non-compliant browsers.

Generally, this method is only recommended if you're using advanced features in your page that break some or all non-compliant browsers. *Breaking* a browser occurs when non-compliant browsers either don't display your page at all or render it in a fashion that severely compromises a user's ability to access and read your page. This is especially true if your page makes use of the W3C's DOM standard (Document Object Model) or ECMAScript (the official standard-compliant version of JavaScript), as well as certain CSS2 features (such as absolute or relative positioning) known to negatively impact page display in non-compliant browsers. This method is called the DOM Sniff method, because it checks to see if the browser version being used supports the W3C's DOM standard. If it does, it gets passed through; if not, it gets redirected.

To add this to your page, just insert the following JavaScript inside of your page's HEAD element:

```
<script type="text/javascript" language="javascript">
<!-- //

if (!document.getElementById) {
    window.location =
        "http://www.webstandards.org/upgrade/"
}

    // -->
</script>
</head>
```

If you're declaring your page to be in "strict" conformance to HTML 4 or XHTML 1, then substitute the following SCRIPT start tag:

```
<script type="text/javascript">
```

If the user is using a non-compliant browser, they're automatically redirected to the WaSP's Browser Upgrade page, as shown in Figure 16.3.

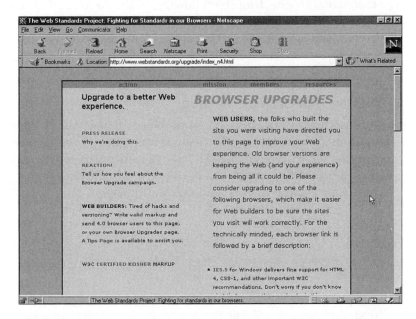

Figure 16.3: *Using the WaSP's DOM Sniff method, users of non-compliant browsers (such as Netscape Navigator 4.7 shown here) are redirected to the WaSP's Browser Upgrade page.*

NOTE

If you previously turned off style sheets in Netscape Navigator 4 to check out using the FONT and other deprecated elements to provide alternative markup for browsers that don't support CSS, you should turn them back on to check out the DOM Sniff method using that browser. Just select **Edit**, **Preferences**, click the **Advanced** option, and then make sure the **Enable style sheets** check box is checked.

In practice, anyone using a "Version 4" or earlier browser (Internet Explorer 4 or Netscape 4, or earlier versions) or Opera 3.5 or earlier, among various other non-compliant browsers, is redirected to the upgrade page.

You can also use a global JavaScript file, which means you only need to create these codes once. Just insert the script lines in a text file, like this:

```
if (!document.getElementById) {
    window.location =
        "http://www.webstandards.org/upgrade/"
}
```

Then save it in your working folder with a .js extension—you might use domsniff.js, for instance. Then you can embed it in any page (within that same folder) by nesting the following to the page's HEAD element:

```
</style>
<script language="javascript" type="text/javascript" src="domsniff.js">
</script>
</head>
```

The Invisible Object Method

This method uses CSS to insert an object that is only visible to users of non-compliant browsers. To users of standards-compliant browsers, however, the object is invisible. The object informs users of non-compliant browsers that the page looks better in a standards-compliant browser, but they can continue to view and access the page if they wish. To add this to your page, first delete the DOM Sniff script you just added to your style sheet:

```
</style>
<script language="javascript" type="text/javascript" src="domsniff.js">
</script>
</head>
```

Next, add a class selector to your style sheet that turns off display of an "invisible" element class:

```
a { color: lime; background: transparent; }
.invisible { display: none; }
```

Next, add the invisible element inside your page's BODY element:

```
<h2 class="invisible">
This site will look much better in a browser that supports
<a href="http://www.webstandards.org/upgrade/" title="Download a browser that
complies with Web standards."> web standards</a>, but it is accessible to any
browser or Internet device.
</h2>
```

Although an H2 element is used here, you can use any other standard element you wish, such as an H1, P, or DIV element, for instance.

This has the effect of displaying the "invisible" object only in older browsers that don't support CSS (or don't support the display: none property). It is important to note, however, that this is not the case in otherwise partially compliant browsers that do support display: none, such as Netscape Navigator 4. It is good, however, for notifying users of earlier browsers (such as Netscape Navigator 3) that they should consider upgrading their browser.

If you want the "invisible" object to also be displayed in Netscape Navigator 4, for instance, the trick is to use an IFRAME element, instead. This works because Netscape Navigator 4 does not support the IFRAME element. Just add the following to your page's code:

```
<iframe class="invisible">
<h2 class="invisible">
This site will look much better
in a browser that supports
<a href="http://www.webstandards.org/upgrade/"
title="Download a browser that
complies with Web standards.">
web standards</a>,
but it is accessible to any browser
or Internet device.
</h2>
</iframe>
```

Be sure to delete the `class="invisible"` attribute in the H2 element. If you don't, it's still invisible in Netscape Navigator 4.7. As Figure 16.4 shows, the invisible object is not displayed in Internet Explorer 5.5, but it is displayed in Netscape Navigator 4.7.

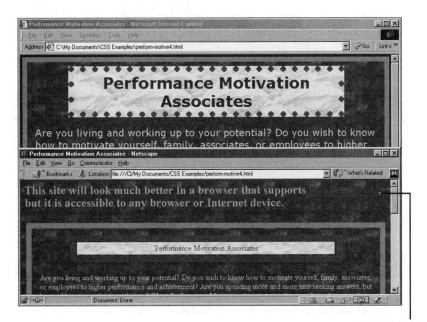

Invisible object (visible in Navigator 4.7)

Figure 16.4: Using the WaSP's Invisible Object method, users of non-compliant browsers (such as Netscape Navigator 4.7 shown here) are notified that the page looks better in a standards-compliant Web browser.

Using the `@import` At-Rule

The `@import` at-rule must be the first rule in a style sheet. It lets you import external style sheets into your page. However, because different browsers have varying degrees of supporting or not supporting this, it can be used to exclude certain browsers from or include certain browser in displaying a specific set of styles.

Use this to block Netscape Navigator 4.x (all platforms), Internet Explorer 3.x (Windows), iCab 2.51 (Mac), Konqueror 2.12, and Amaya 5.1 (Windows):

```
@import url(mystyles.css);
```

Use this to also block Internet Explorer 4 and 5 (Windows or Macintosh):

```
@import url "../styles/mystyles.css";
```

Table 16.1   Browser Support for the **@import** *At-Rule*

Browser	Support
Internet Explorer 3	No[1]
Internet Explorer 4 & 5	Yes, but only in URL form[2]
Opera 3.6 & 5	Yes[3]
Netscape 4	No[4]
Netscape 6	Yes
iCab 2.51 (Mac)	No
Konqueror 2.1.2	No
Amaya 5.1 (Win)	No

1: Internet Explorer 3 Ignores the next ruleset following the &import at-rule. You should thus precede other rulesets with a dummy ruleset:

```
<style type="text/css">
@import url(mystyles.css);
.dummy { color: blue; }
```

2: Internet Explorer 4 and 5 only support the URL form of the @import at-rule, @import url(mystyles.css), but not the non-URL (or string) form, @import "mystyles.css" (or @import 'mystyles.css'). Unfortunately, Internet Explorer 4 for the Macintosh is the exception here, supporting both the URL and string forms of the @import at-rule, meaning that it can't be blocked by using the string form. It is blocked, however, if a relative URL is used to access the style sheet.

3: Although Opera 3.6 and 5 support both the URL and string forms of the @import at-rule, it does have some bugs. The following, for instance, won't be recognized unless "screen" is changed to "all."

```
@import url(media.css) somemediarule, screen;
```

The following also won't be recognized, unless "print" is changed to either "screen" or "all."

```
@import url(media.css) print;
```

4: Some earlier versions of Netscape Navigator 4 (4.06 and earlier) will crash when encountering an @import at-rule. A script could conceivably be used to weed out those implementations of Netscape Navigator, substituting an alternative page or a link to a browser upgrade page.

Because Internet Explorer 4 for the Macintosh does support the `@import` at-rule, but Netscape Navigator 4 doesn't, the primary use for this at-rule is to block Netscape Navigator 4 users from accessing styles that have a deleterious effect in that browser. If you use the string version of the `@import` at-rule, you also block all versions of Internet Explorer 3, plus all versions of Internet Explorer 4 except for the Macintosh version, from accessing the same styles.

You can also deny any version of Internet Explorer 3 or 4 (Windows or Macintosh) by specifying a relative URL to access the style sheet using the `@import` at-rule: `@import url(../styles/mystyle.css)`, for instance.

Using the LINK Element with a MEDIA Attribute

Another way to block out certain browsers is to link to an external style sheet using the LINK element with a MEDIA attribute, like this:

```
<link href="hide3.css" type="text/css" rel="stylesheet" media="all">
```

Use this to block Netscape Navigator 4.x (all platforms) from accessing the specified style sheet. Netscape Navigator 4.x ignores any linked style sheet with a MEDIA value other than "screen" (`media="screen"`). Here's another version:

```
<link rel="stylesheet" href="mystyles1.css" type="text/css" media="screen,
projection" title="My #1 Style Sheet">
```

Finding Out What Works (and Doesn't Work) in Which Browsers

A number of resources on the Web provide charts or feedback on which CSS features are supported by which browsers. Because you're unlikely to want to install every possible browser on your computer or have every possible platform (Windows, Macintosh, Unix/Linux, and so on) available for testing, these can be of invaluable assistance in sorting out which browsers need to be shielded from which style properties. In fact, only one version of Internet Explorer for Windows can be installed on a 32-bit Windows system, so you have to have multiple computers (or multiple copies of Windows installed in separate partitions) to be able to test out your pages in versions of Internet Explorer other than the one you've got installed. Here are descriptions of and links to these resources:

- **WebReview.com's Style Sheet Reference Guide** (`http://www.webreview.com/style/`)—Click the link to the **Master Compatibility Chart** to view support in browsers for all CSS1 properties and features. The chart indicates if a browser's support for a CSS1 property or feature is complete, partial, buggy, quirky, or non-existent. You can also click the link to CSS2 Selectors Chart to check support of the new CSS2 selectors in various browsers.

- **Westciv's House of Style** (http://www.westciv.com/style_master/house/)—Click the **Browser Compatibility** link in the sidebar to access their browser compatibility charts. Browser compatibility is listed for all CSS1, as well as many CSS2, properties and features. In addition to compatibility levels for Internet Explorer, Netscape Navigator, and Opera, compatibility is also listed for WebTV 1.0.

- The comp.infosystems.www.authoring.stylesheets newsgroup can be a great resource for getting down into the nitty-gritty of different browser compatibility issues. You can just lurk or you can solicit responses with a specific query. Before posting, however, be sure to read their FAQs at http://css.nu/faq/ciwas-mFAQ.html and http://css.nu/faq/ciwas-aFAQ.html.

TIP

You can use the Google Groups search engine at http://groups.google.com/ to search all messages that have been posted to the comp.infosystems.www.authoring. stylesheets newsgroup or other newsgroups. This can be a great way to find specific answers to your CSS questions. Just click the Advanced Groups Search link, type the name of the newsgroup in the Newsgroup box, type words or phrases you want to search for in any of the Find messages boxes, and then click the Google Search button.

You can also post a request for others to give you feedback on CSS- or HTML-oriented newsgroups, discussion forums, or mailing lists. Besides the comp.infosystems.www.authoring.stylesheets newsgroup, you can post requests for feedback at:

- **A List Apart's Coders Forum** at http://www.alistapart.com/discuss/coders/. You'll find discussion forums here on Cascading Style Sheets and other subjects to which you can post queries or requests for feedback.

- **The HTML Writers Guild's HWG-Critique** mailing list at http://www.hwg.org/lists/hwg-critique/ is dedicated to allowing HWG members to ask for and provide feedback on their Web pages. A trial membership (good for up to a year) is free; after that membership is $40/year.

The Comment Bug

You can use this bug to shield styles from Internet Explorer 5.0 for Windows (and earlier versions). This does not work, however, to shield styles from Internet Explorer 5.5 for Windows or Internet Explorer 5.0 or 4.x for the Macintosh. If a CSS comment (/* */) immediately follows a selector, Internet Explorer 5.0 for Windows and earlier versions ignores the properties following the CSS comment codes (but other CSS-browsers, including Netscape 4.x, still parse the properties). Here's an example:

```
#selectorid/* */ { color: #ff0; background: transparent; }
```

A Practical Example

In the following exercise, you create a practical example of using the @import at-rule to exclude Netscape Navigator 4 from accessing certain style rules and properties. To get started, first edit perform-motive4.html, as shown here (don't save it yet, however):

```
<style type="text/css">
body { margin: 0;  color: white; background: #660000; }
h1 { color: navy; background: #ffffcc url(paper.gif); text-align: center; margin:
0.15em 10%; padding: 0.1em 5%; border: dotted 12px olive; }
h2, h3 { color: #66ffcc;  background: transparent; }
div.body { font-family: Verdana, Arial, sans-serif; font-size: 1.1em; color:
#ffff99; background: navy url(dark.jpg); border: solid 0.5em #ff9933; margin:
0.5%; padding: 0.2em 1%; }
div.body p { text-align: left; margin-left: 1%; margin-right: 1%; }
div.inset { color: navy; background: url(clouds.jpg) aqua; border: inset 10px
aqua; font-family: Verdana, Arial, sans-serif; padding: 0.2em 4% 0 0; margin: 0
15% 1em; text-align: center; }
a { color: lime; background: transparent; }
.invisible { display: none; }
</style>
<script language="javascript" type="text/javascript" src="domsniff.js">
</script>
</head>
<body text="#ffff99" link="lime" vlink="lime" bgcolor="#660000"
background="dark.jpg">

<iframe class="invisible">
<h2>
This site will look much better
in a browser that supports
<a href="http://www.webstandards.org/upgrade/"
title="Download a browser that
complies with Web standards.">
web standards</a>,
but it is accessible to any browser
or Internet device.
</h2>
</iframe>
```

Go ahead and save this example file in your working folder as **perform-motive5.html**.

Identifying and Excluding Features Problematic in Navigator 4

To identify and exclude properties and features that might be problematic in Netscape Navigator 4.x, go through your style sheet from top to bottom, comparing the properties and features used with one of the compatibility charts mentioned in the previous "Finding Out What Works (and Doesn't Work) in Which Browsers" section. If you have a version of Netscape Navigator 4.x (preferably 4.5 or higher) installed, you can also directly check out your style sheet in that browser, looking for problems. You may also want to consider downloading and installing a version of Netscape Navigator 4, just to use it for testing out how your CSS-styled pages display in that browser. You can find Netscape Communicator 4.78 (which contains Navigator) available for download at Netscape's site at http://home.netscape.com/download/.

As you can see in Figure 16.4, Netscape Navigator 4.7 has a couple problems displaying the H1 (Level-One Heading) element properly. For one thing, the font size for the heading is too small, because this browser incorrectly inherits the font size that is set in that element's parent element (the div.body element). This browser also has a problem with borders and backgrounds applied to block elements (such as the H1 element), inserting a gap between the padding and the border that can't be removed.

Open a separate instance (or window) of your text editor and save the blank file as **nonav4.css**. In the following exercise, you transfer parts of your style sheet that are problematic in Netscape Navigator 4 from perform-motive5.html to nonav4.css. You then import that style sheet, using the @import at-rule, back into perform-motive5.html, shielding Navigator 4 from those styles. First, edit your style sheet in perform-motive5.html, inserting an @import at-rule linking to the external style sheet (nonav4.css), cutting (not deleting) the h1 style rule, and deleting the font-size: 1.1em property from the h2, h3 style rule, like this:

```
<style type="text/css">
@import url(nonav4.css);
body { margin: 0;  color: white; background: #660000; }
h1 { color: navy; background: #ffffcc url(paper.gif); text-align: center; margin: 0.15em 10%; padding: 0.1em 5%; border: dotted 12px olive; }
h2, h3 { color: #66ffcc;  background: transparent; }
div.body { font-family: Verdana, Arial, sans-serif; font-size: 1.1em; color: #ffff99; background: navy url(dark.jpg); border: solid 0.5em #ff9933; margin: 0.5%; padding: 0.2em 1%; }
div.body p { text-align: left; margin-left: 1%; margin-right: 1%; }
```

Next, paste the h1 style rule that you cut into the nonav4.css external style sheet file and type in a div.body style rule specifying only the font-size: 1.1em property you deleted from your embedded style sheet, like this:

Listing 16.3 NONAV4.CSS—External Style Sheet for Shielding Navigator 4

```
h1 { color: navy; background: #ffffcc url(paper.gif); text-align: center; margin:
0.15em 10%; padding: 0.1em 5%; border: dotted 12px olive; }
div.body { font-size: 1.1em; }
```

Now, if you resave both of these files (perform-motive5.html and nonav4.css) and then open perform-motive5.html in Internet Explorer 5.5 and Netscape Navigator 4.7, for instance, what you see should look like what is shown in Figure 16.5.

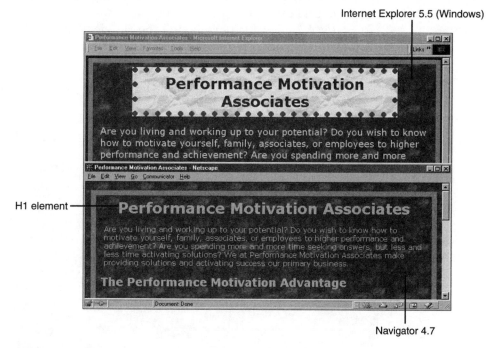

Figure 16.5: You can improve the appearance of your page in Navigator 4.x by shielding it from displaying styles and properties that are wrongly implemented in that browser.

NOTE

Some versions of Netscape Navigator 4 (4.06 and earlier) crash when encountering an @import at-rule in a style sheet. To check out for yourself the result of this example in Netscape Navigator 4, you should use a version of Navigator later than 4.06.

Another method for shielding Netscape Navigator 4 from parsing styles is to include the styles in an external style sheet that is linked to your HTML file using a LINK element with a media="all" attribute (or any value other than "screen").

For more information on this, see the "Using the LINK Element with a MEDIA Attribute" section earlier in this chapter.

If you want to shield as many earlier browsers as possible from accessing certain styles, you can use both methods at the same time. Just insert the styles you want to shield from earlier browsers inside of an external style sheet and import it (using the @import at-rule) into a second external style sheet. Then just link that second external style sheet (using the LINK element with a media="all" attribute) to your HTML file. That way, any browsers that lack support for either of those features will be shielded from accessing those styles.

By moving the problematic H1 element styling, as well as the div.body rule's font-size: 1.1em property, to the nonav4.css external style sheet, Navigator 4.7 now skips displaying the H1 element's border and background and defaults to displaying the H1 element using the deprecated FONT element that you inserted previously.

Figure 16.6 shows the remainder of the perform-motive5.html page as displayed in Navigator 4.7.

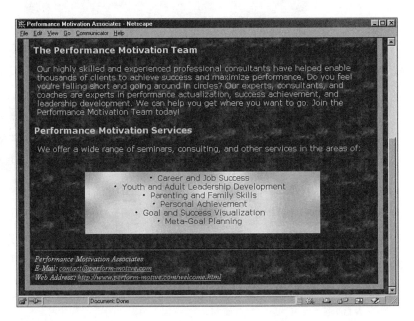

Figure 16.6: *The remainder of perform-motive5.html is at least readable, if not perfect, in Navigator 4.7.*

The point is that you shouldn't strive after perfection in the display of your page in earlier browsers, such as Netscape 4, that only partially or imperfectly support CSS. As long as the display is adequate and the page is readable, that's all that matters. Remember, eventually almost all users will abandon using these browsers in favor of browsers that more fully support CSS, so you shouldn't feel that you have to cater to users of these browsers. You just don't want to shut them out, is all.

Understanding How DocType Switching Works

The most recent CSS-compliant browsers, Internet Explorer 5 for the Macintosh, Internet Explorer 6, and Netscape 6, support what is generally referred to as *DocType switching*. With DocType switching, a browser actually supports two compatibility modes: a *quirks mode* and a *standards mode*. This allows the most current browsers to be fully compliant with the latest HTML and CSS standards, while remaining backward compatible with pages coded to be displayed in earlier, less than fully standards-compliant, Web browsers.

DocType switching is designed to overcome the following problems:

- Web pages coded to display in earlier less than fully standards-compatible browsers may not display well, or at all, in later fully standards-compatible browsers.

- Web pages coded to display in later fully standards-compatible browsers may not display well, or at all, in earlier less than fully standards-compatible browsers.

✔ The mechanism for enabling this, DocType switching, is activated by means of a document's Document Type Declaration (or DocType statement). For background information on Document Type Declarations, see "The Three Flavors of HTML," p. 84 (chapter 4).

DocType switching works roughly in the following manner in Internet Explorer 6 and Netscape 6:

- Any HTML 4.0 or 4.01 "strict" DocType statement triggers standards mode. (Except for Internet Explorer 5 for the Macintosh, which supports 4.01, but ignores 4.0, "strict" DocType statements.)

- A complete HTML 4.01 "transitional" DocType statement (including the standard URL link to the HTML 4.01 DTD) triggers standards mode.

- A less than complete HTML 4.01 DocType statement (either lacking a URL link to the HTML 4.01 DTD or including a link to a different DTD) triggers quirks mode.

- The absence of a DocType statement in a page triggers quirks mode.

Table 16.2 shows some examples of different DocType statements and which mode (standards or quirks) they trigger.

Table 16.2   DocType Switching Modes

DocType Statement	Mode
`<!DOCTYPE HTML PUBLIC "-//W3C//DTD HTML 4.0//EN">`	Standards[1]
`<!DOCTYPE HTML PUBLIC "-//W3C//DTD HTML 4.0//EN"` `"http://www.w3.org/TR/REC-html40/strict.dtd">`	Standards[1]
`<!DOCTYPE HTML PUBLIC "-//W3C//DTD HTML 4.01//EN">`	Standards
`<!DOCTYPE HTML PUBLIC "-//W3C//DTD HTML 4.01//EN"` `"http://www.w3.org/TR/html4/strict.dtd">`	Standards
`<!DOCTYPE HTML PUBLIC "-//W3C//DTD HTML 4.01 Strict //EN">`	Standards
`<!DOCTYPE HTML PUBLIC "-//W3C//DTD HTML 4.01 Strict //EN"` `"http://www.w3.org/TR/html4/strict.dtd">`	Standards
`<!DOCTYPE HTML PUBLIC "-//W3C//DTD HTML 4.01 Transitional//EN"` `"http://www.w3.org/TR/html4/loose.dtd">`	Standards
`<!DOCTYPE HTML PUBLIC "-//W3C//DTD HTML 4.01 Frameset//EN"` `"http://www.w3.org/TR/html4/frameset.dtd">`	Standards
`!DOCTYPE HTML PUBLIC "-//W3C//DTD TML 3.2 file://EN">`	Quirks
`<!DOCTYPE HTML PUBLIC "-//W3C//DTD HTML 4.01 Transitional//EN">`	Quirks
`<!DOCTYPE HTML PUBLIC "-//W3C//DTD HTML 4.01 Frameset//EN">`	Quirks
`<!DOCTYPE HTML PUBLIC "-//W3C//DTD HTML 4.01 Transitional//EN"` `"http://www.myserver.com/myDTDs/myown.dtd">`	Quirks
DocType statement not present	Quirks

1 Internet Explorer 5 for Macintosh only does DocType switching in response to HTML 4.01 and XHTML 1 DocType statements.

This isn't really an issue with XHTML DocType statements. All valid XHTML 1.0 and XHTML Basic DocType statements should trigger standards mode in Netscape 6 and Internet Explorer 6 (although not in Internet Explorer 5 for the Macintosh).

The point of all this is that you *must* have the proper DocType statement inserted at the top of your HTML 4 document if you want to be sure that Netscape 6 and Internet Explorer 6 will adhere to the latest HTML and CSS standards. Otherwise, they revert to quirks mode, effectively meaning that Netscape 6 behaves just like Netscape 4, while Internet Explorer 6 behaves just like Internet Explorer 5.

A simple example of this is how Internet Explorer 5.5 kludges the display of a medium font size setting, setting a small font size as equal to the default font size, while setting a medium font size as one size larger, even though according to the CSS1 specification a medium font size is supposed to be equal to the default font size. Internet Explorer 6, however, as long as standards mode is triggered, follows the standard, displaying a medium font size as equal to the default font size. If quirks mode is triggered, however, Internet Explorer 6 displays a small font size as equal to the default font size, exactly the same as Internet Explorer 5.5 for Windows, along with displaying any other HTML or CSS quirks that Internet Explorer 5.5 displays.

What's Next?

You should now have at least a beginning understanding of the different methods and techniques that can be used to help insure backward compatibility with earlier browsers that either don't support CSS at all or only partially support it. In this chapter, you also got some hands-on experience doing the following: including deprecated elements and attributes to dress up the appearance of pages in browsers that don't support CSS, setting up your pages to participate in the WaSP's Browser Upgrade Initiative, and using @import at-rules and MEDIA value LINK elements to shield Netscape Navigator 4, for instance, from styles that have a harmful or deleterious result in that browser.

This is the final chapter in this book. You should now have a fairly broad understanding of what CSS is, how it works, and how to use it to specify the formatting and appearance of your Web pages. You shouldn't expect to become an expert in CSS overnight, however; but with continuing practical experience implementing CSS in your own Web pages, there's no reason why you can't develop real expertise in using CSS.

For pointers to where you can find out more about using CSS in your Web pages, be sure to check out this book's Web site at http://www.callihan.com/cssbook/.

I've also included a number of appendixes at the end of this book that provide you with further information on CSS, including a CSS quick reference, information on using CSS with other technologies, and a directory of CSS software tools you can download and use.

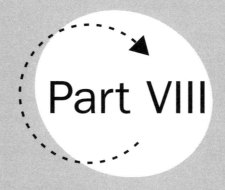

Part VIII

Appendixes

CSS Quick Reference

Using CSS with Other Technologies

Overview of CSS Software Tools

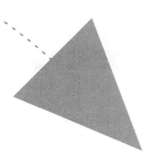

CSS Quick Reference

This appendix is intended as a quick and easy guide to the features and properties included in the CSS1 specification and provides brief descriptions of what is included in the CSS2 specification and is slated to be included in the up-coming CSS3 specification. Included in this appendix is an A to Z listing of all CSS1 properties and their values, along with descriptions and examples.

Containment and Application in HTML

CSS style sheets can be embedded in, linked with, or imported into HTML (HTML 4 or XHTML) documents. The following sections describe the different means for including and applying CSS styles in HTML documents, including HTML elements, at-rules, pseudo-classes, and selectors.

STYLE Element

The STYLE element is nested in the HEAD element and is used to embed styles in a Web page. Example:

```
<style type="text/css">
h1 {color: blue; background: transparent;}
</style>
```

LINK Element

The LINK element is nested in the HEAD element and is used to link an external style sheet to a Web page. Example:

```
<link rel="stylesheet" type="text/css"
href="http://www.myserver.com/style/mystyles.css" TITLE="My Styles">
```

@import At-Rule

The @import at-rule is nested inside the STYLE element, before any other style rules. It is used to import a style sheet into another style sheet. Example:

```
<style type="text/css">
@import url(nonav.css);
h1 {color
</style>
```

STYLE Attribute (Inline Styles)

The STYLE attribute is used to insert styles into HTML elements (inline styles). Example:

```
<h1 style="text-align: center">Coming Events!</h1>
```

Group Selector

A group selector is used to assign properties to a group of elements. Example:

```
h1, h2, h3 {color: blue; background: transparent;}
```

Class Selector

A class selector is used to assign properties to a named class to which elements may be assigned. Example:

```
p.first {font-size: 1.1em}
```

or

```
.first (font-size: 1.1em}
```

This applies the style to the following paragraph (belonging to the "first" class):

```
<p class="first">Welcome to the home page of the Hodges family. Come back
frequently to find out the latest news from John and Tricia and their two
children, Harry and Madge.</p>
```

ID Selector

An ID selector is used to assign properties to an element with a specific ID. Example:

```
p#first {font-size: 1.1em}
```

or

```
#first (font-size: 1.1em}
```

This applies the style to the following paragraph (named with the "first" ID):

```
<p id="first">Welcome to the home page of the Hodges family. Come back frequently
to find out the latest news from John and Tricia and their two children, Harry
and Madge.</p>
```

Note: According to the HTML 4 specification, an ID attribute's value should be unique (not repeated elsewhere in the document).

Contextual Selector

A contextual selector is used to assign properties to an element only within a certain context. Example:

```
div.alert p {color: red; background: transparent;}
```

This applies the style only to a P element that is nested inside of a DIV element belonging to the class "alert":

```
<div class="alert">
<p>To avoid straining his heart, keep the victim lying down. If he regains
consciousness, do not allow him to sit or stand up. If you need to transport him,
carry him in a stretcher.</p>
</div>
```

Anchor Pseudo-Classes

The :link, :visited, and :active pseudo-classes are used to assign properties to different link states (unvisited, visited, and active) of the A (Anchor) element. Examples:

```
a:link {color: green}
a:visited {color: #69c}
a:active {color: #cc00ff}
```

or

```
:link {color: green}
:visited {color: #69c}
:active {color: #cc00ff}
```

Note: CSS2 adds the :hover pseudo-class, which assigns properties that are displayed when the mouse hovers over an object or element. The :hover and :active pseudo-classes should always be listed following any of the other anchor pseudo-classes.

Typographical Pseudo-Elements

The :first-line and :first-letter pseudo-elements are used to assign properties to an element's first line and first letter, respectively. Examples:

```
p:first-line {font-weight: bold}
h1:first-letter {font-size: 1.2em}
```

CSS1 Properties (Alphabetical)

This section contains an alphabetical listing of all CSS1 properties, including their allowed values and characteristics. Short descriptions are included, as well as notes highlighting issues of which you need to be aware.

Legend

To economize on the amount of space required to present this listing, as well as to avoid the repetition of redundant information, I've used the following conventions:

- Many CSS properties specify an initial value that browsers are supposed to utilize or display in the absence of a property declaration. These initial values are highlighted in **bold**. When no initial value is specified, the browser or local system determines the initial value.

- Certain sets of values are available for multiple properties. To avoid having to repeat these each and every time, I make use of key terms, such as <color keyword>, <hexadecimal/rgb>, <url>, <lengths>, <percentages>, and so on. The first time a key term is used, I list the included values, but thereafter I just specify the key term by itself.

- You will also see both singular and plural forms of key terms: <length> and <lengths>, for instance. In the first instance, a single length value can be specified for a property, while in the second instance, multiple length values can be specified.

background

This shorthand property is used to set all of the background properties using a single property declaration. Properties that can be set using the background shorthand property include: `background-color`, `background-image`, `background-repeat`, `background-attachment`, and `background-position`.

Inherited: No   **Applied to:** All

Example:

```
body {color: red; background: black url(blacknight.jpg) fixed;}
h1 {color: lime; background: transparent;}
h2, h3, h4 {color: aqua; background: url(darkwood.jpg);}
div.inset {color: navy; background: #ffcc99;}
```

Note: Because some earlier CSS browsers support the `background` property, but not the `background-color` or `background-image` properties, it is a good idea to stick to using the `background` property for setting both background colors and background images.

background-attachment

This property determines whether a background image remains fixed relative to the canvas or scrolls along with the content.

Values: fixed, **scroll**

Inherited: No   **Applied to:** All

Example:

```
body {color: navy; background: #ffffcc url("ochre.jpg"); background-attachment:
fixed;}
```

background-color

This property sets the background color for an element.

Values: <color keyword>

black, white, silver, aqua, blue, fuchsia, gray, green, lime, maroon, navy, olive, purple, red, teal, white, yellow

<hexadecimal/rgb>, <decimal/rgb>, <percentage/rgb>, **transparent**

Inherited: No   **Applied to:** All

Examples:

```
body {color: white; background-color: black;}
```

The <hexadecimal/rgb>, <decimal/rgb>, and <percentage/rgb> terms refer to specifying RGB colors using hexadecimal, decimal, and percentage values. For examples of using these, see the `color` property.

Note: Background colors are not inherited, but because the initial value for any element's background color is `transparent`, a background color set for an element's parent element, for instance, shows through the current element's transparent background.

Some earlier CSS browsers do not support the `background-color` property, but do support the `background` shorthand property for setting background colors. For that reason, it is a good idea to stick to using the `background` property, rather than the `background-color` property. This has the added value of setting the `background-image` property to none, as long as no background image is declared, because the `background` property resets all undeclared properties to their initial values.

background-image

This property sets a background image for an element.

Values: <url>, **none**

Inherited: No   **Applied to:** All

Examples:

```
body {color: white; background-color: black; background-image:
url("starry.jpg");}
```

The quotes in the URL are optional. The property can just as legitimately be stated as `url(starry.jpg)`, for instance. You can also specify a relative URL, `url(../images/starry.jpg)`, or an absolute URL, `url(http://www.myserver.com/images/starry.jpg)`.

Note: Background images are not inherited, but because the initial value for any element's background color is `transparent`, a background image set for an element's parent element, for instance, shows through the current element's transparent background.

Some earlier CSS browsers do not support the background-image property but do support the background shorthand property for setting background colors. For that reason, it is a good idea to stick to using the background property, rather than the background-image property, when setting background images.

Whenever setting a background image, you should also specify a background color that matches the primary tone and color of your background image as closely as possible—that way, if a viewer turns off display of images, he or she is still see your background color.

background-repeat

This property specifies if and how a background image is repeated (or tiled).

Values: repeat-x, repeat-y, no-repeat, **repeat**

Inherited: No   **Applied to:** All

Examples:

```
body {color: navy; background: #ffffcc url("ochre.jpg"); background-repeat:
repeat-y;}
```

The repeat-x and repeat-y values repeat the background image horizontally and vertically, respectively. The no-repeat value causes the background image to not be repeated (to be displayed only once). The repeat value causes the background image to be repeated both horizontally and vertically.

Note: The background image is positioned flush to the top and left margins, unless the background-position property is set to specify different initial positioning.

background-position

Specifies the position of a background image.

Values: <lengths>

px (pixels), em (em units), ex (x-height), in (inches), cm (centimeters), mm (millimeters), pt (points), pc (picas)

<percentages>

[initial value: **0% 0%**]

<vertical position>

top, center, bottom

<horizontal position>

left, center, right

Inherited: No **Applied to:** Block and Replaced Elements

Examples:

```
body {color: navy; background: #ffffcc url("watermark.jpg"); background-
attachment: fixed; background-repeat: no-repeat; background-position: 50% 8em;}
```

Of the two codes, the first code, 50%, centers the non-repeated background image relative to the left and right margins; the second code, 8em, positions it eight ems down from the top margin.

Note: Using the center value or 50% to vertically position the background image centers it relative to the whole length of the page, not within the browser window. The only way to vertically center a background image within a browser window, and only roughly at that, is to position it down from the top margin.

border

This shorthand property sets the following properties: any of the four border width properties, border-width, border-style, and border-color.

Inherited: No **Applied to:** All

Examples:

```
h1 { border: 0.5em inset green; padding: 1em; margin-left: 2em; margin-right:
2em; text-align: center; color: red; background-color: transparent; font-size:
2em; }
```

border-color

This property sets the color of a border to be drawn around an element.

Values: <color keywords>, <hexadecimal/rgb values>, <decimal/rgb values>, <percentage/rgb values>, [initial value: color property]

Inherited: No **Applied to:** All

Examples:

```
div.alert {border-color: #330099; border-style: solid; padding: 0.5em; margin:
1em; text-align: center;}
div.alert p {text-align: left; font-weight: bold;}
address {border-color: blue silver red; border-style: double none solid; padding:
1em;}
```

One to four color values may be specified:

One color value:	One color is applied to all four sides of the element
Two color values:	One color is applied to the top and bottom and the other color is applied to the right and left sides, respectively
Three color values:	The first and third colors are applied to the top and bottom borders, respectively; the second color is applied to the right and left sides of the element

Four color values: Colors are applied to the top, right, bottom, and left borders, in that order

border-style

This property sets the style of border to be drawn around an element.

Values: dotted, dashed, solid, double, groove, ridge, inset, outset, **none**

Inherited: No   **Applied to:** All

Examples:

```
div.alert {border-style: solid; padding: 0.5em; margin: 1em; text-align: center;}
div.alert p {text-align: left; font-weight: bold;}
address {border-style: double none solid}
```

For the `div.alert` class selector, a solid border is drawn around all four sides of the element's content area and padding. For the `address` selector, a double border is drawn above the element, and a solid border is drawn below it (the right and left borders are set to none).

Note: The `border-style` property can be used alone to draw a border around an element. Because the initial value is `none`, no border is drawn unless the `border-style` property is declared (either by itself or in a `border` shorthand property). If no `border-color` property is declared, the border color is the same as the element's color. The border width defaults to a `medium` width, which different browsers might interpret in slightly different ways (in Netscape 6, a medium border width is three pixels wide; in Internet Explorer 5.5, it is four pixels wide). Also, other than with the solid border style, there is little uniformity among different browsers as to how they treat the other border styles.

border-top, border-right, border-bottom, border-left

These shorthand properties set the following properties for the top, right, bottom, and left borders: any of the four border width properties (`border-top-width`, `border-right-width`, `border-bottom-width`, and `border-left-width`), `border-style`, and `border-color`.

Inherited: No   **Applied to:** All

Examples:

```
div.list { border-top: thick groove blue; border-right: thin solid black; border-
bottom: 0.5em ridge lime; border-left: thin solid black;}
```

BORDER-TOP-WIDTH, BORDER-RIGHT-WIDTH, BORDER-BOTTOM-WIDTH, BORDER-LEFT-WIDTH

These properties set the width of the top, right, bottom, and right borders, respectively.

Values: <length>, thin, thick, **medium**

Inherited: No **Applied to:** All

Examples:

```
div.alert {border-top-width: thick; border-bottom-width: thin; border-color:
#330099; border-style: solid; padding: 0.5em; margin: 1em; text-align: center;}
div.alert p {text-align: left; font-weight: bold;}
address {border-color: blue silver red; border-style: double none solid; padding:
1em;}
```

Note: Different browsers might interpret the meaning of thin, thick, and medium differently, setting different border width sizes for the same border width value. To ensure uniform border widths between CSS browsers, use length values (ems or pixels) to set border width sizes.

border-width

This shorthand property sets the following properties: border-top-width, border-right-width, border-bottom-width, and border-left-width.

Inherited: No **Applied to:** All

Examples:

```
div.alert {border-width: thick thin; border-color: #330099; border-style: solid;
padding: 0.5em; margin: 1em; text-align: center;}
div.alert p {text-align: left; font-weight: bold;}
address {border-width: 0.5em 0 0.25em; border-color: blue silver red; border-
style: double none solid; padding: 1em;}
```

From one to four values can be set for the border-width shorthand property. In the example, for the div.alert selector, the first value sets the top and bottom borders as thick, and the second value sets the right and left borders as thin. For the address selector, the first value sets the top border to 0.5 ems; the third value sets the bottom border to 0.25 ems; and the second value sets the right and left borders to zero widths.

clear

This property causes a following element to clear a floating element—instead of wrapping around a floating element, the cleared element is moved down until the left, right, or both margins are clear (not blocked by the floating element).

Values: left, right, both **none**

Inherited: No **Applied to:** All

Examples:

```
<p><img src="picture1_sm.jpg" style="float: left; width: 300px; height:
203px"></p>
<h1>The Kochanski Family Page</h1>
<p style="clear: left">Welcome to the Kochanski Family page! Look here for
information on birthdays, anniversaries, milestones, graduations, family
gatherings, and other stuff related to our immediate and extended family.</p>
```

color

This property sets a foreground color for an element.

Values: <color keyword>, <hexadecimal/rgb>, <decimal/rgb>, <percentage/rgb>

Inherited: Yes **Applied to:** All

Examples:

```
h1 {color: blue; background: transparent;}
h2, h3 {color: #ff6600; background: transparent;}
h4 {color: #c30; background: transparent;}
p {color: rgb(51,102,0); background: transparent;}
em {color: rgb(0%,20%,40%); background: transparent;}
```

The first line uses a color keyword; the second and third lines use hexadecimal RGB values; the fourth line uses a decimal RGB value; and the fifth line uses a percentage RGB value.

Note: The third line in the example uses a three-digit hexadecimal RGB value, #c30, which is shorthand for a six-digit hexadecimal value, #cc3300.

display

This property specifies whether an element is to be treated as a block, inline, or list-item element.

Values: **block**, inline, list-item, none

Inherited: No **Applied to:** All

Examples:

```
div.side a { display: block; padding: 5px; border: 3px #fc0 outset; margin-
bottom: 0.5em; margin-top: 0.5em; color: #cf6; background-color: #066; font-
weight: bold; text-decoration: none; font-family: arial, sans-serif; }
```

This example declares that A elements (normally treated as inline elements) that are nested inside a "side"-class DIV element are to be treated as block elements.

A value of display: none hides the element and its content.

Note: Although the CSS1 specification states that block is the initial value for this property, in practice, browsers default to inline for inline elements (EM, B, SPAN, and so on) and to list-item for list item elements (UL, OL, and LI).

float

This property causes an element to float at the left or right margins, with the following text or elements flowing around the element. It is most often used to flow text or elements around an inline image, but it can be used with any element.

Values: left, right, **none**

Inherited: No   **Applied to:** All

Examples:

```
<p><img src="picture1_sm.jpg" style="float: left; width: 300px; height:
203px"></p>
<h1>The Kochanski Family Page</h1>
```

Note: If padding is used to add spacing around the image, you shouldn't set a specific image width or height at the same time, due to Internet Explorer's box model formatting bug. Instead, insert the image in a DIV and then float that element while setting the width and height for the IMG element. You can also just use the WIDTH and HEIGHT attributes, which are not deprecated for the IMG element in HTML 4, to set the image height and width.

font

This shorthand property is used to set all of the font properties using a single property declaration. Properties that can be set using the font shorthand property include: font-size, font-style, font-variant, font-weight, and line-height.

Inherited: Yes **Applied to:** All

Percentage Values: Font size percentages are relative to the parent element's font size; line height percentages are relative to the current element's font size

Example:

```
em {font: bold 1.1em/110% Tahoma, Helvetica, sans-serif}
```

Note: In the example, 1.1em/110% sets the font size to 1.1 ems (1.1 times the parent element's font size) and the line height to 110 percent (of the current element's font size). Undeclared properties are reset to their initial values.

font-family

This property is used to assign a specific or generic font, or a list of specific and/or generic fonts, to an element.

Values: <specific-family>

                  Arial, Verdana, "Times New Roman", and so on

                  <generic-family>

                  sans-serif, monospace, serif, cursive, fantasy

                  <combined list>

Inherited: Yes **Applied to:** All

Examples:

```
h1 {font-family: sans-serif}
h2 {font-family: monospace}
div.inset {font-family: Arial, Helvetica, sans-serif}
```

font-size

This property is used to size the font for an element.

Values: <length>, <percentage>

<relative size>

larger, smaller

<absolute size>

xx-small, x-small, small, **medium**, large, x-large, xx-large

Inherited: Yes **Applied to:** All

Percentage Values: Relative to parent element's font size.

Examples:

```
h1 {font-family: sans-serif; font-size: 36px;}
h2 {font-family: monospace; font-size: large;}
blockquote {font-size: 0.9em}
```

Note: For display on the Web, do not use the cm, mm, pt, or pc measurements. These are absolute measurements that have no meaning in a fluid, unfixed medium such as the Web and should be used only when the dimensions of the target medium are known (such as when printing on an 8.5 × 11.5 piece of paper). When setting font sizes, em measurements are preferred, with pixels as the second choice.

For setting font sizes, ems and percentages work exactly the same. A font size setting of 1.5em is equivalent to a setting of 150%. Due to inconsistent implementation among current browsers, both the <relative size> and <absolute size> measurements should be avoided.

font-style

This property applies an italic, oblique, or normal font style to an element.

Values: italic, oblique, **normal**

Inherited: Yes **Applied to:** All

Example:

```
blockquote {font-size: 0.9em; font-style: italic;}
```

Note: Italic fonts are preferable to oblique fonts, in that they are individually crafted; oblique fonts are simply normal fonts that have been slanted. If an italic font isn't available, a browser should default to an oblique font if one is available. Therefore, just specify italic, skipping oblique.

font-variant

This property applies a small caps for normal font variant to an element.

Values: small-caps, **normal**

Inherited: Yes **Applied to:** All

Example:

```
h2 {font-variant: small-caps}
```

Note: Internet Explorer 5.5 for Windows displays elements formatted with the small-caps property in all uppercase.

font-weight

This property is used to set the weight of a font (its boldness or lightness).

Values: bold, bolder, lighter, **normal**

<numerical>

100, 200, 300, 400, 500, 600, 700, 800, 900

Inherited: Yes **Applied to:** All

Example:

```
address a {font-weight: bold}
```

Note: Use only `bold` or `normal`. Netscape 6 does not support `bolder` or `lighter`, displaying them the same (as `bold` or `normal`, respectively). The CSS specifications say that the numerical values of `400` and `700` should be equal to `normal` and `bold`, respectively, which current browsers support, but support for the other numerical values is inconsistent (see Table 7.1, p.xxx).

height

This property sets the height of an element's content area.

Values: <length>, **auto**

Inherited: No **Applied to:** Block and Replaced Elements

Examples:

```
h1 { width: 15em; height: 7em; border: 0.5em inset green; padding: 2em 1em 1em;
margin-left: 5em; margin-right: auto; text-align: center; color: red; background-
color: transparent; font-size: 1.5em; }
```

Note: Internet Explorer 5.5 for Windows, due to a bug in its box formatting model implementation, includes the height of padding and borders within any value set for the height property. The result, if you include padding and borders in your element, is that the height of the element's content area is displayed in a smaller size in Internet Explorer 5.5 for Windows than in Netscape 6 or Opera 5.

letter-spacing

This property is used to increase or decrease the spacing between letters within an element.

Values: <length>, **normal**

Inherited: Yes **Applied to:** All

Examples:

```
h1 {letter-spacing: 3px; }
```

Note: Negative values can be used to decrease the amount of letter spacing.

line-height

This property sets the line height for an element.

Values: <number>, <length>, <percentage>, **normal**

Inherited: Yes **Applied to:** All

Percentage Values: Relative to current element's font size

Examples:

```
blockquote {line-height: 1.5}
div.inset {line-height: 1.2em}
address {line-height: 95%; font-size: 0.95em}
```

Note: Numerical values (1.5, for instance) are measured relative to the current element's font size. Numerical and percentage values otherwise only differ in how they are inherited: if a numerical value, a child element inherits the specified value (1.5); if a percentage value, a child element inherits the computed value.

list-style

This shorthand property is for setting the following properties: list-style-image, list-style-type, and list-style-position.

Inherited: Yes **Applied to:** List item elements

Percentage Values: Relative to current element's font size

Examples:

```
ul { list-style: circle url(goldball.gif) inside; margin-top: -12px; margin-left:
25px; padding-left: 25px;}
li { margin-bottom: 6px; }
```

list-style-image

This property specifies the URL for a bullet image.

Values: <url>, **none**

Inherited: Yes **Applied to:** List item elements

Examples:

```
ul { list-style-image: url(goldball.gif); margin-top: -12px; margin-left: 25px;
padding-left: 25px;}
li { margin-bottom: 6px; }
```

list-style-position

This property specifies whether the list bullet (for UL elements) or list number (for OL elements) is displayed inside or outside the element box.

Values: inside, **outside**

Inherited: Yes **Applied to:** List item elements

Examples:

```
ul { list-style-position: inside; margin-top: -12px; margin-left: 25px; padding-
left: 25px;}
li { margin-bottom: 6px; }
```

A value of `inside` causes the bullet character, bullet image, or number to be displayed inside of any border or padding set for the impacted list item element. A value of `outside`, the initial value, places the bullet character, bullet image, or number outside and to the left of any border or padding.

list-style-type

This property specifies whether the list bullet (for UL elements) or list number (for OL elements) is displayed inside or outside the element box.

Values: circle, square, **disc**, **decimal**, lower-roman, upper-roman, lower-alpha, upper-alpha, none

Inherited: Yes **Applied to:** List item elements

Examples:

```
ul {list-style-type: square; margin-top: -12px; margin-left: 25px; padding-left:
25px;}
ol {list-style-type: upper-roman}
li { margin-bottom: 6px; }
```

Note: For bulleted lists (the UL element), the initial value is disc; for numbered lists (the OL element), the initial value is decimal.

margin

This shorthand property is used to set all of the margin properties using a single property declaration. Properties that can be set using the margin shorthand property include: margin-top, margin-right, margin-bottom, and margin-left.

Inherited: No   **Applied to:** All

Examples:

```
body {margin: 1em}
h1 {margin: 0 0.5em}
div.announce { margin: 0 1em 0.5em 1em; padding: 0.5em; border: solid red 3px;
text-align: center;}
div.announce p {margin: 0.5em 1.5em 0.3em; text-align: left; font-weight: bold;}
```

The first example sets spacing of one em for all four margins. In the second example, the first margin value sets zero spacing for the top and bottom margins, and the second value sets spacing of half an em for the right and left margins. In the third example, the four margin values set spacing individually for all four margins (top, right, bottom, and left, respectively). In the fourth example, the first and third margin values set the top and bottom margins, but the second value (in the absence of a fourth value) sets both the right and left margins (to 1.5 ems).

margin-top, margin-right, margin-bottom, and margin-left

These properties set the amount of margin that is displayed around the top, right, bottom, and left sides of an element.

Values: <length>, <percentage>, auto, [initial: **0**]

Inherited: No   **Applied to:** All

Percentage Values: Relative to the width of the closest block ancestor element

Examples:

```
body {margin-top: 10px; margin-right: 10px; margin-bottom: 10px; margin-left:
10px;}
p {margin-top: 5px; margin-right: 10px; margin-bottom: 5px; margin-left: 10px;}
h1 {margin-left: -5px}
```

Margin spacing is set outside of the content area, padding, or borders of an element.

Note: Horizontal margins for nested elements are concatenated; vertical margins of adjacent elements are collapsed to the largest margin value.

Negative values can be specified to reduce the amount of margin spacing that would otherwise be displayed.

padding

This shorthand property is used to set all of the padding properties using a single property declaration. Properties that can be set using the padding shorthand property include: padding-top, padding-right, padding-bottom, and padding-left.

Inherited: No   **Applied to:** All

Examples:

```
div.announce { padding: 0.5em 0.7em; margin: 0 1em 0.5em 1em; border: solid red
3px; text-align: center;}
```

You set padding values in exactly the same manner as you set margin values, with a single padding value setting all four padding values, for instance.

padding-top, padding-right, padding-bottom, and padding-left

These properties set the amount of padding that is displayed between an element's content area and any border or margin that might be set for an element.

Values: <length>, <percentage>, auto, [initial: **0**]

Inherited: No   **Applied to:** All

Percentage Values: Relative to the width of the closest block ancestor element

Examples:

```
div.announce {padding-top: 0.5em; padding-right: 0.5em; padding-bottom: 0.5em;
padding-left: 0.5em; margin-left: 1em; margin-right: 1em; border: solid red 3px;
text-align: center;}
div.announce p {text-align: left; font-weight: bold;}
```

Padding spacing is set between the content area of an element and any borders or margins that are set for an element.

Note: Negative values are not allowed for setting padding values.

text-align

You use this property to specify how text is horizontally aligned within an element.

Values: left, right, center, justify

Inherited: Yes   **Applied to:** Block Elements

Examples:

```
h1 {text-align: center}
h2, h3, h4 {text-align: right}
p {text-align: justify}
```

Note: Horizontal alignment is relative to the width of the element, not to the canvas.

text-decoration

You use this property to specify how an element is to be decorated (or highlighted).

Values: underline, overline, line-through, blink, **none**

Inherited: No   **Applied to:** All

Examples:

```
h1 {text-decoration: overline; color: navy; background: transparent;}
```

Note: Although not inherited, the text decoration should span any child elements; underline, overline, and line-through should maintain any foreground color that is set, even if different colors are set for child elements. Consider carefully before using blink, since some users are liable to consider blinking text as rude.

text-indent

This property specifies the amount to indent the first line of an element.

Values: <length>, <percentage>, [initial: **0**]

Inherited: Yes **Applied to:** Block Elements

Percentage Values: Relative to parent element's font size

Examples:

```
p {text-indent: 1em}
```

text-transform

This property enables you to transform the case in which an element is presented.

Values: capitalize, uppercase, lowercase, **none**

Inherited: Yes **Applied to:** All

Examples:

```
h1 {text-transform: uppercase}
```

Note: These values capitalize the first letter of each word, set all letters to uppercase, or set all letters to lowercase. A value of none (the initial value) leaves any capitalization as it is.

vertical-align

This property vertically aligns an element relative to its parent element.

Values: sub, super, top, middle, bottom, text-top, text-bottom, **baseline**, <percentage>

Inherited: No **Applied to:** Inline Elements

Percentage Values: Relative to current element's line-height value.

Examples:

```
h1 { text-align: center; color: red; background-color: transparent; font-size:
2em; }
h1 em { font-size: 1.5em; vertical-align: middle;}
```

This causes an EM element nested inside of the H1 element to be aligned vertically with the middle of the H1 element.

Note: The text-top, text-bottom, and middle values align the element relative to the top, bottom, and middle of the parent element's font; the top and bottom values align the element relative to the tallest and lowest element on a line, respectively.

white-space

This property specifies how white space within an element is to be treated.

Values: pre, nowrap, **normal**

Inherited: No **Applied to:** Block elements

Percentage Values: Relative to the width of the parent element

Examples:

```
div.code {white-space: pre; font-family: monospace;}
```

This example causes text nested inside of a "code"-class DIV element to be treated as though it were nested in a PRE element, with all spaces displayed (and not collapsed) and all hard returns treated as line breaks.

Note: CSS1-compliant browsers are not required to support the white-space property and can legally default to normal when either pre or nowrap is specified.

width

This property sets the width of an element's content area.

Values: <length>, <percentage>, **auto**

Inherited: No   **Applied to:** Block and Replaced Elements

Percentage Values: Relative to the width of the parent element.

Examples:

```
h1 { width: 15em; height: 7em; border: 0.5em inset green; padding: 2em 1em 1em;
margin-left: 5em; margin-right: auto; text-align: center; color: red; background-
color: transparent; font-size: 1.5em; }
```

Note: The sum of the element's content area, left and right padding widths, left and right border widths, and left and right margin widths must equal 100 percent of the total element width. The width property is supposed to set the width of the element's content area, exclusive of any padding, borders, or margins. Internet Explorer 5.5 for Windows, however, due to a bug in its box formatting model implementation, also includes the width of padding and borders within any value set for either the width or height property. The result, if you include padding and borders in your element, is that the width or height of the element's content area is displayed in a smaller size in Internet Explorer 5.5 for Windows than in Netscape 6 or Opera 5.

word-spacing

This property enables you to increase or decrease the spacing between words within an element.

Values: <length>, **normal**

Inherited: Yes **Applied to:** All

Examples:

```
h1 {letter-spacing: 3px; }
```

Note: Negative values can be used to decrease the amount of word spacing. Internet Explorer 5.5 for Windows treats any <length> value the same as normal (allowed for in the CSS1 specification), so you might want to avoid setting word spacing.

CSS2 Positioning Properties

Although current browsers are only required to be CSS1-compliant, in practice some CSS2 features and properties are supported by current browsers. The most important of these are the positioning properties that enable you to absolutely or relatively position elements on the page.

position

This property declares how an element is to be positioned on a page, either absolutely in relation to the element's containing block or relatively in relation to the element's current position.

Values: absolute, relative, fixed, **static**, inherit

Inherited: No **Applied to:** All elements (except generated content)

Examples: (See the top, right, bottom, and left properties for an example)

All current browsers (Netscape 6, Opera 5, Internet Explorer 5.5 for Windows, and Internet Explorer 5 for the Macintosh) support absolute and relative positioning. Only a few browsers (Opera 5, Internet Explorer 5 for the Macintosh, and recent builds of the Mozilla browser) support fixed positioning.

Note: Generally, absolutely positioned element boxes are positioned relative to the browser window (or viewport). An absolutely positioned element with values of zero for the left and top properties is positioned flush with the left and top sides of the browser window. Likewise, with values of zero for the bottom and right properties, it is positioned flush with the bottom and right sides of the browser window. The exception is if the absolutely positioned element is nested within another positioned element with a position value other than static, in which case the content dimensions of that ancestor element forms the containing block.

top, right, bottom, left

These properties specify the position of a positioned element either relative to the edges of the page or relative to the normal position within the current block (relative positioning).

Values: <number>, **auto**, inherit

Inherited: No **Applied to:** Positioned elements

Examples:

```
div.side { position: absolute; top: 4em; left: 0; width: 145px; height: 315%;
padding-top: 0.5em; margin-left: 0.6em; background-color: #099; }
div.main { position: absolute; top: 4em; left: 155px; height: 315%; margin: 0
0.5em; padding: 0.5em; background-color: #fec; }
```

In the examples, the position: absolute properties specify that the element is to be positioned absolutely relative to the top, right, bottom, or left of the element's containing block. Assuming that the "side"-class DIV element is contained by the BODY element, then in the example it is absolutely positioned four ems down from the top margin and zero space in from the left margin of the BODY element. The "main"-class DIV element is then positioned four ems down from the top margin and 155 pixels in from the left margin of the BODY element. Notice that the width (145 pixels) is set for the "side"-class DIV element, and the width of the "main"-class DIV element is left undeclared (defaulting to the initial value of auto).

A position: relative property works the same way, except that the positions are stated relative to the current element position (relative to the normal flow). For instance, the following would cause an H1 element to be positioned down one em and in from the left two ems from its normal position:

```
h1 {position: relative; top: 1em; left: 2em;}
```

It is important to note that the absolute or relative positioning of an element does not result in the repositioning of containing or adjacent elements. It is possible to overlap one element over another element using positioning, which might or might not be what you want.

z-index

This property establishes the stack level of a positioned box within the current stacking context.

Values: <number>, **auto**, inherit

Inherited: No   **Applied to:** Positioned elements

Examples:

```
div.bottom-right {position: absolute; right: 0; top: 300px; z-index: 2; width:
300px; height: 300px; border: solid 2px green; color: white; background: navy;}
div.top-left {position: absolute; left: 0; top: 0; z-index: 1; height: 300px;
color: black; background: #ffffcc;}
```

Normally, a positioned element that follows after another positioned element overlaps and is displayed on top of the preceding element. The second element, in this case, is said to be "stacked" on top of the first element. By using the z-index property, you can change the stacking order of elements on the page. Elements with higher z-index values are stacked on top of elements with lower z-index values. For instance, the div.bottom-right selector has a z-index value of 2 assigned to it, and the div.top-left selector has a z-index value of 1 assigned to it. This means that the "bottom-right"-class DIV element is stacked on top of the "top-left"-class DIV element, because of its higher z-index value, even if it follows the latter element on the page.

Finding Out More About CSS1 and CSS2

It is important to understand that CSS2 does not replace CSS1 as much as it supplements it. Although CSS2 includes a few changes to the CSS1 specification, by and large CSS1 survives unchanged within CSS2. You should think of the different levels of CSS as being like the layers of an onion, in other words.

A number of CSS2 features and properties have been used or referenced in this book's examples. Unless otherwise noted, any CSS2 properties used in this book's examples are supported by current CSS browsers. Current CSS browsers, however, are only required to be compliant with CSS1—many of the new CSS2 features and properties can't really be used yet, due to lack of support in all or some current CSS browsers. Here's a quick rundown on some of the new features and functionality that are included in CSS2:

- **The `@media` at-rule**—Current CSS browsers support the use of the STYLE element's MEDIA attribute, but the new CSS2 `@media` at-rule is inconsistently supported.

- **The `inherit` property value**—When added to a property declaration, this strengthens the likelihood that it will be inherited by child elements.

- **The `!important` property value**—While this is a CSS1 property value, its function has been altered in CSS2. In CSS1, an author's `!important` value trumps the same value set by a user; in CSS2 a user's `!important` value trumps the same value set by an author.

- **The `@page` at-rule**—This allows the formatting of paged documents, including setting page size, margins, two-sided pages, page breaks, orphan/widow controls, and more.

- **Aural style sheets**—A special set of properties and values is defined for use in style sheets targeted at speech browsers and synthesizers.

- **Internationalization features**—These include international list numbering styles, support for bi-directional text, and language-specific quotation marks.

- **The `@font-face` at-rule**—This allows for intelligent font matching, user-specified font synthesis, and the display of downloadable fonts. The `font-size-adjust` and `font-stretch` properties have also been added.

- **Ability to specify system colors and fonts**—This enables you to integrate the appearance of CSS-styled documents with a user's local system settings.

- **Table formatting model**—Extensive new features are added for controlling the appearance of tables.

- **Relative, absolute, and fixed positioning**—See "CSS2 Properties" earlier in this appendix.

- **New values for the display property**—These include compact and run-in.

- **The overflow, clip, and visibility properties**—These give you further control over the visual presentation of content.

- **The min-width and min-height properties**—These properties are used to specify minimum and maximum widths and heights.

- **Additional selectors**—Universal selectors, child selectors, adjacent sibling selectors, and attribute selectors are all available.

- **New pseudo-classes**—These include the :first-child, :hover, :focus, and :lang pseudo-classes.

- **New pseudo-elements**—These include :before and :after.

- **Generated content, automatic counters and numbering, and additional list marker controls**—These include the :before and :after pseudo-elements, the content property, the quotes property, the counter-reset and counter-increment properties, the marker-offset property, and additional list-style-image property numbering values (including international numbering styles).

- **The ability to set text shadows**—The text-shadow property lets you set shadow-effects to be displayed behind an element's text. The vertical and horizontal position, color, and blur radius can be set for the effect. Multiple shadow-effects can be applied to the same element.

- **The ability to control the appearance of the cursor**—The cursor property lets you control how the cursor is displayed, as well as providing the ability to retrieve a custom cursor file.

- **Dynamic outlines**—Outlines, unlike borders, do not take up space or cause reflow of following text or elements.

Because almost all of CSS1 is supported by current CSS browsers, any time spent studying the CSS1 specification is not wasted. Even after CSS4 (for instance) might be introduced, CSS1 will still be fully relevant. You can find the W3C's CSS1 specification at http://www.w3.org/TR/REC-CSS1.

If you want to find out more about what is included in the CSS2 specification, you can find the W3C's CSS2 specification at http://www.w3.org/TR/REC-CSS2.

A Look Ahead at CSS3

Here's a brief rundown on some of the features slated to be included in CSS3:

- New selectors, pseudo-classes, and pseudo-elements, along with a new concept, namespaces

- Dynamic properties

- Floating boxes to top or bottom of page

- Color profiles and transparency for embedded images

- A line box model for controlling the content of inline elements and the inline content of block elements

- Copy-fitting, auto-sizing, and auto-spacing controls

- New internationalization features, such as enabling the presentation of vertical Japanese, Arabic, and so on

- New paged media features, including running headers and footers, page numbers, cross-references, and gutters

- New features for rendering forms

- Media queries that allow limiting the scope of a style sheet for specific media, including setting widths and heights, color-depth, and other requirements

To find out more about CSS3 and follow its continuing development, see http://www.w3.org/Style/CSS/current-work.

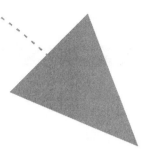

Using CSS with Other Technologies

You've already seen many examples of using CSS with another technology—HTML, to be specific. Although the CSS examples in this book utilize HTML 4 code, they work exactly the same way with XHTML code. I've stuck with using HTML 4 code in this book because it is still much more widely known and used than is the case with XHTML. The purpose of this book, after all, is to teach CSS and not specifically HTML (HTML 4 or XHTML). The following subjects are discussed in this appendix:

- Using JavaScript with CSS
- Creating dynamic styles with Dynamic HTML
- Using CSS with XML (Extensible Markup Language)

Using JavaScript with CSS

There are two primary ways in which you might utilize JavaScript in conjunction with CSS: swapping browser-specific style sheets and creating dynamic styles triggered by the user or other actions.

A couple of problems, however, sometimes occur when using a browser sniffer to redirect users to the correct style sheet based on their browser:

- There are no consistent browser-identification standards, meaning that some browsers are liable to be misidentified, no matter how carefully you think you've crafted your script.

- Browser sniffer scripts have to be updated and maintained to account for new browsers. This can be a headache.

One approach that you might find useful, however, was covered in Chapter 16, "Providing for Backward Compatibility," where the section, "Participating in the Web Standards Project," p. 385 (Chapter 16), discusses using the WaSP DOM Sniff script to test whether a browser supports the W3C's DOM (Document Object Model) or not. If not, the user is redirected to the WaSP's browser upgrade page (or to a browser upgrade page of your own).

If you're still of a mind to try using a browser sniffer, here are some places where you can find them:

- RichInStyle.com's Free Browser Detection Script at `http:// RichInStyle.com/free/detection.html`

- Browser Compatibility at `http://www.webreference.com/js/column6/`

- The Ultimate JavaScript Client Sniffer at `http://www.mozilla.org/ docs/web-developer/sniffer/browser_type.html`

- Browser Detection and Redirection at `http://netmechanic.com/news/ vol3/javascript_no15.htm`

- JavaScript Browser Detection at `http://www.w3schools.com/js/ js_browser.asp`

Creating Dynamic Styles with Dynamic HTML

The term *dynamic styles* was coined by Microsoft to denote the aspect of Dynamic HTML that encompasses using JavaScript to dynamically assign style properties to elements based on the W3C's DOM (or Document Object Model). *Dynamic HTML* is not a specific technology, but rather the interoperation of three technologies: CSS, JavaScript, and the DOM. Through the

DOM, programs and scripts can access, change, delete, or add any object within a document.

The methods shown here for creating dynamic styles work in the following browsers: Netscape 6 and Internet Explorer 4 (or greater). They do not work in Netscape 4 (or earlier) or in Opera 5. Ultimately, however, as more browsers support the W3C's DOM, support for creating dynamic styles will become much more universal.

The following sections cover two basic methods for creating dynamic styles:

- Applying dynamic styles using class selectors
- Applying dynamic styles directly to document elements

Applying Dynamic Styles Using Class Selectors

Using this method, you assign properties to alternative class selectors that you can then dynamically reassign. This involves

- Creating alternative class selectors to specify different style properties to be used for the same elements.
- Using HTML 4 event handlers (onMouseOver, OnMouseOut, and so on) that use JavaScript to dynamically assign a CLASS name to an element in response to user actions or other events.

For this method to work, in addition to applying initial styles to an element using a simple, group, or contextual selector, you need to define one, two, or more class selectors that are used to dynamically alter styles for the element. For instance, you define a simple selector for the H1 element, assigning foreground and background colors, changing the font size, and specifying the specific or generic font family to be displayed. You then define two additional class selectors, defining properties to be displayed when the mouse passes over or off the element, for instance.

To do this example, you can use the provided example code—just open kochanski.html and edit it to match the following example code—or you can use any other HTML file that you've already created (as long as it includes H1, H2, P, and UL elements). Resave the file (name it **dynastyle.html**, for instance).

In the following example, simple selectors are created to assign properties to the H1, H2, and P elements that are initially displayed in the document. For each of these elements, two class selectors are also created to assign properties that can then be dynamically assigned to these elements in response to mouse actions or other events. Just type the style sheet in, and then edit the body of the document, as shown here:

Listing B.1 DYNASTYLE.HTML—Dynamic Styles Example

```
<!DOCTYPE HTML PUBLIC "-
//W3C//DTD HTML 4.01 Transitional//EN"
"http://www.w3.org/TR/html4/loose.dtd">

<html>
<head>
<title>Kochanski Family Page</title>
<style type="text/css">
body { color: black; background: url(tanback.jpg); }
h1 { color: purple;  background: transparent; font-family: serif; font-size: 2em;
}
h1.over1 { color: aqua; background: url(dark.jpg); font-family: sans-serif; text-
align: right; }
h1.off1 { color: yellow; background: green; font-size: 2em; text-align: center; }
h2 { color: purple;  background: transparent; font-size: 1.5em; }
h2.over2 { color: lime; background: url(dark.jpg); font-family: sans-serif; text-
align: right; }
h2.off2 { font-size: 1.5em; }
p { padding-left: 10px; }
p.over3 { color: navy; background: transparent; border: red solid 5px; padding:
5px; font-weight: bold; }
p.off3 { border: transparent; }
</style>

<body>
<h1 onMouseOver="this.className = 'over1'" onMouseOut="this.className =
'off1'">The <em>Kochanski Family</em> Page</h1>

<p onMouseOver="this.className = 'over3'" onMouseOut="this.className =
'off3'">Welcome to the <em class="middle">Kochanski Family</em> page! Look here
for information on birthdays, anniversaries, milestones, graduations, family
gatherings, and other stuff related to our immediate and extended family.</p>

<p>George and I will also be presenting the latest information and details about
our own lives and careers, as well as the latest info on our two wonderful kids,
Joe and Sue (or at least what we've been able to wring out of them!).</p>

<h2 onMouseOver="this.className = 'over2'" onMouseOut="this.className =
'off2'">The Kochanski Family Gathering</h2>
<p>You'll all be pleased to know that the annual Kochanski family gathering has
been scheduled for next July 1st. It will be held at Ford Park at Stove #24
starting at 12 noon. Back by popular demand, George will be handling the barbecue
(ribs and hot dogs), but others are encouraged to contribute other dishes and
items to eat or drink.</p>
```

All of these work the same way, just using different alternative class selectors. For instance, for the H1 element, the h1 simple selector assigns the initial properties to be displayed for the element, the h1.over1 class selector assigns properties to be displayed for the element when the mouse pointer passes over it, and the h1.off1 class selector assigns properties to be displayed when the mouse pointer passes off of the element.

In the body of the document, the onMouseOver and onMouseOut event handlers call JavaScript script strings swap in different CLASS names for the elements, triggered by when the mouse passes over and passes off of an element. Figure B.1 shows the page as it appears when first loaded, while Figure B.2 shows the result when the mouse pointer passes over the H1 element. Figure B.3 then shows the result when the mouse pointer passes off of the H1 element.

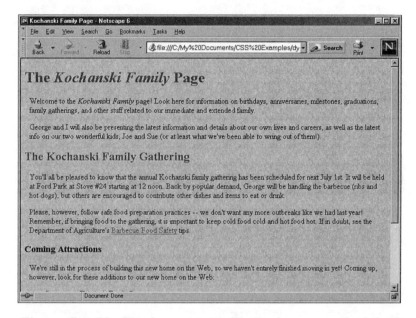

Figure B.1 *The H1 element initially displays a purple, left-aligned, two-em high, serif font against a transparent background (allowing the BODY element's background image to show through).*

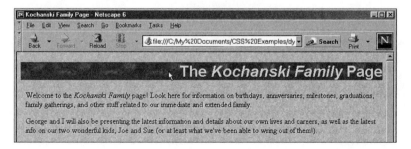

Figure B.2 *With the mouse pointer passing over it, the H1 element displays an aqua, right-aligned, sans-serif font against a dark background image.*

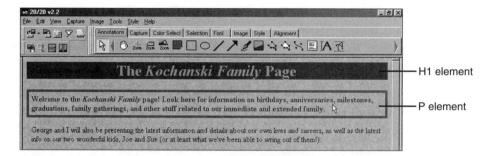

Figure B.3 *With the mouse pointer passed off of it, the H1 element displays a yellow, center-aligned, serif font against a green background; with the mouse pointer passed over the first paragraph, it is displayed in a bold navy font and outlined with a red border.*

As Figure B.3 shows, when the mouse pointer is passed over the first text paragraph, it is changed to a bold navy-colored font and is surrounded by a red border.

NOTE

Although this isn't required in Internet Explorer (4 or higher), to have your dynamic styles work in Netscape 6, don't use inline styles to set the initial property values for elements for which you want to apply dynamic styles using class selectors. This is because Netscape 6, quite properly, treats inline styles as having greater specificity, and thus greater weight, than styles set using class selectors. Set the initial styles in your style sheet, not inline, for elements you want to dynamically change by swapping in and out different class names.

Although it's not shown in the figures, you can also pass the mouse over and off the first H1 element to see style changes dynamically applied to that element.

Applying Dynamic Styles Directly to Document Elements

You can also dynamically apply style properties directly to elements, without first setting them in a class selector. Here's a fairly simple example of doing that:

Listing B.2 DYNASTYLE.HTML—Dynamic Styles Example (Part 2)

```
<div onclick="this.style.color = 'blue'; this.style.fontSize = '1.25em';
this.style.backgroundColor = '#ffffcc';" ondblclick="this.style.color = 'black';
this.style.fontSize = '1em'; this.style.backgroundColor = 'transparent';">
<ul>
```

Listing B.2 continued

```
<li>George and Kristine's Family Room
<li>Sue's Teddy Bear Haven
<li>Joe's Hideaway (we hardly ever see him!)
<li>Other Family News and Events
</ul>
</div>
```

In this case, when you click anywhere within the bulleted list (the UL element that is nested inside of the DIV element), the color of the bulleted list's text is switched to blue, its font size to 1.25 ems, and its background color to #ffffcc, as shown in Figure B.4.

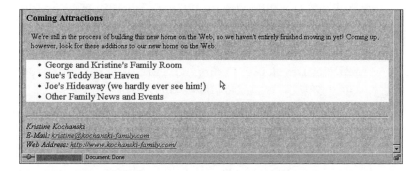

Figure B.4 *After clicking anywhere inside the bulleted list, its color, font size, and background color dynamically change.*

To change the element's properties back to their initial settings, just double-click anywhere within the bulleted list.

TIP

Values in JavaScript strings shouldn't contain hyphens. To reference a CSS property name that includes a hyphen in a dynamic style, just eliminate the hyphen and then capitalize the first following letter. For instance:

```
background-color = backgroundColor
background-image = backgroundImage
border-style = borderStyle
font-family = fontFamily
font-weight = fontWeight
margin-left = marginLeft
text-align = textAlign
```

Finding Out More About the Dynamic HTML and the DOM

The examples shown here just barely scratch the surface of what is possible when using JavaScript and the DOM to apply dynamic styles to your documents. Although it isn't the case now, it won't be long before all of the current major browsers will be fully compliant with the W3C's DOM. Here are some places you can look to find out more about Dynamic HTML and the DOM:

- The W3C's Document Object Model page at `http://www.w3.org/DOM/`.

- Dynamic HTML Central at `http://www.dhtmlcentral.com/`.

- The MSDN Library at `http://msdn.microsoft.com/library/`. Relevant table of contents entries include "Cascading Style Sheets" and "HTML and Dynamic HTML."

- The Dynamic HTML Guru at `http://www.htmlguru.com/`.

- ZDNet Developer: Coding/DHTML at `http://www.zdnet.com/devhead/filters/0,,2133215,00.html`.

- The Web Developer's Virtual Library (WDVL): Dynamic HTML at `http://WWW.Stars.com/Authoring/DHTML/`.

- Internet Related Technologies (irt.org) at `http://irt.org/`. See relevant sections on Cascading Style Sheets, Dynamic HTML, and JavaScript.

- Advanced HTML: DHTML, XML, SMIL at `http://www.webdeveloper.com/advhtml/`.

- DHTML Lab at `http://webreference.internet.com/dhtml/`.

- Project Cool's Dynamic HTML Developer Zone at `http://www.projectcool.com/developer/dynamic/`.

Using CSS with XML

CSS can be used with XML documents, as well as in conjunction with HTML and XHTML documents . XML documents have no formatting at all and require either an XSL (Extensible Stylesheet Language) or a CSS style sheet if they are to be displayed at all.

Although XSL provides functionality beyond CSS (such as element reordering, for instance), CSS is simpler and easier to implement. According to the original XSL proposal, "CSS will be used to display simply-structured XML documents and XSL will be used where more powerful formatting capabilities are required or for formatting highly structured information such as XML structured data or XML documents that contain structured data." (See `http://www.w3.org/Submission/1997/13/Overview.html`.)

A CSS style sheet can be linked directly in an XML document. For instance, to include a CSS style sheet, `MyStyles.css`, in an XML document, just include the following codes in the document's prolog:

```
<?xml version="1.0" standalone="yes"?>
<?xml-stylesheet type="text/css" href="MyStyles.css"?>
```

Another role for CSS is in formatting XML documents after they've been transformed (by XSLT, or XSL Transformations) into HTML documents.

Covering XML in any detail is far beyond the scope of this book. The following is a fairly simple example of using CSS and XML to create an online bibligraphy. First, create an XML file containing the content of your bibliography, saving it as **biblio.xml** in your working folder:

Listing B.3   BIBLIO.XML—CSS/XML Example

```
<?xml version="1.0" standalone="yes"?>
<?xml-stylesheet type="text/css" href="biblio.css"?>
<bibliography>
 <page_title>A Bibliography: Middle Eastern History</page_title>
 <listing>
  <title>The Arab Conquest of Egypt and the Last Thirty Years of the Roman
Domination</title>
  <author>Alfred Joshua Butler</author>
  <publisher>Clarendon Press</publisher>
  <location>Oxford</location>
  <year>1902</year>
 </listing>
 <listing>
  <title>The Mohammedan Dynasties</title>
  <author>Stanley Lane-Poole</author>
  <publisher>Constable</publisher>
  <location>London</location>
  <year>1894</year>
 </listing>
 <listing>
  <title>The Arab Heritage</title>
  <author>Nabih Emin Faris (ed.)</author>
  <publisher>University Press</publisher>
  <location>Princeton</location>
  <year>1944</year>
 </listing>
 <listing>
  <title>History of the Islamic Peoples</title>
  <author>Carl Brockelmann</author>
  <publisher>G. P. Putnam's Sons</publisher>
  <location>New York</location>
  <year>1947</year>
 </listing>
</bibliography>
```

Next, create the external style sheet that is referenced in the XML document, saving it as **biblio.css** in your working folder:

Listing B.3   BIBLIO.XML — CSS/XML Example

```
bibliography {
  color: navy; background; white;
  display: block;
  margin: 5%;
}
page_title {
  font-size: 2em;
  color: blue; background: transparent;
  display: block;
  float: left; clear: left;
  width: 89%;
  text-align: center;
  padding-bottom: 0.25em;
  border-bottom: red solid 3px;
  margin-bottom: 1em;
}
listing {
  border-bottom: navy solid 2px;
  display: block;
  float: left; clear: left;
  width: 89%;
  padding-left: 0.5em;
  margin-bottom: 1em;
}
title {
  color: green; background: transparent;
  font-style: italic;
  font-weight: bold;
  display: block;
  float: left;
  clear: left;
}
author {
  color: red; background: transparent;
  display: block;
  float: left; clear: left;
}
publisher {
  display: block;
  float: left; clear: left;
}
location {
  display: block;
  float: left; clear: left;
```

Listing B.3   continued

```
}
year {
  display: block;
  float: left; clear: left;
  margin-bottom: 1em;
}
```

Figure B.5 shows what this looks like in Internet Explorer 5.5 for Windows.

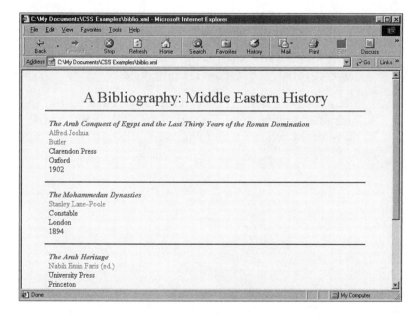

Figure B.5 *The XML file, biblio.xml, defines the structure and the content of the document, an online bibliography, while the external CSS style sheet, biblio.css, entirely controls its appearance.*

Because XML doesn't specify any formatting characteristics, the CSS style sheet has to control every aspect of the presentation of the document's elements. For instance, the elements are all specified as block elements (`display: block`), the `float` property causes each element to be displayed flush with the left margin, and the `clear` property causes each element to clear the previous floating property. Without these, the elements would all be displayed on the same line, plus property values that can only be assigned to block elements wouldn't work.

If you'd like to learn more about XML, and using CSS with XML, the following links are good starting points:

- The W3C's XML page at `http://www.w3.org/XML/`.

- XML 101 at `http://xml101.com/`.

- Using XSL and CSS Together at `http://www.w3.org/TR/NOTE-XSL-and-CSS`.

- CSS 2 Tutorial at `http://zvon.org/xxl/CSS2Tutorial/General/htmlIntro.html`. This site provides a tutorial on applying CSS2 style sheets to XML documents.

- Displaying XML with CSS at `http://javertising.com/webtech/cssxml.htm`.

- How Should My XML Look? Using Style Sheets with XML at `http://html.about.com/library/weekly/aa110600a.htm`.

- The XML Cover Pages at `http://xml.coverpages.org/`. This site features extensive documentation on XML, XSL, XSLT, XHTML, CSS, and other related technologies.

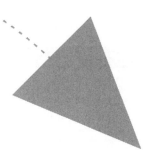

Overview of CSS Software Tools

Many CSS software tools that you can download and try out are available on the Web, including style sheet editors, HTML editors, Web publishing suites, and CSS conversion tools.

continues

Style Sheet Editors

Although it is a good idea to first become familiar with crafting your own style sheets, after you've earned your CSS spurs, you might want to check out some of the following style sheet editors:

Windows

- **CoffeeCup StylesSheet Maker at** `http://www.coffeecup.com/style/`—15-day evaluation version; $30 to register.

- **Dutch's Cascading Style Sheets at** `http://www.bee.net/dutch/`—15-day evaluation version; $19.95 to register.

- **EasyStyle (included with EasyASP) at** `http://www.easyasp.org/about_easystyle.html`—Free.

- **Prime Style at** `http://www.pconsulting.com.au/style/`—20-use evaluation version; $25 to register.

- **Sheet Stylist** `http://homepages.tcp.co.uk/~drarh/Stylist/`—40-use evaluation version; $15 to register.

- **StyleMaker at** `http://www.danere.com/StyleMaker/`—15-day evaluation version; $29.95 to register.

- **StyleMaster at** `http://www.westciv.com/style_master/index.html`—31-day evaluation version; $29 (StyleMaster) and $49 (StyleMaster Pro) to register.

- **Style Studio at** `http://www.xsstudio.net/`—30-day evaluation version: $29.95 to register.

- **TopStyle at** `http://www.bradsoft.com/topstyle/`—Shareware; $49.95 to register.

Macintosh

- **Cascade Style Sheets Editor at** `http://interaction.in-progress.com/cascade/`—Free.

- **StyleMaster at** `http://www.westciv.com/style_master/index.html`—31-day evaluation version; $29 (StyleMaster) and $49 (StyleMaster Pro) to register.

Other Platforms

- **JustStyle at** `http://juststyle.mastak.com/`. 30-day evaluation version; $20 to register. (Java)

CSS-Supporting HTML Editors and Web Publishing

Following are lists of HTML editors and Web publishing suites that support CSS.

Windows

- **AceHTML at** `http://www.visicommedia.com/acehtml/`—Freeware; $49.95 to register (AceHTML Pro).

- **Adobe GoLive at** `http://www.adobe.com/products/golive/main.html`— 30-day evaluation version; $284 to register.

- **Amaya at** `http://www.w3.org/Amaya/`—The W3C's combination browser and authoring tool. Free.

- **Microsoft FrontPage at** `http://www.microsoft.com/frontpage/`— 30-day trial version available for $9.95 U.S./$14.95 CAN; $169 (standalone), $239 (MS Office XP Standard), $329 (MS Office XP Professional), and $479 (MS Office XP Professional Special Edition).

- **HomeSite at** `http://www.allaire.com/products/homesite/`—30-day evaluation version; $89 to register.

- **HoTMetaL Pro at** `http://www.hotmetal.com/`—30-day evaluation version; $99 to register.

- **Layout Master at** `http://www.westciv.com/layout_master/`—30-day evaluation version; $49.99 to register.

- **Macromedia Dreamweaver at** `http://www.macromedia.com/software/dreamweaver/`—30-day evaluation version; $299 to register.

- **XMetaL at** `http://www.xmetal.com/`—XML editor with support for CSS. 30-day evaluation version; $495 to register.

- **XML Spy Suite at** `http://www.xmlspy.com/`—includes an integrated development environment for creating XML documents. 30-day evaluation version; $399 for single-user license. (Windows)

Macintosh

- **Adobe GoLive** at `http://www.adobe.com/products/golive/main.html`—30-day evaluation version; $284 to register.

- **BBEdit** at `http://www.barebones.com/products/bbedit.html`—24-use evaluation version; $119 to register.

- **Layout Master** at `http://www.westciv.com/layout_master/`—30-day evaluation version; $49.99 to register.

- **Macromedia Dreamweaver** at `http://www.macromedia.com/software/dreamweaver/`—30-day evaluation version; $299 to register.

- **PageSpinner** at `http://www.optima-system.com/pagespinner/`—21-day evaluation version; $29.95 to register.

- **WebDesign** at `http://www.ragesw.com/`—Supports HTML, XHTML, CSS, and JavaScript. Evaluation version; $29.95 to register.

Other Platforms

- **Amaya** at `http://www.w3.org/Amaya/`—The W3C's combination browser and authoring tool. (Linux/Unix)

- **Bluefish HTML Editor** at `http://bluefish.openoffice.nl/`—Beta version. (Unix/Linux with the GTK libraries).

- **Quanta Plus** at `http://quanta.sourceforge.net/`—Pre-release version. (KDE 2/Linux)

Text Editors

To create HTML, XML, and CSS files, you only need a text editor. Following are selections of text editors that are available for Windows, the Macintosh, and other platforms.

Windows

- **EditPad Pro** at `http://www.editpadpro.com/`—Shareware; $29.95 to register.

- **EditPad Classic** at `http://www.editpadpro.com/editpadclassic.html`—Postcardware (almost free).

- **HTML-Kit** at `http://www.chami.com/html-kit/`—A full-featured text editor optimized for HTML, XML, and script authors. Evaluation version; $25 to register.

- **GWD Text Editor at** `http://www.gwdsoft.com/`—Shareware; $29 to register.

- **Muli-Edit at** `http://www.multiedit.com/`—Evaluation version; $139 to register.

- **NoteTab Light at** `http://www.notetab.com/`—Freeware.

- **NoteTab Pro at** `http://www.notetab.com/`—Shareware; $19.95 to register.

- **TextPad at** `http://www.textpad.com/`—Shareware; $27 to register.

- **UltraEdit at** `http://www.ultraedit.com/`—Shareware; $30 to register.

Macintosh

- **BBEdit Lite at** **http://www.barebones.com/products/bbedit_lite.html**—Freeware.

- **FinalWord at** `http://www.ragesw.com/`—Evaluation version; $15.95 to register.

- **Pepper at** `http://www.hekkelman.com/pepper.html`—Shareware; $45 to register. (OS 9/X)

- **Tex-Edit Plus at** `http://www.nearside.com/trans-tex/`—Shareware; $15 to register.

- **Texter at** `http://www.lightheadsw.com/`—Demo version; $10 to register (and activate all its features).

Other Platforms

- **asWedit at** `http://www.advasoft.com/asWedit.html`—Free for non-commercial use. (Linux/Unix)

- **Elvis at** `http://elvis.the-little-red-haired-girl.org/`—Free. (Linux/Unix)

- **gedit at** `http://gedit.sourceforge.net/`—Free. (Linux/Unix)

- **jEdit at** `http://www.jedit.org/`—Free. (Java)

- **NEdit at** `http://nedit.org/`—Free. (Linux/Unix)

- **TED at** `http://www.geocities.com/SiliconValley/Bridge/8617/ted.html`—Free. (Linux)

- **VIM (Vi Improved) at** `http://www.vim.org/`—Free. (Linux/Unix)

- **Xcoral at** `http://www.multimania.com/lfournigault/xcoral.html`—Free. (Linux/Unix)

Miscellaneous Utilities

Here are some additional utilities you might find useful:

- **Back to Font Web Color Picker at** `http://www.markup.co.nz/colorpicker/back_to_font_home.htm`—A JavaScript-based CSS-color picker.

- **Cool Web Scrollbars at** `http://www.harmonyhollow.net/cws.shtml`—Automates creating colorized scrollbars using CSS.

- **CodeLifter.com at** `http://www.codelifter.com/`—A source code viewer that lets you see all of the code residing behind the presentation of http://-generated HTML page. Bypass no-right-click scripts, see past windows without file menus or url boxes, and sniff out referrer pages that cannot be seen in your browser. You can also access external CSS style sheets, external JavaScript files, and any other text file at an http:// address. Evaluation version; $25 to register. (Windows)

- **SVGFont at** `http://www.steadystate.co.uk/svg/`—A utility that generates SVG (Scaleable Vector Graphic) font definitions from TrueType fonts. (Java)

- **Style-O-Matic at** `http://builder.cnet.com/webbuilding/pages/Authoring/CSS/ss12.html`—A free online utility that lets you interactively generate CSS styling code.

- **DHTML Menu Builder at** `http://software.xfx.net/utilities/dmbuilder/`—Create snazzy pull-down menus for your Web pages, without having to write a single line of code. Evaluation version; $65 to register. (Windows)

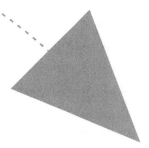

Index

A

absolute line height, 161
absolute positioning, 233–241
  block elements and, 213
  menus and, 314
absolute size of fonts, 127, 131, 138, 139–140
absolute values, 102–105
absolute vs. relative measurement in Web page, 189
A:hover pseudo class, hypertext links/hyperlinks and, 175
address block, 47, 61–64, 329
  centering, 62
  colors for, 62–64
  horizontal rule for, 61
  hypertext links/hyperlinks and in, 173–174
ADDRESS element, 61–64, 173
Adobe Photoshop, 115
Adobe PostScript (See PostScript)
agents, user, 91
alignment, 155, 156–159
  block elements and, 213
  block elements and, horizontal, 214–219
  block elements and, specific-width elements in, 217–219
  menus and, 305
  tables and, 273, 285–286
ALINK attribute, 111, 174, 176–177
ALT attribute, 220, 221
anchor pseudo classes for, 174–175
Anchor tag, 171–172
aspect ratio of font, 142
asterisk, as comment delimiter, 80

At rule for fonts, 151–153
attributes, 64, 68
author as source of style information, 90–95
author/user balance, 89, 95

B

BACKGROUND attribute, 111
BACKGROUND attribute, 119–125, 119
Background shorthand property, 109, 125
backgrounds, 25
  Background shorthand property for, 109, 125
  borders and images as, 204
  browser support for, 125
  color of, 37–39, 51, 92, 102, 109, 111–119
  columns in table using, 288–289
  fixed images as, 123–125
  fixed sidebar as, 330–337
  images as, 109, 119–125, 240, 328, 334–337, 353
  menus and, 311
  newspaper columns and, 351
  padding in, 196–197
  positioning images for, 121–123
  repeat value for, 121
  repeating images as, 109
  rows in table using, 287–288
  tables and, 295–296
  text vs. background colors, 113
  transparent watermarks, 124
  watermark as, 122–124
backward compatibility, 18, 377–399
  A List Apart's Coders Forum and, 392
  "breaking" a browser and, 386
  browser sniffers for, 384–385